AN INTRODUCTION TO CATHOLIC
SOCIAL THOUGHT

Michael Hornsby-Smith offers an overview of Catholic social thought focusing particularly on recent decades. While drawing on official teaching such as papal encyclicals and the pastoral letters of bishops' conferences, he takes seriously the need for dialogue with secular thought. The book is organized in four stages. Part I outlines the variety of domestic and international injustices and seeks to offer a social analysis of the causes of these injustices. Part II offers a theological reflection on the characteristics of the kingdom of God which Christians are urged to seek. Part III reviews Catholic social thought in six main areas: human rights, the family and bioethical issues, economic life, social exclusion, authentic development and war and peace. Part IV completes the cycle with a consideration of appropriate social action responses to the injustices which the author has identified and analyzed.

MICHAEL P. HORNSBY-SMITH is Emeritus Professor of Sociology, University of Surrey. He is author of *Roman Catholic Beliefs in England* (1991) and editor of *Catholics in England 1950–2000* (1999) and he has published around 160 articles, mainly on the sociology of religion.

AN INTRODUCTION TO CATHOLIC SOCIAL THOUGHT

MICHAEL P. HORNSBY-SMITH

CAMBRIDGE
UNIVERSITY PRESS

CAMBRIDGE UNIVERSITY PRESS
Cambridge, New York, Melbourne, Madrid, Cape Town, Singapore, São Paulo

Cambridge University Press
The Edinburgh Building, Cambridge CB2 2RU, UK

Published in the United States of America by Cambridge University Press, New York

www.cambridge.org
Information on this title: www.cambridge.org/9780521681995

First published 2006

Printed in the United Kingdom at the University Press, Cambridge

A catalogue record for this publication is available from the British Library

ISBN-13 978-0-521-86339-1 hardback
ISBN-10 0-521-86339-2 hardback
ISBN-13 978-0-521-68199-5 paperback
ISBN-10 0-521-68199-5 paperback

Cambridge University Press has no responsibility for
the persistence or accuracy of URLs for external or
third-party internet websites referred to in this publication,
and does not guarantee that any content on such
websites is, or will remain, accurate or appropriate.

Contents

Tables and figure

Acknowledgements

In the writing of this book I have been given encouragement and help by many people. I would particularly like to record my thanks to Brian Davies and Michael Walsh who read and commented critically and helpfully on the whole text. I am also grateful to those who made helpful suggestions on individual chapters: Valerie Flessati, Bruce Kent, Ian Linden, Pat Logan, Dominic McDonnell, David McLoughlin, Brian Wicker, and Frs. Adrian Graffy, Kevin Kelly, John Sherrington and Jim Sweeney. Helpful advice and suggestions at various stages of this project were also generously given by Christine Allen, Peter Askonas, Jeremy Boutwood, John Collins, Matthew Dell, Gordon Ferns, Mary Grey, Jo Kitterick, Roger O'Toole and Ian Pritchard, and Frs. Bob Dixon, Owen Hardwicke, Jim Hug, Michael McGlade and Eamonn O'Brien. I also wish to acknowledge the constructive comments made by a number of anonymous readers. They have all helped correct some of my grosser errors.

I am aware that in attempting to cover such a wide range of issues I will inevitably have failed to take on board the latest evidence and thinking in the large number of disciplines relevant for this study. For this reason I view this book as a first attempt to address what I feel sure is an intimate connection between domestic and international issues of injustice. Hopefully it offers an approach which can be corrected, improved and built on by others more qualified than I am. Those errors which remain are entirely my own responsibility.

I would like to acknowledge with gratitude permissions to quote widely from official papal and episcopal sources in *Catholic Social Thought: The Documentary Heritage* edited by David J. O'Brien and Thomas A. Shannon and published by Orbis in 1992.

Thanks are due to the US Conference of Catholic Bishops to quote from several of their pastoral letters. The sources I have used differ marginally from the official text. I am also grateful for permission to quote from the *Catechism of the Catholic Church*, published in 1994 by Geoffrey Chapman, copyright administered by Continuum. Scriptural quotations have generally been taken from *The New Jerusalem Bible*, published and copyright 1985 by Darton, Longman and Todd Ltd and Doubleday, a division of Random House Inc. and used by permission of the publishers. While I have attempted to use gender-inclusive language, there is an inherent sexism in the English language versions of all official Catholic documents. On the whole, but with apologies, I have left quoted texts in their official form.

To Dr Kate Brett at Cambridge University Press a very special thanks is due for her enthusiastic and helpful advice throughout the publication process. I am very grateful to her for her support. My thanks, too are due to Sara Barnes, Gillian Dadd and Jackie Warren for their care and attention throughout the publication process.

Finally, I must acknowledge with love and gratitude, the endless patience and support given me during the long five years of this book's gestation by my wife, Lennie, best friend and companion for nearly fifty years. I will always be grateful that she gave me the space to hide in my study for long hours while she faithfully undertook all the domestic chores of a busy household, which should have been more evenly shared. I am very conscious of the gendered nature of our division of labour and hope that with this confession I might be forgiven.

To Lennie
With all my love
and to our four grandchildren,
Luke, Benedict, Katie and Douglas,
in the hope that one day they will take up the challenge
to struggle for justice and peace,
here on earth as in heaven.

Abbreviations and acronyms

AI	Amnesty International
AIDS	Acquired Immune Deficiency Syndrome
ARVs	Antiretrovirals
ASI	AntiSlavery International
CAAT	Campaign Against the Arms Trade
CAFOD	Catholic Agency for Overseas Development
CAP	Church Action on Poverty
CAP	Common Agricultural Policy
CASC	Catholic Agency for Social Concern (now merged into Caritas-Social Action)
CBCEW	Catholic Bishops' Conference of England and Wales
CBI	Confederation of British Industry
CDF	(Sacred) Congregation for the Doctrine of the Faith
CEDAW	(UN) Convention on the Elimination of All Forms of Discrimination Against Women
CERD	(UN) Convention on the Elimination of All Forms of Racial Discrimination
CFC	Chlorofluorocarbon
COMECE	Commission of the Bishops' Conferences of the European Communities
CPAG	Child Poverty Action Group
CRC	(UN) Convention on the Rights of the Child
CSO	Civil Society Organisation
DESO	Defence Export Services Organization
ECPAT	End Child Prostitution, Pornography and Trafficking
ECRI	European Commission Against Racism and Intolerance
EU	European Union
FCCC	Framework Convention on Climate Change
GATT	General Agreement on Tariffs and Trade
GDP	Gross Domestic Product

GNI	Gross National Income
HDI	Human Development Index
HIPC	Heavily Indebted Poor Countries
HIV	Human Immunodeficiency Virus
IANSA	International Action Network on Small Arms
IBRD	International Bank for Reconstruction and Development
ICT	Information and Communications Technology
IDA	International Development Association
IDP	Internally Displaced Person
IIED	International Institute on Environment and Development
IMF	International Monetary Fund
INGO	International Non-Governmental Organization
IOM	International Organization for Migration
JPIC	Justice and Peace and the Integrity of Creation
MAW	Movement for the Abolition of War
MNC	Multinational Corporation
NGO	Non-governmental organization
NHS	National Health Service
NJPN	National Justice and Peace Network
NT	New Testament
OCIPE	Catholic European Study and Information Centre
OECD	Organization for Economic Cooperation and Development
OT	Old Testament
PLC	Public Limited Company
PPP	Purchasing Power Parity
SCM	Student Christian Movement
SMO	Social Movement Organization
SVP	St Vincent de Paul Society
THOMAS	Those on the Margins of Society
TNC	Transnational Corporation
TRIPS	Trade Related Intellectual Property Rights (Agreement)
UK	United Kingdom
UNCTAD	United Nations Conference on Trade and Development
UNDP	United Nations Development Programme
UNHCR	United Nations High Commission (or Commissioner) for Refugees
UN(O)	United Nations (Organization)
UNRWA	United Nations Relief and Works Agency
US(A)	United States (of America)

USCCB	US Catholic Conference of Bishops
WB	World Bank
WCC	World Council of Churches
WDM	World Development Movement
WEF	World Economic Forum
WIPO	World Intellectual Property Organization
WSF	World Social Forum
WTO	World Trade Organization
YCW	Young Christian Workers

VATICAN COUNCIL DOCUMENTS ETC

AA	*Apostolicam Actuositatem* (Decree on the Apostolate of the Laity)
DH	*Dignitatis Humanae* (Declaration on Religious Freedom)
GS	*Gaudium et Spes* (Pastoral Constitution on the Church in the Modern World)
CCC	*Catechism of the Catholic Church*

PAPAL ENCYCLICALS ETC

Indicated by the initials of their Roman titles, e.g.

RN	*Rerum Novarum* (Leo XIII, 1891)
PIT	*Pacem in Terris* (John XXIII, 1963)
OA	*Octogesima Adveniens* (Paul VI, 1971)
LE	*Laborem Exercens* (John Paul II, 1981)
SRS	*Sollicitudo Rei Socialis* (John Paul II, 1987)
CA	*Centesimus Annus* (John Paul II, 1991)
VS	*Veritatis Splendor* (John Paul II, 1993)

PART I

Social reality and social analysis

CHAPTER I

Introduction

JUSTICE-SEEKING IN A CHANGING WORLD

This book by a Catholic layperson and sociologist has been written with the aim of contributing to the on-going and developing debate about the search for social justice. I commenced writing it in the week following the devastating attack on the World Trade Centre in New York on 11 September 2001. This was a brutal act of violence which shocked the world but which also raised important issues of justice. It demonstrated the interrelatedness of the issues of peace, human rights, economic structures and inequalities, the uses and misuses of technologies, and power differentials in a global context. It pointed to the need not only to react with compassion but also to analyze and understand the causes of the persistent structures of injustice and the conflicts and violence they promote.

When there are evident injustices the traditional Christian response has been one of compassion for the poor, suffering and oppressed and the attempt to ameliorate their suffering. But in recent years there has been a growing awareness that this is not enough. The *causes of persistent structures of injustice* and sin need to be analyzed and understood so that social, political and economic policies to address those causes can be sought. It is the first aim of this book to offer such an analysis, however tentative, as an aid to those seeking a more just society and world.

In recent years various social movements and non-governmental organizations (NGOs) have emerged, many of them inspired by Christian beliefs and commitment, to raise awareness about a wide range of matters from homelessness, poverty, racism and social exclusion in our own society to the arms trade, international trade relations, starvation and ill health in developing societies.[1] In practice most of the Christian NGOs in the areas of both domestic and international justice are working in strategic alliances

[1] Mich 1998.

with other Church and secular bodies. They all campaign for changes in social and economic policies in the area of their special concerns. This may retard the development of a more comprehensive understanding of unjust and sinful structures within the Christian community with the consequence that the imperative to seek the kingdom of God 'on earth as in heaven' fails to become a central feature of the commitment of Christians and of the Church.

The result is that the real interconnections between local and international structures of injustice, are not clearly made or perceived. Examples of this are legion. The terrible atrocity at the World Trade Centre in New York was seemingly associated with Arab resentment at the failure of the USA to push for a just settlement between its client state, Israel, and the Palestinians and to the continuing influence of the USA in the 'Gulf States' a decade after the first Gulf War. Arms production in the major industrial nations is a major source of foreign earnings and of employment but these arms are frequently used by authoritarian regimes to oppress their own populations. The flood of refugees, asylum seekers and economic migrants to 'fortress Europe' can only be understood in the context of the historical legacies of colonialism and imperialism. The striving for cost reductions by transnational corporations (TNCs) and the ease of transfer of capital from one part of the world to another means that the opening of new plants in one country often means the closing of similar plants in another. And so on.

A second aim of this book, therefore, is to seek to show to what extent *national and international structures of injustice are intimately connected* and to argue that this needs to be recognized if a proper analysis is to be undertaken as a preface to an informed social action response. The interdependence of all the peoples on earth now, and, particularly when considering ecological concerns, cross-generationally, is an integral part of a Christian belief that we are all children of the one creator God, made in His image and likeness. Following the tsunamis in 2004, people all over the world intuitively understood this and there was a 'globalization of compassion'.

A third aim of this book is to offer *a Roman Catholic contribution* to the debates about justice-seeking. This is not to retreat into a confessional defensiveness but to stress that there is a long and dynamic tradition of Catholic social thought which is intrinsically valuable and relevant to our present concerns with the structures of sin and injustice which disfigure our society and today's world. In a recent essay Stanley Hauerwas offered some 'unsolicited advice from a Protestant bystander' and pleaded: 'I do not want Catholics to be good ecumenical citizens – I want them to be Catholics . . . Catholics have been so anxious to be like us that they have failed in their ecumenical task of helping us see what it means for any of us to be faithful to the Gospel on which our unity depends'.[2] It is in that spirit that I hope, therefore, that this book might be of value not only to students of Catholic social thought and justice and peace activists, but also to politicians and other decision-makers and to all those of good will, not only fellow Christians but also those of other faiths or none, who are concerned with the struggle to make our world a better place not only for present generations but also for those generations still to come.

This is a large task and in a book such as this can only be addressed in outline. It involves a wide range of disciplines including Church history, economics, philosophy, political science, sociology and theology. I am very conscious of my many inadequacies in all of these areas. While I hope this book will be of value to a wide readership, there will be many who will wish to take the analysis much further. Hence a fourth aim of the book is to offer *suggestions for further reading and study* and invite contact with the multiplicity of NGOs working in specific areas. These often publish informative journals, periodicals and reports with more detailed analyses and information about them is readily available on the internet. I hope this book will be a valuable resource for all those who are seeking to further God's kingdom here on earth by striving for justice for poor, deprived and oppressed people.

Against those who suggest that religion is entirely a private affair and should have nothing to do with politics, this book holds with the Synod of Bishops who taught in 1971 that:

Action on behalf of justice and participation in the transformation of the world fully appear to us as a constitutive dimension of the preaching of the Gospel, or, in other words, of the Church's mission for the redemption of the human race and its liberation from every oppressive situation.[3]

Justice-seeking is no optional extra but an essential element in Christian discipleship.

The world has changed significantly in the four years this book has been in the writing. There have been wars in Afghanistan and Iraq, and terrorist atrocities in places as far apart as Bali, Istanbul, London, Madrid and Beslan. The World Social Forum of grass-roots organizations and a global justice movement aiming to 'make poverty history' are now beginning to challenge the decisions taken by economic institutions set up to serve the interests of powerful nations half a century ago. The possibilities of cloning human beings draws ever closer. Recent legislation has been seen as

---

[2] Hauerwas 1995: 221.   [3] O'Brien and Shannon 1992: 289.

legalizing euthanasia by starvation and neglect. The 'people of God' are having to interpret the meaning of the teaching of Jesus in circumstances never met before in human history. In these changing times, how can Catholic social thought help people make key moral choices? What key principles underpin this thought and how can they be translated into social, economic and political policies which are faithful to the call to 'bring the Good News to the poor' and oppressed both in our own society and, indeed, throughout the whole world?

In recent years it has become increasingly apparent that we live in a relatively fragile world and that, for better or worse, our lives and those of others who share our planet are inextricably linked. For decades after the Second World War most people in the northern hemisphere were conscious of the dangers of nuclear war and that its consequences would be far more catastrophic than the world had ever experienced in historical times. Recent developments in communications technology, particularly the ubiquitous television with its instant coverage of news of famines or disasters all over the world, have exposed people to the realities of suffering, need and oppression throughout the whole world. In spite of some 'compassion fatigue', it is clear that the awareness of needs and injustices has also generated attempts to respond both by ameliorating suffering and need and by attempting to prevent them happening by understanding their causes and responding politically. Thus there has been the emergence of an environmental movement concerned to address such problems as climate change and the loss of animal species resulting from our present economic arrangements. More recently, the awareness of a widening of the gap between rich and poor countries has led many to challenge the acceptability of our present institutional arrangements for regulating trade and investment and the present distribution of political and economic power which serves to maintain such injustices. The terrorist attacks of 11 September 2001 demonstrated as never before that traditional assumptions about power and security were obsolete and that in order to tackle transnational terrorism, it was necessary to construct international coalitions. In a very real sense we are all interconnected and we increasingly sense this.

For Christians this comes as no surprise. They believe that all people on earth have been born in the image of their creator God. Not that human history has demonstrated a deep consciousness of our common humanity and brotherhood with our Saviour over the two millennia since Jesus of Nazareth became our Emmanuel, God-with-us. The Holocaust is under one lifetime ago. Historically, Christians have frequently failed adequately to love their neighbours as themselves. In the past this may have resulted partly from ignorance of things happening on the other side of the world about which they knew nothing. But in the modern world, this is no longer the case and there is an increasing awareness that the way we live our lives, the consumer choices we make, the energy we consume and the trade relations and regulations concerning migration flows we tolerate, all impact on the lives of others, sometimes with extremely harmful consequences. So how should Christians respond?

This book has been written on the basis of six major convictions:

1. There are numerous *social injustices* in the world in which we live, from torture and discrimination to poverty and social exclusion, and from war and oppression to unequal development and environmental damage.

2. These different types of injustice are all, in some way, interlinked and related to the dynamics of *liberal capitalism*, and this has become increasingly the case as the processes of globalization have accelerated in recent years.

3. Quite apart from the personal injustices and evil of individuals, there are *sinful social structures*, such as trade relations or discriminatory laws, which are unjust and evil.

4. There are two distinct types of compassionate response to social need or suffering:
   - *amelioration* of the suffering or satisfaction of the need, such as feeding the hungry or providing shelter for the homeless; and
   - *seeking justice* by addressing the causes of injustices and changing the structures which oppress. It is the latter which is the main concern of those who thirst for justice and it is essentially a political response involving advocacy and struggle with those who wield political or economic power.

5. The Christian imperative to love our neighbour as ourselves is best developed through a social action cycle which consists of four successive and interlinked stages:
   - the identification of the *social reality*: needs and social injustices;
   - the *social analysis* of their causes and the concrete reality;
   - *theological reflection* on these in the light of scripture and the developing social thought of the Church and its members; and
   - the *social action* response to the needs and injustices in the light of the social analysis and Christian reflection.

6. While in recent years, Christians and people of good will and a social conscience have increasingly worked closely together, Catholics have a *special contribution* to make on the basis of their rich heritage of social thought which is worth sharing.

These six convictions have determined the structure of this book and the sequence of its argument which is offered to all people of good will and to all who are involved in various ways in what Catholics call the Justice and Peace Movement. This chapter offers a brief account of the social realities in our contemporary world and aims to provide an overview of both domestic and international injustices. Chapter 2 will endeavour to provide some tools for a social analysis of the causes of these injustices, necessary if appropriate responses are to be identified. It will introduce a consideration of processes of globalization and the current dominant model of liberal capitalism. It will also point to issues of social, economic and political power which serve to perpetuate and extend structures and patterns of injustice both domestically and throughout the world.

Part II aims to provide a set of tools for Christian reflection on the social realities we face in our present world. Chapter 3 will offer an account of the kingdom of God which Jesus urged his followers to seek and which exists but remains to be fully realized. Chapter 4 will address some key themes in secular pluralist societies such as the entitlements and responsibilities of citizenship and the three great revolutionary aims of freedom, equality and solidarity. In Chapter 5, an outline of Catholic social thought as it has developed over the centuries, but especially since the Second Vatican Council, will be presented and a number of key principles identified.

The multitude of social injustices which face us in the modern world have been clustered in Part III under six broad headings. Each of them will be considered in the light of the principles and resources identified in Part II. Chapter 6 will address the challenges of human rights, including such issues as torture, the death penalty, asylum seekers, and racism. Prominence has always been given in Catholic social thought to the family as the primary social unit of all societies. In Chapter 7, some of the issues of concern, including abortion, euthanasia, social and welfare policies affecting the family, recent developments in genetic engineering and bioethical issues will be considered. Chapter 8 will outline Catholic approaches to economic life. The right to private property, work and employment and to associate in trade unions will be discussed. Issues of social exclusion, including poverty and inequality, homelessness, discrimination and participation, will be addressed in Chapter 9. Chapter 10 will consider the range of matters involved in the notions of authentic and sustainable development. Apart from issues of trade relations and aid, and the role of the major international institutions for the regulation of global trade, investment and financial flows, consideration will also be given to the concerns for the environment and climate change. Chapter 11 will address the issues of war and peace and the impact of the trade in arms. It will also consider the challenges of international terrorism and the need for appropriate international institutions for the regulation of conflicts between nations and ethnic groups.

Chapter 12, which constitutes Part IV of this book, will attempt to draw some conclusions for social action responses to the injustices outlined in Part III. In particular, it will note the large number of NGOs, many of them Christian in origin and in their operative ideologies, which together constitute at least an embryonic global social justice movement. While there are numerous activists involved in 'doing good' in particular areas, it is a major plea of this book that their actions as committed Christians will be greatly enhanced to the extent that there is a growing awareness of and conversion to a continuous process of social analysis and theological reflection on social needs and action responses to them in the light of that reflection.

This book aims to offer *a* Roman Catholic contribution to justice-seeking. While it will include an account of 'official' Catholic social teaching, insofar as it has been articulated in recent years in papal encyclicals or pastoral letters from Bishops' Conferences, it also aims to offer a lay critique of such teaching and indicate in addition a range of theological and secular analyses of both domestic and international injustices. The focus will be on the situation in the UK, though some account will also be taken of the special position of the USA. Reference will also be made to key writings from other (mainly Christian) traditions and also to relevant secular contributions.

Before commencing this task a few words about the changing nature of Catholicism is appropriate. In the first place, it must be admitted at the outset that the historical role of institutional Catholicism has been ambiguous. In the past it was often closely associated with ruthless, violent and destructive secular quests for imperialist expansion, for example in South America, or with authoritarian forms of social control, as in European fascism. It has also frequently had a strong bias in favour of established secular powers, however corrupt and unjust they might be. For the better part of two centuries it resisted the forces of modernity as articulated in the Enlightenment and the democratic impulses of the French and American revolutions. But the ravages of the Industrial Revolution gradually led to a more dialogical relationship between Catholicism and the modern world.

A major transformation can be dated from the Second Vatican Council in 1962–65 which recognized the contribution of scientific advances and by interpreting the Church as the People of God, encouraged the legitimate autonomy of lay people in their special tasks of bringing the world closer to the vision of the kingdom of God proclaimed by Jesus. Furthermore, the Council recognized that God's spirit was at work in the world, in history and in society. It was the task of the Church to discern the 'signs of the times'. Hence it encouraged the emergence from a fortress model of the Church, embattled against the evils of a secular world, to a more respectful, though critical, relationship with it and a greater readiness to work with other people of good will. Thus there has been a great development of ecumenical collaboration in recent decades, not only in terms of individual contacts but also institutionally, in order to address specific needs and injustices ranging from poverty and homelessness to international development and famine relief.

CATHOLIC APPROACHES

There is clearly a need for a serious consideration of the ethical dilemmas posed by contemporary social and economic arrangements. Catholic approaches to injustices and evils have historically emphasized individual sin and responsibility. An awareness of 'structural sin' is relatively recent. It can perhaps be traced from the Second Vatican Council though it was not fully embraced until Pope John Paul II's encyclical *Sollicitudo Rei Socialis* (§§36–39) in 1987. It recognized flaws in the social order resulting 'in part from the natural tensions of economic, political, and social forms' though it saw these as flowing 'from man's pride and selfishness, which contaminate even the social sphere' (*GS* §25). There is, however, a 'risk of conservative bias' and attachment to the *status quo* in too individualistic an approach to social injustices. What is necessary to counter structural injustices is collective action, organized pressure to amend legislation, and the mobilization of countervailing power.[4] The South African theologian, Albert Nolan, has pointed out that 'all sin has a social dimension because it has social consequences. Sin affects other people and becomes institutionalized in the structures, laws, and customs of society. In turn, society then shapes and influences the sinner'.[5] Similarly the Dutch theologian, Edward Schillebeeckx has insisted that 'the Christian understanding of sin ... includes the recognition of systematic disruptions of communication like sexism, racism and fascism, (and) antisemitism' and that 'Christian love which is the basis of community ... (requires) deep involvement in present-day work of political, cultural and social emancipation'.[6]

---

[4] Boswell 2000: 102.   [5] Quoted in Fuellenbach 1995: 86.   [6] Ibid: 88.

   The main elements of Catholic social thought have been outlined in the three chapters of Part II which presents the fundamental values and principles of this thought as it has developed over the past twenty centuries.[7] In general terms two different approaches have been used in this development: scripture, which privileges faith, and notions of natural law, in principle accessible to all people of good will. The relative emphases between these two approaches has varied over time. The articulation of official papal and episcopal social *teaching* can be seen to be largely *reactive* to the major problems of the day: the condition of the working class at the height of nineteenth-century industrialization, and authentic development and environmental concerns in the last decades of the twentieth century. Many people have contributed to the emergence of this teaching including popes, bishops and theologians but also lay people with relevant expertise.

   Our starting point is the understanding that Jesus came to preach and initiate the kingdom of God, 'on earth as in heaven'. This kingdom, which is both present among us but not yet fully realized, is the subject of Chapter 3. This is a kingdom of justice, truth, freedom, love, peace and joy. In this chapter particular attention is paid to the notion of justice, seen as 'love structured in society'. The biblical concept of justice has to do with *right relations*, in the sense of what God intended, with God and with our neighbours throughout the world. God's justice is, challengingly, more than fairness, as is clear in the parable of the vineyard. It has a transformative and restorative quality and is subversive of popular views which take existing social arrangements as deserved and proper. This chapter also reviews some important secular approaches to justice such as those proposed by the philosopher, John Rawls, who saw justice as fairness, and Friedrich Hayek who, on the other hand, saw the striving for justice as corrosive of personal freedom.

   Catholic social thought is dialogical in that it has emerged in implicit dialogue with key secular ideas. Chapter 4 aims to take this dialogue seriously. For example, what does it mean to be a citizen of the kingdom of God, in terms of rights but also responsibilities? It is suggested that the secular concept of citizenship, which is still very much in the process of development, offers a valuable framework for the exploration of civil and legal, political, economic and social, and even environmental, citizenship and dimensions of justice in a global context. The chapter also explores the

[7] Throughout this book reference will be made to the *Compendium of the Social Doctrine of the Church* published by the Pontifical Council for Justice and Peace in 2004. See also the two documents *Prosperity with a Purpose* published by Churches Together in Britain and Ireland in 2005.

utility of the three key slogans deriving from the French Revolution: liberté, égalité and fraternité, and suggests that these are also key characteristics of the kingdom of God. Yet it must be acknowledged that these concepts have not yet been fully incorporated into Catholic social thought. The fact that the Church only finally acknowledged the right of religious freedom at Vatican II (1962–65), and that it has barely come to grips with the claims of equality, other than the platitude that we are all equal in the sight of God, and that the Vatican has reacted nervously to the challenges of liberation theology, indicates that there is a great deal of scope for further dialogue with secular thought. Pope John Paul II, however, put the claims of human solidarity firmly at the front of his social teaching.

Chapter 5 offers a brief introduction to Catholic social thought as it has emerged historically on the basis of scriptural exegesis and natural law thinking. It summarizes the key developments especially since Pope Leo XIII's encyclical *Rerum Novarum* in 1891 and more especially since Pope John XXIII and the Second Vatican Council in the 1960s. Apart from papal encyclicals, reference is also made to conciliar documents, the statement arising from the Synod of Bishops in 1971, the conclusions of two major meetings of the bishops in Latin America in 1968 and 1979, and the two major pastoral letters on peace and the economy by the US bishops of 1983 and 1986. Attention is also drawn to 'non-official' (in the sense of non-episcopal) contributions from priests, theologians and lay people. The chapter concludes by suggesting that there are six key concepts in Catholic social thought in addition to those deriving from secular thought. These are regarded as key criteria and guiding principles for the evaluation of social policies and processes. These are:

- *Human Dignity*: regarded as inviolable since every human person has been created by God in His image.
- *Common Good*: which recognizes the social character of all human beings and their interdependence and mutuality.
- *Subsidiarity*: which recognizes the rights of the family and intermediate organizations in relation to the state.
- *Preferential Option for the Poor*: which is solidly rooted in both the Old and New Testaments.
- *Solidarity*: which recognizes a responsibility to all other human beings and which rejects extreme forms of individualism.
- *Preferential Option for Non-Violence*: which is solidly rooted in Jesus' teaching and example.

These principles underpin the approach of Catholic social thought to the six major issues which we will consider in Part III of this book. They are suggested as criteria for the evaluation of existential social conditions as well as proposed social policies. Chapter 5 concludes with a brief evaluation of the present state of Catholic social thought and draws attention to some weaknesses, such as its neglect of women and of ecological concerns and its failure to address concretely the overwhelming power of major economic institutions which dominate the lives of so many people.

SOCIAL NEEDS AND INJUSTICES

As we have noted, the first stage on our journey seeking to respond as Christians and people of good will to the social realities of our contemporary world is to *identify* the social needs and injustices. One only has to listen to the latest news bulletin or open a newspaper to be swamped with a multiplicity of social needs and evidence of a wide range of injustices, both at home and across the world. In this book these have been subsumed under the six main justice issues which will be treated in detail in Part III of this book:

- *Human Rights* (Ch. 6) will include a consideration of the death penalty, torture, violence, racism and refugees.
- *The Family* (Ch. 7) will include gender issues and the emergent issues of bioethics such as IVF, cloning and the ethics of euthanasia.
- *Economic Life* (Ch. 8) will include such issues as work, employment and unemployment, private and public property, and trade unions.
- *Social Exclusion* (Ch. 9) is multifaceted and includes not only poverty and homelessness but also various forms of marginalization and participation.
- *Authentic Development* (Ch. 10) includes a consideration of international inequalities, international debt, population pressures and ecological concerns.
- *War and Peace* (Ch. 11) considers the issues of conflict and violence, disarmament and the arms trade.

STRUCTURAL INJUSTICES

It seems clear that this wide range of injustices, both at home and internationally between nations, are very largely interconnected and the consequence of the operation of the differential power of decision-making between the rich and the poor, people as well as nations, and the ability of the former to determine the rules of the game, taxation and welfare policies, immigration rules and restrictions, trade regulations, favoured groups, corporations or nations, institutional arrangements such as the International Monetary Fund (IMF), World Bank (WB) and World Trade Organization (WTO), and so on. Since the economic crises in the 1970s and the collapse of the Soviet Empire in the late 1980s, free market theories have increasingly determined both domestic and global economic policies. We are living in a period of liberal capitalist hegemony. There is today a growing awareness of the global reach of many economic, social, technological, cultural, military and political forces. Globalization is increasingly identified with liberal capitalism. The widening gap between rich and poor, both within and between nations, is in stark contrast to frequently expressed claims that economic growth will inevitably result in 'trickle-down' effects which will eventually benefit the poor.

What is it that maintains such injustices? Are they the inevitable consequence of placing too much reliance on Adam Smith's 'hidden hand' which supposedly promotes the good of society? The answer that they are simply the consequence of individual greed, selfishness, violence and evil is incomplete and fails to take account of the social dimension of all human action. An individual immigration officer at Gatwick operating the regulations of the state as a dutiful bureaucrat might do so in a way which respects the dignity of the traveller in a polite and sensitive way. The same regulations might provide an opportunity for vicious and thoroughly unpleasant treatment by a racist officer. The point, however, is that the regulations themselves might be unjustly discriminatory. Similarly, quite independently of differences of ability, women continue to be paid at a much lower rate than men for the same job. Poor people frequently have to borrow, for example to get into the housing market, at higher rates of interest on a loan or mortgage. International trade regulations and huge subsidies to farmers prevent poor countries exporting their cheaply produced food to rich countries. The free market is everywhere extolled but not in the case of poor people who wish to move to rich countries in search of employment. Examples are endless.

Whatever the undoubted achievements of the global economy, for example in increased life expectancy and greater literacy and hence access to labour markets in recent decades, discerning critics are concerned about the implications of a pervasive individualism and consumer mentality among western peoples. They argue that communal values needed for social cohesion have been diluted. Concerns have been growing at the ravages inflicted on ecosystems by cavalier and unregulated forms of liberal capitalism. Among the consequences of present economic arrangements is the loss of large numbers of animal species. Climate changes threaten millions of people in low-lying areas of the world as the tsunami and Hurricane Katrina illustrated only too clearly. Political and economic power inequalities have drawn attention to the undemocratic influence of huge multinational corporations (MNCs).[8]

What the above examples indicate is that there are social structures of injustice which have social consequences, quite apart from the personal faults of individuals. Unjust structures are frequently erected by powerful individuals or groups to further their own interests. Once in place they are maintained by the same or similar interests. People are socialized to treat them as inevitable, 'the way things are' and indeed ought to be. In time, strident claims will be made that 'there is no alternative'. Unjust structures become institutionalized. Unjust structures of inequality or dominance become rigid and legitimated by those with the power to assert their inevitability or desirability. What is being argued here is that it makes sense to talk and think in terms of unjust structures and institutionalized patterns of human behaviour as well as of unjust people.

A good example of structural injustices in the world at the beginning of the third millennium is provided by the workings of the international political economy which operates in the interests of the most powerful state, the USA. The consequence of the structural inequalities produced by such arrangements is likely to be disaffected new generations of young people who are prone to revolt. The 'structural arrangements that replicate a grossly unequal world have to be redesigned, so that markets working within the new framework produce more equitable results'.[9] As one commentator has put it: 'In a world of global dependencies with no corresponding global polity and few tools of social justice, the rich of the world are free to pursue their own interests while paying no attention to the rest'.[10]

In order to challenge such *social* structures of injustice it is necessary to take some form of *social* action. In other words, in order to remove social injustices it is necessary to mobilize people to struggle to change or amend the structures of law, rules and regulations which serve to maintain the injustices, by whatever political means are appropriate. In our democratic society this means by political lobbying, mobilizing public opinion in favour of whatever changes are necessary. Some suggestions for social action responses to injustices will be offered in Chapter 12. The structural aspects of injustice under liberal capitalism and in a globalizing world will be considered further in Chapter 2.

---

[8] Hertz 2001.　[9] Wade 2002.　[10] Bauman 2001: 56.

ACTION RESPONSES

So what actions can be taken in response to the structural injustices which can be identified? Modern technologies of instant TV news conveyed into our living rooms have enabled us to see far beyond our own personal experiences. However, while our compassion may be raised, the big challenge for Christians today is to know how to respond adequately to the suffering and need, both local and global, which can be seen.

We noted earlier that there are two distinct types of compassionate response to social need or suffering: the *amelioration* of suffering or the satisfaction of some need, on the one hand, and the removal of the causes of that suffering and need by means of political action. The charismatic Archbishop of Recife in north-east Brazil, Helder Camera, is once said to have observed sadly that 'when I feed the hungry they call me a saint, but when I ask why they are hungry, they call me a communist'! Catholics have always been enjoined to perform 'corporal acts of mercy'. As the 1994 *Catechism of the Catholic Church* (*CCC*) puts it, these 'consist especially in feeding the hungry, sheltering the homeless, clothing the naked, visiting the sick and imprisoned, and burying the dead' (*CCC*, §2447). Amelioration is generally uncontroversial and highly regarded. It also tends to be individual and personal and relatively local. Typically, parish branches of the St Vincent de Paul Society (SVP) quietly help poor people or those recently bereaved in their own area and local inter-Church groups collaborate in setting up overnight shelters for the homeless.

In contrast, *seeking justice* is altogether more controversial, challenging and threatening, as Helder Camera observed. It tends to be much more communal and because it addresses sinful structures, it tends to be social and political and hence much more national and international. Almost inevitably, since it questions existing social arrangements, laws, regulations and norms, it generates conflict with those who have an interest in those arrangements. In its official and formal statements, the Catholic Church has tended to be extremely wary of emphasizing the political implications of seeking justice, typically by means of lobbying those with economic or political power. However, as we shall see in subsequent chapters, in recent years individual pastors, bishops' conferences and social movements with transnational networks have been increasingly vocal in calling for structural changes.

In practice, both 'direct service' and 'social action' are necessary, compassionate responses. In recent years this has been depicted by CAFOD as 'the two feet of social concerns', both being necessary in order to walk. The

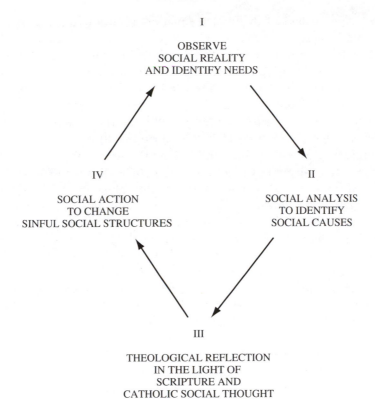

I

OBSERVE
SOCIAL REALITY
AND IDENTIFY NEEDS

IV

SOCIAL ACTION
TO CHANGE
SINFUL SOCIAL STRUCTURES

II

SOCIAL ANALYSIS
TO IDENTIFY
SOCIAL CAUSES

III

THEOLOGICAL REFLECTION
IN THE LIGHT OF
SCRIPTURE AND
CATHOLIC SOCIAL THOUGHT

Figure 1.1   The four stage cycle of social action

former aims to help people survive a present crisis, such as homelessness, earthquakes, famines and refugee crises, as well as traditional parochial care programmes such as visiting or shopping for the elderly. Social Action proper aims to remove the causes of structural problems and injustices by means of advocacy and lobbying; empowering groups to organize themselves to deal with their own problems, such as the needs of tenants or the marketing of farm produce; and by consciousness-raising events, writing letters, non-violent protest, and so on.

In recent years a four-stage pastoral cycle, as indicated in Figure 1.1, has been developed by Catholic social activists and movements.[11] John Fuellenbach notes that if we admit a 'kingdom-process' which 'is in some sense incarnated in human history, then we would be justified in using

---

[11] Holland and Henriot 1983: 7–30.

sociological analysis of the human situation as an interpretative tool for understanding this incarnation'. He insists that 'theology cannot be done independently from society and history'.[12] In line with this conviction, the social needs and injustices identified in the first stage of this methodology are subject to social analysis in the second stage. This seeks to identify the social causes of those injustices and is a process of 'conscientization', that is deepening the awareness of the socio-cultural reality and the capacity of human agency to transform it. This, in turn, requires a third stage of theological reflection on the injustices and their causes in the light of scripture and emerging Catholic social thought. Paolo Freire[13] stressed the need for both 'action' and 'reflection'. He argued that without action there is just 'verbalism' or idle chatter. Without reflection there is 'activism' which makes true dialogue with others impossible. Dialogue is necessary to liberate people from oppression. Finally, in the fourth stage, a pastoral response in actions aimed at eradicating the injustices by political action which addresses the root causes of injustices is encouraged.

The important point to note is that religiously inspired social action is cyclical and in a real sense unending. Each stage leads on to the next with the spiral deepening in its understanding and commitment. Social analysis and theological reflection sharpen the awareness of the imperfections of the world in which we live and help us to transcend the boundaries of our own limited experiences and identify new issues. Social action alongside the poor or oppressed and a deeper awareness of their experiences challenge us to develop an interpretative social analysis on these and to reflect on them theologically in the light of scripture and the developments in Catholic social thought. This four-stage process will be discussed further in Chapter 5. Increasingly important, too, in this process is the place of prayer and spirituality as part of the scriptural and theological reflection and their consequent impact on the lifestyles and witness of actors.

SUMMARY

This chapter has introduced the six convictions which provoked this book. It has suggested that an inductive method which starts from the realities of lived experiences of people and proceeds to analyze the causes of injustices and suffering and to reflect on them in the light of faith reflection in order to plan and undertake social action, is the appropriate way to respond to the manifest injustices in our world today. This appears to be the way Jesus

---

[12] Fuellenbach 1995: 57.   [13] Freire 1972: 60.

taught, for example in the parables. It is to be preferred to an earlier deductive approach which starts from Church teaching and then attempts to apply them to specific realities. The possibilities of human action are infinite and no deductive theory can address them all in their different circumstances. For example, the dangers of nuclear war or the potential of genetic engineering are new problems to which Christians have had to respond only within the last generation.

This chapter has presented in outline a schedule of social needs and injustices both domestically and internationally, which are a challenge to the Christian conscience. These have been clustered under six main headings, each of which will be addressed in more detail in Part III of this book. It is argued that it is important to context such deliberations historically, economically, socially and culturally. In the contemporary world, the hegemonic forces of neo-liberal capitalism in an increasingly global context have been boosted not only by the collapse of Soviet Communism but also by significant technological advances in recent years. Both economic developments and bitter resistance to them in recent terrorist attacks, have drawn attention to the fact of our interconnectedness in the modern world. Yet an essential element in the current social reality is that the world in which we live has one superpower and its current administration has no qualms in asserting explicitly its intention to act unilaterally in its own interests.

Recent Catholic approaches to social injustices have insisted on their structural causes. Hence any social action responses need to be grounded in serious social analyses of these causes. In Chapter 2 a framework for the social analysis of the causes of social needs and injustices is offered. This will focus in particular on the nature of capitalism and the extent to which it can be regulated in the interests of the common good. The contemporary version of globalization and the implications for poor people not only in developing countries, but also for labour in our own society will also be considered. Apart from tools for an appropriate social analysis, for the Christian there are the additional resources offered by theological reflections on social reality which are rooted in scripture and the developing contributions of Catholic social thought. These will be the foci of the three chapters in Part II.

CHAPTER 2

Capitalism in a global context

THE SOCIAL CONTEXT

In the previous chapter a significant number of instances of need or seeming injustices, both domestically within our own society and internationally between nations, were identified. The next stage is to provide an analytical framework for understanding injustices and an attempt to explain them in terms of some theory or understanding of causality. What is it that 'causes' social injustices such as increased income inequality between rich and poor both within and between nations? Why are people poor or homeless in affluent societies? What institutions determine major global economic decisions? Whose interests do they favour? Why are there so many asylum seekers from specific countries and refugees from other countries? Why are there migration flows of people seeking employment far from their own homes? What social policies appear to be harmful to families? Whose interests are being served by the international arms trade and what are its consequences?

These are basically sociological questions seeking explanations for the social outcomes of our existing social, economic and political decisions and the task of answering them is that of social analysis. In setting out on this quest it is relevant to note, in particular, four historical and contextual events which together constrain the way we look at the world at the beginning of the twenty-first century. The first is the Second World War, which generated the possibility of nuclear annihilation on a global scale, and which triggered the ending of the period of European colonialism and imperialism, the emergence of new nations and new international agencies such as the UN and its Security Council, and the division of the world into two major blocs led by two super-powers, the USA and the Soviet Union. The second key event was the sudden collapse of the Communist regimes in the Soviet Union and Central and Eastern Europe in 1989 and the resulting triumph of liberal capitalism led by the USA. The third key event was the terrorist attacks in the USA on 11 September 2001 which resulted initially in a sympathetic international coalition against the al-Qaeda terrorist organization in Afghanistan but then, very rapidly to the development of an aggressively unilateralist stance by the USA in its relations with the rest of the world.

A fourth contextual reality which Christians in western liberal democracies must face is that in spite of the historical legacy of Christianity, committed Christians today are often minorities in pluralist and secular, even post-Christian, societies. Not only is there a plurality of religious beliefs and practices, with large numbers of adherents to other faiths, such as Islam and Hinduism, as a result of recent migration flows, but increasing numbers of people in western societies deny that they have any religious beliefs at all. Contemporary society is distinctly secular and often pagan and is characterized by religious indifference and toleration of a wide range of beliefs and practices. Religion has largely become a purely private affair as secularization theorists have pointed out.

In recent times technological developments in information and communications technology (ICT) have speeded up and facilitated the possibilities of operating economically and culturally on a global scale. Major TNCs, such as Coca Cola and Nike, are familiar across the globe. Flows of capital, trade and labour have a global reach. This is not a new phenomenon but the pace and range of global transactions have increased dramatically. In recent decades there has also been a growing awareness of the global dimension of environmental concerns. Holes in the ozone layer or the impact of the general consumption of fossil fuels on global warming have had unexpected impacts on weather patterns all over the world. Even the nature of violence has achieved global significance with the discovery of global networks of terror. All of these processes are commonly referred to as exemplifying the processes of 'globalization'.

It seems clear that since the collapse of Communism there has been a growing tendency to promote economic liberalization with the removal of regulations controlling the free exercise of market forces globally in trade, investment and finance. The production of goods in a system of market competition with prices of all goods, including labour, determined by the balance between supply and demand, has in general resulted in the more efficient use of human and capital resources and resulted in higher average standards of living more successfully than alternative forms of state-controlled economic systems. But capitalist systems also tend to be more inequitable and this can generate resentments, conflicts and a lack of minimum levels of cohesion necessary for their successful operation.

In recent years a vocal anti-globalization movement has focused attention on a growing range of discontents about the consequences of economic liberalization for poor, developing countries, the growing gap
between poor and rich countries, the policies imposed on poor countries
by international institutions and their sense of powerlessness and lack of
political clout in the face of global forces. Such concerns require us to focus
on the many forms of power: military, political, economic, cultural,
technological, social and symbolic. In the world in which we live we
must take particular account of the enormous power of the US to achieve
its will either by the direct use of its military or economic power or through
its dominant control of international agencies such as the UN Security
Council or the IMF, WB or WTO, or culturally through its dominant
control of the world media.

In the following sections the four concepts: globalization, capitalism,
power and secular pluralism will be considered briefly. Together these
describe the world we are living in early in the twenty-first century and
provide a framework for the analysis and understanding of the range of the
domestic and international injustices which will be the focus of Part III of
this book. The attempt to understand and explain why these injustices exist
is a necessary first step in seeking to respond to them as Christians.

GLOBALIZATION

What is the meaning of 'globalization' and what are its advantages and
disadvantages? Basically it means that increasingly all social life is undertaken on a global scale. We can see glimpses of this in the fact that people
all over the world wear the same clothes (e.g. jeans), eat the same foods (e.g.
at McDonald's) and drink the same drinks (e.g. Coca Cola), watch the
same TV programmes, films and videos, recognize the same logos, suffer
from the effects of global climate change, utilize the same technologies (e.g.
computers), share the same goods (e.g. the same plastic toys in markets all
over the world), and are able to communicate virtually instantaneously (by
satellite or email) with people all over the globe. Rapid improvements in
transport (particularly air travel) have facilitated the mobility of labour to
different parts of the world and massive developments in tourism have
introduced increasing numbers of people to other cultures, traditions and
lifestyles. The recent spontaneous response to the tsunami disaster in Asia
illustrated the globalization of compassion.

In one sense, though, globalization is not a new phenomenon, for trade
in goods and ideas and the migration of peoples goes back at least to

biblical times and more recently to the discoveries of the Americas, Africa and Asia by European nations since the fifteenth century. What seems clear, however, is that in the past two decades, globalization has been dramatically accelerated by developments in ICT. One consequence has been that contemporary problems, such as Third World debt, climate change and terrorism, and indeed collaborative responses to them, are increasingly seen as global in their reach. In recent years groups concerned about the global impact of policies promoted by liberal capitalism on poor people throughout the world have been able to use the internet to mobilize huge protests from Seattle to Gleneagles. Since 11 September 2001, it has also become apparent that terrorist and disaffected groups also have a global reach.

Most discussion of globalization focuses on economic factors such as the growing international mobility of goods, capital and technology. But, as Giddens has pointed out, 'Globalization is political, technological and cultural, as well as economic'.[1] The term 'globaloney' has been coined to distinguish between real and imagined effects of recent changes and a former Director General of the Confederation of British Industry (CBI) has stressed that 'states still retain a high degree of freedom to choose between alternative social, environmental and indeed foreign-policy options'.[2] Hirst and Thompson distinguished strong and weak forms of globalization. They, too, stressed the evidence for the continued salience and power of decision-making by the nation state. They suggested that in its 'strong', deterministic form, globalization 'is a myth suitable for a world without illusions, but it is also one that robs us of hope'.[3] What was going on, they suggested, was closer to 'internationalization' as illustrated by the fact that most trade and foreign direct investment was 'intra-triadic', i.e. between the three great economic powers: the United States, the European Union and Japan.

In their analysis of historical patterns of globalization, David Held et al.[4] showed that globalization was 'best understood as a multifaceted or differentiated social phenomenon' which certainly could not be understood as linear or deterministic. Summarizing the patterns of globalization in the post-war period they concluded that in most dimensions, contemporary patterns had both quantitatively surpassed those of previous periods but

---

[1] Giddens 1999: 10.   [2] Turner 2001: 16.

[3] Hirst and Thompson 1999: 6. It might be noted that Christians are essentially people of hope in the redeemability of people and society and so reject deterministic explanations such as a strong version of globalization with immense independent causal power to generate social and economic outcomes. They would insist on some measure of social agency or responsibility for action, whether by individuals, groups, nation states or international regulatory bodies.

[4] Held et al. 1999: 27, 425.

also displayed significant and unique qualitative differences, particularly in the areas of politics, law and governance, military affairs, transport and communications, cultural linkages, human migrations, economic activity and shared global environmental threats. In economic relationships there was an unprecedented and growing intensity and complexity of production and trading networks.

In a paper prepared for UNCTAD, Martin Khor pointed out that in the last two decades the processes of globalization have been greatly accelerated by the liberalization of financial flows, trade and foreign investment.[5] He noted that 'a major feature of globalization is the growing concentration and monopolization of economic resources and power by transnational corporations and by global financial firms and funds'. There has also been a 'globalization of policy-making' and a reduction in the autonomy of national economy policy capacity in favour of international institutions such as the WB, the IMF and the WTO.

What seems to be apparent is that processes of globalization are social facts. It would make as much sense to deny them as it was for Canute to deny that the tide would come in. It seems clear, therefore, that in an important sense the antagonism of anti-globalization protesters is thoroughly misconceived. It is not that globalization *per se* harms the poor or pollutes the globe so much as its dominant and unregulated forms in the world today. It follows that what needs to be looked at much more closely are the structures which exist for the regulation of globalizing processes and the effectiveness of the controls of these processes in order to prevent the exploitation of the weak by the powerful. The dominant institutions of contemporary globalization are those of liberal capitalism.

LIBERAL CAPITALISM

Since the collapse of Communism in the former Soviet Union and Eastern Europe in 1989, global capitalism has reigned triumphant. The only serious alternative economic system, based on centralized state control and planning, had been defeated. Whilst Statist Centralism had served useful purposes in reducing inequality and virtually eliminating unemployment, it was economically inefficient, failed to motivate workers at all levels, and was riddled with contradictions.[6] The triumph of liberal capitalism was global in its reach as former communist societies, including China, increasingly introduced elements of market competition into their economies.

[5] Khor 2001: 7–16.   [6] Hutton 2002; Saunders 1995.

It is the hegemony of liberal capitalism and what John Gray has called 'the delusions of global capitalism'.[7] which have caused much soul-searching and spawned a plethora of anti-globalization coalitions[8] to protest at the harm being done to many of the poorest people in the world in the name of trade expansion and the assumed advantages of liberalization, such as the claims that the advantages of economic growth will 'trickle down' to poor people.

Peter Saunders[9] has defined capitalism as 'a system in which individuals or combinations of individuals compete with each other to accumulate wealth by buying the rights to use land, labour and capital in order to produce goods or services with the intention of selling them in a market at a profit'. He noted that capitalism pre-dated the industrial revolution and traced it at least as far back as the eleventh century. He argued that it was 'the most dynamic economic system the world has ever witnessed' and had three fundamental elements: the private ownership of property, the systematic and self-interested pursuit of profit, and the exchange of goods and services on the basis of market prices.

But it is important to note that there are numerous different versions of capitalism. As Saunders put it: 'Capitalism is not the same in Scandinavia as in Hong Kong, not the same in Germany as in the United States, not the same in nineteenth-century England as in twenty-first century Thailand'. John Gray[10] has emphasized that Roosevelt's New Deal capitalism of the 1930s was quite different from Bush's version of capitalism in the 2000s. He has also shown that the American global *laissez-faire* project of minimal state regulation is quite different from East Asian capitalisms.

Several analysts of contemporary capitalism have in different ways focused on comparisons between capitalism in the United States and Europe. Turner, for example, has suggested that the capital intensity per hour worked and labour productivity are higher in France and Germany compared to the United States. But hours worked per capita are much higher in the USA so that GDP per capita is higher there.[11] Both Peter Saunders and Will Hutton contrasted contemporary USA forms of free market capitalism with the more social market forms to be found in Europe.[12] Saunders noted that in the social market model in Germany, collective success and cooperation and longer-term concerns were more important and argued that 'capitalism cannot sustain a healthy society of happy individuals unless it is underpinned by some sort of shared moral

[7] Gray 1998.
[8] Christie and Warburton 2001; Duchrow 1995; Hertz 2001; Jacobs 1996; Klein, 2001, 2002.
[9] Saunders 1995: 1–9.   [10] Gray 1998: 130.   [11] Turner 2001: 135.   [12] Hutton 2002; Saunders 1995.

framework'.[13] While the American model of capitalism 'has degenerated into selfishness and corruption', the European model places greater emphasis on training and the role of trade unions and welfare. But he suggested that it was under threat for both economic reasons, such as low-cost competitors, and for political reasons, such as the appeal of USA media and culture and because of a relative openness to migrants in spite of a culture of conformity.

Although Michael Novak and others have attempted to demonstrate 'that the capitalist market system is consistent with Judeo-Christian ethics, and that the profit motive does not imply a disregard for the needs of others',[14] Saunders feared that the traditional values which previously underpinned American capitalism had begun to disintegrate in the face of unrestrained individualism and moral relativism. Hutton's book[15] was a sustained polemic against the ideology of American Conservatism with its assertion of the primacy of market forces as a human right. He argued that its claims were false because there were alternative and more benign forms of capitalism, such as potentially a modern version of the Roosevelt New Deal or the capitalism which generated the post-war Marshall Plan for the reconstruction of devastated Europe. Another model was that of the European Social Market, variants of which have been followed in many of the countries of the European Union since the Second World War. Table 2.1 presents a comparison between American Conservative and European Social Market forms of capitalism based on Hutton's analysis.

While both forms of capitalism shared a commitment to democracy, human rights and market capitalism, there were major differences in their core values and goals. American Conservatism was driven by a belief in uncontrolled individualism and a minimalist state. The *rights* of ownership took precedence over *duties* to share. Individual success was seen as the reward for hard work and virtue so that minimal obligations to the poor and needy were acknowledged. The public realm and need for some sort of social contract were barely considered. Social welfare was regarded as an individual responsibility and public provision was minimal. The European Social Market was premised on quite different values. The security and prosperity of the community as a whole and social justice concerns promoted by a facilitative state were valued. The wealthy were regarded as having obligations towards the less fortunate and the need for a social contract between different stakeholders, such as shareholders and trade unionists, was regarded as essential for the cohesion of society.

---

[13] Saunders 1995: 109–12.   [14] Ibid.: 119; Novak 1991.   [15] Hutton 2002.

Table 2.1. *A comparison between American Conservatism and the European social market (based on Will Hutton's analysis)*

	American Conservatism	European social market
Public goods	Uncontrolled individualism Minimalist state	Security, prosperity and social justice Facilitative state
Commitment to:		
a. democracy	Yes	Yes
b. human rights	Yes	Yes
c. market capitalism	Yes	Yes
Core values:		
a. obligations of propertied to society	No	Yes
b. need for social contract	No	Yes
c. centrality of public realm	No	Yes
Citizenship values (after Marshall):		
a. civil/legal	Yes	Yes
b. political	Limited	Yes
c. social/welfare	Minimal	Yes
Social awareness:		
a. interdependence	Little	Greater
b. reciprocity of obligations	Little	Considerable
c. global interest	Little	Greater
Social justice concerns	Minimal; detracts from self-interest	Significant; arises from reciprocity
Role of state:		
a. emphasis	Security; minimal intervention	More interventionist and pro-active
b. regulative	Minimal control of corporate capital	Stronger regulation of corporate capital
c. international	Unilateralist	Multilateralist
Taxation policy	Lower; favours rich; regressive	Higher; progressive; redistributive
Welfare policy	Minimalist; seen as disabling poor	Citizen rights; human capital investment
Corporate goal	Maximum profits for shareholders	Balance stakeholders' interests
Trade Unions	Low density; regarded with suspicion	Higher density; regarded as stakeholders
Employment protection	Minimal; seen as challenge to liberty	Higher; seen as part of social contract

Table 2.1. (*cont.*)

	American Conservatism	European social market
Inequality of wealth & income	High and increasing; of no cultural concern	Lower and social concern to reduce
Health	Relatively poor; highly inequitable	Relatively good; less unequal
Unemployment	Relatively low	Relatively high
Social mobility	Relatively low	Some
Key exemplars		
a. economists	Hayek; Friedman	Keynes; Beveridge
b. political scientists	Strauss; Nozick	Tawney; Rawls
c. politicians	Reagan; Thatcher	Roosevelt; Delors

Source: based on Will Hutton, *The World We're In*, London: Little, Brown, 2002

The public realm was salient for this reason and citizenship values were important.

Such concerns have relevance for the UK where successive British governments, from Thatcher through to Blair, have to a large extent followed American conservative economics, the pursuit of flexible labour markets, constraints on trade union activity and the privatization of public services. To a very real extent American Conservativism has achieved global hegemonic status. It is important to note, however, that it is but one model of capitalism, and one that has serious consequences for the pursuit of social justice both at home and internationally.

It is only proper that any analysis of liberal capitalism attempts a fair 'social audit' of the advantages and disadvantages of liberal capitalism. Thus Peter Saunders[16] has insisted that 'capitalism is a growth machine' which has resulted in huge increases in living standards and improved shelter, health, mortality and morbidity standards for an increasing number of people over recent decades. Even colonialism brought rational systems of law and administration, necessary preconditions for economic development. TNCs brought capital, skills and new technologies. Less convincingly, he offered a defence of the environmental impact of capitalism and argued that 'market capitalism and environmental quality are not inherently incompatible'.

---

[16] Saunders 1995: 10–12, 29–51, 34, 38, 75 and 100.

Against the positive consequences of capitalism must be set the negative consequences of the commodification of people's everyday lives. Thus Saunders admitted that 'self-actualization through paid employment is systematically undervalued in capitalist societies' and was largely sought in the home and in leisure. It is also clear that the current form of Anglo-American capitalism has seen very significant increases in inequality both within societies (such as the UK or the USA) and internationally between the developed and less-developed societies. More than half of the biggest economic entities in the world are TNCs, many with turnovers greater than all but a few nation states. Their increasing power has also raised concerns about proper democratic control of corporate capital generally,[17] especially in the light of recent scandals such as Enron and WorldCom in the USA, and Maxwell and Shell in the UK.

Any attempt to understand and explain the prevalence of domestic and international injustices must take into account the hegemony of liberal capitalism which in the early years of the twenty-first century is manifesting itself in a peculiarly extreme form. Its powerful tentacles intrude into all aspects of human social and economic life, from relationships within families and between different social classes, ethnic groups and genders, to relationships in the workplace, between organizations and between rich and poor nations. Market relationships intrude into all aspects of both private life and the public 'commons' such as education and health. These relationships reflect great power differentials between rich and poor people and nations.

POWER

Held et al. note that 'Globalization concerns the expanding scale on which power is organized and exercised, that is, the extensive spacial reach of networks and circuits of power. Indeed, power is a fundamental attribute of globalization'.[18] We may not like it but military, economic, political, social and cultural power differentials are facts of life. Any attempt to redress injustices must face the fact that prolonged struggle against the entrenched forces of domination is inevitable.

What is 'power'? Essentially, as Max Weber pointed out, power is the possibility of imposing one's will over others. In the world in which we live and in spite of attempts to regulate political relationships between states through the UN, and economic relationships through such international institutions as the IMF, the WB and the WTO, it is difficult to avoid the

[17] Hertz 2001; Klein 2001, 2002.   [18] Held et al. 1999: 28.

conclusion that the power of the USA is hegemonic. The world has much to thank the USA for, notably its crucial role in the defeat of Nazism in the Second World War and for its assistance, with Marshall Aid, in the reconstruction of a ravished Europe. But great power is rarely used altruistically and any serious attempt to understand the causes of injustice in the world must take into account the interests of the USA and of American corporate capitalism in general.

The USA under President George W. Bush has repudiated the anti-ballistic missile treaty and the Kyoto climate change protocol, scorned the Earth Summit in Johannesburg, refused to recognize the International Court of Justice, introduced tariff protection for the American steel industry and for farmers while insisting on trade liberalization for weak nations, scorned the multilateralism of the UN, initiated a war in Iraq in spite of the concerns of practically every other nation on earth, and so on. For some time the current USA administration, inspired by the principles of the *Project for the New American Century* which was established in 1997, has been asserting a unilateralist right to strike pre-emptively whatever the UN might say. As the world's only remaining superpower, no one can stop it. It has overwhelming military might and technological sophistication to ensure that it can impose its will if it wishes to do so. It also has enormous economic power which it can use to coerce smaller nations into collaboration or compliance. The military, economic, political and cultural power of the USA is a social fact in the world as we know it and under the present political regime, its contempt for any efforts at multinational regulation or conciliation has been defiantly asserted with the repudiation of previous treaties and agreements on arms control, environmental issues and trade relations.

Robert Hunter Wade has demonstrated how the USA has structured the world economy to serve its own interests.[19] He argued that a combination of six policies enabled the USA to consume far more than it produced and ensured that while international economic organizations gave a veneer of multinational legitimacy, they were financed in a way which ensured American control. These six policies were: free capital mobility; free trade (except where imports threatened American industries and jobs); free international investment (with no protection for weak or embryonic indigenous industries); the dollar as the main reserve currency; no constraint on creating dollars (for example by any dollar–gold link); and international lending at variable interest rates in dollars. This system operated in the interests of the richest individuals and most powerful

---

[19] Wade 2002.

corporations. The USA had also used its economic and political clout in the WTO in favour of a general agreement on trade in services, such as health care, welfare, pensions, education and water, 'which will undermine political support for universal access to social services in developing countries' but will be in the interests of private corporations. Wade suggested that 'these power relations and exercises of statecraft are obscured in the current talk about globalization. The increasing mobility of information, finance, goods and services frees the American government of constraints while more tightly constraining everyone else. Globalization enables the US to harness the rest of the world to its own rhythms and structure'.

He concluded by warning that while the USA and its allies could defeat specific groups by force or bribery, 'in the longer run, the structural arrangements that replicate a grossly unequal world have to be redesigned'. The history of all previous empires suggested that the present American policies of unilaterally determining its own rules and policies without concern for the rest of the world were unsustainable.

The three international organizations responsible for the promotion and regulation of economic affairs on a global scale, the IMF, the WB and the WTO, all have their origins in the attempts to construct appropriate regulatory structures in order to prevent a repetition of the collapse of the economic system in 1929.[20] The IMF is a membership organization of 184 countries but voting rights are weighted according to subscription quotas. The United States has 17 per cent of votes, Germany and Japan 6 per cent each, the United Kingdom and France just under 5 per cent each, and other EU countries 14 per cent. It is, therefore, not surprising that this has been described as a plutocracy, i.e. rule by the rich. It has been pointed out that 'in the system where an 85 per cent majority is required for important decisions, the United States has a de facto veto right'. The IMF purports 'to promote international monetary cooperation, exchange stability, and orderly exchange arrangements; to foster economic growth and high levels of employment; and to provide temporary financial assistance to countries to help ease balance of payments adjustment'. The reality has not been so benign and Joseph Stiglitz has recently published a damning critique of IMF policies.[21]

The second key organization in the world economy is the 'World Bank', which refers to the International Bank for Reconstruction and Development (IBRD) and the International Development Association (IDA). The WB 'is one of the world's largest sources of development

[20] Duchrow 1995: 95–106.   [21] Stiglitz 2002: 19.

assistance. It is the largest funder of education and also funds major health programmes, including HIV/AIDS programmes. The WB is governed by its 184 member countries represented by a Board of 24 Executive Directors. But again, voting is on the basis of subscription shares. The five countries with the largest number of shares, France, Germany, Japan, the United Kingdom and the United States, each appoint one director. The remaining countries are clustered into groups which each select a director to serve for two years. It has been tacitly accepted that the head of the IMF is a European and that of the WB an American. Clearly, these 'institutions are not representative of the nations they serve'. Africa, for example, has few votes because it is poor.

The third of the major international organizations is the WTO which deals 'with the rules of trade between nations. At its heart are the WTO agreements, negotiated and signed by the bulk of the world's trading nations and ratified in their parliaments. The goal is to help producers of goods and services, exporters, and importers conduct their business'. The WTO, which had 144 member countries in 2002, was created by the Uruguay Round of negotiations in 1995 and is the successor of the General Agreement on Tariffs and Trade (GATT) founded in 1947. The post-war multinational trading system is said to have promoted exceptional growth rates in trade which in 1997 was fourteen times the level of 1950. Recent rounds of negotiations have included not only tariff reductions but also anti-dumping measures, and wide-ranging liberalization measures including information technology, financial services, and currently, attempts to liberalize access to the education and health sectors and services such as water, energy and telecoms.

But, as before, the rules appear to operate in favour of the rich and powerful nations. Duchrow notes that 'free trade under GATT/WTO means freedom for the strong to make inroads into the national economies of the weak – protectionism by the strong against competitive products of the weak (the best-known example being the EU's Common Agricultural Policy)'.[22] He also points out that the UN is more democratic on the basis of one vote for each member state but that its Conference on Trade and Development (UNCTAD) 'has been gradually sidelined by the institutions of the rich, i.e. the IMF, the World Bank and GATT'. Stiglitz has also pointed out that the WTO negotiations are carried out in secret so that the influence of corporate interests is hidden and environmental concerns are

---

[22] Duchrow 1995: 104. Recent examples have included President Bush's protectionist measures to defend American steel producers and cottongrowers.

given little attention.[23] Rather than accept the claim that 'there is no alternative' to economic liberalization and the unfettered promotion of global capital, many have sought to find ways in which some form of control and regulation can be put in place, perhaps under UN auspices, to ensure that the benefits of increased trade are more fairly distributed and that the poorest and weakest people are not disadvantaged.[24]

The world today is changing rapidly in ways which are difficult to predict. Certainly, the USA is hegemonic on most dimensions at the beginning of the twenty-first century, but China and other Far East countries are becoming more powerful every day. The EU, too, in May 2004 welcomed the accession of ten new members and further expansion is anticipated. It may well provide an alternative and more multilateralist model to the United States in its relations with the rest of the world. The asymmetries of military, economic, political and cultural power both within our own societies and internationally, which are, to a large extent intrinsic to the nature of capitalism, are facts of life. That the powerful are not invulnerable has, however, been demonstrated not only by the non-violent opposition of anti-globalization protesters but also horrifically by recent terrorist attacks, resistance to the occupation in Iraq and Hurricane Katrina. Seekers after justice have to address not only the legitimacy of huge power differentials but also the consequences of domestic and global injustices.

SECULAR PLURALISM

The Second Vatican Council (1962–65) recognized that God's Spirit was at work in society. No longer was Catholicism to be *in opposition to* the world but rather in *critical dialogue with* it. But as with all forms of human interaction, the social context is important if we are to understand the nature of that dialogue and the relative power and influence of the different parties.

What seems to be undoubtedly the case in Britain, and more generally in Europe, is that there has been a decided process of secularization *in the public domain* and in social life generally. This means that the Christian Churches are no longer regarded as the major legitimate exponents of social morality but rather as but one of a whole variety of special interest groups aiming to influence public opinion and social policy. The world we live in today has changed dramatically since the early post-war years when the

[23] Stiglitz 2002: 227–28.   [24] Hirst and Thompson 1999; Monbiot 2003; Turner 2001.

Church had a status and authority which ensured it would be listened to. Now the right to be listened to must be earned by demonstrable commitment and expertise, for example through work with the poor or the competence of background research. Any attempt to dialogue with the world must recognize the changing context within which that dialogue takes place.

There are several different aspects of the changing position of religion in our society at the beginning of the twenty-first century. Firstly, whereas at the end of the Second World War 'religion' in western societies generally meant Christianity, that is no longer the case. As a result of the large migrations which have taken place since the ending of the colonial period, there are now large numbers of Moslems, as well as Hindus, Sikhs and adherents of other Eastern religions in Western Europe. In the United States there are huge numbers of 'Hispanics' from Central and South America. There are large numbers of adherents to a wide variety of 'New Age' religions. In Europe an increasing proportion of the population affirm that they belong to no religion and secular humanism is widely practised. In other words, there is a plurality of religious beliefs and practices, all of which make claims to some sort of legitimacy. Religious pluralism is a social fact in our current social context.

Secondly, personal and social morality is much less likely to be dictated by some religious or other authority figure or by tradition or social custom than it used to be. With increasing levels of education more and more people are making up their own minds on more and more issues and moral dilemmas than used to be the case. At the Second Vatican Council even the Catholic Church finally affirmed the primacy of the individual conscience, even though it insisted that such a conscience ought to be 'informed' by an awareness of official Church teaching. People are less likely to make decisions on difficult moral issues on the basis solely of what authority figures, such as the Pope or parish priest, might tell them. Part of the contemporary reality, therefore, is a strong element of subjectivism based on real or imagined experiential knowledge.

Thirdly, and related to this, is a strong cultural element of relativism, i.e. that the morality of an act depends on the circumstances and may change over time and between different cultures. This pervasive view challenges the traditional Christian position that there are absolute moral truths, often referred to as the 'natural law' which is binding on free human beings. This was a major theme of Pope John Paul II's encyclical letter *Veritatis Splendor* in which the pope warned against 'today's widespread tendencies towards subjectivism, utilitarianism and relativism ... (which claim) full cultural and social legitimacy'.[25] The prevalent view would deny that there is any way in which one person's view of what is 'natural' can be verified above that of anybody else's conflicting view. For believers, the Ten Commandments provide important guidelines though even here there are exceptions: the poor have the right to take and eat someone else's food if they are starving, and the State has the right to kill in legitimate defence.

Part of a common contemporary perception is that religion is not always benign. Religious conflicts have been pervasive throughout history. In our own times we have experienced the vicious 'troubles' between Catholics and Protestants in Northern Ireland; between Catholic Croats, Orthodox Serbs and Moslems in Bosnia; Moslems and Hindus in Kashmir; and Moslems and Jews in Israel. Secular humanists see these conflicts as clear evidence of the evil consequences of strongly held religious beliefs. Nor can it be claimed that all forms of Christianity are benign. People in the justice and peace movement would certainly want to distance themselves quite firmly from extremist forms of fundamentalism, for example those articulated by some elements of the 'new Christian right' in the Southern States of the USA and possibly fundamentalist House Churches in Britain.

All of these factors, suspicions concerning the 'fruits' of religion, the fact of a plurality of at least partially conflicting faiths, no universally accepted authority on moral issues, the emphasis on experientialism, subjectivism and relativism, a pragmatic utilitarianism, and a growing secularization of public life in spite of any religious transformations and revitalization, are all part of the contemporary climate within which the Christian religion must operate today. In this context it is only proper that Catholic social thought should make its contribution.

GLOBAL INTERDEPENDENCE

This chapter has suggested some basic themes and concepts which might be helpful in the attempt to offer a *social* analysis of the injustices, both domestic and international, which we briefly pointed to in Chapter 1. The world in which we are living at the beginning of the twenty-first century has changed quite dramatically in the decades since the Second World War. With the ending of colonialism and of the Soviet era, and as a

---

[25] John Paul II 1993: §106; also §§98–101.

result of a whole series of wars and ethnic conflicts, Europe experienced huge flows of refugees and economic migrants. Inevitably the population has become more heterogeneous, both socially and religiously. Post-war technological advances in transport and communications exposed the world to extremely rapid flows of capital, finance and ideas which have increased the potential for economic and social instability. The technology of war advanced at a frightening rate. Economically, after a long post-war period of economic growth, recent decades have witnessed the triumph of an extreme liberal form of capitalism which appears not to have operated always in the best interests of the poorest people or nations. Politically, for four decades the world was dominated by the Cold War between two superpowers. With the collapse of Communism, the USA was left as the triumphant leader of the capitalist world. Militarily, the balance between two competing superpowers in the Cold War period has been replaced by American hegemony and unilateralism. Alarmingly the asymmetries of power have in the past few years been challenged not only by emerging grassroots, non-violent, social movements, such as the World Social Forum or the Make Poverty History campaign, but also by new forms of international terrorism. Culturally, the USA, through its control of the mass media, has disseminated American values worldwide. This, then, in broad outline, is the social context in today's world.

The world is currently experiencing a multifaceted social phenomenon of growing global interconnectedness. It has been noted that power is a basic characteristic of globalization, and in our present world, the overwhelming military, political, economic and cultural power of the USA has been reflected in the present dominance of deregulated market capitalism. This model has been articulated through international agencies which were for long periods dominated by the 'Washington Consensus'.

The atrocity at the World Trade Centre on 11 September 2001, drew attention to an ugly side of the globalizing processes. People and nations all over the world woke up to the fact that small numbers of committed terrorists with a perceived grievance and an ideology which justified violence against 'westernization' could threaten not only large numbers of people anywhere in the world, but also the stability of the global economy itself, and with it the livelihoods of billions of people. The perception of the violence as a global threat to all might have generated a remarkable coalition of previously hostile nations in seeking an appropriate response. It seemed to point to the interdependence of all people on earth. Sadly, the opportunity to promote a multilateral response through the UN was lost in the second Iraq war.

The former US President, Bill Clinton, with the benefit of hindsight, has offered some reflections on the challenges facing the rich nations.[26] 'The great question of this new century', he wrote, 'is whether the age of interdependence is going to be good or bad for humanity. The answer depends upon whether we in the wealthy nations spread the benefits and reduce the burdens of the modern world'. He noted that optimists drew attention to the fact that the global economy 'had lifted more people out of poverty around the world in the past 30 years than at any time in history', the phenomenal growth in information technology, the potential contributions towards disease eradication resulting from advances in the biological sciences, and the explosion of democracy and ethnic and religious diversity.

Against this, pessimists and people in poor countries point out that 'the global economy is the problem, not the solution. Half of the world's people live on less than $2 a day; . . . 1 bn people go to bed hungry every night; a quarter of the world's people never get a clean glass of water; every minute one woman dies in childbirth'. Furthermore the world is likely to be consumed by an environmental crisis with global warming wrecking devastation and creating millions of new refugees. There is also a global health crisis with the danger that the spread of AIDS will create 'the biggest public health problem since the black death killed a quarter of Europe in the 14th century'. Clinton concluded with a healthy dose of pragmatism that in order to reduce the risk of disaffected terrorists, it seems fundamental 'that we cannot have a global trading system without a global economic policy, a global healthcare policy, a global education policy, a global environmental policy and a global security policy'.[27]

At this point a word of caution is appropriate. In their book on *Global Transformations*, Held et al. warned against 'the dangers of eliding globalization with concepts such as interdependence, integration, universalism and convergence'. They pointed out that 'whereas the concept of interdependence assumes symmetrical power relations between social and political actors, the concept of globalization leaves open the possibility of hierarchy and unevenness; that is, a process of global stratification'.[28] This is a useful distinction. It can scarcely be argued that power relations between the rich and the poor, or between developed and developing

[26] *Guardian Saturday Review*, 26 January 2002.
[27] The need for appropriate regulatory institutions at the global level has been a significant theme in much recent papal teaching.
[28] Held et al. 1999: 28.

countries are symmetrical. This means that references to 'interdependence' should be treated cautiously, perhaps as aspiration rather than reality. Christians would see the goal of interdependence as something called for by their common humanity as children of God. They would interpret the manifestation of the interdependence of people and of nations, both now and across time transgenerationally, as a sign of the coming of God's reign here on earth.

We are living in a world of rapid social change, increasing complexity and interconnectedness, a world of high risk but also of great opportunities, a world of great injustices but also one where the awareness of such injustices is becoming increasingly apparent. Many people work with compassion to alleviate the suffering of the poor, deprived and oppressed peoples in the world (the ameliorative 'sticking plaster' response). But it is also necessary to seek to understand the causes of these injustices, both current and historical, and endeavour to respond to them by lobbying for changes in the social and economic policies of governments, industrial and commercial corporations, and international regulatory institutions (the response of justice seeking). It is important to ask whose interests are served by existing social arrangements and who has the power of decision-making. It is suggested that the answers are to be found in the nature of capitalism and the struggles over the extent to which it is regulated in the interests of the common good. This book aims to contribute to this process by focusing, in particular, on the approaches to social justice which can be found in the rich tradition of Catholic social thought.

In his review of 'the modern process of globalization of Catholicism' José Casanova observed that the Catholic Church 'has remained one of the public voices left still questioning capitalist globalization and demanding the humanization and moralization of market economies and a more just and fair international division of labour and distribution of world resources'.[29] This questioning process is conducted not only from 'a radical structure centred in Rome' but also by means of a large number of transnational Catholic networks, exchanges and movements which cross national and regional boundaries and often bypass Rome. Increasingly important is the growing role of NGOs, including Catholic NGOs, working through UN institutions and western governments.

The aim of this book is to outline a Roman Catholic approach to seeking justice and peace both domestically and internationally. Western liberal, tolerant, secular, pluralist societies allow free choices between a multitude

---

[29] Casanova 2001: 433–34.

of competing views on issues of justice and peace. This is the world in which the Church's voice is to be heard. The Church has no privileged status in such societies and its voice is likely to be heard only to the extent that its message resonates with people of good will, whether committed members of the Church or not. In its dialogue with the world, its social analysis must be persuasive. But it has the advantage of being able to draw on the rich deposit of Catholic social thought based on scripture and twenty centuries of theological reflection. Part II of this book aims to introduce these resources.

PART II

Theological resources

CHAPTER 3

The kingdom of God

SETTING OUT

In the previous chapter we suggested a basic framework for the social analysis of the causes of injustices and the ways in which they are structured in enduring institutions, structures of power and domination, and pervasive cultural attitudes and values. The next step is to review the theological resources available to Christians in order that they might make a considered action response. In the three chapters of Part II we will outline recent understandings from scripture scholars and theologians, and the developing tradition of Catholic social thought, often in response to developments in secular thinking, especially since the onset of industrialization and Pope Leo XIII's encyclical *Rerum Novarum* (1891).

We will commence our reflections by considering two key passages from the Sermon on the Mount. Firstly, St Matthew recounts that Jesus urged people to trust in providence, stop worrying about everyday concerns and seek the kingdom of God *first*, and God's saving justice (Mt. 6: 33). The importance of seeking the kingdom was affirmed strongly in the Second Vatican Council's Pastoral Constitution on the Church in the Modern World (*Gaudium et Spes*: 72): 'Whoever in obedience to Christ seeks first the kingdom of God, will as a consequence receive a stronger and purer love for helping all his brothers (and sisters) and for perfecting the work of justice under the inspiration of charity'.

Yet traditional Catholic piety has often been very individualistic and focused on personal salvation. This has tended to give it an 'other-worldly' flavour with little practical concern to seek 'kingdom values' and address the causes of social injustices. This book is an attempt to respond to Jesus' call to seek the kingdom and argue that it has clear social implications for his followers.

Secondly, Christians typically pray the Lord's Prayer every day: 'Thy kingdom come, thy will be done, *on earth* as it is in heaven' (Mt. 6: 10). Yet before Pilate, Jesus insisted that his kingdom was not of this world (Jn 18:36). The words are so familiar that they tend to trip off tongues easily and unthinkingly. How can the two statements be reconciled? What did Jesus mean when he prayed that God's kingdom be realized here on earth and how should Christians respond to his call today? Is the kingdom to be interpreted solely in religious terms or does it have a social and political dimension? Vatican II taught that to the extent that earthly progress 'can contribute to the better ordering of human society, it is of vital concern to the kingdom of God'. So another purpose of this book is to seek a kingdom of truth, life, justice, love and peace (*GS* 39). How can the emergence of these 'kingdom values' be encouraged?

In this chapter we will reflect on Jesus' proclamation of the kingdom of God and on its meaning and implications for Christians today. This will be followed by a brief overview of the contribution of political theologians and their relevance for our purposes. Finally, we will suggest that a key characteristic of the kingdom of God is social justice and consider some valuable contributions from secular writers.

JESUS' PROCLAMATION OF THE KINGDOM

There seems to be substantial agreement among scripture scholars that 'the proclamation of the near arrival of God's kingdom is the central message of Jesus'.[1] Furthermore, this was 'a reality open to everyone, including the destitute poor, the sick, and the crippled, and tax collectors, sinners, and prostitutes'.[2] What this proclamation might mean and what its significance might be for Christians today is a matter of much debate. Three issues in particular are stressed: the eschatological concern with the full cosmic realization of the reign of God; that this realization is God's work; and whether the mission of the Church is political or not.

'Already' but 'not yet'

Both the instruction to seek the kingdom first and the Lord's prayer are clearly future-oriented and eschatological. In other words they reflect 'the sense that history is essentially open ended and incomplete until it finds its consummation in the aim God has set for it in the very act of creation'.[3] And yet, Jesus also told us that 'the kingdom of God is among you' (Lk 17: 21). 'The time of eschatological fulfilment is here and God's kingdom of

---

[1] B. Y. Viviano in Brown et al. 1991: 639.   [2] McBrien 1994: 449.   [3] In Dwyer 1994: 343.

glory is near'.[4] Jesus inaugurated the kingdom of God which is present here and now but it remains to be fully realized at the end of time when Satan's powers of domination and oppression are finally defeated by God's power of service and freedom.[5] Fuellenbach,[6] following an extensive discussion of the two aspects of the kingdom, the 'already' and the 'not yet', concludes that they 'must be held in dialectical tension'. After much reflection since the time of the Fathers he notes that three theological interpretations have emerged in recent years:

- *Other-worldly and future-orientated*: suggested around a century ago. This view, associated with Johannes Weiss and Albert Schweitzer, discounts any present realization of the kingdom.

- *This-worldly and present*: proposed around the 1950s and 1960s by C. H. Dodd ('realized eschatology') and Rudolf Bultmann ('existential eschatology'), tried to show the relevance of the kingdom message here and now but tended to neglect any future realization.

- *This-worldly but future*: often referred to as the 'already and not yet' position came to prominence in the 1960s and 1970s and was associated with the writings of Joachim Jeremias, Rudolf Schnackenburg and Oscar Cullmann. Fuellenbach notes that 'while almost all Catholic scholars maintain *both* the "already" *and* the "not yet" of the kingdom as a biblical reality, there is still considerable difference of emphasis among them'. Some argue that Matthew supports the 'not yet' position while Luke supports the 'already' position.

Jesus took the expression 'the kingdom of God' (or 'heaven' in Matthew) for granted and it appeared to be something which every Jew understood and longed for. According to the editors of *The New Jerusalem Bible*[7] the whole of Matthew's Gospel is a 'dramatic account in seven acts of the coming of the kingdom of heaven' which it mentions no fewer than fifty-five times:[8]

---

[4] Schnackenburg 1963: 213. [5] Nolan 1977: 69.

[6] Fuellenbach 1995: 206, 188–94. Fuellenbach gives a valuable and readable overview of the debates among scripture scholars about the kingdom of God.

[7] Wansborough 1985: 1606. Others interpret Matthew differently. Adrian Graffy, for example, suggests that 'Matthew superimposes on the basic gospel five major speeches of Jesus' which he considers to be 'a deliberate reflection on the five books of the Pentateuch ... The five speeches suggest Matthew's concern to present Jesus as a new and greater Moses'. (2001: 128, 129).

[8] Fuellenbach 1995: 4. It is also significant that while the Gospels mention the 'kingdom' 115 times, they mention 'church' only twice. In his Apostolic Exhortation *Evangelii Nuntiandi*, Pope Paul VI wrote that 'as an evangelizer, Christ first of all proclaims a kingdom, the Kingdom of God; and this is so important that, by comparison, everything else becomes "the rest", which is "given in addition". Only the Kingdom therefore is absolute, and it makes everything else relative'. (1975: §8).

- The *preparation* of the kingdom in the person of the child-Messiah (Chs. 1–2).
- The *proclamation* of the kingdom by Jesus in the Sermon on the Mount (Chs. 5–8).
- The *preaching* of the kingdom by missionaries (Chs. 8–10).
- The *obstacles* which the kingdom will meet (11:1–13:52).
- Its embryonic *existence* among the first disciples (13:53–18:35)
- The *crisis* provoked by the hostility of the Jewish leaders (Chs. 19–25)
- The *coming* effected through Jesus' Passion and Resurrection (Ch. 26–28).

Jesus did not define what He meant by 'the kingdom of God' but 'presented its meaning in symbolic actions such as table fellowship with sinners, healings and exorcisms ... (and) disclosed its significance in parables, similes, images, and metaphors'.[9] The parables are Jesus' distinctive way of teaching and they 'provide a vision of the kingdom that calls for immediate action aiming at the transformation of the world in its present state'. They tell stories which challenge the 'taken-for-granted', have different levels of meaning, aim to persuade and convert to a new vision of truth, which may be shocking and subversive, and lead to new forms of action and a change in lifestyle. They testify to a compassionate God 'who cares, loves, forgives'. They 'challenge us to act and to live in accordance with this gratuitous experience' of the kingdom. Jeremias concludes his classic study of Jesus' parables by observing that they all compel his hearers to come to a decision about him and his mission. For they are full of the secret of the kingdom of God, that is the recognition of 'an eschatology that is in the process of realization' and a 'veiled christological self-attestation of the historical Jesus'.[10]

For Pope John Paul II

The proclamation and establishment of God's kingdom are the purpose of Jesus' mission: 'I was sent for this purpose' (Lk 4:43). But that is not all. Jesus himself is the 'good news', as he declares at the very beginning of his mission in the synagogue of Nazareth ... Since the 'good news' is Christ, there is an identification between the message and the messenger, between saying, doing and being. His power, the secret of the effectiveness of his action, lies in his total identification with the message he announces: he proclaims the 'good news' not just by what he says or does, but by what he is.[11]

Daniel Harrington has written an appropriate conclusion to the theological problem of reconciling the present and future realization of the

---

[9] Fuellenbach 1995: 70–76.   [10] Jeremias 1963: 230.   [11] John Paul II 1991b: §13.

kingdom of God. He sees these as held in tension throughout the New Testament. When Jesus taught his disciples to pray 'Your kingdom come', the fundamental hope in the full realization of God's kingdom in the future was maintained. But there was also a growing awareness that in Jesus' ministry, death and resurrection the kingdom was also a present reality. The kingdom had been initiated. In sum, 'Christians live in the tension between the "already" and the "not yet" '.[12]

God's work

The second matter which deserves attention relates to the appearance of the kingdom of God in our present-day world and lives. To what extent can we speak of 'building up the kingdom'? At the Second Vatican Council *Gaudium et Spes* affirmed that through their labour, men and women were 'contributing by their personal industry to the realization in history of the divine plan' (§34). Ten years later Pope Paul VI's apostolic exhortation *Evangelii Nuntiandi* (§13) also affirmed the importance of human activity and building up the kingdom. In *Redemptoris Missio* Pope John Paul II taught that 'building the kingdom means working for liberation from evil in all its forms ... the kingdom of God is the manifestation and the realization of God's plan of salvation in all its fullness' (§15).

Yet it is important to note that scripture scholars stress that realizing the kingdom of God on earth is God's work and cannot be built simply on the basis of human endeavours. Schnackenburg, for example, regards the phrase 'building up the kingdom of God' as unbiblical.[13] Meier insists that 'God is now beginning to assert his rightful claim over his rebellious creatures and will soon establish his rule fully and openly'.[14] Brown points out that 'Jesus did not proclaim a social programme but the kingdom of God in the sense of God's coming to transform people and rule in the last times'.[15] Finally, Fuellenbach also insists that 'we cannot create or build the kingdom of God. It is God's work and gracious gift, but our actions on earth make a difference ... We are God's cooperators, but the kingdom remains God's until its final coming'.[16] In other words, it will only come about if we accept it willingly and actively. In this process, human beings are given the gift and challenge of freedom, to collaborate or not. In this

---

[12] In Dwyer 1994: 511.
[13] Schnackenburg 1963: 354. On the other hand Johann Baptist Metz (1969) and Jon Sobrino (1985) have no inhibitions about 'building the kingdom'.
[14] Meier 1991: 1320. [15] Brown 1997: 827. [16] Fuellenbach 1995: 203, 205, 34.

sense 'the coming kingdom must be looked upon not merely as a gracious gift but also as a task'.

This leads us to a consideration of the third issue of significance: the perspectives of political theology and of the Latin American liberation theologians and their Vatican critics. As Fuellenbach notes, there are ambiguities in recent Church teaching in the use of terms such as 'building up' the kingdom.[17] But an important strain of socio-political thinking has emerged in recent years which seems relevant to the theme of building up or realizing more fully the values of God's kingdom on earth. This includes both the European political theology of Jürgen Moltmann and Johann Metz as well as the Latin American liberation theology of Gutiérrez, Assmann, Boff and Sobrino. Both Moltmann and Metz call for a radical discipleship which challenges structural injustice and strives for the transformation of the world and the realization of justice, freedom and humanity in the light of the Christian hope in the promised future reign of the risen Christ. The liberation theologians, on the other hand, start from the social reality of oppression, exploitation and dependence and construct a theology on the basis of liberation from these evils and injustices in ways which may begin to approximate more closely to the values of God's kingdom of full human life and dignity.

St Mark tells us that after the arrest of John the Baptist, Jesus went to Galilee and in his first reported words said: 'The time is fulfilled, and the kingdom of God is close at hand; repent, and believe the gospel' (Mk 1: 15). In Luke's account (4: 18) of Jesus' visit to Nazareth, Jesus reads the text from Isaiah (61:1–2): 'The spirit of the Lord is on me, for he has anointed me to bring the good news to the afflicted. He has sent me to proclaim liberty to captives, sight to the blind, to let the oppressed go free, to proclaim a year of favour from the Lord'.

Both Matthew and Luke report that John the Baptist sent two of his disciples to ask if he was the 'one who is to come'. In his reply Jesus said: 'Go back and tell John what you have seen and heard: the blind see again, the lame walk, those suffering from virulent skin-diseases are cleansed, and the deaf hear, the dead are raised to life, the good news is proclaimed to the poor . . .' (Lk 7: 22) The first thing that strikes one about the proclamation and Jesus' reply to John is their emphatic social dimension: compassion for

[17] Ibid.: 197.

the poor and afflicted, prisoners, the disabled and oppressed, and his commitment to do something about it, to tackle the sources of their suffering and oppression, to cancel accumulated debts and end exploitation as in the Jubilee traditions of the Mosaic Law.[18] In this way God's will is to be done. This, it seems, is Jesus' manifesto for the kingdom.

All the same, 'Jesus seems to have had no concrete plan of how the kingdom would be realized. He left that to God, who would determine the time, as well as the way it would unfold'.[19] According to St Paul: 'it is not eating and drinking that make the kingdom of God, but the saving justice, the peace and the joy brought by the Holy Spirit' (Rom 14: 17). These are 'the fundamental values of the kingdom'. The challenge to Christians today is how to bring about a world permeated with such values. This challenge was taken up by political and liberation theologians.

Thus Johann Baptist Metz called for an engaged discipleship concerned about the structural injustices between the rich North and the poor South. This discipleship necessarily had a double structure with *both* spiritual and political dimensions. Thus he argues that

the praxis of discipleship should therefore not remain limited to individual moral praxis, for individual moral action is in no way societally neutral or politically innocent. Any Christology of discipleship therefore must inquire into the societal and political context of such discipleship. In this sense, it is – necessarily – *political Christology* . . . The Church must . . . increasingly become in itself a sign of protest against the dominance of a mere market society . . . where no ideal of justice is publicly admitted other than the justice of the market.[20]

For Metz, the Christian should not simply speak of hope but actually offer it in his or her praxis. Elsewhere he writes:

The eschatological City of God is *now* coming into existence, for our hopeful approach *builds* this city. We are workers building this future, and not just interpreters of this future . . .. The Christian is a 'co-worker' in bringing the promised universal era of peace and justice. The orthodoxy of a Christian's faith must constantly *make itself* true in the 'orthopraxy' of his actions orientated toward the final future, because the promised *truth* is a truth which must be *made* (see John 3:21ff).[21]

The theology of hope of the Protestant theologian Jürgen Moltmann is similar to that of Metz. He writes that 'hope finds in Christ a consolation *in* suffering, but also the protest of the divine promise *against* suffering . . .

---

[18] Lev. 25: 8–17.   [19] Fuellenbach 1995: 129, 156.   [20] Metz 1978: 140.
[21] Metz 1969: 94–95; quoted in McBrien 1994: 1146.

Those who hope in Christ can no longer put up with the reality as it is, but begin to suffer under it, to contradict it. Peace with God means conflict with the world'. The resistance of Christians to an unjust world should show 'them to be a group that is incapable of being assimilated' to their own society and to be seriously seeking 'the eschatological *hope of justice*, the *humanizing* of man, the *socializing* of humanity, the *peace* for all creation'.[22]

Liberation theologians from Latin America are actually quite critical of the Vatican Council's *Gaudium et Spes*, of European theology in the post-Vatican period, Pope Paul VI's encyclical *Populorum Progressio* (1967) and his apostolic exhortation *Evangelii Nuntiandi* (1975), and even of the documents arising from the CELAM meeting at Medellin (1968). While there is general approval of the 'new political theology' of Metz and Moltmann, there are criticisms that it is based on an inadequate social analysis of the structures of domination, that it is reformist and 'palliative', too defensive of the *status quo* and tolerant of existing structures of injustice, inadequately prophetic, and too concerned about internal eccle-sial matters rather than the realities of 'unrelenting forces of domination'.[23]

In *A Theology of Liberation*, Gustavo Gutiérrez, starts out by noting that 'the gift of the kingdom of God (is) in the heart of human history'. Liberation theology is 'open – in the protest against trampled human dignity, in the struggle against the plunder of the vast majority of people, in liberating love, and in the building of a new, just, and fraternal society – to the gift of the kingdom of God'. For Gutiérrez the elimination of misery and exploitation, oppression, servitude or alienated work, the evil and scandal of poverty 'will signify the coming of the kingdom'.[24]

In his *Christology at the Crossroads*[25] Jon Sobrino insists that 'orthopraxis must take priority over orthodoxy' if it is not to remain abstract. He notes that 'Jesus equates "proclaiming God" with "realizing God's reign in practice"' and that he emphatically denounced structural sin. 'Individuals become Christians through their efforts to fashion the kingdom into a reality'. This presupposes renewal in human hearts, societal relationships and the cosmos at large. It means doing justice, renouncing power and aiming for universal reconciliation.

[22] Moltmann 1967: 324, 329.
[23] See, e.g., Assmann 1975: 30–31, 92–96; Gutiérrez 1974: 215–25; Sobrino 1978: 28–33; 1985: 341 (FN 23).
[24] Gutiérrez 1974: 11, 15, 167–68, 295. For a critical review see Charles 1998b: 244–49.
[25] Sobrino 1978: 45–46, 95,119, 121–22, 391.

Leonardo Boff continues with the same themes but focuses on the historical Jesus whose praxis could be regarded as 'a liberation in process'. Justice occupied a central place in Jesus' proclamation. 'The primary function of the messianic king is to do justice to the poor and to defend the rights of the weak. He also rejects wealth, viewing it dialectically as a result of the exploitation of the poor . . . Equally liberative is his criticism of all power exercised as domination over others'. People enter the kingdom of God 'by breaking with this world and changing it, not by prolonging its existing structure'.[26]

In a later book Sobrino summed up Jesus' mission of fidelity to the Father as proclaiming the kingdom of God, denouncing sins against the kingdom and therefore 'every form of oppression that was practised by the economically strong, the intellectuals, the religious leaders, and the political leaders', and by his actions in bringing about the kingdom as a reality, by showing the signs of its realisation in miracles, exorcisms, and unity with outcasts, as well as in the prophetic signs of its absence (such as the merchants in the temple).[27] Gutiérrez brings us back strongly to the theme of urgently seeking the kingdom of a God who liberates and gives life in its fullness, does justice, is holy and faithful to the covenant.[28]

In 1977 the South African Dominican theologian, Albert Nolan, wrote his well-known study *Jesus Before Christianity*.[29] Nolan argued that Jesus condemned the political and social structures of this world as evil and belonging to Satan. 'When God's kingdom comes, God will replace Satan'. 'Jesus dared to hope for a kingdom or world-wide community which would be so structured that there would be no rich and no poor', where there was no stratification of prestige and no social distinctions, where 'a new universal solidarity' replaced old group solidarities, where every form of domination and slavery will have been abolished in the kingdom of mercy and compassion, service and freedom.

The teaching authority of the Catholic Church was concerned about secularist interpretations of the coming of an earthly kingdom of justice arising from some elements in liberation theology. Thus the Sacred Congregation for the Doctrine of the Faith (CDF) in *Libertatis Nuntius* warned in 1984 that 'There is a tendency to identify the kingdom of God and its growth with the human liberation movement, and to make history

---

[26] Boff 1980: 282–88. A critical account of Boff's later book *Church, Charism and Power* (1985) which was notified as being 'in error' by the CDF in 1985, is given in Charles 1998b: 311–14.
[27] Sobrino 1985: 238.   [28] Gutiérrez 1991.   [29] Nolan 1977: 48, 53–54, 63, 69–71.

itself the subject of its own development, as a process of the self-redemption of man by means of the class struggle'. Furthermore, they were alarmed at the notion of class conflict and judged there was 'a disastrous confusion between the *poor* of the Scripture and the *proletariat* of Marx'. Liberation theology has also been criticized by Third World feminist theologians for its failure to address the injustices experienced by women.[30]

However, at the instigation of the Vatican's Secretariat of State, the CDF published *Libertatis Conscientia*,[31] a more positive assessment, two years later. It claimed that 'the quest for freedom and the aspiration to liberation, which are among the principal signs of the times in the modern world, have their first source in the Christian heritage'. It argued for 'a Christian practice of liberation', seen as a development of the social doctrine of the Church, 'in accordance with the changing circumstances of history' and 'the supreme commandment of love of God and neighbour in justice'. Among the fundamental principles for reflection are four which will be considered further in Chapter 5: human dignity, subsidiarity, solidarity and the common good. Liberation theologians would agree with these principles and simply insist on social action to implement them. These principles are the basis for judging social situations, structures and systems. However, in my view, the document is so concerned to stress the primacy of persons over structures and to distance itself from Marxist analyses that it makes the strange and inaccurate observation that 'the Church's social doctrine is opposed to all forms of collectivism'. In spite of this, it admits that 'the fight against injustice is meaningless unless it is waged with a view to establishing a new social and political order in conformity with the demands of justice'.

It is my judgement that the contribution of liberation theologians to the social analysis and scriptural and theological reflection on the multitude of social injustices in the contemporary world has been immense. They continue to offer one of the most fruitful, challenging and prophetic perspectives to Christians as they struggle to promote social justice. Their approach fits in well with the main theme of this chapter which is that Jesus came to proclaim and inaugurate the kingdom of God on earth and that it is the task of the followers of Christ to seek this kingdom where God reigns in peace, justice and joy.

[30] CDF 1984: IX 3, 10; McBrien 1994: 143; Charles 1998b: 303–311.
[31] CDF 1986: §§5, 72–80; McBrien 1994: 143; Charles 1998b: 311–325.

JUSTICE IN THE KINGDOM OF GOD

But first, let us consider some of the essential characteristics of the kingdom of God. We will begin by suggesting that justice is essential for the realization of the kingdom of God. In the Sermon on the Mount, Jesus challenges: 'if your uprightness does not surpass that of the scribes and Pharisees, you will never get into the kingdom of Heaven' (Mt 5: 20). This points to a 'fuller justice' which is deeper than and goes beyond the law.[32] Justice is an essential characteristic of the kingdom of God.

The *Catechism* (*CCC* §§1807, 1928–1948) regards justice as one of the four cardinal virtues and defines it as 'the moral virtue that consists in the constant and firm will to give their due to God and neighbour . . . Justice toward men disposes one to respect the rights of each and to establish in human relationships the harmony that promotes equity with regard to persons and to the common good'. Society is said to ensure social justice 'when it provides the conditions that allow associations or individuals to obtain what is their due, according to their nature and their vocation. Social justice is linked to the common good and the exercise of authority'. It has respect for the essential and equal dignity of each human person and their God-given rights. The *Catechism* admits that there are 'sinful inequalities . . . in open contradiction of the Gospel'.

This is very general and unspecific and frequently 'an occasion of serious contention'.[33] 'Justice demands a special concern for the disadvantaged and the marginalized, for the orphan, the stranger, the widow and the poor'.[34] The just community is characterized not only by fairness and impartiality but also by generosity beyond the reciprocity of doing unto others what you would have them do to you. The parable of the labourers in the vineyard expands our notion of justice. Generosity is also expressed in mercy and forgiveness. Justice is manifested 'in a community of restored relationships and healed memories'. The Judeo-Christian understanding of justice looks forward in eschatological hope to God's kingdom of justice and love which is in stark contrast to Francis Fukuyama's claim[35] that liberal democracy is the only legitimate hope left for the world.

The Christian can draw on the resources of scripture to point the way forward. As we have noted already, St Paul teaches that it is 'the saving justice, the peace and the joy brought by the Holy Spirit' that make the kingdom of God (Rom 14: 17). The kingdom of God aims 'to liberate the

[32] Graffy 2001: 134–135.   [33] John XXIII, *Mater et* Magistra, 1961: §206.
[34] Forrester 1997: 210, 231–234.   [35] Fukuyama 1992; Forrester 1997: 252.

whole of creation' from the rival kingdom of evil and it will manifest itself as 'a liberating force that aims at restructuring human society in terms of justice, peace, and joy'.[36] The biblical concept of justice (or righteousness) has to do with *right relations* 'to God, to oneself, to one's neighbour both as individual and as part of society, and to creation as a whole'. But what is meant by 'right relations'?

The Old Testament is full of references to the ideal Covenant relationship in which 'I will be your God and you will be my people'. According to Micah (6:8), the Israelites were told that Yahweh only wanted them 'to act justly, love tenderly, and walk humbly with your God'. Over and over again the errant Israelites were told that more important than ritual worship and holocausts was for them to act justly especially to the poor, orphans, widows and foreigners.[37] It is important that we recognize that the biblical idea of justice is about God treating people, not according to their deserts but according to their needs. The biblical sense of justice 'is to sort out what belongs to whom, and to return it to them'. God's justice has a transformative quality and causes things to change so that there is abundant life.[38]

This theme of 'giving things back' has its origins in the Mosaic Covenant and the institution of the Great Jubilee in Leviticus (Lev 25: 1–28). The Israelites were instructed that even the land must keep a sabbatical year of rest every seven years. Every fifty years they were to return to their ancestral properties, thus preventing the creation of land monopolies. 'Land will not be sold absolutely, for the land belongs to me' says Yahweh. In Deuteronomy (Deut 15: 1–11) the Israelites were instructed to remit all debts every seven years. This was the inspiration behind the Jubilee 2000 campaign and the theology of relinquishment of 'one's claim to what others need'.[39]

The central message of Jesus 'must be seen as aiming first at the restoration of Israel to the Covenant ideal, which in turn would lead to the transformation of all human structures in favour of justice and the rights of the poor'.[40] This implies the 'life-creating and life-sustaining' relationships which express God's intention for creation. The Covenant was originally egalitarian and participative so that its restoration requires the conversion of people to the Covenant ideal and the restructuring and

---

[36] Fuellenbach 1995: 88–89, 157.
[37] See, e.g., 1 Sam 15: 22; Prov 21: 3; Is 1: 16–17; Is 42: 6–7; Is 58: 6–11; Jer 22: 16; Hos 6: 6 (quoted twice in Mt 9:13 and 12: 7); Amos 5: 23–24; Ps 51: 17.
[38] Fuellenbach 1995:159, quoting W. Brueggemann.   [39] Neal 1977: 105.
[40] Fuellenbach 1995: 69, 138–139, 162–167; 171–172; 224–225; 255–256.

transformation of socio-political structures and institutions to realize it. This is the significance of Jesus' opposition to the Temple aristocracy which had created a society of security and oppression in place of 'the free God of the Exodus'. It was Yahweh's intention to create a 'counter-community with a counter-consciousness that matches the vision of God's freedom'. This model would be a 'subversive kingdom . . . (which) seeks to replace society's dominant values and structures with those of the kingdom of God . . . in radical obedience to the gospel and in opposition to the powers of the present age . . . (and which) shows particular concern for the poor and oppressed, the victims of society . . . the widow, the orphan, and the alien'.

Fuellenbach and others have stressed that the Christian concept of justice embraces the notion of the 'integrity of creation' and respect for the interrelatedness and interconnectedness of God's creation and of our role as stewards. The fruits of justice include peace and joy, fullness of life and abundant love. In the development of Catholic thinking on justice there is a close relationship between love and justice.

The Greek and Latin Fathers of the Church in the fourth century, particularly Basil, Ambrose and Augustine were concerned about the origin and nature of political authority, 'rendering to Caesar' what was his due. For Augustine, the 'tranquillity of order' depended on justice. For Basil, if wealth were distributed justly, there would be no rich and no poor. For Ambrose, the sharing of riches was a duty and a matter of justice since God had given the fruits of the earth for common use. The social responsibilities of ownership and wealth were addressed by Thomas Aquinas in the thirteenth century. People needed a sufficiency of material goods in order to live a fully human way of life. Extreme inequalities created discontent because they offended a human sense of justice. It was the task of the State to seek justice in the interests of the common good. It was from Aquinas that the distinctions between general and particular, distributive, commutative and legal justice were derived.[41]

Thus the *Catechism* notes that 'one distinguishes *commutative* justice (which regulates exchanges between persons in accordance with a strict respect for their rights) from *legal* justice which concerns what the citizen owes in fairness to the community, and from *distributive* justice which regulates what the community owes its citizens in proportion to their contributions and needs' (*CCC* §2411).

[41] Charles 1998a: 80, 88, 91, 209–210.

Social justice is clearly a multifaceted concept as is indicated in the developments in Catholic social doctrine over the past century and more. In Leo XIII's encyclical *Rerum Novarum* (1891) the law of (distributive) justice 'ordains that each shall have his due' (§§27, 34) and this included the notion of the 'just wage'. Forty years later Pius XI in *Quadragesimo Anno* (§§47, 110, 137) referred to the right to property which 'belongs to what is called commutative justice faithfully to respect the possessions of others, and not to invade the rights of another, by exceeding the bounds of one's own property'. These principles must also regulate the relations between capital and labour. 'The public institutions of the nations should be such as to make all human society conform to the requirement of the common good, that is, the norm of social justice'. Pius XI notes interestingly that 'justice alone, even though most faithfully observed, can remove indeed the cause of social strife, but can never bring about a union of hearts and minds'. This will only come about 'when all sections of society have the intimate conviction that they are members of a single family and children of the same Heavenly Father'.

A great leap forward in Catholic social thinking was inspired by Pope John XXIII who in *Pacem in Terris* (1963) taught that relations between nations should be regulated by justice which 'implies, over and above recognition of their mutual rights, the fulfilment of their respective duties' (§91). Two years later in *Gaudium et Spes*, the Second Vatican Council pointed out that 'peace is not merely the absence of war ... Instead it is rightly and appropriately called "an enterprise of justice". Peace results from that harmony built into human society by its divine Founder, and actualized as they thirst after ever greater justice' (§78, quoting Is.32:7).

Pope Paul VI's encyclical letter *Populorum Progressio* (1967) urged the three duties of human solidarity, social justice and universal charity (§44). Four years later, in his Apostolic Letter *Octogesima Adveniens*, Pope Paul pleaded that 'there is a need to establish a greater justice in the sharing of goods' and in international exchanges which were based on force. This meant that 'the most important duty in the realm of justice is to allow each country to promote its own development, within the framework of a cooperation free from any spirit of domination, whether economic or political' (§43).

As we noted in Chapter 1, the 1971 Synod of Bishops firmly indicated that the search for justice is no optional extra but an integral part of Christian witness and the vocation to evangelize and preach the 'Good News' of salvation and liberation from sin and injustice. In their pastoral letter on *The Challenge of Peace*, the United States bishops referred to the *comparative* justice of the claims of two warring adversaries (§92). In their later pastoral letter *Economic Justice for All* they described *contributive* justice as stressing the duty of all who are able to help create the goods, services, and other nonmaterial or spiritual values necessary for the welfare of the whole community (§71).

Some have claimed that justice has been recognized in Catholic social thought since the time of the early Church. But the working out of what it might mean in practice in specific instances, such as slavery or war, or the paying of a just wage, or the right to religious freedom, or appropriate relations between political leaders and citizens, or the rights of migrants and indigenous people, or the acceptability of nuclear deterrence theory, or the boundaries of genetic engineering, have all taken centuries of theological reflection to develop and articulate. Thus it was only towards the end of the nineteenth century, some decades after socialists had grappled with the plight of industrial workers, that modern Catholic social thought began to address the social consequences of industrialization. And it has only been since the 1960s that the Church has begun to address the social and economic consequences of development processes and economic relations between rich and poor nations. The Church, insofar as it is incarnated in a specific social and historical context, is inevitably likely to be strongly influenced by that context as it strives to address its particular challenges, however much it attempts to do so from the perspectives of faith.

There is clearly continuing scope for the development of doctrine as the Church struggles to interpret the mind of its founder. Some measure of pluralism seems inevitable. Apart from methodological and theological pluralism, there is a pluralism of social analyses, and 'the very complexity of the issues argues against the possibility of claiming with absolute certitude that there is only one possible Christian approach or solution' on ethical issues.[42] Indeed, Pope Paul VI acknowledged a pluralism of options in *Octogesima Adveniens* when he admitted that it was difficult to offer a solution to problems 'which has universal validity'. He went on to say: 'It is up to the Christian communities to analyse with objectivity the situation which is proper to their own country, to shed on it the light of the Gospel's unalterable words and to draw principles of reflection, norms of judgment and directives for action from the social teaching of the Church' (§4; see also §§50–52).

Pope John Paul II, in his encyclical *Centesimus Annus* (1991), which celebrated the centenary of *Rerum Novarum*, affirmed that 'the "new

---

[42] Curran 1978: 158–159.

evangelization", which the modern world urgently needs ... *must* include among its essential elements a proclamation of the Church's social doctrine' (§5; emphasis added). It seems that justice is most frequently appealed to in terms of its perceived absence among the poor, oppressed or afflicted or in 'a network of domination, oppression, and abuses which stifle freedom and which keep the greater part of humanity from sharing in the building up and enjoyment of a more just and more fraternal world'.[43] As support for the Make Poverty History campaign in 2005 showed, people recognize that in a world of great plenty there is injustice in poverty, that torture and genocide are evil, that the arms trade and discriminatory trade relations between developed and developing nations and the widening gap between rich and poor are unjust.

SECULAR APPROACHES TO JUSTICE

It is clear that there are difficulties in making concrete judgements about exactly what is social justice. Is it 'an eye for an eye', capital punishment for the murderer? What do we mean by a 'just wage' or 'fair price' or just distribution of wealth or income or trade between nations? How seriously ought we take fears of the 'nanny' or 'social assistance' state and a 'culture of dependency'? What criteria are relevant in the search for distributive justice? What is the just way of responding to genocide or terrorism? Can there be a 'just war' with modern weapons and mobilized populations? Brief reference will be made here to the contrasting perspectives of the Harvard philosopher, John Rawls, and the Nobel Prize winner in economics, Friedrich Hayek.

In his enormously influential treatise on justice as fairness, Rawls enunciates two principles for institutions:[44]

- *First Principle*: Each person is to have an equal right to the most extensive total system of equal basic liberties compatible with a similar system of liberty for all.
- *Second Principle*: Social and economic inequalities are to be arranged so that they are both (a) to the greatest benefit of the least advantaged ... and (b) attached to offices and positions open to all under conditions of fair equality of opportunity.

Rawls then adds two 'priority rules' and a 'general conception':

- *First Priority Rule* (The Priority of Liberty): The principles of justice are to be ranked ... and therefore liberty can be restricted only for the sake

---

[43] *Justice in the World*, 1971, in O'Brien and Shannon 1992: 288.   [44] Rawls 1973: 302–303.

of liberty . . . (a) a less extensive liberty must strengthen the total system of liberty shared by all, (and) (b) a less than equal liberty must be acceptable to those with the lesser liberty.

- *Second Priority Rule* (The Priority of Justice over Efficiency and Welfare): The second principle of justice is . . . prior to the principle of efficiency and to that of maximizing the sum of advantages; and fair opportunity is prior to the difference principle . . . an inequality of opportunity must enhance the opportunities of those with the lesser opportunity . . .
- *General Conception*: All social primary goods – liberty and opportunity, income and wealth, and the bases of self-respect – are to be distributed equally unless an unequal distribution of any or all of these goods is to the advantage of the least favoured.

Duncan Forrester[45] offers a detailed and extended critique of Rawls' thesis and suggests there are significant differences between Rawls' 'original position' and subsequent developments. Whereas the former aimed to secure 'some kind of objectivity in reasoning about justice, rising above narrow and short-term self-interest', Rawls later stressed that his account made no claims to universality or truth and was, rather, rooted in the consensus of most people in modern liberal democracies. Forrester correctly points out that a consensus of most people about justice may be false, as in Nazi Germany. Consensus is likely to be built on self-interest. Even Rawls' 'difference principle', which Forrester sees as derived from the Judeo-Christian tradition and a secular version of the 'preferential option for the poor' would not necessarily generate a response to poverty and deprivation if it was not in the interest of the rich and powerful. In spite of such criticisms, Forrester affirms four elements in Rawls' theory:

- the priority given to justice over efficiency and prosperity;
- the assumption of human equality;
- the 'difference principle' as at least a partial expression of a preferential option for the poor which seeks 'to mitigate the influence of social contingencies and natural fortune on distributive shares' by providing 'basic structural conditions . . . necessary for fair equality of opportunity';[46]
- the importance of fairness as an essential component of justice.

However, as Forrester rightly points out, 'fairness is not enough' within unchanged and unjust social structures: 'But a society or a polity in which the fundamental principle of justice has been narrowed down to fairness, in

---

[45] Forrester 1997: 120, 122–124, 128–130, 133–134, 113–139.   [46] Rawls 1973: 73.

which justice is not in some obvious sense an expression of love, is impoverished and inhumane ... A justice which is more than fairness demands just societies and just social institutions. The justice that the Lord requires is more than fairness'.

Others, such as Friedrich Hayek, regard the very pursuit of social justice as a 'humbug' which would inevitably erode freedom and lead along *The Road to Serfdom*.[47] 'As long as the belief in "social justice" governs political action, this process must progressively approach nearer and nearer to the totalitarian system'.[48] Hayek believed that striving for social justice would have 'highly undesirable consequences, and in particular lead to the destruction of the indispensable environment in which traditional moral values alone can flourish, namely, personal freedom'.

Forrester suggests that 'the ideological nature of Hayek's theory of justice is betrayed by the fact that it leaves the wealthy and the powerful undisturbed and unchallenged provided that they obey the simple rules of fair dealing'.[49] We might add that unjust or sinful social structures fundamentally constrain the access to social goods and opportunities of the poor, disadvantaged or oppressed, and hence their access to the substantive freedoms which would be a mark of a just and free society. Critics, such as John Gray, go further and point to Hayek's 'neglect of the destructive impact of free markets on social cohesion' and claim that this 'confirms that liberal ideals of personal autonomy require an active, enabling state, not the minimal government of classical liberal theory', for 'in the circumstances of the late modern world personal autonomy and a stable, cohesive society are not alternatives'.[50]

CONCLUDING REFLECTIONS

This chapter has shown that the kingdom of God, both already here among us and to come in the fullness of time, were at the core of Jesus' proclamation to bring the good news to the poor. The scriptural roots of the kingdom of God and its various characteristics and manifestations were indicated in outline. Theologians reflecting on apparently contradictory sayings attributed to Jesus have expressed the tensions between the present and future manifestations of the kingdom in the phrase 'already but not yet'. The contributions of European political theology and Latin American liberation theology were found to resonate well with eschatological notions

[47] Hayek 1944: 81–84; 164–169.   [48] Hayek 1982: 67–68.   [49] Forrester 1997: 151.
[50] Gray 1998: 161.

of the kingdom of God. While the realization of the kingdom is God's work, followers of Jesus are called to transform society in ways which will bring it closer to God's intentions for His people.

It was then suggested that justice was an essential sign of the existence of the kingdom of God. The biblical concept has to do with 'right relations' with God and with our neighbour but the understanding of what that might mean in concrete situations continues to be worked out today. The scriptures showed that God's justice had to do with a special concern for the poor, orphans, widows and foreigners, with ensuring their full participation in the life of the community, and with a periodic redistribution of land and property in order to restore a primordial equality and harmony amongst all God's people. Further insights from the early Fathers of the Church and from Thomas Aquinas have led to current understandings. Since the time of Pope Leo XIII at the end of the nineteenth century, successive popes have articulated the developing mind of the Church on the issues and have attempted to define aspects of distributive, commutative, comparative and contributive forms of social justice, but difficulties remain in specifying what these might mean in any real, empirical and concrete situation.

The Second Vatican Council encouraged a much more open stance towards secular thought but to date there have been relatively few examples of genuine dialogue between theologians and scripture scholars, on the one hand, and social scientists and philosophers, on the other. One of the most influential contributions to the understanding of social justice in recent years has been that of John Rawls. At the other end of the political spectrum Frederick Hayek has been a major critic of the very idea of social justice. Both have been the subject of a valuable critique by Duncan Forrester. In the chapters which follow we will return to their contributions in our search for the justice dimensions of the kingdom of God in our world, both at home and abroad. But first, we will explore in Chapter 4 more secular interpretations and analyses of the concept of citizenship (of the kingdom) and of such values as freedom, equality and solidarity in any realization of the kingdom of God on earth as in heaven.

Christian citizenship

CITIZENSHIP

In the previous chapter we saw that there are considerable scriptural and theological resources available for reflecting on the imperative to seek the realization of the kingdom of God here 'on earth as in heaven' and to strive for social justice. But there are other valuable resources, notably key values, principles and ideologies which have arisen in secular society, some of which were bitterly resisted for decades by the Church and which have only in recent years come to be accepted. In this chapter, we will consider the concept of citizenship and the rights and obligations it implies. St Paul reminded the Christians of Ephesus (2:19) that they were 'fellow-citizens with the holy people of God and part of God's household'. The traditional Catholic position has always been to stress the dignity of each individual human person created in the image of God and to be suspicious of any tendency to reduce that to the status of citizen of a state. The state exists for the benefit of its citizens and not vice-versa. Cardinal Cormac Murphy O'Connor has stressed that the Catholic sense of citizenship is to be found in seeking the 'Common Good'. In this chapter we will discuss the participation of citizens in God's kingdom and also the three characteristics of citizenship which emerged out of the French Revolution of 1789: freedom, equality and, to use the modern papal term, solidarity. Our aim is to offer a Christian perspective in dialogue with secular approaches.

In his Introduction to the statement by the Catholic Bishops' Conference of England and Wales (CBCEW) on *The Common Good* (1996) Bishop Konstant stated that 'we want to be open in our approach. We are eager to listen to ideas from other Churches and indeed anyone who wants to contribute, Catholics or not' (§§15, 41). Part I of the document was entitled 'Christian Citizens in Modern Britain'. It affirmed 'that in the spirit of good citizenship all members of the Catholic Church must accept their full responsibility for the welfare of society'. Furthermore, 'all Catholic citizens need an informed "social conscience" that will enable them to identify and resist structures of injustice in their own society'. In 1986 the United States Catholic bishops in *Economic Justice for All* taught that 'the virtues of citizenship are an expression of Christian love more crucial in today's interdependent world than ever before' (§66). What citizenship actually consists of is, however, rather glossed over in both documents.

Bryan Turner argued that 'the universalist element in the Abrahamic faiths laid the ideological foundation for a universalistic definition of social membership not based on blood or kinship'.[1] While the concept of citizenship could be found in the Greek city-state and the works of Plato and Aristotle, modern versions usually date from the French Revolution of 1789. Turner suggested that there were three reasons why the French Revolution remained critically important. Firstly, it was linked to debates about universal citizen rights as requiring both equality and community. Secondly, it was linked to the notion of the nation state with subjects called citizens. Thirdly, it offered political liberation for minority groups and against colonial and other dominating powers. Turner emphasized in particular the link between citizenship and the emergent needs of capitalism to overthrow traditional forms of hierarchy and ascription in favour of relationships of economic exchange.

T. H. Marshall had argued in 1950 that in England there were three stages in the development of citizenship. In the eighteenth century there had been the emergence of civil (or legal) rights, that is 'the rights necessary for individual freedom – liberty of the person, freedom of speech, thought and faith, the right to own property and to conclude valid contracts, and the right to justice'.[2] In the nineteenth century there was an extension of political rights, i.e. 'the right to participate in an exercise of political power, as a member of a body invested with political authority or as an elector of such a body'. Civil and political rights were both relevant for the emergence of the individual wage-worker of liberal capitalism. Thirdly, in the twentieth century, with the development of the welfare state, attempts were made to identify and extend a range of social rights, to education, health, welfare and social security.

Marshall acknowledged, and subsequent commentators have emphasized, that the realization of civil, political and social rights had always been the product of struggle. As Turner pointed out,[3] 'the (capitalist) economy tends to generate inequalities in income and wealth whereas

---

[1] Turner 1986: 13–15; 19; 21–25. [2] Quoted in Bulmer and Rees 1996: 5. [3] Turner 1986: 6, 136.

the (democratic) political system is based on the egalitarian principle of citizenship'. In other words, there were contradictions between the three dimensions of citizenship so that the struggle to extend social rights was ongoing and indeed reversible. Turner argued that : 'The claims to individual rights which were first used by the bourgeoisie against the aristocracy are now used by workers against employers, by women against men, by children's advocates against parents and by migrant workers against their host communities'.

Bulmer and Rees pointed out the continuing 'robust usefulness'[4] of Marshall's categories to the critique of inequalities not only of class and income, but also of race and gender and to contemporary debates about inclusion and exclusion within a society. The notion of citizenship implied some form of closure, for example against migrants or asylum seekers. Different nations, for example Britain, France and Germany, have historically developed quite different concepts of nationality and citizenship and hence exclusion of some groups of immigrants. In an era of increasing consciousness of globalization, extending the concept of citizenship to all people on earth replicates the struggles which once took place within one society. Thus Howard Newby[5] argued that there had been the emergence of struggle for 'environmental citizenship' in a context where global citizens might be 'institutionally disenfranchised' and fragmented when faced with global environmental change.

Bryan Turner[6] suggested that Christianity was inherently egalitarian and that since all people were equal in the sight of God, it was difficult to justify inequality. He also noted that a succession of social movements had worked to extend universalistic citizenship rights to new categories of beneficiaries. The first wave of citizenship extended rights to non-property holders, the second to women, the third to (age and disability) dependants. Of course, some rights would be in conflict: workers and employers; the right to bear arms and freedom from violence; women's rights over their own bodies and the rights of children, especially unborn children. A fourth wave attempted to extend quasi-citizenship rights to animals and to dissolve the boundaries between all living creatures and the natural environment.

PARTICIPATION

One obvious right of citizenship is that of participation in key areas of social life. This includes participation in the political life of society, in the

---

[4] Bulmer and Rees 1996: 283; 15–16.   [5] Newby 1996.   [6] Turner 1986: 67; 75; 138; 105; 97–100.

election of representatives, decision-makers and civil authorities, and the determination of social policies; in the economic life of society, normally through paid employment which provides self-respect and a wage necessary to bring up a family and accumulate property; and in the social and cultural life of society. Participation as a right derives from the notion of the intrinsic dignity of each individual human being who, for Christians, is called to participate in the extension of God's creation through productive work and to contribute to the common good. Participation also implies and is related to the notions of individual freedom and equality. Thus, Pope Paul VI noted that with social and technological change and better education 'two aspirations persistently make themselves felt . . . the aspiration to equality and the aspiration to participation, two forms of man's dignity and freedom' (*OA*, 1971: §22).

A concern in Catholic social thought for participation, and the related themes of partnership or co-partnership and democracy, seems to have emerged as salient only relatively recently. Roger Charles suggested that up to the time of Pius XII in the post-war era, the popes' direct experience of democratic governments in Europe following the French Revolution had not inspired trust since they had sought to destroy the Church in France and had introduced unacceptable forms of totalitarianism in Italy and Germany. He argued that representative government was acceptable provided that it operated under just law which safeguarded the rights and dignity of all people and allowed for the peaceful transfer of power. This had not been the experience in Europe but the papacy had not had contact with the older tradition in Britain and the United States, 'which was derived from the theories and practices of Western Christendom in the Middle Ages'.[7] Pope John Paul II gave much more emphasis to the notion of participation and stressed the responsibility of the Christian citizen to participate. However, he expressed concerns that where basic Christian assumptions about an absolute moral order had been undermined by secularism, relativism and subjectivism there was a danger of a democratic totalitarianism.[8]

Participation, then, is seen as a right of human beings to determine legitimate political authority and policy decisions. We can discern a gradual shift in papal thinking over the past seventy years. Thus, Pius XI in 1931, building on earlier proposals for co-partnership and codetermination,

---

[7] Charles 1998b: 106. See also pp. 27, 114–115, 178, 363.
[8] John Paul II, *Centesimus Annus* 1991: §46; *Veritatis Splendor* 1993: §101; *Evangelium Vitae* 1995: §§20, 71. See also Rico 2002: 159–60, 171, 205.

proposed that 'the workers and executives become sharers in the ownership or management, or else participate in some way in the profits' of productive enterprises (*QA*, §65). Thirty years later, Pope John XXIII noted the increasing complexity of modern life so that 'in many areas of activity, rules and laws controlling and determining relationships of citizens are multiplied'.[9] Arguing from a personalist emphasis on the dignity of human beings and the need to seek the common good, he urged that people be encouraged to participate in the affairs of their group. 'Justice is to be observed not merely in the distribution of wealth, but also in regard to the conditions under which men engaged in productive activity have an opportunity to assume responsibility . . .' Later he repeated the view that 'the dignity of the human person involves the right to take an active part in public affairs and to contribute one's part to the common good of the citizens'.[10] The Vatican Council's document, *Gaudium et Spes* (§§68, 75), again from a 'personalist' perspective, urged that both 'active (economic) participation of everyone in the running of an enterprise should be promoted' and that political participation in 'juridical-political structures' should, 'without any discrimination, afford all their citizens the chance to participate freely and actively in establishing the constitutional bases of a political community, governing the state, determining the scope and purpose of various institutions, and choosing leaders'. In 1971, as we noted above, Pope Paul VI recognized that participation was a legitimate human aspiration.

The argument has since been taken further. In 1981, ninety years after Leo XIII's *Rerum Novarum* had asserted the right of workers to organize collectively in defence of their own interests, Pope John Paul II, in *Laborem Exercens*, bluntly noted that 'rigid' capitalism remains 'unacceptable' and reaffirmed proposals for 'joint ownership of the means of work, (and) sharing by the workers in the management and/or profits of businesses' and personalist arguments favouring a sense that the worker is working 'for himself'(*LE*, §§14–15). By 1985 the pope was drawing attention to the consequences of denying participation, seen now as a basic right, not only in the workplace but also in broader context. He warned: 'future violence and injustice cannot be avoided when the *basic right* to participate in the choices of society is denied'.[11]

In *Centesimus Annus* he argued that 'democratic participation in the life of society' contributed 'to deliver work from the mere condition of a

---

[9] John XXIII, *Mater et Magistra* 1961: §§62, 65, 82.   [10] John XXIII, *Pacem in Terris* 1963: §26.
[11] John Paul II, *World Day of Peace Message* 1985: §9.

"commodity", and to guarantee its dignity' (*CA*, §19). Against both state and liberal forms of capitalism, the pope rather sought 'a society of free work, of enterprise and of participation . . . not directed against the market, but (one that) demands that the market be appropriately controlled by the forces of society and by the state, so as to guarantee that the basic needs of the whole of society are satisfied' (§35). The pope suggested that Catholic social teaching 'recognizes the legitimacy of participation in the life of industrial enterprises so that, while cooperating with others, and under the direction of others, they can in a certain sense "work for themselves" through the exercise of their intelligence and freedom' (§43). Turning to political participation, the pope affirmed that 'the Church values the democratic system inasmuch as it ensures the participation of citizens in making political choices, guarantees to the governed the possibility both of electing and holding accountable those who govern them, and of replacing them through peaceful means when appropriate'. But, he warned, 'authentic democracy is possible only in a state ruled by law, on the basis of a correct conception of the human person'. Structures of participation and shared responsibility must be based on a respect for truth and objective morality because 'a democracy without values easily turns into open or thinly disguised totalitarianism' (§46).

In his World Day of Peace message in 1999, the pope expressed the generally shared conviction today that 'all citizens have the *right* to participate in the life of their community' (§6). The following year he seemed to suggest that it was also a matter of self-interest since 'experience seems to confirm that economic success is increasingly dependent on a more genuine appreciation of individuals and their abilities, on their fuller participation, on their increased and improved knowledge and information, and on a stronger solidarity'.[12]

The Catholic resistance to excessive demands on its citizens and the suppression of individual rights and dignity by a powerful state has already been noted. A concern for justice towards non-citizens (such as economic migrants and asylum seekers) and of core citizenship rights for those on the periphery (such as ethnic minorities) is also central to the Catholic search for social justice. This search requires us to consider the three central claims of secular humanism as formulated at the time of the French Revolution: liberty, equality and fraternity.

---

[12] John Paul II, *World Day of Peace Message* 2000: §16. Similar themes had been expressed by the United States bishops in *Economic Justice For All* 1986: §§15, 68–76, 78, 295–325.

FREEDOM

The Church was extraordinarily slow to come to a realization of the importance of freedom in God's world. In the mind of the popes, the democratic stirrings of the American and French Revolutions at the end of the eighteenth century were interpreted as invitations to social chaos and challenges to the monarchical rights of the popes as rulers of the Church and of the Papal States. It was not until the final session of the Second Vatican Council in 1965 that the age-old antipathy to religious freedom was finally laid to rest. So we must appreciate that we are talking here of a very recent development in Catholic social thought, one which has hardly begun to be fully digested and understood. It continues to be regarded with some suspicion, as the recent Vatican concerns about liberation theology suggested,[13] and is an area in which there is clear scope for a further development of doctrine.

Arguably, individual freedom is 'the human person's most precious gift'. It goes back to the Creation stories in Genesis. God commanded man: 'You are free to eat of all the trees in the garden. But of the tree of the knowledge of good and evil you are not to eat' (Gen 2: 16–17). Offending against this prohibition was a claim to moral independence and a refusal to recognize his status as a created being. Human beings were free to choose to obey God or not, but in Catholic thought they were also obligated to seek the truth, to recognize their total dependence on God, and faithfully to conform to God's will, guided by His authentic interpreters and teachers in the institutional Church. The parables of the sower and the wedding feast can be interpreted as showing that the good news of the kingdom is preached to all but that people have the freedom to determine to what extent they respond.

This raises the question of the relationship between individual conscience and the Church's magisterium. In a recent study Linda Hogan[14] argued that 'the Catholic approach to conscience is deeply ambiguous'. While for St Augustine conscience was never binding, for St Thomas Aquinas 'every conscience, true or false, is binding, in the sense that to act against conscience is always wrong'. In spite of the primordial gift of freedom, Hogan endeavoured to confront 'the many confusions and contradictions' in the Catholic tradition. These had been illustrated over the centuries by the savage war against the Albigensians, the use of torture and the Inquisition, the slowness with which the Catholic Church opposed

[13] CDF 1984; 1986.   [14] Hogan 2001: 2, 4, 26, 31, 80–81, 115–118.

slavery, its bitter resistance to the democratic ideals of the American and French Revolutions, the lateness of its acceptance of religious freedom, the matter of conformity to papal teaching about contraception and women priests. The continuing tendency to authoritarianism and the suppression of debate and dissent, all pointed to a certain ambiguity when considering the relationship between the individual conscience and Church teaching and the place of freedom in the kingdom of God.

In *Quanta Cura* (1864) Pope Pius IX had referred to the opinion that 'liberty of conscience and worship is each man's personal right' as 'erroneous' and 'fatal in its effects on the Catholic Church and the salvation of souls' and recalled that Pope Gregory XVI had regarded it as 'an insanity'. In an appendix to the encyclical, known as *The Syllabus of Errors*, Pius IX condemned many of the tenets of 'liberalism' including freedom of worship and the separation of Church and state.[15]

Hogan[16] suggested that there were two competing versions of moral theology, both of which had supported their positions with selective readings of the theology and history of conscience. She argued that in spite of a number of continuing ambiguities in the treatments of conscience in *Gaudium et Spes* and *Dignitatis Humanae*, the Second Vatican Council signalled a paradigm shift from a legalistic or 'manualist' tradition of moral theology to a more 'personalist' model which respected the role of conscience for a person with free choice and took into account factors such as context and circumstances, goals, intentionality and consequences of actions.

As with all 'revolutionary' paradigm shifts, there were major conflicts between those who stuck firmly to the older paradigm and those who favoured the emergence of the new. She illustrated this with a consideration of Pope John Paul II's encyclical *Veritatis Splendor* (1993) which expressed fears of excessive individualism, privatization and subjectivism. Hogan[17] suggested that the pope in this encyclical followed a 'legalistic model' of morality which seemed to allow only a limited role to personal moral judgement. Against this view, she argued in favour of a 'personalist model' which she claimed was in tune with the teaching of Vatican II. This 'prioritizes the personal autonomy and responsibility of individuals in moral matters'. She believed that individuals were attempting to act in a responsible and mature way which took account of their own experiences and in awareness of the Christian encounter with God's law of love of God and neighbour. But this process was 'always subject to the limitations of human understanding and discernment' and hence error.

---

[15] Quoted in Burns 1994: 26, 28.   [16] Hogan 2001: 100–126.   [17] Ibid.: 25, 29.

The notion that 'error has no rights' appeared to have been derived from a serious distortion of Augustinian thinking during the struggle against the Albigensians. Pope Gregory IX 'put the seal on the use of force against error in 1231, when he absorbed into canon law the imperial legislation which decreed the burning of convicted heretics by the secular power'.[18] Against *Veritatis Splendor*, Hogan[19] argued that the Church had historically been mistaken in claiming to be 'the *only* reliable interpreter of moral law' as its approach to the torture of heretics illustrated. 'Conscience too has a primary role'. In sum, 'the task of conscience involves scrutinizing one's intention, evaluating all the relevant circumstances and informing oneself of Church teaching and other sources of moral wisdom'.

Pope John XXIII signalled a development of doctrine in his encyclical *Pacem in Terris* (1963) which took as its starting point the dignity of each individual human person created in the image of God. He wrote that 'the dignity of the human person also requires that every man enjoy the right to act freely and responsibly . . . human society is bound together by freedom, that is to say, in ways and means in keeping with the dignity of its citizens, who accept the responsibility of their actions, precisely because they are by nature rational beings' (*PIT*, §§34–35).

Two years later the Vatican Council promulgated its final official texts, the Pastoral Constitution on the Church in the Modern World (*Gaudium et Spes*) and the Declaration on Religious Freedom (*Dignitatis Humanae*).[20] The former taught that 'only in freedom can man direct himself towards goodness . . . For its part, authentic freedom is an exceptional sign of the divine image within man' (*GS* §§16–17). Hogan suggested that there remained ambiguities between obedience and discernment in *Gaudium et Spes* and in its relationship to *Dignitatis Humanae* which resulted from what the great American Jesuit theologian, John Courtney Murray, called 'the greatest argument on religious freedom in all history'.[21] He pointed to the substantial shift in teaching in the century following Pius IX's *Quanta Cura* (1864) and saw it as an area of major development of doctrine which 'still remains to be explained by theologians'. 'In all honesty', he writes, 'it must be admitted that the Church is late in acknowledging the validity of the principle of religious freedom. The victories won in the West for the cause of constitutional government and the rights of man owed little to the Church . . .'[22]

---

[18] Duffy 1997: 115; see also Phan 1994: 62.   [19] Hogan 2001: 26, 28, 30, 32.
[20] For an analysis of Pope John Paul II's interpretation of *Dignitatis Humanae* see Rico 2002.
[21] Murray in Abbott 1966: 672–673.   [22] Murray 1966: 601.

Dignitatis Humanae (§§1–2) 'intends to develop the doctrine of recent Popes on the inviolable rights of the human person and on the constitutional order of society'. People have a right to religious freedom free from external coercion or constraint. This was 'in accordance with their dignity as persons' created in the image of God. John Courtney Murray summarized the Declaration's three doctrinal tenets:

- the *ethical* doctrine of religious freedom as a human right (personal and collective);
- a *political* doctrine with regard to the functions and limits of government in matters religious; and
- the *theological* doctrine of the freedom of the Church as the fundamental principle in what concerns the relations between the Church and the socio-political order.[23]

It seems that Murray considered that further development of doctrine was necessary on political and juridical aspects of freedom and on the relationship between religious liberty and freedom of conscience.

The dignity of the human person requires not only their religious freedom but also that governments 'create conditions favourable to the fostering of religious life . . . in order that society itself may profit by the moral qualities of justice and peace which have their origin in men's faithfulness to God and to His holy will' (*DH*, §6). It was concerns such as these that led in the 1970s to the emergence of liberation theology, one of the great creative and prophetic challenges to the Church since Vatican II. Reflecting on their experiences of injustice and oppression in nominally Catholic countries, and subject to immense economic forces associated with unregulated processes of development, Latin American theologians began to argue that Jesus came to liberate people from sinful structures which oppressed and impoverished them. The persistence of dehumanizing poverty was a scandal against which the Church should struggle.

Some liberation theologians used Marxist categories of social analysis in terms of class conflict and it was this that drew forth concerns of the CDF. In its *Instruction on Certain Aspects of the Theology of Liberation* (1984) it first acknowledged that

Liberation is first and foremost liberation from the radical slavery of sin. Its end and its goal is the freedom of the children of God, which is the gift of grace. As a logical consequence, it calls for freedom from many different kinds of slavery in the cultural, economic, social and political spheres, all of which derive ultimately

---

[23] Abbott 1966: ibid.: 672–673; emphases added.

from sin, and so often prevent people from living in a manner befitting their dignity.[24]

The Instruction[25] noted the wide use of the Exodus story which 'represents freedom from foreign domination and from slavery' but insists that it 'cannot be reduced to a liberation which is principally or exclusively political in nature'. It admitted 'there are structures which are evil and which we must have the courage to change' but these 'are the result of man's actions and so are consequences more than causes' and the need was to convert 'free and responsible' people 'to live and act as new creatures in the love of neighbour and in the effective search for justice'. The Instruction expressed concern about the 'tendency to identify the Kingdom of God and its growth with the human liberation movement'.

Two years later the Congregation issued a complementary *Instruction on Christian Freedom and Liberation.*[26] While the previous document had been interpreted as rather negative, this aimed to present a more positive view of Christian freedom. As such, it had much value though, like many Vatican documents, it occasionally made wild claims and assertions which were hard to justify in terms of empirical experience. For example, the Instruction claimed that 'the reality of the depth of freedom has *always* been known to the Church, above all through the lives of a multitude of the faithful, especially among the little ones and the poor'. As we have seen, this simply is not true historically. Other statements such as 'the Church, in her docility to the Spirit, goes forward faithfully along the paths to authentic liberation' beg the question as to what is 'authentic' and who does the defining! But these reservations aside, the Instruction did present a useful statement of the official Church's current rhetoric about freedom.

The core teaching is that 'the truth will make you free' (Jn 8: 32).[27] The Instrument presented a theological reflection on the Church's understanding of freedom. This was that 'through His Cross and Resurrection, Christ has brought about our Redemption, which is liberation in the strongest sense of the word, since it has freed us from the most radical evil, namely sin and the power of death'. The Instruction noted that 'the quest for freedom and aspiration for liberation . . . are among the principal signs of the times in the modern world' and claimed expansively and unconvincingly that they (including the Renaissance, Luther, the Enlightenment and French Revolution) 'have their first source in the Christian heritage'. It warned against 'serious ambiguities' in the modern processes of liberation

[24] CDF 1984: 3.   [25] Ibid.: §§IV 3; IV 15; IX 3; 35.   [26] CDF 1986, §§21, 57.
[27] Ibid.: §§3, 5, 10–19, 24.

such as 'new forms of servitude', 'new relationships of inequality and oppression' between nations, 'unscrupulous regimes or tyrannies' and 'new forms of slavery'. 'The liberating capacities of science, technology, work, economics and political activity will only produce results if they find their inspiration and measure in the truth and love . . . revealed to men by Jesus Christ'.

The next section of the Instruction[28] seemed to be grounded in Natural Law thinking, an emphasis on seeking the 'common good', and right relationships to God and neighbour. Thus 'freedom only truly exists where reciprocal bonds, governed by truth and justice, link people to one another'. 'Authentic freedom is the "service of justice"'. 'God calls man to freedom' 'to do good', that is avoid sin and recognize total dependence on God. In a consideration of scriptural sources, the Instruction acknowledged that 'the Exodus . . . has a meaning which is both religious and political. God sets His People free and gives them descendants, a land and a law, but within a Covenant and for a Covenant'. 'The situation of the poor is a situation of injustice *contrary to the Covenant*'. The salvific and ethical treasures of (Mary's) *Magnificat* are stressed rather than the temporal and 'this-worldly' concerns of social justice. The Instruction looked forward to the kingdom of God 'which will receive its completion at the end of time with the resurrection of the dead and the renewal of the whole of creation'.

The official teaching of the Church gives priority to individual sin as the cause of poverty and injustice.[29] It appears that there is a reluctance to embrace the concept of structural sin. Even so, the Instrument claimed that 'through her social doctrine . . . she has sought to promote *structural* changes in society so as to secure conditions of life worthy of the human person'. Christ has redeemed us and assigned us the task of realizing 'the great commandment of love'. This 'leads to the full recognition of the dignity of each individual, created in God's image. In the light of the image of God, freedom, *which is the essential prerogative of the human person*, is manifested in all its depth'.

The contemporary teaching on human freedom is summarized in the *Catechism of the Catholic Church* (§§1730–1748):

- 'There is no true freedom except in the service of what is good and just. The choice to disobey and do evil is an abuse of freedom and leads to "the slavery of sin"'.
- 'Every human person, created in the image of God, has the natural right to be recognized as a free and responsible being. . . . The *right to the*

[28] Ibid.: §§26, 30, 37, 44, 46, 48, 58, 60, 97.   [29] Ibid.: §§67, 68, 71, 73; emphases added.

exercise of freedom, especially in moral and religious matters, is an inalienable requirement of the dignity of the human person . . .'

- There are, however, threats to freedom and 'the economic, social, political and cultural conditions that are needed for a just exercise of freedom are too often disregarded or violated. Such situations of blindness and injustice injure the moral life and involve the strong as well as the weak in the temptation to sin against charity . . .'
- '. . . authentic freedom is an exceptional sign of the divine image within man. For God has willed that man . . . can seek his Creator spontaneously . . .'

So far we have considered Catholic social thought on human freedom from a largely theological point of view. It remains briefly to note two dimensions of secular concern: political freedom and economic liberalism. Thus Pope John Paul II, particularly in *Centesimus Annus* (1991), stressed that, in spite of encouragement for private enterprise and criticisms of the 'social assistance state' (§§39–40, 48), 'economic freedom is only one element of human freedom'. There is a 'risk of an "idolatry" of the market . . . which ignores the existence of goods which by their nature are not and cannot be mere commodities'. There is emphatically no encouragement in Catholic social thought for neo-liberalism or extreme forms of individualism which take no account of human relationships, the link between freedom and solidarity, and the common good. Thus there should be juridical limits to the operation of free markets and concerns about increasing inequality both within and between countries.

St John's Gospel records that Jesus told the Jews who believed in Him that they would come to know the truth and 'the truth will set you free'. When they asked Him what this meant, He replied: 'In all truth I tell you, everyone who commits sin is a slave' (Jn 8: 32, 34). Real freedom is the absence of slavery to sin. But it is not just 'freedom from' but also 'freedom to' – freedom 'to exercise responsibilities towards other people and to the rest of creation'. The understanding of 'freedom' in Catholic social thought is not that of the 'sovereign individual' but that freedom given by the Creator to each individual human being to seek the truth about God and to pursue the 'good' in conformity with God's will and moral law. It is such freedom which is the mark of the human being created in the image of God.

In practice, how this is interpreted has been subject to a development of doctrine. As we have seen, even after Vatican II's *Declaration on Religious Freedom*, there remain areas requiring further development. But the essential element in Catholic thought has been derived from the dignity of the human person. As we have seen, the Catholic sense of freedom is radically different from individual licence or uncontrolled economic liberalism because they fail to take into account the dignity of people. Real freedom is absence from both individual and social sin and is a mark of the kingdom of God which has already been revealed to us by Jesus, but which remains to be sought and witnessed to in our temporal existence.

EQUALITY

Let us consider next the second of the three great slogans of the French Revolution, equality. There is inevitably some overlap in the treatment of the concepts of justice and equality. Others have gone further and stressed the intimate interconnectedness in Catholic social thought of the notions of freedom, equality, solidarity, rights and justice.[30] The concept of equality is perhaps the least developed and least promoted characteristic of the kingdom of God in Catholic social thought. In this section, I will reflect on the relative lack of concern positively to promote equality (as opposed to the rather unspecific advocacy of reduced inequalities) in Catholic social thought, and argue, however tentatively, that equality is an essential characteristic of the kingdom of God and therefore a good which it is incumbent on the followers of Christ to seek and strive for.

The reasons for the Church's resistance to any affirmation of equality (or of democracy) have to be found in the long history of the papacy. There has always been an emphatic insistence that the Church is not a democracy and is intrinsically hierarchical and so unequal. This view continues to be central to papal thought as Eamon Duffy pointed out in *Saints and Sinners*.[31] He showed that for fifteen centuries the papacy was in a perpetual struggle with the political leaders of Europe – emperors and kings – over their respective jurisdictions and authority, the appointment of bishops, and their relative powers. The papacy came (wrongly) to assume the necessity of monarchical rights over the papal states for their spiritual independence.

The violence and destruction of the old ways heralded by the French Revolution appalled the popes of the eighteenth and nineteenth centuries. They came to associate demands for equality with the destruction of monarchical forms of social organization, of civilization, and of religion itself. Hence the reactionary stance of the papacy which lasted until the Second Vatican Council. The result, I suggest, was to devalue the centrality of equality in the understanding of God's basic intentions for His kingdom. Only with Vatican II did the Church begin the process of dialoguing with the modern world and learning to appreciate equality which had been

---

[30] Boswell 2000: 109, and Coleman in Boswell et al. 2000: 273.   [31] Duffy 1997.

promoted as a secular value for well over a century and a half. It seems clear that there is very considerable scope for developments in theological reflection and substantive policy propositions in the consideration of equality as a basic value in the kingdom of God.

In the previous chapter we noted the debate with John Rawls' theory of justice as fairness. He concluded that 'all social primary goods – liberty and opportunity, income and wealth, and the bases of self-respect – are to be distributed equally unless an unequal distribution of any or all of these goods is to the advantage of the least favoured'.[32] On the face of it, then, equality is an essential feature of justice.

In 1929 the Christian socialist R. H. Tawney wrote his classic essay on *Equality*. He was concerned that inequality was almost a religion in England, and that as a result of periodic adjustments to rising discontents about extreme forms of inequality, things continued to be accepted as the way things were. An indifference to inequality was a national characteristic and a blind eye was turned on privilege.[33] The injustices of capitalism were denounced but largely maintained by would be capitalists. For Tawney, it was not so important that equality should be completely attained as that it should be sincerely sought. He contended that a society which seriously valued equality would attempt to reduce the significance of economic and social differences. These were essentially man-made and hence capable of addressing by removal of the structural causes in unjust privileges and social institutions. Formal legal equality needed to be buttressed by equality of opportunity and the addressing of hereditary inequalities. He regarded inequalities of educational opportunity based on differences of wealth as a 'barbarity'. Against the general view that liberty and equality were antithetical, he retorted that 'freedom for the pike is death for the minnows' and argued that 'measures which, by diminishing inequality, have helped to convert . . . nominal rights into practical powers, have made, in the strictest sense, a contribution to freedom' and turned it from an abstract notion into a sober reality.

The Nobel prize winner, Amartya Sen, commenced his important re-examination of inequality by asking 'equality of what?' Human beings were clearly not equally endowed in terms of their economic, social, cultural and political capital. So what sort of equality should be sought? To what extent is there sense in Marx's slogan 'from each according to his ability, to each according to his need'?[34] Sen's approach was to focus on an

---

[32] Rawls 1973: 302–303.   [33] Tawney 1964: 39–40, 41, 56, 58, 145, 164, 235.
[34] In his 1875 *Critique of the Gotha Programme*, in Feuer 1969: 160.

individual's 'capability to achieve functionings that he or she has reason to value'.[35] What he sought was a form of 'diverse egalitarianism' which recognized that different people have different priorities and that equality on one priority (such as freedom) often resulted in inequality on another variable (such as income). He also made the distinction between achieved equality and the freedom to achieve (equality of opportunity). There were also variations of people's 'ability to convert resources into actual freedoms . . . even when we have the same bundle of primary goods', such as income or wealth. These may differ according to age or gender. 'Equality of freedom to pursue our ends cannot be generated by equality in the distribution of primary goods'. Thus, as Sen affirmed, his capability approach both drew on Rawls's analysis of fairness and of responsibility, and criticized its dependence on the holding of primary goods, such as income or education, as opposed to the freedoms and capabilities that persons enjoy. It was important to take account of the real freedoms that people *in fact*, and not just *in principle*, enjoy.

In his recent analysis of *Inequality and Christian Ethics*, Douglas Hicks[36] contrasted the 'human capability' approach of Amartya Sen and the concentration on primary goods, such as income and wealth, in John Rawls' theory of justice. Both addressed the questions, inequality and equality of what and among whom. But whereas Rawls's reliance on primary goods placed emphasis on the *means* to freedom and the *means* to well-being, and not those ends themselves, Sen's capability and functioning were *ends*. Sen asserted that the ability of people to *convert means into desirable ends* varied to a significant degree. This was illustrated with respect to gender differences. Thus 'Sen's point is that because of the variability in conversion rates [from means to ends], equality in the space of primary goods means unacceptable inequality in the capability to function'. Hicks considered 'that as the discussion of equality and inequality moves from moral theory into empirical application and analysis, the central issue becomes not one of absolute equality in any social good, but rather the level of inequality that is morally acceptable in the distributions of various social goods . . . absolute equality is not necessarily required in any good'. On the other hand, 'moral equality does require an absolute equality in political and legal spaces', for example one vote for each adult citizen. In sum, 'Rawls's discussion of primary goods and Sen's discussion of basic social functionings are moral arguments that articulate *social, political, and economic conditions under which particular inequalities are not so great as to impair any persons from being treated as moral equal*'.

---

[35] Sen 1992: 4–5; 85–87; 148–149.   [36] Hicks 2000: 27–28, 30–31.

Duncan Forrester has presented what he called a 'Christian vindication of equality'. First of all, he pointed out that it was often modern *opponents* of equality who stressed the biblical and Christian roots of equality.[37] These were traced back to the Creation story which affirmed that '*all* human beings are created in the image of God, they all share equally in this crucial, definitive characteristic'. The Fall, reported in Genesis 3, showed that 'inequality is a *punishment*'. God was Father of all and treated all His children equally (Job 31:13–28). Forrester pointed out that the laws in Deuteronomy and Leviticus

constantly enjoined special consideration for the poor and weak, reflecting God's partiality and compassion for them. Legislation relating to the Year of Release (Deut. 15), and the Year of Jubilee (Lev. 25) provide for the release of Hebrew slaves, the cancelling of debts, and the redemption of land – all involving a recognition that inequalities are subversive of the kind of fellowship God wills for His people.

Furthermore, the Israelites were reminded that strangers (aliens and migrants) were entitled to equal treatment with the Jew since they were once aliens in Egypt. The prophets constantly reminded that structures of equality and justice are the clear will of God.

John Fuellenbach interpreted the original Covenant with the Israelites as one of an egalitarian and participative 'counter-society' in contrast to Pharaoh's society of oppression and slavery.[38] In the New Testament there was a greater emphasis on the universalistic norm of treating everyone alike, as in the parable of the good Samaritan,[39] and in the way that 'Jesus broke through the barriers of status, and purity, of rank and power, of race and gender which keep people apart' and rebuked the disciples for their status claims. In the parable of the labourers in the vineyard (Mt 20: 1–16) the landowner paid the labourers hired at the end of the day the same as the wage agreed as just by those employed at the beginning of the day. As Forrester noted: 'they are given exactly the same pay, independently of their desert, or ability, but in relation to their equal need'. On the face of it, and in human terms, this seems unfair and inequitable. But God's ways are not the same as ours. The parable, which illustrates God's unconditional love, is a prophetic challenge to us to give serious consideration to the notion of equality.

Paul taught the Galatians (3: 28) that 'there can be neither Jew nor Greek, . . . neither slave nor freeman, . . . neither male nor female – for you

---

[37] Forrester 2001: 79, 83–84, 86–89.   [38] Fuellenbach 1995: 224–225.
[39] Forrester 2001: 93, 95–98, 100–101, 104–106, 134.

are all one in Christ Jesus'. In the early Church (Acts 4: 32) all were equal and there were no class distinctions. 'No one claimed private ownership of any possessions, as everything they owned was held in common'. Paul invited the prosperous Church in Corinth (2 Cor 8: 13–14) to share their surplus with poorer Churches. St James (2: 1–6) warned against class or status distinctions in the assemblies for worship. In spite of the fact that 'the early Church in New Testament times did not press for organic social reform or any kind of revolutionary change in institutions such as slavery, the state, or the family ... the equality of the practice and teaching of Jesus was subversive of received notions of order, and was not easily or quickly assimilated within the Church'. Forrester continued to argue that 'this disturbing egalitarian memory and expectation' was drawn on in later developments such as the American Declaration of Independence (1776) which declared 'we hold these truths to be self-evident, that all men are created equal ...' and in Article I of the Universal Declaration of Human Rights (1948) which proclaimed that 'all human beings are born free and equal, in dignity and rights'.

When reading through the documentary heritage of Catholic social thought, one cannot but notice how little treatment there is specifically on the theme of equality. Pope John XXIII, in his encyclical *Pacem in Terris* (1963: §44) acknowledged 'the conviction that all men are equal by reason of their natural dignity'. As we noted above, Pope Paul VI in his Apostolic Letter, *Octogesima Adveniens* (1971: §22) referred to equality and participation as 'two forms of man's dignity and freedom'. But such assertions of a general cultural value do not put it in the forefront of Catholic social thought or identify it as a goal to be sought. Reflecting on what he called 'the silences of Catholic social thought', Jean-Yves Calvez referred to 'the very structure of unequal capitalism' and the need 'to revert periodically in some systematic way to the degree of equality'. He concluded: 'it seems impossible to keep silent in such an important area'.[40]

At the Second Vatican Council the Church attempted to come to terms with the implications of modernity. In *Lumen Gentium* (§32) it taught that the People of God 'share a common dignity from their rebirth in Christ ... There is in Christ and in the Church no inequality on the basis of race or nationality, social condition or sex ... All share a true equality with regard to the dignity and to the activity common to all the faithful for the building up of the Body of Christ'. In *Gaudium et Spes* (§29), it was stressed that: 'since all men possess a rational soul and are created in God's likeness, since

---

[40] In Boswell et al. 2000: 10–11.

they have the same nature and origin, have been redeemed by Christ, and enjoy the same divine calling and destiny, the basic equality of all must receive increasingly greater recognition'. While it is undoubtedly the case that people differ in their attributes, 'nevertheless, with respect to the fundamental rights of the person, every type of discrimination ... is contrary to God's intent'. All are equal in the sight of God. It seems evident that equality is an essential characteristic of the kingdom of God.

Forrester considered the contribution of liberation theology to have 'been one of the major factors in encouraging Roman Catholic official social teaching to move significantly towards an affirmation of human equality as integral to Christian faith'.[41] He agreed that the main challenge facing the Church in many parts of the world was not that of unbelief but an unconcern with economic, social, political and cultural structures which dehumanized people. Hicks,[42] too, in his consideration of Christian approaches to equality before God, usefully analyzed the contribution of Gustavo Gutiérrez. As a liberation theologian Gutiérrez was concerned about the 'non-person' and the social reality that produced 'non-persons'. Hicks pointed to Gutiérrez's recognition that 'social sin and structures are rooted in the personal wills of people who are sinning against God and human beings' so that the criticisms of the two documents from the CDF (1984; 1986) seemed rather heavy handed. Hicks drew four implications of equality before God in the liberationists' interpretations of sin and creation:

- 'the human dignity that God has bestowed equally on all people is blocked for everyone by the spiritual and material effects of sin ...';
- 'the degree of impact of social sin is *disproportionately* felt by people (or "non-persons") at the bottom of the socioeconomic (and political) distributions. Oppressors and the oppressed each need liberation, but by definition the former group benefits from the latter's lack of social power or agency. The effects of sin are thus not only distinct across socioeconomic distributions, they are also unequal ...';
- 'all people are sinners, equally unable to effect their own liberation or salvation without God's help. No one group, including the "poor" is morally superior to any other group ...';
- 'severe political, social, or economic deprivation can block the attainment of human relationality intended for all people as children of God and as siblings to one another. A commitment to equality can thus call for praxis to overcome forms of deprivation (either relative or absolute) that dehumanize'.

[41] Forrester 2001: 137.   [42] Hicks 2000: 140–142, 148, 159.

Hicks concluded his review of the approach of Gutiérrez by noting that 'equality before God is a claim about one's moral status; it is not a claim advocating sameness in any moral, cultural, or social sense. The liberationist account rejects oppression, marginalization, and deprivation, but not differences'. Forrester concluded his review of the Christian shape of equality by reviewing official Catholic social teaching about equality since Vatican II, structured more around scriptural themes than natural law thinking accessible to all rational beings, but he criticized its tendency to neglect 'its own contextuality and time boundedness'.[43]

In a recent collection, Jonathan Boswell insightfully reflected on the mutual relationships between diversity, equality and solidarity. In the local parish or basic Christian community, 'Catholics are bound to a central event, the Mass, as God's gift of Himself made equally to every person, binding diverse characters and gifts into One Body. In the Eucharist they see a Real Presence offered to all without qualification or distinction'.[44] He proceeded to reflect on these correlates in the case of the Trinity: 'The Three Divine Persons, according to creedal orthodoxy, are a) diversely distinct, b) absolutely equal, and c) perfectly loving and united (in solidarity) . . .' The kingdom of God ought to reflect these characteristics of the Trinity. The citizens of the kingdom were diversely distinct, equal and had parity of esteem in the sight of God, and related to each other in fraternal love and solidarity.

SOLIDARITY

The third of the great slogans of the French Revolution was 'fraternité' which might roughly be translated as 'solidarity'. The concept of solidarity, which has important secular roots, has been much stressed in modern Catholic social teaching, especially by Pope John Paul II.

The Second Vatican Council's Pastoral Constitution on the Church in the Modern World (*GS* §§3, 4, 32, 57, 84) commenced by asserting 'its solidarity with the entire human family . . . by engaging with it in conversation' about the various problems facing the modern world. Although there was 'a very vivid sense of . . . needful solidarity', where 'everyone, as members . . . would render mutual service according to the different gifts bestowed on each' and where there was 'a sense of international solidarity' and a 'spirit of true fraternity' among international agencies, sadly there were often grievous conflicts between different groups which needed to be addressed.

---

[43] Forrester 2001: 163.   [44] In Boswell et al. 2000: 108–109.

In 1967 Pope Paul VI took these ideas further in his encyclical letter *Populorum Progressio* (§§17, 43, 44, 48, 80, 85). He argued that 'there can be no progress toward the complete development of man without the simultaneous development of all humanity in the spirit of solidarity'. He insisted that 'the reality of human solidarity, which is a benefit for us, also imposes a duty'. 'The same duty of solidarity that rests on individuals exists also for nations'. He concluded that 'it is time for all men and all peoples to face up to their responsibilities'. Pope Paul pleaded that we follow Christ with 'an enlargement of heart . . . (and) a more brotherly way of living with a truly universal human society'.

The concept of solidarity was a major theme in the teaching of Pope John Paul II who had been so influential in the rise of the non-violent workers' movement, Solidarity, in Poland. Support for worker solidarity appeared in his encyclical *Laborem Exercens* (§8). The call to worker solidarity was ethically justified as a 'just social reaction' to unjust working conditions and exploitation and continued to be necessary where workers were degraded or subject to new forms of injustice.

In 1987 in his social encyclical *Sollicitudo Rei Socialis* (§§9, 17, 36–40) he reaffirmed the 'moral duty of solidarity . . . considered in the perspective of universal interdependence'. When the interdependence between the First, Second, Third and Fourth Worlds was disregarded, it had disastrous consequences for the weakest. When considering 'structures of sin' the pope suggested that there was a 'growing awareness of *interdependence* among individuals and nations'. The virtue, solidarity, 'is not a feeling of vague compassion . . . (but) *a firm and persevering determination* to commit oneself to the *common good*; that is to say to the good of all and of each individual, because we are *all* really responsible *for all*'. John Paul II saw 'peace as the fruit of solidarity' and considered that

in the light of faith, solidarity seeks to go beyond itself, to take on the *specifically Christian* dimension of total gratuity, forgiveness and reconciliation. One's neighbour is then not only a human being with his or her own rights and a fundamental equality with everyone else, but becomes the *living image* of God the Father, redeemed by the blood of Jesus Christ and placed under the permanent action of the Holy Spirit.

Pope John Paul II returned to the concept briefly in his encyclical *Centesimus Annus* (§10) and he regarded the mutual support between the partners and generations in the family as 'a community of work and solidarity' (§49). He observed that the principle of solidarity was one of the fundamental principles of the Christian view of social and political organization. It was related to the term *friendship* used by Leo XIII, *social charity* used by Pius XI, and Paul VI's '*civilization of love*'.

A recent study of non-official Catholic social thought has added useful insights. Verstraeten has pointed out that the usage of the term 'solidarity' in Catholic social teaching, in bearing 'radical witness to our love of our neighbour', went far beyond any form of 'enlightened self-interest'.[45] Boswell argued that solidarity was 'at the peak and the other values are found to inter-penetrate and inter-relate in the light of solidarity'. It included 'relationships of community, sociability, conviviality, civility, *fraternité*, civic friendship, social consciousness, public spirit'. He claimed that without it an understanding of other values such as justice, human rights, freedom and subsidiarity in Catholic social thought was impossible.[46] Coleman suggested that solidarity and the preferential option for the poor were 'biblically and metaphorically soaked, rich root images in the imagination of social Catholicism'.[47]

In sum, the concept of solidarity, with its suggestive secular roots in French revolutionary history and worker movements for social justice, has been elaborated in much recent social thought as an awareness of the interdependence of peoples has become more apparent under globalization. But it also has important biblical roots which have been articulated, notably by recent popes, in contemporary Catholic social thought.

CONCLUSIONS

In this chapter we have reviewed five major values in contemporary secular thought. We have seen that each of them can be said to characterize the kingdom of God of peace and justice, altruism and love. We are all called to be citizens of the kingdom which is marked by participation, freedom, equality and solidarity. Each of these concepts has been shown to have deep scriptural roots, even if for long periods of history they have been forgotten and even resisted. Today they are among the defining principles of Catholic social thought. We will draw on them as we consider each area of injustice or social concern in Part III of this book.

There has clearly been considerable development with Catholic social teaching over the past century and especially since Vatican II. Thus there has been a remarkable reconciliation with the secular strivings from the time of the Reformation in the sixteenth century, and the Enlightenment thinking and French Revolution in the eighteenth century. We have come

---

[45] Verstraeten 2000: 74–75.   [46] Boswell 2000: 104–106.   [47] Coleman 2000: 276.

increasingly to realize that apart from justice, the kingdom of God is manifested by collaborative participation and in the revolutionary themes of liberty, equality and fraternity.

Jesus taught that the kingdom of God is among us (Lk 17: 21) and is implicitly realized when 'the good news is proclaimed to the poor' (Mt 11: 5). As Fuellenbach noted: 'what counts is people ... compassion and justice, not holiness and purity. Love is at the heart of the Reign of God'.[48] 'The kingdom remains God's work ... Our task is to *witness* to this presence of the kingdom, to make it felt by our concern for "justice, peace, and joy" where we live and work, and to challenge every human society to restructure itself according to the kingdom's principles ... Our task is to set up signs on the way to the kingdom'. In this chapter we have suggested that these signs include the citizenship values of participation, freedom, equality and solidarity.

Teaching nearly 2000 years ago, Jesus did not tell us how to cope with the injustices of international debt, nuclear, chemical and biological warfare, genetic engineering or how to tackle the problems of social exclusion or climate change. Christians have to work out their responses for themselves on the basis of the reflections of the Christian communities over the past twenty centuries, and guided by the Church. Catholic Social Thought, which is dynamic and has on occasion changed dramatically since the time of Jesus, is the subject of the next chapter.

---

[48] Fuellenbach 1995: 95, 205–206.

CHAPTER 5

Catholic social thought

INTRODUCTION

This chapter offers an introduction and outline of Catholic social thought[1] as it has developed since the time of Jesus who did not have to address such contemporary issues as the morality of nuclear deterrence, or the Common Agricultural Policy, or international debt, or global warming or genetic engineering. It offers brief reflections on the place that natural law thinking has in Catholic social thought. It then outlines some key historical developments particularly since Leo XIII's encyclical *Rerum Novarum* in 1891. Six key principles of Catholic social thought, around which there is much consensus, are then suggested. This is followed by an evaluation of the strengths and weaknesses of this body of thought. The chapter concludes with an overview of the theological resources suggested in Part II of this book and available for reflection on the six main areas of injustice to be considered in Part III.

One of the first things to note about Catholic social thought is that it is not static but dynamic in response to changing circumstances and needs. Indeed, on certain matters, such as democracy, co-ownership, human rights and conscientious objection, earlier positions have been reversed. Secondly, Catholic social thought for the past century and a half has sought to articulate a path between statist socialism and liberal capitalism and has insisted that the economy is to serve the needs of people. Thirdly, two different approaches have been used in the development of Catholic social thought: scripture (and the appeal to revelation) and natural law theory (in principle accessible to all people of good will). The relative emphases between these two approaches has changed over the years.[2] Fourthly, it is important to understand that Catholic social thinking flows from

---

[1] Attention is drawn to the Pontifical Council for Justice and Peace's *Compendium of the Social Doctrine of the Church* 2004.
[2] Curran 1991; 2002.

numerous sources. It is generally regarded as part of standard moral theology and as such has been discussed since the time of the evangelists.

Michael Schuck,[3] for example, claims that modern Catholic social thought is the product of three main groups in the Church: the Church hierarchy, writers and academics, and leaders of social movements. Roger Charles[4] distinguishes four sources: scripture; the apostolic tradition as articulated by popes and theologians; the experience of the Church; and relevant findings of the human and social sciences. It might be helpful to elaborate this and note six influential sources at the beginning of the twenty-first century:[5]

- the teaching of the Second Vatican Council (especially in *Gaudium et Spes* and *Dignitatis Humanae*);
- papal encyclicals (which may simply articulate in an authoritative way the 'mind of the Church' as it has emerged in an ever changing social, economic, cultural and political context);
- collegial teaching such as the Synod of Bishops' statement on *Justice in the World* and such major pastoral letters as those of the United States bishops on peace and defence issues and on the economy; the teaching of the Latin American bishops following their meetings especially at Medellin and Puebla on the 'preferential option for the poor'; and the statements of the Bishops of England and Wales on *The Common Good* and *Cherishing Life*;
- the insights of liberation theologians from Latin America, Asia and Africa;
- insights articulated by the burgeoning number of both Catholic and secular non-governmental organizations[6] both at home and abroad, and the wide-ranging coalitions seeking debt relief or reform of international institutions such as the International Monetary Fund and the World Trade Organization.

---

[3] Schuck 1994.   [4] Charles 1998a: xiii.

[5] A particularly valuable basic source is the collection edited by O'Brien and Shannon (1992), which introduces the texts of Vatican II's *Gaudium et Spes*, and ten main social encyclicals over the hundred years from *Rerum Novarum* to *Centesimus Annus* as well as the 1971 Synod statement on *Justice in the World* and the two major statements of the United States bishops on *The Challenge of Peace* and *Economic Justice for All*. The Pontifical Council for Justice and Peace have recently published *The Social Agenda* (Sirico and Zięba 2000) and a *Compendium of the Social Doctrine of the Church* (2004). Charles (1998a and 1998b) provides a comprehensive review of the historical developments of Catholic social teaching from biblical times to the present. Dorr (1992) and Curran (2002) offer critical analyses of developments since *Rerum Novarum*. DeBerri and Hug (2003) provide a helpful introduction for study purposes.

[6] e.g. Housing Justice and Church Action on Poverty; CAFOD, CIIR; Make Poverty History.

- academic theologians, philosophers and social scientists producing critical analyses and evaluations of Catholic social thought.[7]

In his encyclical *Centesimus Annus* (§54), Pope John Paul II saw Catholic social thought as part of the Church's evangelising mission when he argued that:

today, the Church's social doctrine focuses especially on man as he is involved in a complex network of relationships within modern societies ... However, man's true identity is only fully revealed to him through faith, and it is precisely from faith that the Church's social teaching begins. While drawing upon all the contributions made by the sciences and philosophy, her social teaching is aimed at helping man on the path of salvation.

Recent reviews of Catholic social thought have indicated something of the complexity of the historical, philosophical and theological issues which are involved. Catholic social thought embraces not only 'social doctrine', which outlines 'universal moral principles articulated by the Church hierarchy'; 'social teaching' which includes both social doctrine and 'the hierarchy's prudential policy choices'; and 'social ethics' resulting from 'the work of professional Catholic ethicists'.[8] A useful distinction is that between 'Catholic social teaching' and 'Catholic non-official social thinking'.[9] Furlong and Curtis[10] suggested that the distinctive contribution of the Catholic synthesis in the century since *Rerum Novarum* lies in the emphasis given to three themes: (1) the organic nature of the relationship between state and society; (2) the importance of moral values in modern social and political activity, and (3) the balance between state and market in modern government. In the United States, John Coleman[11] similarly reviewed the tradition focusing in particular on the issues of the family, work and peace.

ON NATURAL LAW

Charles Curran has provided a useful introduction to the two different methodologies which have been used in the development of Catholic social teaching on ethical issues. In the first place, when primarily addressing members of the Church, there has been a strong emphasis on scriptural sources and what Curran called 'appeals to the Christian warrants of creation, sin, redemption, and, to some extent, eschatology'.[12] He pointed

---

[7] Boswell et al. 2000, which celebrates Catholic non-official social thinking.
[8] Schuck 1994: 614. [9] Boswell et al. 2000. [10] Furlong and Curtis 1994: 3–4.
[11] Coleman 1991b. [12] Curran 1991: 73, 74, 86; see also 2002.

out that the Second Vatican Council's *Pastoral Constitution on the Church in the Modern World* appealed to scriptural roots (*GS* §§12–39) as have more recent encyclicals. Alternatively, especially when aiming to address all people of good will, the emphasis had been on the notion of natural law, accessible to all people using their human reason to guide the practical ordering of human activity and relationships. The theological foundations of Catholic natural law theories were laid by Thomas Aquinas. Curran argued that there was 'only one social moral order and all humankind, including Christians, are called to work for the same social justice'. He noted the interesting reversal in papal encyclicals over the past century when he observed that 'the natural-law method of the earlier encyclicals made them in principle open to all other human beings, but as a matter of fact they were not specifically addressed to all humankind. Now, even though appeals are often made to scripture and Christian warrants, the letters where applicable are addressed to all humankind'. Whether Catholic or not, all people 'are called to work together in solidarity for authentic human development and liberation'.

Curran observed that John XXIII's encyclical *Pacem in Terris* (1963) 'was the last document to employ an exclusively natural-law approach'. Natural law theory had its origins in the writings of the Greek philosophers in the fourth and fifth centuries BC. It was developed in the jurisprudence of Roman jurists and given its classical formulation by Cicero in the first century BC. God was the author of this law which was eternal for all places and all times. Knowledge of this law was available to all people through the use of right reason, as St Paul noted in his epistle to the Romans (2: 14–15). The early Fathers of the Church spoke of it and it was passed down through the ages until given its classic formulation by St Thomas Aquinas in the thirteenth century.[13] Natural law thinking implied the 'rejection of total arbitrariness'[14] in morality.

The *Catechism of the Catholic Church* (§§1954–1960) outlined the current official Catholic teaching on the natural law. St Thomas Aquinas is quoted as writing that 'The natural law is nothing other than the light of understanding placed in us by God; through it we know what we must do and what we must avoid. God has given this light or law at the creation'. The *Catechism* continued: 'The natural law, present in the heart of each (person) and established by reason, is universal in its precepts and its authority extends to all . . . It expresses the dignity of the person and determines the basis for his fundamental rights and duties'. The *Catechism* then quoted

[13] Charles 1998a: 75–77. [14] Fuchs 1994: 669.

Cicero, the Roman stoic and philosopher, who lived in the century before Christ: 'For there is a true law: right reason. It is in conformity with nature, is diffused among all (people) and is immutable and eternal; its orders summon to duty; . . . To replace it with a contrary law is a sacrilege'.

The obvious empirical fact that people in different cultures and at different times have *not* interpreted this natural law in the same way is clearly admitted in the *Catechism*. As Gerard Hughes put it in his commentary on this section: 'The *catechism* is carefully nuanced'.[15] It admits that:

application of the natural law varies greatly; it can demand reflection that takes account of various conditions of life according to places, times, and circumstances. Nevertheless, in the diversity of cultures . . . the natural law is *immutable* and permanent throughout . . . history . . . (and) provides the solid foundation on which man can build the structure of moral rules to guide his choices . . . The precepts of natural law are not perceived by everyone clearly and immediately. In the present situation sinful man needs grace and revelation so (that) moral and religious truths may be known by everyone . . . with firm certainty . . .

Indeed, it was necessary to 'keep in mind that all attempts at natural-law thinking are never more than human attempts and thus are always exposed to the danger of mistaken understanding and/or ideological presuppositions'. Josef Fuchs[16] has pointed to some of the problematics of natural law thinking. Early Christian thinking, he suggested, was influenced more by the Roman Stoics with their pantheistic worldview than by the more 'eternal' ideas of Greek philosophers such as Aristotle. 'It was Thomas Aquinas who . . . in the 13th century attempted to transpose and integrate the ideas of the Greek world (Aristotle), and especially of Roman philosophy and Roman law, into Christian philosophy and theology and into their understanding of morality and law'.

But there were two main variants of the Roman understanding of natural law. Some, such as Cicero, 'considered that which is distinctively human . . . namely, reason, to be the primal source of ethical and legal knowledge'. Others, such as Ulpian, 'understood physical nature, which is *the same in human and animal*, to be that which is most "natural" . . . and to be the deepest guideline in human nature for correct behaviour'. There clearly lay in this dispute the potential for major disagreements in areas such as sexual relations. It was also the basis of Aquinas' distinction between 'in keeping with reason' and 'in keeping with nature' and led to inconsistencies because he paid attention to Ulpian. While human persons

[15] Hughes 1994: 341.   [16] Fuchs 1994.

were obligated to do good and avoid evil, how that works out in concrete instances has to be interpreted in each new situation. Since a person's 'capacity to interpret, evaluate, and orientate himself/herself . . . changes to a certain extent (over time) . . . it follows that it would be an error to hold that a definitive codex of the legal and ethical norms of natural law could be drawn up with equal validity for all times'. Fuchs concluded that there had been a historical tendency to understand natural law in the more contingent and voluntarist interpretation of Duns Scotus than in Aquinas' understanding.

Fuchs noted that between the mid-nineteenth and mid-twentieth centuries, the Roman Catholic Church's magisterium largely accepted the Thomistic distinction between 'nature' and 'reason'. Some teachings, such as those relating to matters of life, death and sexuality were considered to belong to an ethical order given by nature (and hence by God) and therefore to be immutable. The morality of social and political issues, however, must be discovered by reason. Fuchs concluded that 'this twofold understanding of natural law is not satisfactory'. He suggested that there were indications in the Second Vatican Council's *Gaudium et Spes* and in recent social encyclicals of a shift away from 'formulated laws and norms . . . to the God-given task of more fully humanizing the human person and the world'. Finally, Fuchs was critical of the claims of the magisterium to give an 'authentic interpretation and exposition of the natural law in its concrete totality' because this was not properly part of the deposit of faith.

In their statement on *The Common Good* (1996) the bishops of England and Wales noted that the insights of natural law thinking were accessible to people of other faiths and none as well as to Catholics. They regarded the Common Law principles of natural justice as expressions of natural law. They recognized that 'the interpretation and application of natural law is rarely straightforward and often controversial . . . On the other hand, to ignore natural law, for instance by organizing society so that in effect it serves the interests of a few rather than the common good, is to collaborate with the structures of sin' (§47).

In his important critique of weaknesses in neo-Thomist formulations of natural law ethics, Frank McHugh claimed 'it is possible to reconstruct natural law ethics, articulated in connection with its ontological suppositions, as a reflexive and rich ethics that encourages human flourishing, uncovers a place for creativity and offers a structural dimension which gives it purchase on the social realities of a globalized world'.[17] John Coleman[18]

---

[17] McHugh 2000: 57.   [18] Coleman 2000, especially pp. 276–280.

usefully summarized much recent debate about the Catholic interpretation of natural law. He drew attention to the fact that natural law theory was pre-Christian in its origins and that the medieval notion was theologically informed. This dimension tended to get lost in pre-Vatican II Catholic moral theology so that some fundamental revisions and a renewed attention to the scriptural roots of theology, and a greater awareness of the salience of historical context were necessary. As Coleman succinctly put it: 'A totally unchanging human nature seems difficult to accept'.

Natural law thinking has always been an essential component in Catholic social thought. But it has been historically contexted. As we have seen, in its origins it was influenced by Greek philosophy and Roman jurisprudence. In the classical formulations of Thomas Aquinas it was profoundly influenced by scripture and theological understandings of God's creation. In the centuries following the Reformation it was given an extremely rigid interpretation in manuals of moral theology. In concrete situations in today's fallible and sinful world, the understanding of what is against nature and intrinsically evil (e.g. genocide) increasingly finds expression in the striving for a just international order. Finally, one might note that some Protestant critics have welcomed the Catholic natural law tradition and urged that it not be diluted in ecumenical dialogue.[19]

HISTORICAL DEVELOPMENT OF OFFICIAL TEACHING

We have noted that Catholic social thinking is not static but dynamic in response to changing circumstances and needs. 'It is an arena, preeminently, of the development of doctrine'.[20] John Coleman traced its roots in the life and words of Jesus; patristic insistence in the early Christian centuries on caring for the poor; medieval theologians and the conditions for a just war; later thinkers forging the rudiments of international law; and papal responses to modern liberalism and development.

Michael Schuck[21] rejected the common starting point of Leo XIII's encyclical *Rerum Novarum* of 1891. Instead he proposed a threefold periodization: pre-Leonine, from the pontificate of Benedict XIV in 1740 to 1877; Leonine, from the accession of Leo XIII in 1878 to 1958; and post-Leonine, from the accession of John XXIII in 1958 to the present.

---

[19] Hauerwas 1995.
[20] Coleman 1991b: 2–3, 6. A useful overview is given in the *Compendium* 2004: §§87–104.
[21] Schuck 1994: 616–622.

The pre-Leonine period witnessed the violent upheavals associated with the ending of the period of feudalism and absolute monarchs, the economic stimulation of imports from the Americas, the onset of the industrial revolution, the upheavals of the French Revolution, socialist revolutions, and unification movements in Italy and Germany, and the intellectual revolution of the Enlightenment. Catholic responses to these challenges varied. In 1740 Pope Benedict XIV initiated the practice of writing encyclicals and prior to Leo XIII, nine popes wrote no fewer than seventy-seven. Several popes in this period suffered imprisonment by Napoleonic armies. Some reaction against the turbulence of the times was, therefore, only to be expected. Gregory XVI (1831–46), for example, condemned the notion of freedom of conscience in religion and Pius IX (1846–78) in *Quanta Cura* (1864) and its appendix, the *Syllabus of Errors*, declaimed against 'liberal' culture. In 1870 Vatican I proclaimed the doctrine of papal infallibility but the Council was suspended when Italian forces captured Rome. But among the signs of hope in this pre-Leonine period were popular Catholic social movements, such as Frederick Ozanam's Society of St Vincent de Paul (SVP), and Bishop Ketteler's creation of the German Centre Party.

Schuck refers to the period from the accession of Leo XIII in 1878 through to the death of Pius XII in 1958 as the Leonine period. The earlier part of this period was characterized by the antagonism of European nation states to the Church, aggressive and competitive colonialism in Africa and Asia, the First World War and the Russian Revolution. This was followed by political instability and both fascist and communist forms of totalitarianism. A period of deep economic depression preceded the Second World War and the beginnings of the Cold War between two major blocs. This period experienced the developments of major technical inventions such as the car, aeroplane, radio, television, nuclear power and mass production. Among the influential thinkers of this period were Keynes, Nietzsche and Freud. Schuck argued that in this period the popes acquired a 'a broadened sense of pastoral responsibility for the whole of Western civilization, a greater preoccupation with specific moral issues, and a stronger claim to religious and moral authority'.[22] The nine popes of this period wrote no fewer than 185 encyclicals, many of them on social matters. In response to

[22] Ibid.: 619. Note that Gene Burns (1994) argues that with the loss of the papal states and the Church's changed status in relation to the nation states, the popes have asserted moral authority over individual personal morality, such as contraception, while tending to act pragmatically, for example by signing concordats with states and in matters of social morality where they lacked power or influence.

the unprecedented changes during this period, Leo XIII initiated an institutional revival of Thomistic studies but 'discordant' theological and philosophical principles were condemned by Pius X in his attack on 'modernism' in *Pascendi* (1907) and by Pius XII in *Humani Generis* (1950). During the eighty years of this period, the popes wrote extensively about such matters as political liberty, nationalism, war and peace, family life, the rights and duties of employers and employees, the right to private property, and the importance of intermediate organizations such as trade unions. Pius X and Pius XI both encouraged 'Catholic Action' by the laity under the direction of the hierarchy but Joseph Cardijn founded the lay-led Young Christian Worker movement in 1925 with its well-known 'see; judge; act' methodology.

After the death of Pius XII in 1958, Pope John XXIII called the Second Vatican Council (1962–65) which Schuck regarded as 'the watershed between the Leonine and post-Leonine periods'. The latter period spanned the major pontificates of John XXIII, Paul VI and John Paul II. The Council opened up the Church to alternative theological and philosophical thought, encouraged greater attention to scripture and patristic studies, and even admitted a grudging recognition of the value of the social sciences.

The period witnessed not only the development of the ideas and thrust of the Second Vatican Council but also the new challenges of liberation and feminist theologies. During this period western nations experienced unprecedented economic growth until the sudden collapse of the centralized economies in the former Soviet bloc in 1989. Since then, extreme forms of economic liberalism achieved hegemonic status throughout most of the world. Schuck noted that alongside those who valued Thomist thought, such as Roger Charles, Johannes Metz 'has developed a political theology informed not by natural law but the theological concept of the kingdom of God'. Major innovations included the liberation theology of Gustavo Gutiérrez and others while Michael Novak and others insisted on the merits of the capitalist market economy. Feminist theologies of Rosemary Radford Ruether and others 'have criticized the long-standing link in Catholic thought between human beings' reproductive biology and their social role'. The conciliar document *Dignitatis Humanae* reversed previous papal teaching and endorsed freedom of conscience in religion. The Synod of Bishops in 1971, in their statement on justice in the modern world, explicitly declared that 'action on behalf of justice' was 'a constitutive dimension of the preaching of the Gospel'; seeking justice was no optional extra for the Christian.

Table 5.1 identifies some of the most important official Church documents since Leo XIII's encyclical *Rerum Novarum* on the condition of the

Table 5.1. *Major church documents on justice and peace, 1891–2004*

Year	Author[a]	Document	Key themes	Reference[b]
1891	Leo XIII	*Rerum Novarum*	The condition and rights of labour	OBS: 12–39
1931	Pius XI	*Quadragesimo Anno*	Justice, common good, subsidiarity	OBS: 40–79
1961	John XXIII	*Mater et Magistra*	Just distribution; aid; neo-colonialism	OBS: 82–128
1963	John XXIII	*Pacem in Terris*	Human rights; participation; arms race	OBS: 129–162
1965	Vatican II	*Gaudium et Spes*	Social person; justice and development	OBS: 164–237
1965	Vatican II	*Dignitatis Humanae*	Religious freedom; conscience; dignity	WMA: 675–696
1967	Paul VI	*Populorum Progressio*	Global justice; aid; peace; development	OBS: 238–262
1968	Paul VI	*Humanae Vitae*	Family life; affective love; birth control	CTS: Do 411
1968	CELAM II	*Medellin*	Basic Christian communities	USCCB, 1979
1971	Paul VI	*Octogesima Adveniens*	Action for justice; social responsibility	OBS: 263–286
1971	Synod	*Justitia in Mundo*	Justice seeking as evangelization	OBS: 287–300
1975	Paul VI	*Evangelii Nuntiandi*	Evangelization; liberation; solidarity	OBS: 301–345
1979	CELAM III	*Puebla*	Preferential option for the poor	CIIR, 1980
1979	John Paul II	*Redemptor Hominis*	Human dignity; human rights	CTS
1980	John Paul II	*Dives in Misericordia*	Human dignity; justice and love	CTS
1981	John Paul II	*Laborem Exercens*	Human work; labour and capital	OBS: 350–392
1983	USCB	*The Challenge of Peace*	Pacifism; just war principles	OBS: 492–571
1986	USCB	*Economic Justice for All*	Justice and common good for all	OBS: 572–680
1987	John Paul II	*Sollicitudo Rei Socialis*	International relations; solidarity	OBS: 393–436
1991	John Paul II	*Centesimus Annus*	Limits of market capitalism	OBS: 437–488
1993	John Paul II	*Veritatis Splendor*	Universal and unchanging moral norms	CTS: Do 616
1994	John Paul II	*Tertio Millennio Adveniente*	Good News; preferential option	CTS: Do 627

Table 5.1. (*cont.*)

Year	Author[a]	Document	Key themes	Reference[b]
1995	John Paul II	*Evangelium Vitae*	Value and inviolability of human life	CTS: Do 633
1996	CBCEW	*The Common Good*	Human dignity; common good	Gabriel
2001	John Paul II	*Novo Millennio Ineunte*	International debt; poverty; ecology	CTS
2004	CBCEW	*Cherishing Life*	Health and medical care; bioethics	CTS

Notes:
[a] CELAM: Conference of Latin American Bishops; USCB: US Catholic bishops; CBCEW: Catholic Bishops' Conference of England and Wales.
[b] OBS: D. J. O'Brien and T. A. Shannon (eds.) (1992) *Catholic Social Thought: The Documentary Heritage*, Maryknoll, New York: Orbis. CTS: Catholic Truth Society; CIIR: Catholic Institute for International Relations; Gabriel Communications; USCCB: US Conference of Catholic Bishops; WMA: W. M. Abbott (eds.) *The Documents of Vatican II*, London: Geoffrey Chapman, 1966.

industrial working classes in 1891. Many of them commemorate anniversaries, especially of *Rerum Novarum*, and were written in quite different historical, social and cultural contexts. Leo XIII had written for an insecure church only twenty years after the loss of the Papal States as the Church struggled to get to grips with the French and industrial revolutions in what appeared to be a confident and secure world. Forty years later, in *Quadragesimo Anno*, Pius XI at the time of the great depression, spoke for a more triumphalist Church to a world on the point of despair. Thirty years later, addressing a wearied and worried world still recovering from the devastation of the Second World War and the Holocaust and fearing nuclear catastrophe, John XXIII spoke for a more humble and chastened Church. In doing so he reopened the door to participation in liberal and pluralistic societies on the basis of natural law principles which had been tentatively opened by Leo XIII, though within the post-Vatican I Catholic ultramontanist, anti-modernist, centralist and authoritarian subculture. After the changes of the Second Vatican Council, especially the *Declaration on Religious Liberty*, Catholics could begin to dialogue with secular pluralist society more easily.[23]

[23] O'Brien 1991: 23–24.

It is not possible here to provide a detailed review of all these documents.[24] They will be introduced where relevant to the specific issues of injustice to be considered in Part III. Here I will simply draw attention to some of the more significant aspects of the main documents. Pius XI in *Quadragesimo Anno*[25] is chiefly remembered for his enunciation of the important principle of subsidiarity: 'it is an injustice and at the same time a grave evil and a disturbance of right order, to transfer to the larger and higher collectivity functions which can be performed and provided for by lesser and subordinate bodies'. The encyclical was critical of the capitalist economic regime and despotic economic domination and called on the state to ensure that 'human society conform to the requirements of the common good, that is, the norm of social justice'. While bitterly opposed to communism, for the first time reference was made to a 'mitigated socialism'.

Another thirty years were to pass before the great surge of new thinking which John XXIII initiated with his two encyclical letters *Mater et Magistra* (1961) and *Pacem in Terris* (1963). He noted the changing social context and, in particular, scientific, technological and economic developments, the extension of systems of social security, greater participation in public life, and the ending of colonialism. He 'began the process of breaking the long alliance between Roman Catholicism and socially conservative forces'.[26] He favoured worker participation in management and affirmed the regulative function of the State in pursuit of the common good. John XXIII was at ease with post-war developments of the welfare state His approach was reformist and exhortatory. He was the first pope to address the issue of international development.[27] In *Pacem in Terris*[28] he invoked natural law arguments in favour of human rights including the right to life and a reasonable standard of living, freedom of speech, to access to education and culture, to religious freedom, to choose freely one's state in life, to property and to work, to free assembly, to migrate, and to political and legal rights. These rights had their corresponding duties: of the individual in society and towards the State, of states towards each other and, finally, of both individuals and states within the entire world community. This assertion of human rights, based both on natural law and

---

[24] Useful summaries of most of the documents can be found in Walsh 1984; Dorr 1992; O'Brien and Shannon 1992; Charles 1998b; Curran 2002; and DeBerri and Hug 2003.

[25] *Quadragesimo Anno 1931*: §§59, 71, 79, 103–110, 113, 117, 120, 137.

[26] Dorr 1992: 138, 145–147.

[27] *Mater et Magistra 1961*: §§46–49, 53–58, 79, 91–92, 115, 117, 152, 172.

[28] *Pacem in Terris 1963*: §§11–38, 56, 65.

reinforced on scriptural grounds, 'was new in the official pronouncements of the Catholic Church'.

At the very end of the Second Vatican Council (1962–65), two major documents, the Pastoral Constitution on the Church in the Modern World, *Gaudium et Spes*,[29] and the Declaration on Religious Freedom (*Dignitatis Humanae*) were approved. At the beginning of the Council the bishops had 'insisted that the two great problems facing the Church were peace and social justice'. *Gaudium et Spes* set out to dialogue with the people of the modern world and taught that peace was bound up with justice. Like most people at the time, the Constitution appeared to believe that economic development would resolve many of the problems of poorer nations. It is chiefly remembered for its unqualified condemnation of 'total war' and its judgement that the arms race was a 'treacherous trap'. *Dignitatis Humanae*[30] was considered to be one of the biggest U-turns in the history of the Church. The Declaration 'declares that the right to religious freedom has its foundation in the very dignity of the human person ... known through the revealed Word of God and by reason'. People are obliged to follow their consciences without restraint or coercion but 'in the formation of their consciences, the Christian faithful ought carefully to attend to the sacred and certain doctrine of the Church'.

Paul VI developed the teaching of John XXIII but with a more critical edge. In his encyclical letter 'On the Development of Peoples', *Populorum Progressio* (1967)[31] he agonized over 'the scandal of glaring inequalities' of possessions and power, 'stifling materialism', and 'moral underdevelopment'. He called for a fully human 'authentic development' and relief from 'oppressive social structures'. He was critical of 'unchecked liberalism', and urged the 'duty of solidarity' on developed nations. The arms race was 'an intolerable scandal'. He concluded by proclaiming that 'the new name for peace is development'. In the following year Paul VI delivered his ill-fated encyclical *Humanae Vitae* (1968)[32] which reaffirmed the traditional teaching on 'artificial' birth control. As is well known, the pope had discarded the considered advice of the pontifical commission, initiated by Pope John, which he had expanded to advise him. The issue created an uproar in the Church in western societies and a major loss of confidence in the authority of the papacy. The unfortunate Paul VI, seemingly shaken by the hostility

---

[29] *Gaudium et Spes* 1965; see §§1, 2, 4, 9, 12, 17, 26, 29, 32, 47–52, 64–68, 78, 80–83, 86.
[30] *Dignitatis Humanae* 1965; see §§2–3, 6–7, 13–14. For a critical analysis see Rico 2002.
[31] *Populorum Progressio* 1967; see §§9, 18–21, 26, 44, 53, 58, 87.
[32] *Humanae Vitae* 1968: §4. See Kaiser 1987; Hebblethwaite 1993; Marshall 1999.

his encyclical had aroused, was to write no other encyclical in the remaining decade of his pontificate. But influenced by the deliberations of the Conference of Latin American Bishops (CELAM) at Medellín in 1968[33] he wrote an Apostolic Letter, *Octogesima Adveniens*[34] in 1971. This further developed 'papal theorizing about world affairs' and drew particular attention to the problems of urbanization, the role of women, the 'new poor' on the margins of society, environmental concerns and the unregulated power of multinational enterprises. Pope Paul noted the contemporary aspirations to equality and participation and insisted on the need for greater justice in the sharing of goods, both within and between nations.

In 1971 a Synod of Bishops meeting in Rome produced *Justitia in Mundo*.[35] Perceiving a world of networks of domination and injustice, they made the remarkable statement that we have noted previously that action on behalf of social justice is an integral element in the Church's mission of evangelization. 'Unless combated and overcome by social and political action . . . economic injustice and lack of social participation keep (people) from attaining (their) basic human and civil rights'. This recognition of structural injustices requiring political action was strong stuff and marked a new stage in the development of the Church's social teaching in response to the new challenges in the modern world. The next Synod in 1974 was devoted to evangelization. It decided to remit its findings to the Pope who published *Evangelii Nuntiandi* on the tenth anniversary of the ending of Vatican II.[36] Of particular note was the remark that 'as the kernel and centre of his Good News, Christ proclaims salvation, this great gift of God which is liberation from *everything* that oppresses man'. *Evangelii Nuntiandi* was not a guide for action but 'a profound theological statement of the Church's commitment to the struggle for justice'.

Shortly after the CELAM II meeting at Medellín, Latin American theologians began to reformulate Christian theology from the viewpoint of the liberation of the poor.[37] In the run-up to the CELAM III Conference in 1979 at Puebla there was a major clash between liberation theologians and conservative opponents. In spite of the resistance, the concluding statement of CELAM III included important references to human dignity and human rights and 'the promotion and integral liberation of human

---

[33]   CELAM II Conclusions 1979; Smith 1991: 18–24.
[34]   *Octogesima Adveniens* 1971, §§2, 8–22, 24, 31, 34–35, 40, 43–44; Walsh 1984: xv.
[35]   *Justice in the World* 1971, in O'Brien and Shannon 1992: 287–300.
[36]   *Evangelii Nuntiand*, 1975: §9; Walsh 1984: xvii.
[37]   Gutiérrez 1974; Assman 1975; Segundo 1977; Sobrino 1978; Boff 1980.

beings in terms of both their earthly and their transcendent dimensions'.[38] It recognized the need to overcome not just personal sin but also 'sinful structures'. It affirmed 'the need for conversion on the part of the whole Church to a preferential option for the poor, an option aimed at their integral liberation'. Puebla was an important source of collegial teaching and, in spite of the subsequent Vatican criticisms of liberation theology which we discussed earlier, it remains one of the most important threads of post-Vatican theological thinking about social injustices.

Another important thread has been the social teaching of Pope John Paul II. Before commenting on his more overtly social encyclicals, brief mention must be made of his two earlier encyclicals. *Redemptor Hominis* (1979) on the redemptive work of Christ had much to say about the dignity of the human person,[39] freedom as necessary for this dignity, and about human rights. The pope made clear his concerns about the absence of an 'authentically humanistic plan'. He called for 'social love', solidarity and concern for the common good in view of the essential dignity of every human person. In 1980 Pope John Paul II issued *Dives in Misericordia* about divine mercy.[40] Following a moving reflection on the parable of the prodigal son, the pope again pointed to contemporary anxieties about the threat of nuclear war, the fear of abuses of power, oppression, and the increases of inequalities between individuals and nations. But he warned against distortions of some movements in pursuit of justice which replaced one tyranny with another. The experiences of our own lifetime had shown us that 'justice alone is not enough . . . if that deeper power, which is love, is not allowed to shape human life in its various dimensions'.

Following the practice of previous popes, Pope John Paul II issued his encyclical *Laborem Exercens*[41] to mark the ninetieth anniversary of *Rerum Novarum*. This encyclical marked a distinct break with the natural law arguments of previous papal encyclicals. It was, rather, a biblically-grounded philosophy and a theology of work. What was important was that work exists for man, and not the other way round. It was seen as a sharing in the activity of the divine creator and represented a response to the biblical calling to 'subdue the earth'. The pope called for 'a constructive revision both in theory and practice' of the dogma of the exclusive right to the private ownership of the means of production and encouraged various

---

[38] CELAM III 1980: §§156, 281, 321, 475, 648, 1134.
[39] *Redemptor Hominis* 1979: §§8–12, 15, 17; in Walsh and Davies 1984: 243–261.
[40] *Dives in Misericordia* 1980: §12 in Walsh and Davies 1984: 262–270.
[41] *Laborem Exercens* 1981: §§4, 6–10, 12–14, 16–27; Walsh 1984: xviii.

forms of joint or social ownership. The encyclical dealt extensively with the rights of workers, particularly the rights of women[42] and migrant workers. The encyclical concluded with an outline for a scripturally-based spirituality of work.

At this point reference must be made to the two important pastoral letters written by the United States bishops in the 1980s. These were of much more than local interest, not only for their content, but also because they were the product of a dialogical methodology which involved a much wider range of secular sources and interests than had probably ever been consulted previously. O'Brien and Shannon provided a useful introduction to their contribution to the Church worldwide and noted that while the letters 'express a critical distance' between the Church and American society, and 'while valuing prophetic witness, the bishops take their stand within and not apart from American society' in a non-judgemental way while seeking the 'goals of equality, justice, security, and peace'.[43] *The Challenge of Peace* (1983), which was scripturally-based, addressed 'many concrete questions concerning the arms race, contemporary warfare, weapons systems, and negotiating strategies', such as the policy of nuclear deterrence. Three years later the United States bishops issued their pastoral letter, *Economic Justice for All.*[44] While the letter drew on a long tradition of Catholic thought on the moral dimensions of economic activity, it also addressed the specifically American context. Nevertheless, this document was an immensely important resource for those seeking justice in social and economic life.

Pope John Paul II issued his encyclical *Sollicitudo Rei Socialis*[45] twenty years after Pope Paul's encyclical *Populorum Progressio*. The pope developed the idea of the authentic development of human beings and of nations as including not only economic and social dimensions, but also cultural identity and openness to the transcendent. The pope offered a theological reading of modern problems and recognized the legitimacy of speaking of 'structures of sin', though he insisted that they were 'rooted in personal sin ... and the concrete acts of individuals'. He sought a 'conversion' of individuals and nations and saw signs of it in a growing awareness of

---

[42] Ibid.: §19; the pope calls for 'a social re-evaluation of the mother's role' and adds that 'the true advancement of women requires that labour should be structured in such a way that women do not have to pay for their advancement by abandoning what is specific to them and at the expense of the family, in which women as mothers have an irreplaceable role'.
[43] O'Brien and Shannon 1992: 489–491.   [44] USCBC 1986: §§13–18, 28–294.
[45] *Sollicitudo Rei Socialis* 1987, §§28, 32, 36–38, 40, 42–44. See also Dorr 1992: 317–339.

economic, cultural, political, and religious interdependence, and of the virtue of gratuitous solidarity. He urged the need for reforms of the international trade system, the world monetary and financial system, technological exchanges, the international juridical order, and democratic and participatory political institutions.

Four years later Pope John Paul II issued *Centesimus Annus* to celebrate the centenary of *Rerum Novarum*.[46] The encyclical was published two years after the collapse of the Soviet empire in Central and Eastern Europe. The pope constantly returned to the themes of human dignity, freedom and human rights, solidarity and the need for struggle against injustice, marginalization and suffering. He reaffirmed 'the positive value of an authentic theology of integral human liberation'. The right to private property was confirmed with the proviso that the right was not absolute and was limited by the common purpose of goods. He acknowledged the positive aspects of the modern business economy but drew attention to its risks and problems such as dehumanizing work, the marginalization of people, and uncontrolled urbanization in developing countries. He warned against 'an "idolatry" of the market' and stressed that some collective and qualitative needs could not be satisfied by market mechanisms. A strong juridical framework for the free market economy of capitalism was necessary. With the collapse of totalitarian systems he called for a democracy with 'an authentic and solid foundation' of human rights, including 'the right to life, an integral part of which is the right of the child to develop in the mother's womb from the moment of conception'. The encyclical recognized the right of the state to regulate and coordinate but had some harsh criticisms to make of the 'social assistance state' which failed to pay due attention to the principle of subsidiarity. He called for 'fraternal support' for those in need. In order to overcome the contemporary 'individualistic mentality', what was required was a concrete solidarity and charity, within the family but also between nations. This might mean significant 'changes in established lifestyles, in order to limit the waste of environmental and human resources'.

Two years later the pope addressed his encyclical letter *Veritatis Splendor* (1993) to his fellow bishops regarding the Church's moral teaching. It contained relatively few references to social questions but is of relevance here for its strong affirmation of the tradition of universality and immutability of natural law in the Church.[47] It warned against the exaltation of freedom 'almost to the point of idolatry' and offered a lengthy treatment of

[46] *Centesimus Annus* 1991, §§22–30, 33, 40, 42, 48–52. See Dorr 1992: 340–350 and Curran 2002: 13–14.
[47] *Veritatis Splendor* 1993: §§42–64, 79–83, 98, 100–101.

the judgement of conscience, which 'is not an infallible judge', may be 'culpably erroneous', and needs to be properly 'informed' with help from 'the Church and her Magisterium'. There was an extended treatment of the notion of 'intrinsic evil' and Paul's teaching that 'it is not licit to do evil that good may come of it'. There was a brief and unspecific reference to 'the need for a radical personal and social renewal capable of ensuring justice, solidarity, honesty and openness'. The pope taught that 'reducing persons by violence to use-value or a source of profit is a sin against their dignity as persons and their fundamental rights'. Finally he warned of 'the risk of an alliance between democracy and ethical relativism'. In this encyclical the pope frequently referred to the new *Catechism of the Catholic Church* (1994).

In his apostolic letter in preparation for the Jubilee year 2000, *Tertio Millennio Adveniente* (1994),[48] Pope John Paul II reflected on the custom of jubilees going back to Old Testament times and pointed out that 'one of the most significant consequences was the general "emancipation" of all the dwellers on the land in need of being freed'. In preparation for the millennium he encouraged 'forms of counter-witness and scandal', and a serious examination of conscience for the responsibility of 'so many Christians for grave forms of injustice and exclusion'. He asked that since Jesus came to 'preach the good news to the poor' (Mt 11:5; Lk 7: 22), how could we fail to lay greater emphasis on the Church's preferential option for the poor and the outcast? Indeed, he suggested, a commitment to justice and peace in a world marked by so many conflicts and intolerable social and economic inequalities, was a necessary condition for the preparation and celebration of the Jubilee.

In 1995 John Paul II published *Evangelium Vitae*, 'the Gospel of Life'.[49] He expressed alarm at new threats to human life, including abortion, euthanasia and 'techniques of artificial reproduction', and the 'more sinister character' of the contemporary 'culture of death' which threatened the human dignity of the weakest members of society. In a deeply scriptural analysis he reflected that Jesus came that we might have life to the full and that 'life is always a good'. This embraced the 'ecological question' as well as the dignity of the unborn child, and the sick and elderly. The pope reflected on legitimate defence and the death penalty and argued that all innocent human beings have an equal right to life. He appealed to modern genetic science to respect the human being as a person from the moment of

---

[48] *Tertio Millennio Adveniente* 1994: §§12, 33, 36, 51.
[49] *Evangelium Vitae* 1995: §§7–28, 34, 42, 44–47, 57, 60, 62–63, 66, 70.

conception. Hence not only was abortion 'a grave moral disorder' but 'the use of human embryos or fetuses as an object of experimentation constitutes a crime against their dignity as human beings'. Euthanasia, suicide and assisted suicide were seen as rejections of 'God's absolute sovereignty over life and death'. The pope was sharply critical of the ethical relativism which many regarded as 'an essential condition of democracy' and affirmed the moral objectivity of the natural law. He concluded by appealing for a new culture of human life.

At the close of the Great Jubilee of 2000 and the commencement of the 'third millennium' John Paul II signed the apostolic letter *Novo Millennio Ineunte* encouraging Christians to 'put out into the deep' and 'go forward in hope'.[50] This optimistic letter noted that the jubilee had provided 'the opportunity to voice a strong call to correct the economic and social imbalances present in the world of work and . . . ensure that the processes of economic globalisation give due attention to solidarity and the respect owed to every human person'. He affirmed the Church's commitment to make a 'preferential option' for the poor and urged 'a new "creativity" in charity . . . by "getting close" to those who suffer'. The social question had assumed a global dimension; he mentioned an ecological crisis, catastrophic wars, the contempt for fundamental human rights of so many people, especially children, 'respect for the life of every human being, from conception until natural death', and advances in biotechnology which 'must never disregard fundamental ethical requirements'.

Finally, reference must be made to two statements recently made by the Catholic Bishops' Conference of England and Wales (CBCEW) on *The Common Good* (1996) and *Cherishing Life* (2004). The former was a valuable and readable outline of Catholic social teaching. Interestingly, it welcomed dialogue with anybody who wished to participate. It claimed that the Church had earned a voice since it was already contributing to the good of society in welfare and education. It suggested that all Christians had a duty to take seriously the 'option for the poor' and expressed concern about such issues as poverty, stark inequality and human rights. It asserted the importance of such values as the common good, solidarity and subsidiarity. It believed the Church's teaching would appeal to many because it had been shaped by 'natural law'. The statement addressed most of the main areas of injustice and contemporary social concern though there were surprisingly no references to the issues of war, terrorism or defence policy. It concluded challengingly that 'the political arena has to be reclaimed in

---

[50] *Novo Millennio Ineunte* 2001, §§1, 10, 14, 49–52, 58.

the name of the common good' even against strong economic forces that would deny it.[51] A subsequent document, *Cherishing Life*,[52] included an overview of Catholic teaching on healthcare, medical research, transplantation and gene therapy, abortion, embryo experimentation, suicide and euthanasia, and a brief reference to the issues of war and peace.

It is clear from the above review that official Catholic social thinking is not static but dynamic in response to changing circumstances and needs. Indeed, on certain matters, such as democracy, co-ownership and human rights, earlier positions have been reversed. Catholic social thought has been historically-contexted and reactive to changing social circumstances. There is no need to be overly defensive about this. Scientific and technological innovations and social, economic, political and cultural developments inevitably pose questions which earlier generations had never had to face. In response and in each generation charismatic and heroic individuals, such as Dorothy Day and Oscar Romero, and movements, such as the Young Christian Worker (YCW) movement, Pax Christi and CAFOD, have initiated innovative approaches to bring closer the realization of kingdom values.

KEY CONCEPTS IN CATHOLIC SOCIAL THOUGHT

Having reviewed the most significant contributions to Catholic social thought as we embark on the third Christian millennium, it might be opportune to summarize the six key concepts or 'guiding principles' which permeate and define it. There is general agreement on these amongst a variety of recent commentators.[53] They are interconnected and dynamic but 'although these may be good guiding principles, they still need a lot of working through and connecting, by way of middle-level thinking, to ideas for policy'.

Human dignity [54]

The first concept, which Curran regarded as 'the basis of official Catholic social teaching',[55] is that of 'the inviolable dignity of every human person'[56] which is 'a transcendent value, always recognized as such by those who

---

[51] CBCEW, *The Common Good* 1996: §119.   [52] CBCEW, *Cherishing Life* 2004.
[53] See, e.g., Boswell et al. 2000: xvi–xvii; 227; 267 and 273.
[54] The dignity of the human person is a major theme in the Vatican's *Compendium* 2004: §§105–151.
[55] Curran 1991: 79. See also Siroco and Zięba 2000: 21–24.   [56] *Christfideles Laici* 1988: §37.

sincerely search for the truth'.[57] This suggests a natural law claim until it is expressed in terms of the creation story and the revelation that every human person has been 'created by God in His image and likeness as well as redeemed by the most precious blood of Christ, . . . called to be . . . a living temple of the Spirit, destined for the eternal life of blessed communion with God'. Pope John XXIII had constructed his argument for the recognition of human rights on the basis of 'the dignity of the human person in the light of divinely revealed truth'.[58]

Common good

The second concept is that of the common good[59] which recognizes the interdependence of human beings and 'rejects the individualistic presuppositions of that form of liberal thought rooted in the Enlightenment notion of human autonomy'. In *Gaudium et Spes* (§26) the common good referred to 'the sum total of social conditions which allow people, either as groups or as individuals, to reach their fulfilment more fully and more easily'. It presupposed respect for individual people and social groups and their access to what was necessary to lead a fully human life, and a stable, secure and just social order. The bishops of England and Wales, in their statement on *The Common Good* referred to Pope John Paul II's teaching on the need for conversion which would affect attitudes and behaviour towards neighbours, human communities, animals, and the whole natural world, all of which are involved in the common good. They continued: 'That common good is the whole network of social conditions which enable human individuals and groups to flourish and live a fully, genuinely human life, otherwise described as "integral human development". All are responsible for all, collectively, at the level of society or nation, not only as individuals' (§48).

Subsidiarity

The third principle, subsidiarity,[60] teaches that 'a community of a higher order should not interfere in the internal life of a community of a lower order, depriving the latter of its functions, but rather should support it in

---

[57] John Paul II, *World Day of Peace Message* 1999: §2.   [58] *Pacem in Terris* 1963: §10.
[59] *Compendium* 2004: §§164–170; Siroco and Zięba 2000: 82–86; Hollenbach in Dwyer 1994: 192–196; Coleman 2000: 289–292.
[60] *Compendium* 2004: §§185–188; Sirico and Zięba 2000: 69–71; Allsopp in Dwyer 1994: 927–929.

case of need and help to co-ordinate its activity with the activities of the rest of society, always with a view to the common good' (*CA* §48). It defends the right to associate and organize and the rights of individuals and families in their relationships with the state. From Pius XI's *Quadragesimo Anno* (1931) it encouraged the establishment of a healthy plurality of intermediate associations such as trade unions. The principle has been appealed to by nations in their relationships with the European Union and to the internal life of local Churches.[61]

Preferential option for the poor

The fourth principle, the preferential option for the poor[62] emerged with liberation theology in Latin America in the 1960s. In *Sollicitudo Rei Socialis* (§42) Pope John Paul II referred to 'the preferential option or love of preference for the poor … a special form of primacy in the exercise of Christian charity'. Donal Dorr has recently interpreted this as part of a Vatican 'counter-offensive' against the concept.[63] He stressed that this option commits Christians to resist 'the injustice, oppression, exploitation, and marginalization of people that permeate almost every aspect of public life … (and) to disengage from serving the interests of the powerful and instead to take the side of those who are relatively powerless'.[64] The notion is solidly rooted in both the Old and New Testaments.

Solidarity

The fifth principle of Catholic social thought is that of solidarity which we have already discussed at length in the previous chapter. As we noted, solidarity[65] was strongly emphasized by Pope John Paul II. In reaction to liberal capitalism and extreme individualism it stresses our common humanity and responsibility for others. It aims to apply natural law understandings of human beings as essentially social in modern contexts. It relates not just to workers within societies but also to relationships between developed and developing nations. In *Sollicitudo Rei Socialis* (§38), solidarity 'is not a feeling of vague compassion … at the misfortunes of so many

---

[61] Quinn, J. R., 'The Claims of the Primacy and the Costly Call to Unity', *Briefing*, Vol. 26 (8), 15 August 1996: 18–29, espec. 27–28.

[62] *Compendium* 2004: §§182–184, 449; Sirico and Zięba 2000: 159–162; Dorr 1992; 1994: 755–759; and 2000: 249–262.

[63] Dorr 2000: 255.   [64] Dorr 1994: 755.

[65] *Compendium* 2004: §§192–196; Sirico and Zięba 2000: 66–69; Lamb in Dwyer 1994: 908–912.

people, . . . (but) a firm and persevering determination to commit oneself to the common good'.

Verstraeten observed that its significance in Catholic social thought went beyond enlightened self-interest 'to signify an attitude which finds its image in the common fatherhood of God and the brotherhood of all in Christ – a solidarity which finds its concrete expression in bearing radical witness to the love of our neighbour, so that it makes us ready for sacrifice'.[66] Boswell argued that solidarity is open in the direction of love, and is the lead value for all the other interdependent values. He saw Catholic beliefs in the Trinity's diverse distinctness, absolute equality and perfect love as fostering 'a desire for diversity, parity and love to be combined *even* in the temporal world'.[67] Coleman, too, argued that 'the constellation and inter-penetration of concepts (in Catholic social thought) is distinct: of human dignity, solidarity, subsidiarity, social justice, the option for the poor, the common good, justice as participation, etc'.[68]

Preferential option for non-violence

It has been suggested that an emerging sixth principle in Catholic social thought is that of a preferential option for non-violence. The *Compendium* does not advocate non-violence as a positive good, though negatively it does admit that 'violence is never a proper response' (§496). Though it does not appear to have been expressed explicitly in this way, a preference for non-violence clearly is implicit in recent Catholic thought about war and peace. The traditional conditions for a 'just war' increasingly fail to be met in modern, technologically sophisticated warfare where the evidence is of a rapidly increasing proportion of non-combatant deaths. This was reflected in the Vatican Council's explicit condemnation of 'total warfare' (*GS* §80). In just war thinking war has traditionally been seen as a response of last resort after all attempts at reconciliation have failed. Given the indiscriminate destructive power of modern weaponry a preferential option for non-violence clearly ought to be regarded as a basic principle of Catholic social thought.

EVALUATION

Of course these six principles, and the citizenship concepts we considered in the previous chapter, do not exhaust the riches and resources of Catholic

[66] Verstraeten 2000: 75.   [67] Boswell 2000: 103–110.   [68] Coleman 2000: 273.

social thought. But they provide a basic starting point for our reflections on specific policy areas where it is hoped to contribute to the 'middle-range' thinking called for by the Von Hugel collection.[69]

In the final chapter of *Option for the Poor*,[70] Donal Dorr suggested that between 1891 and 1961 Catholic Social Doctrine developed a coherent body of teaching around two basic themes:

- a particular concern for the poor and the powerless, together with a criticism of the systems that leave them vulnerable; (and)
- a defence of certain personal rights (above all, the right to private property) against collectivist tendencies.

Dorr suggested that throughout this period the popes were consistently critical of both liberal capitalism and socialism. They also 'put forward certain *fundamental principles* about human nature and the nature of human society in its economic, political, social, cultural and religious aspects', particularly

- the right of the individual to own property;
- the right of workers to join trade unions;
- the right of the head of a family to be paid a family wage;
- the obligation of mothers to care for their children in the home;
- the duty of the citizen to obey lawful authorities;
- the duty of governments to work for the common good;
- the right of citizens to resist oppression by lawful means;
- the obligation of governments and the rich and powerful to help the poor;
- the duty of governments and larger agencies to respect the principle of subsidiarity;
- the right of believers to freedom of worship; and
- the right of the Church to carry out its functions and to speak out on issues of public morality.

Dorr continued to argue that since Pope John XXIII's *Mater et Magistra* in 1961 there has been 'a decisive move away from the right' and a change in the 'Catholic ethos' alongside the poor in the struggle for justice, though this was a locus of struggle within the Church. Dorr identified a number of *strengths* of Catholic Social Teaching:

- it is humanistic and appealing to all people of good will;
- it focuses on two key humanistic values: participation and solidarity;
- it is pluralistic;
- it is based on much social analysis (i.e. is 'grounded' in social reality);

---

[69] Boswell et al. 2000.   [70] Dorr 1992: 352–3, 355, 366–377.

- it has a strong scriptural basis; and
- it is prophetic 'in the sense of being radically challenging and inspirational'.

Before leaving this outline we might note that both Donal Dorr and John Coleman have drawn attention to some of the weaknesses of Catholic social thought. Dorr noted that it remained somewhat ethnocentric and western and had a limited model of development, was insufficiently ecological, neglected women and the role of the Church in politics, failed to offer an adequate analysis of the root causes of social injustice, failed to address issues of confrontation and conflict or injustices within the Church, and failed to listen effectively to the *sensum fidei*. Coleman[71] added that it paid too little attention to productivity as a social good; assumed social harmony and overlooked pluralism, embraced the *status quo* and failed to suggest alternatives.[72] As I have indicated above, in my view, it also fails to offer positive advocacy of equality and non-violence.

It may be appropriate at this point to note that there appears to be some tension between two different theological approaches to seeking social justice. One theology starts from the nature of the human person in God's plan of love, with a conscience, moral norms and virtues in the human community, and the place of the Church in it. This broadly speaking has been the perspective running through the papal encyclicals of the past hundred years. The recently published *Compendium* clearly articulates this perspective. The alternative approach, which has been favoured in this book because it is grounded in social reality and the scriptural testimony that Jesus came to proclaim the reign and kingdom of God, seeks to work out what the realization of 'the kingdom is among you' might mean in the real world. This approach has been favoured by liberation theologians with their more critical concepts of liberation and dependency which make empirical sense of our fallen world. Within this perspective it is perfectly possible to locate the six guiding principles we have identified.

While the *Compendium* is worthy of the respect due to a formal outline of the current social doctrine of the Church, unlike this present book it contains no social analysis backed by empirical evidence. It reflects the teaching of Pope John Paul II and marginalizes all conflicting or alternative views, is overwhelmingly personalist and tends to dilute the analysis of the *social* causes of injustices. It fails to address the issue of the *social* power of

---

[71] Coleman 1991a: 39–41; 2000: 286–292.
[72] Against the more critical evaluations of Dorr and Coleman, noted above, George Weigel has offered a rather generous evaluation of the emergence of modern Catholic social doctrine which reflects an American liberal ideology in Grasso et al. 1995: 257–258.

institutions (such as the IMF) which are never named. Its claim to be 'in friendly dialogue with all branches of knowledge' is belied by the fact that not one of the 1232 footnotes refers to secular thought. In sum, the *Compendium* is a statement of a position, not an argued thesis. It presents a 'top-down' approach to social justice whereas liberation theologians and social justice activists endeavour to pursue a more dialogical, inductive and 'bottom-up' approach from the perspectives of the poor and oppressed in seeking appropriate responses to their social injustices and needs.

In *Centesimus Annus*, too, Pope John Paul II wrote that 'in order better to incarnate the one truth about man in different and constantly changing social, economic and political contexts, (the Church's social teaching) enters into dialogue with the various disciplines concerned with man' (§59). Yet a cursory look at papal documents will make it painfully obvious that the overwhelming bulk of references to previous work is to previous papal and other Church writings. There is practically never any reference to the writings of lay people or any engagement with the major thinkers of the time. Even the diatribes against communism rarely, if ever, refer to Marx or Engels directly, and references to the great philosophers of the Enlightenment, or to Keynes or Freud or John Rawls, or to the authors of huge advances in astrophysics or biogenetics in our own times are negligible. This hardly demonstrates an openness to the modern world or to a willingness to dialogue about the marvels as well as the challenges of modern science.

It is beyond the scope of this Introduction to respond to this at length but the recent symposium at the Von Hugel Institute, Cambridge, helpfully reviewed much relevant literature.[73] Lay writers who have influenced social thought include Jacques Maritain (on Pope Paul VI, the United Nations and post-war Christian Democracy),[74] Barbara Ward[75] (on the Pontifical Justice and Peace Commission), and Michael Novak (with his contribution to the United States bishops' pastoral letter on the economy and his spirited defence of democratic capitalism).[76] A number of writers have added notably to recent debates about communitarianism and the role of religion in the economy and public life.[77] Important contributions to Catholic social thought have been made by priests such as John A. Coleman, Charles E. Curran, David Hollenbach and John Courtney Murray,[78] by liberation theologians such as Leonardo Boff, Gustavo

---

[73] Boswell et al. 2000; Coleman 1991a; 2000: 273–275; Stiltner 1999; Curran 2002.
[74] Hebblethwaite 1993: 121–122; Maritain 1951.   [75] Ward 1962; 1972.   [76] Novak 1991.
[77] Boswell 1994a, 1994b; Casanova 1994; Grasso et al. 1995.   [78] Murray 1960.

Gutiérrez and Jon Sobrino, and by feminist theologians and writers on Christian ethics such as Rosemary Ruether and Lisa Cahill. All these thinkers have contributed to the climate of opinion and the development of doctrine both within the Church and in the wider society, which is increasingly global in its scope.

We have previously noted a certain oscillation in the relative emphasis in official Catholic social teaching between natural law claims and scripture. Some tension between the two positions seems inevitable. In arguing for a 'conception of natural law as transcendental equity', Frank McHugh suggested that the 'essential elements' of Catholic social thought – 'justice, solidarity, subsidiarity and an option for the poor – facilitate debate with our post-modern contemporaries, who are preoccupied with the same questions'.[79] He proposed the term 'common social wisdom' which better expressed the tradition 'which encourages rigour of thought, the importance of common human experience, the motivating force of theological imagination and the *praxis* of ecclesial communities'.

Natural law thinking is likely to be historically-contexted.[80] This is, perhaps, most obvious in its unqualified emphasis on the value of private property at the expense of the common good, or its undiscriminating rejection of Marxian analysis of class conflict and uncritical advocacy of corporatism[81] and bias in favour of the political and economic *status quo*. This has resulted in a view of society 'as basically a satisfactory organic system that must be preserved and perfected'. But this is ahistorical, and dialectical sociologies which see class conflict as inevitable in a developing society, as expressing a vision of those 'from below', and see society 'as inadequate, badly structured, full of conflict and in need of transformation', seem more appropriate in the analysis of contemporary reality.[82] A strong scriptural emphasis with claims to a privileged interpretation by the Church's magisterium, on the other hand, is unlikely to convince non-believers. It is not surprising, therefore, that a number of Catholic writers have expressed concerns about the failure to dialogue effectively with contemporary secular thought.[83] It is to be hoped that as Catholics move out of the defensive, pressure group politics of an 'immigrant Church' they

---

[79] McHugh 2000: 54, 56.   [80] Walsh 1984: xviii–xxi.
[81] Coleman 1991b: 6.   [82] Walsh 1984: xx.
[83] Charles Curran 2002: 250, instances the fact that 'the most respected proponent of philosophical liberalism', the late John Rawls, had not mentioned 'until recently the social thought of the most renowned Catholic writer on political theory', John Courtney Murray. John Coleman treats of 'Catholic Social Thought in Dialogue with Contemporary Thought' in Boswell et al. 2000: 286–292.

will increasingly become 'a voice trying to persuade through reason and deliberation'.[84]

THEOLOGICAL RESOURCES: CONCLUDING REFLECTIONS

In the *Catechism of the Catholic Church* (§1807) justice is seen as one of the four 'cardinal' moral virtues that 'consists in the constant and firm will to give their due to God and neighbour'. The just man is said to be 'distinguished by habitual right thinking and the uprightness of his conduct toward his neighbour'. This begs a number of questions; what is 'right thinking'? In practice, the Catholic notion of 'justice' is certainly not the same as 'fairness' as perhaps the parable of the workers in the vineyard (Mt 20: 1–16) makes clear. The Catholic interpretation of justice would see itself as part of an evolving and refining Judeo-Christian ethic. It would regard the teachings of Jesus as an important turning point. Thus the injunction not to take 'an eye for an eye' (Ex 21: 24) but to 'turn the other cheek' (Mt 5: 39).

Considerable attention is still paid to the prophetic writings in the Old Testament, especially Isaiah, Amos, Hosea and Micah, and in the notions of jubilees and sabbaticals (Lev 25: 10). The Exodus account of a pilgrim 'People of God' on a journey to the promised land is strongly emphasized by liberation theologians.[85] But however much the Old Testament tradition is drawn upon, the primacy of the new law to love is emphatic, as in the parable of the good Samaritan (Lk. 10: 29–37). A key text here is the parable of the Last Judgement (Mt 25: 31–46) where eternal life or damnation are decided in terms of the extent to which the individual has fed the hungry, given drink to the thirsty, welcomed strangers, clothed the naked, and visited the sick or imprisoned.

The emerging social justice paradigm has been much influenced by Latin American liberation theologians and the two major meetings of the Latin American bishops at Medellin in 1968 and Puebla in 1979 which provided a legitimation for the slogan 'the preferential option for the poor'. These were building on *Gaudium et Spes*, the Second Vatican Council's Pastoral Constitution on the Church in the Modern World. There is a strong emphasis on liberation, primarily from sin, and that includes the social sin of slavery to oppressive and unjust socio-economic systems. For the first time there are references to 'sinful social structures' (*SRS* §§36–39)

---

[84] Curran 2002: 251. In England and Wales, the response to the bishops' statement *The Common Good* in 1996, suggested that they had made some progress in this respect.
[85] e.g. Gutiérrez 1991: 3–6.

and 'a *structural* conflict between the oppressor and the oppressed, between the rich and the poor'.[86] Thus the call to justice includes giving a 'preferential option for the poor', mindful of the preaching of Jesus at Nazareth to 'go and preach the good news to the poor' (Lk 4: 18; Is 61: 1–2).

In sum, the emerging paradigm sees justice in right relationships with God and neighbour and a recognition that ultimately all are dependent on God for the gifts of this life so that no one can claim absolute property rights over the goods of the earth. Even so, there is a struggle to realize this in practice and to convince the membership of the Church that the pursuit of justice lies at the heart of what it means to be a Christian today. Many of these perspectives are shared with members of other Christian Churches.[87]

In Part I of this book we attempted to provide a brief overview of domestic and international injustices and suggest a framework for an appropriate social analysis leading to their understanding and explanation. The three chapters of Part II have endeavoured to review the range of theological resources available for any systematic critique of the social, political, economic, technological and cultural arrangements in our contemporary world which give rise to social injustices. In Chapter 3 we considered the scriptural vision of the kingdom of God which was revealed in the life of Jesus of Nazareth 2,000 years ago. Jesus came to call us to realize this vision in our temporal world. Because of sin and evil in the world, this will always be a struggle and will never be completed until the end of time. That it is utopian to think that a perfect just and peaceful world is attainable does not absolve followers of Jesus from seeking to bring its realization closer. Chapter 4 attempted to dialogue with contemporary secular values such as citizenship, and the revolutionary values of liberty, equality and fraternity. It argued that all of these values are compatible with a contemporary Christian understanding of the kingdom of God.

Finally, in the present chapter, a review of Catholic social thought has been offered. This has been shown to have had two distinct roots in scripture and natural law theory. Catholic social thought has evolved over twenty centuries in reaction to the major challenges and problems of the time. Thus it has been historically-contexted and frequently biased and is clearly an arena for the development of doctrine. There have been many developments since the time of Pope John XXIII and the major theological shifts legitimated by the Second Vatican Council. As we enter the third Christian millennium, the themes of human dignity, the common good, subsidiarity, the preferential option for the poor, solidarity

---

[86] Nolan 1984: 9.   [87] CTBI 2005a, 2005b.

between people and nations, and the preferential option for non-violence, provide valuable concepts and principles for the working out of appropriate social policies which seek to eliminate or at least alleviate the multitude of injustices both at home and internationally. In Part III of this book we will consider six main areas where Catholic social thought might make a valuable contribution.

PART III

Justice issues

CHAPTER 6

Human rights

RIGHTS AND REALITY

The first main area of need and justice is that of human rights in its broadest sense. Recent claims have included the right to walk the streets naked, women's absolute rights over their embryos, parents' claim to choose the gender of their children, gay and lesbian couples' demand to be able to adopt children, the right to privacy and to a good night's sleep under the flight path to a nearby airport, the right of women and ethnic minorities to equal treatment at work, children's right not to be smacked, the right to paid employment, and to choose the time of death. Campaigning groups make claims on behalf of asylum seekers or refugees in terms of intrinsic human rights. The founding fathers of the USA saw the right to life, liberty and the pursuit of happiness as inalienable. The UN Universal Declaration on Human Rights recognized the equal dignity and rights of all people and their right to life, liberty, personal security and the right not to be tortured (Articles 1, 3 and 5).

The right to life itself, from conception to natural death, is a long way from being achieved. Many countries continue the practice of executions for certain crimes and Amnesty International has reported clear evidence of torture by state authorities in many countries. The World Bank reported that the mortality rate of children under five in developing countries was over twelve times that in high income countries. Thousands of people have been killed as a result of war or terrorist activities.

The claim to a life of security can also be seen in the growing numbers of refugees and asylum seekers. Most refugees are to be found in some of the poorest countries of the world. In 2002 the UNHCR reported that there were around 20 million people 'of concern', including around 12 million refugees and nearly one million asylum seekers. Other desperate people have migrated from their homelands for economic reasons in order to support their impoverished families. The remittances of foreign workers to their families in their home countries was second only to oil in world trade in the mid-1990s.[1] Ethnic minorities and economic migrants are frequently the targets for violent attacks, discrimination and racism. In 1999 the Macpherson Report into the murder of Stephen Lawrence in 1993 accused the Metropolitan Police of 'institutional racism'[2] and similar charges could be levelled against other institutions such as schools and Churches.

Five 'generations' of human rights thinking have recently been distinguished including civil and political rights, economic, social and cultural rights. This is a formidable list of claims.

THE EMERGENCE OF HUMAN RIGHTS DISCOURSE

The concept of human rights has been traced from England's Bill of Rights of 1689 and the American Declaration of Independence of 1776. Article I of the French Revolution's Declaration of the Rights of Man and the Citizen of 1789 asserts that 'Men are born and remain free and equal in rights'. In response, Thomas Paine wrote *The Rights of Man* in 1791.[3] In 1948 the General Assembly of the United Nations adopted and proclaimed the *Universal Declaration of Human Rights*.[4] Two years later the member states of the Council of Europe signed the *Convention for the Protection of Human Rights and Fundamental Freedoms*. In Britain the Human Rights Act became law in 1998. Members of the European Union proclaimed the Charter of Fundamental Rights in 2000.

The current official teaching of the Church's Magisterium[5] on human rights is of fairly recent origin as we noted in previous chapters. In *Pacem in Terris* (§§9–30) Pope John XXIII indicated the basis of Catholic beliefs on human rights in both natural law and Christian revelation when he wrote that 'every human being is a person; that is, his nature is endowed with intelligence and free will. Indeed, precisely because he is a person he has rights and obligations flowing directly and simultaneously from his very nature'. These are 'universal and inviolable, so they cannot in any way be surrendered'. Furthermore the dignity of human beings has been enhanced by having been 'redeemed by the blood of Jesus Christ'. The pope proceeded to identify a number of specific rights: to life and a worthy standard

---

[1] Castles and Miller 1998: 4–5.   [2] Macpherson Report, Cm 4262-I 1999. London: Stationery Office.
[3] Davies 1996: 678–679, 713–714.
[4] The Catholic Bishops of England and Wales produced *Human Rights and the Catholic Church* 1998, to mark the fiftieth anniversary of the UN Declaration.
[5] Compendium 2004: §§152–159. On 'Magisterium', see N. J. Rigali 1994; on non-official contributions which have a different authority, see Boswell et al. 2000.

of living; to a good reputation and freedom in searching for truth and of expression of opinion and to a basic education; to religious freedom in accordance with one's conscience; to choose freely one's state of life with equal rights to men and women; to a free choice of marriage partner; to opportunities to work without coercion; to assembly and association; to freedom of movement and to emigrate; and to political rights. But natural rights are inseparably connected with corresponding duties to take account of the common good and 'rights as well as duties find their source, their sustenance and their inviolability in the natural law'.

The notion of human rights was emphatically endorsed by the Second Vatican Council in *Gaudium et Spes* and *Dignitatis Humanae* and was a major theme in the teaching of John Paul II, notably in his encyclical *Centesimus Annus*. What has been termed 'the Catholic human rights revolution' represented a U-turn in official Church teaching following 'the papal struggle with liberalism'.[6] José Casanova[7] pointed out that 'Pope Pius VI in his 1791 papal Brief *Caritas* adamantly condemned the Declaration of the Rights of Man by the French National Assembly, arguing that the rights to freedom of religion and freedom of the press, as well as the Declaration on the Equality of all Men, were contrary to the divine principles of the Church'. Pius IX in 1864 included the principle of human rights and most modern freedoms, including religious freedom, in his *Syllabus* of errors. 'Vatican II's Declaration on Religious Freedom, *Dignitatis Humanae*, radically changed the Catholic course by recognizing the inalienable right of every individual to freedom of conscience, grounding it in the *sacred* dignity of the human person'. It should, perhaps, be pointed out that this new emphasis on human rights in official Catholic social teaching does create difficulties. Casanova, for example, points out that one historical consequence 'in the long run (is) the incompatibility of a dogmatic conception of authoritative tradition and the principle of freedom of conscience'.[8] An obvious example is the clash between a 'woman's right to chose' and an embryo's 'right to live'.

Julie Clague has reviewed some of the philosophical difficulties of a stress on individual rights taken out of a context of social relationships. She noted that Alasdair MacIntyre and others saw the Enlightenment view of the person-as-individual as 'a corruption of and antithetical to the classical conception of the person-as-social fundamental to Christianity'. In spite of

[6] Burns 1994: 22–46. Note, however, that in *Rerum Novarum* in 1891, Leo XIII taught that there were rights to free association and to a just wage.
[7] Casanova 2001: 432–433.   [8] Casanova 1994: 72.

such difficulties, Clague concluded that 'provided they are supported by a sufficiently rich Christian anthropology – human rights can serve an important purpose in public discourse by providing a means by which the requirements of justice can be articulated to the modern world'.[9]

It is worth reflecting on the fact that an emphasis on the right to private property and on political liberty, while ignoring the social and economic rights of the poor, served the interests of the West in the Cold War period. Furthermore, 'as cases under the Human Rights Act in the United Kingdom have already begun to show, it is the rich and powerful (human and corporate) who gain disproportionately from entrenching rights in an unequal society'.[10] Nevertheless, the insistence on human rights embodies a claim that every person has an intrinsic worth no matter how vulnerable, down-trodden or defenceless they might be. In plural societies disagreements about rights and responsibilities are inevitable. It seems that human rights are not so much moral absolutes as conventions regarding minimum standards of human behaviour.

To mark the fiftieth anniversary of the Universal Declaration of Human Rights, the Commission of the Bishops' Conferences of the European Communities (COMECE) published a Special Issue of their monthly publication *Europe Infos* on the theme *Human Rights and Human Dignity*. This usefully distinguished four generations of human rights thinking:[11]

- first generation civil and political rights, such as the right to life, the prohibition of torture and slavery, freedom of religion, expression, and association;
- second generation economic and social rights, such as the right to work, social security, protection of the family, necessary for the development of the human person;
- third generation rights to solidarity, to a healthy environment and to development;
- fourth generation rights to safeguard human dignity from abuses of technology and biomedicine.

The Nice summit meeting of the EU in 2000 introduced what might be called a
- fifth generation of rights to freedom of scientific research and enterprise, protection of intellectual property, to proper administration, children's

---

[9] Clague 2000: 125–126. See also Hollenbach 1979, 1998; Drinan 2001.
[10] Gearty, C. in a review of Drinan 2001 in *The Tablet*, 7 July 2001.
[11] *Euro Infos* February 1999: 16–18. It might be noted that for Marxists, second generation rights must come before first generation rights or they will not work.

rights, access to utilities, protection in the event of unfair dismissal, to individual equality before the law and between men and women.

THE RIGHT TO LIFE AND THE DEATH PENALTY

The Catholic bishops of England and Wales in *The Common Good* suggested that 'the study of the evolution of the idea of human rights shows that they all flow from the one fundamental right: the right to life (§37)'. The fifth commandment given to Moses was 'You shall not kill' (Exod 20: 13; Deut 5: 17).[12] It is evident that this commandment continues to be broken in every war and fatal act of violence everywhere. For the moment we will address the matter of the death penalty and legal execution of those deemed to have been serious offenders.

The Universal Declaration of Human Rights asserted 'Everyone has the right to life, liberty and security of person' (1948: Article 3). Similarly the European Union's Charter of Fundamental Rights asserted that '(1) Everyone has the right to life. (2) No one shall be condemned to the death penalty, or executed' (2000: Article 2).

In 2002 the Death Penalty Information Center[13] reported that eighty-four countries still retained the death penalty. According to Amnesty International, during 2001, at least 3,048 prisoners were executed in 31 countries and 5,265 were sentenced to death in 69 countries, though the true figures are likely to have been much higher. Ninety per cent of all known executions took place in China, Iran, Saudi Arabia and the USA. 'Seven countries since 1990 are known to have executed prisoners who were under 18 years old at the time of the crime'.

According to Robert Drinan, the abhorrence of 'cruel and inhuman treatment or punishment' first appeared in the English Bill of Rights of 1689. Since then there has been a steady emergence of customary international law, similar to that which eventually brought about the end of slavery and piracy, to abolish the death penalty as a form of punishment.[14] Drinan traced the struggle to abolish capital punishment in the United States. One interesting source of international pressure on the USA relates to its observer status at the Council of Europe (CoE). 'It

---

[12] The commandment 'covers deliberate and accidental homicide but not capital punishment and the killing of animals for food, both practised in Israel'; see Brown et al. 1991: 98.
[13] http://www.deathpenaltyinfo.org/dpicintl.html; http://web.amnesty.org/rmp/dplibrary.nsf; *Amnesty* Issue 117. January/February 2003: 14–17.
[14] Drinan 2001: 130, 148–153.

is now a precondition for accession to the CoE that States institute an immediate moratorium on executions with a view to abolition of the death penalty in the long term'. Serious consideration is being given to the attachment of similar conditions to those states with observer status, including the USA.

There are several reasons on humanistic grounds to abhor the death penalty. Perhaps the main one is the danger of executing the innocent. The UN Secretary General, Kofi Annan, when presented with a petition in 2000 for a moratorium on executions, observed wisely that 'the forfeiture of life is too absolute, too irreversible, for one human being to inflict it on another, even when backed by legal process. And I believe that future generations throughout the world will come to agree'. Furthermore, research for the UN in 1988 and 1996 concluded that there was no 'scientific proof that executions have a greater deterrence effect than life imprisonment' or that abolition of the death penalty results in any increase in crime rates.

Old Testament justice stresses the equality of offence and punishment and a limit to retaliation. Three times it is stressed: 'life for life, eye for eye, tooth for tooth' (Exod 21: 24; Lev 24: 20; Deut 19: 21). Yet Jesus authoritatively transcended this earlier morality. After insisting that he had come not to abolish the Law or the Prophets but to complete them (Mt 5: 17), Jesus gives six examples of new standards higher than the old (Mt 5: 21–48). Thus he replaces the law of retaliation expressed in the phrase 'life for life' with the ethic of forgiveness (Mt 6:14–15) and his radical challenge to love enemies. Christians believe that criminals have also been redeemed by Jesus the Saviour and that all people are called to repent their faults and sin no more.

Whereas the Church has traditionally allowed for capital punishment in order to uphold the common good of society and as a form of legitimate defence, it seems clear that there is now a strong presumption to seek alternative forms of punishment. Thus the *Catechism* (§2267) states that 'if bloodless means are sufficient to defend human lives against an aggressor and to protect public order and the safety of persons, public authority should limit itself to such means, because they better correspond to the concrete conditions of the common good and are more in conformity to the dignity of the human person'. In *Evangelium Vitae* (§§26–27, 56) Pope John Paul II saw the growing public opposition to the death penalty as a positive sign and argued that the execution of offenders ought to be reverted to only 'when it would not be possible otherwise to defend society. Today however . . . such cases are very rare, if not practically non-existent'.

THE RIGHT TO LEGAL JUSTICE

In this section we shall consider a range of issues which can broadly be grouped under the heading of legal justice. This includes in the first place a system of justice which is fair and impartial and which treats all who are brought before the courts as of equal human dignity and deserving of respect. Secondly, whatever punishments for wrongdoing are determined, they must be seen to be appropriate while continuing to respect the dignity of the prisoner. Thirdly, given freedom of conscience and the right to dissent which follows from the intrinsic dignity of each human being created in the image of God, there must be concern about the incarceration of political prisoners. Fourthly, for the same reason the use of torture as an instrument of policy must be strongly opposed. Fifthly, in the same way there can be no place for institutions of slavery.

The right to a fair trial

The ancient writ of *habeas corpus* requiring an arrested person to be brought to court to investigate the lawfulness of his or her detention, a common law right thought to predate Magna Carta in 1215, seems clearly to have been breached both at the United States base at Guantanamo Bay and in the UK Belmarsh high security prison. It is important that Christians consider the morality of such forms of imprisonment justified in the name of national security.

In the pursuit of legal justice, the first thing to be sought is a legal system which is both formally in the legal codes themselves and in operational practice, just in its treatment of people of different statuses and power. It should ideally be impartial and resistant to political pressures and the interests of the powerful, whether individuals, corporations or states. Article 6 of the Universal Declaration asserted that 'Everyone has the right to recognition everywhere as a person before the law' and Article 7 that 'All are equal before the law and are entitled without any discrimination to equal protection of the law . . .' Article 10 laid down that 'everyone is entitled to full equality to a fair and public hearing by an independent and impartial tribunal, in the determination of his rights and obligations and of any criminal charge against him'. Article 6(1) of the European Convention included the phrase that 'everyone is entitled to a fair and public hearing . . .' Article 20 of the European Charter stated simply that 'everyone is equal before the law' and Article 21(1) prohibited 'any discrimination based on any ground such as sex, race, colour, ethnic or social origin, genetic features, language, religion or belief, political or any other opinion, membership of any national minority, property, birth, disability, age or sexual orientation . . .'

Such secular charters of human rights claims are operationalizing injunctions in the Mosaic laws. In the book of Exodus it was laid down that 'You will not cheat the poor among you of their rights at law. Keep clear of fraud. Do not cause the death of the innocent or upright, and do not acquit the guilty. You will accept no bribes, for a bribe blinds the clear-sighted and is the ruin of the cause of the upright. You will not oppress the alien . . .' (Exod 23: 6–9). In Leviticus (19: 15) Yahweh spoke to Moses and said: 'You will not be unjust in administering justice. You will neither be partial to the poor nor overawed by the great, but administer justice to your fellow-citizen justly'. The Third Isaiah (56:1) wrote: 'Thus says Yahweh: Make fair judgement your concern, act with justice'. Wicked and unscrupulous rulers and judges were warned by the psalmist (Ps 82: 2–3). The crookedness of the two judges of Susanna who tried to bring about her unjust execution was exposed by Daniel and punished according to the law (Dan 13). The political expediencies of the high priest, Caiaphas, who sought to bring about the death of Jesus (Jn 11: 50, 18: 14) and of Pilate, the Roman procurator, who allowed it (Jn 18: 28–19: 16) have been universally condemned.

Yet in reality, the justice systems of most, if not all, countries are often deeply flawed. In Britain there have been several high profile cases of injustice in recent years including the execution of the innocent, wrongful imprisonment, or the inadequate prosecution of the guilty. Black people have been disproportionately stopped and searched, harassed, wrongfully arrested, imprisoned. A number of police officers have been convicted of taking bribes from drug dealers and other criminals. Extremely complex financial fraud cases and white collar crime generally seem to be disproportionately difficult to prosecute. For the rich and powerful, and for corporate capital generally, it is regarded as a legitimate goal to avoid contributing to the common tax revenue. An adversarial legal system favours those who can afford the cleverest lawyers. In sum, there is differential access to justice. Even the most impartial judges carry with them biases of culture and upbringing.

The requirement in justice for a fair and impartial legal system and a judiciary of integrity has a long and explicit warrant in Judeo-Christian ethics. It is seen as a requirement for the kingdom of God. In our own times organizations such as Amnesty International and Liberty are in the forefront of struggles for legal integrity and accountability both domestically and internationally. As Robert Drinan argued, 'human rights depend on an independent judiciary'.

The right to a fair punishment

The notion of punishment for wrong-doing was clearly warranted in the Old Testament. The prophet Hosea, for example, warned that Yahweh 'will punish Jacob as his deeds deserve' (Hos 12: 2–3). But punishments were always strictly limited and controlled.[15] The codification of the Book of the Covenant (Exod 20:22–23:33) provided in detail for appropriate punishments for a wide range of crimes. It was summed up in the well-known code of limited vengeance: 'eye for eye, tooth for tooth'. But Jesus, in his six antitheses, replaced the law of retaliation with the obligation to forgive wrongdoers and love enemies. It has taken many generations to discern just what this means in practice. Over many centuries there has been a general revulsion against the death penalty, torture, and physical forms of punishment, such as flogging. But various forms of incarceration remain with substantial public support though they are a challenge to a Christian sense of human dignity, even in the case of the most hardened criminals.[16]

There are numerous purposes in punishing criminals: deterrence of others; retribution for harm done to others; restoration of the situation before the fault; the rehabilitation of the criminal, and so on. The Christian ethic would lead us to seek a shift in the purposes of punishment away from retribution towards rehabilitation and restoration. The aim should be the forgiveness of criminals and their re-inclusion into mainstream society.

In Britain the number of people in prisons has reached record levels. There are now over 80,000 prisoners, the highest number in Europe. Many of them are incarcerated three to a cell for 23 hours each day. In the USA nearly 2 million people are imprisoned and hundreds have spent many years on death row.[17] Such conditions are inhuman and degrading and fail to provide for legitimate prisoners' human rights. They are a challenge to a proper Christian conscience concerned to respect the dignity of every human being. There are well-attested alternatives to imprisonment, for instance community action and systematic forms of re-education such as are provided in some Scandinavian countries, which decisively shift the

---

[15] Article 49(3) of the EU Charter of Fundamental Rights declared that 'the severity of penalties must not be disproportionate to the criminal offence'.
[16] See the excellent CASC Jubilee Paper No.1, *Women in Prison*, 1999.   [17] Drinan 2001: 141.

balance from retribution to rehabilitation and which have been shown to have resulted in lower rates of recidivism and crime.

Imprisonment implies a significant reduction in the human right to freedom. A Christian response to crime would put far more emphasis on the achievement of reconciliation with the victims and the making of reparations in order to restore the situation as far as possible to that existing before the crime. Attempts to do this seem to have had promising results. It is, perhaps, time for Christians to address such matters more forcefully.

The right to dissent: prisoners of conscience

Among the many human rights which have been increasingly recognized worldwide are those of protest and of free expression. Thus, Article 18 of the UN Declaration declared that 'everyone has the right to freedom of thought, conscience and religion' and Article 19 that 'everyone has the right to freedom of opinion and expression'. Article 20 acknowledged 'the right to freedom of peaceful assembly and association'. Parallel statements are to be found in Articles 9–11 in the European Convention and Articles 10–12 in the European Charter which also recognized the 'right to conscientious objection . . . in accordance with the national laws governing the exercise of this right'. The Human Rights Act 1998 included Article 10 (1) which recognized that 'everyone has the right of freedom of expression. This right shall include freedom to hold opinions and to receive and impart information and ideas without interference by public authority and regardless of frontiers'. But Article 10 (2) continued to specify limits to this right in the interests of national security and public order or safety. In other words, Article 10 was a 'qualified right'.

Sadly, this right is frequently and crudely put aside by powerful and corrupt states and political dissidents are ubiquitous. As Peter Benenson noted at the foundation of Amnesty International: 'What matters is not the rights that exist on paper in the Constitution, but whether they can be exercised and enforced in practice'.[18] Amnesty defined a prisoner of conscience as 'any person who is physically restrained (by imprisonment or otherwise) from expressing (in any form of words or symbols) an opinion which he honestly holds and which does not advocate or condone personal violence'. In 1999 fifty-one countries were conducting unfair trials for

---

[18] *The Observer Weekend Review*, 28 May 1961, reproduced in the *Observer Life Magazine*, 27 May 2001 which celebrated Amnesty's 40th birthday. A Special Birthday Issue was published in *Amnesty*, Issue 107, May/June 2001.

political prisoners and people were arbitrarily arrested and detained or in detention without charge or trial in sixty-three countries. Sixty-one countries were holding or believed to be holding prisoners of conscience. Amnesty's logo, a candle wrapped in barbed wire, was inspired by an old Chinese proverb: 'It is better to light a candle than to curse the darkness'. The letter-writing of ordinary people to authorities is a most important contribution to campaigns for structural change and the ending of both individual and structural oppression. Many thousand political dissidents owe their lives and freedom to the cumulative efforts of thousands of ordinary letter-writers.

Society is enormously enriched by its dissidents, those who keep open the flame of freedom or testify to values other than those expected by authoritarian states or powerful political, military or other interests. Vaclav Havel, the former Czech President and dissident during the period of Soviet totalitarianism, observed that 'human beings can be accomplices in their own bondage, and the appeal of a totalitarian system is that it is nourished by the fear of human autonomy'.[19] Commenting on Havel's analysis of the readiness to 'live a lie', Fuellenbach noted, however, the 'unquenchable thirst for human dignity and freedom (which) makes itself felt in the dissident voice of the powerless ... (who create) a network of integrity and free action ...'

The right to freedom from torture

The UN Universal Declaration (Article 5), the European Convention (Article 3) and the EU Charter (Article 4) all agree that 'No one shall be subjected to torture or to cruel, inhuman or degrading treatment or punishment'. Between 1997 and mid-2000, Amnesty had 'received reports of torture and ill-treatment inflicted by state agents in over 150 countries'.[20] People had reportedly died as a result in over eighty countries. Torture occurs not only in authoritarian regimes but also in democratic countries.[21] Victims include 'criminal suspects as well as political prisoners, the disadvantaged as well as the dissident, people targeted because of their identity as well as their beliefs. They are women as well as men, children as well as adults'.

[19] Quoted in Fuellenbach 1995: 11.
[20] A range of reports can be found on http://www.stoptorture.org and on Amnesty's web site http://web.amnesty.org/ai.nsf/index
[21] It is difficult to avoid the conclusion that the treatment of prisoners from Afghanistan in Guantanamo Bay amounted to torture.

It was reported that rape and sexual abuse were also widespread. In the former Yugoslavia, central Africa and Sierra Leone, 'mass rape of women from the "enemy" population is a favoured weapon of war'. The torture of innocent and vulnerable children is particularly shocking. Electric shock treatment, the suspension of the body, beating on the soles of the feet, suffocation, mock executions or death threats, and prolonged solitary confinement were reported in many countries. Judicial amputations are known to have been carried out in at least seven countries and judicial floggings in fourteen countries. There was evidence of physical, mental and sexual abuse by Coalition forces in Abu Ghraib prison in Iraq. Amnesty reported a 'clear link between racism and torture'. Those most at risk are the poorest and most marginalized; despised social, ethnic or political minorities; immigrants, migrant workers and asylum-seekers; and gays, lesbians, bisexuals or transgendered people. It is highly probable that there is a great deal of under-reporting of torture in all these cases.

The Amnesty report *Stopping the Torture Trade* pointed out that 'torture does not happen in a vacuum'. Torture was usually systemic and associated with specific social, economic, political and cultural contexts. Governments could stop torture if they had the political will. But 'manufacturing, trading and promoting equipment which is used to torture people is a money-making business' and there was an equally profitable business 'in providing devices and expertise which are ostensibly designed for security or crime-control purposes, but which in reality lend themselves to serious abuse'.[22]

The ethical case against torture, whether practised by individuals or by states, rests on its cynical abuse of the proper dignity of the human person. Not only is it the responsibility of governments to address such abuses but it is also incumbent on Christians and people of good will to struggle to abolish them and so bring closer the kingdom of God with its proper respect for the dignity of human persons, and their God-given freedom and equality.

The right to be free from slavery

Article 4 of the Universal Declaration stated that 'no one shall be held in slavery or servitude; slavery and the slave trade shall be prohibited in all their forms'. The European Convention's Article 4 went further and added: 'no one shall be required to perform forced or compulsory labour'.

---

[22] *Stopping the Torture Trade* 2001. London: Amnesty International Publications, p. 1.

The EU Charter in Article 5 added still further: 'trafficking in human beings is prohibited'. It may seem astonishing that in the modern world slavery continues to exist. But clearly the forced labour of Filipino servants in London or Saudi Arabia and the trafficking in young girls to the UK or Kuwait are forms of slavery. Other forms include child soldiers, early and forced marriage.

The concept of forced or compulsory labour is problematic. In one sense most people in employment are 'wage slaves', largely dependent on retaining employment in order to pay for accommodation and to bring up a family. The right to 'go elsewhere' may be more formal than substantive, especially in areas where there is only one major employer, but in principle it is there. Nevertheless, wherever workers are tightly bound to an employer, for example in 'tied accommodation' or by contract or custom, there are forms of slavery.

AntiSlavery International (ASI) reported[23] that trafficking was the fastest growing means by which people are forced into slavery today. This 'involves the movement of people through violence, deception or coercion for the purposes of forced labour, servitude or slavery-like practices ... This includes (traffickers) controlling their freedom of movement, where and when they will work and what pay, if any, they will receive'. Trafficking is global in its reach and 'one of the most lucrative forms of international crime'. A United States Government report in 2002 estimated that at least 700,000 people worldwide are trafficked each year. In the UK the Home Office estimated in 2000 that several hundred women are trafficked each year. While prostitution is one form of slave labour, the exploitation of child labour in West Africa, Chinese and Vietnamese women in the Pacific islands, and men from Mexico to work on farms in the USA are all significant forms of trafficking. In 2002 ASI published a report which 'makes recommendations on such areas as investigation and prosecution, residency status, protection from reprisals, in-court evidentiary protection, support and assistance, and legal redress and compensation'. Evidence of the trafficking of children into and through the UK for sexual purposes has recently been reported.

Roger Charles in his comprehensive history of the development of Catholic social teaching pointed out that in spite of the teaching about the equality of all people, 'slave and free' in the New Testament, the institution of slavery remained because, following the Aristotelian theory of the natural inequality of men, it did not occur to people that it could be

[23] http://www.antislavery.org/homepage/antislavery/trafficking.htm

dispensed with; it was too necessary to the maintenance of society as they understood it. Slavery as an institution was not challenged by the Stoics, the Roman jurists, or the early Christian Fathers. The Church 'did not oppose the institution of slavery as such, on the grounds that it seemed permanently embedded in human society'.[24] On the other hand, the abolitionist movement was fed from many sources including Duns Scotus in the thirteenth century, valiant campaigns by priests working in Africa and Spanish South America, and papal condemnations of the slave trade from the fifteenth century. Christians only gradually came to realize that slavery was an institution which deprived the human person of that freedom and dignity which was their God-given right. It is, therefore, incumbent upon them to be sensitive to its contemporary forms and in justice seek to abolish them.

THE RIGHT TO MIGRATE

In the 1971 Synod statement *Justice in the World* the case of migrants was given as an illustration of the 'voiceless victims of injustice', forced to leave their homes in search of opportunities to support their families, and subject to discrimination, insecurity and loneliness.[25] Recently the Church has, for natural law reasons, made much of the right to migrate, in contrast to free marketers who want freedom of movement of goods and capital but not people! There is a Pontifical Council for the Pastoral Care of Migrants and Itinerant People (*Cor Unum*) and the Pope delivers a message on each annual World Day of Migrants and Refugees.[26] There is a need to hear the cries of those subject to discrimination and oppression either as a cause of their migration or as a consequence of it.

There are at least four major reasons for migration from one's home-land. First of all, there are enterprising people who periodically travel to other countries in pursuit of trade, the expansion of markets, and profits. This can be seen as realizing the scriptural injunction to 'be fruitful, multiply, fill the earth and subdue it' (Gen 1: 28). Secondly, there are refugees who are escaping from the ravages and dislocations of war or persecution in their homeland. Thirdly, there are political dissidents threatened by totalitarian, authoritarian or oppressive regimes who seek asylum elsewhere. Fourthly, there are seasonal or long-stay migrant

[24] Charles 1998a: 49–50, 77–79, 261–2, 270–272, 349.   [25] In O'Brien and Shannon 1992: 291.
[26] http://www.vatican.va

workers who may be escaping from famine or starvation and so have left their homeland in pursuit of work in order to support their families.

The UN Universal Declaration is rather coy about the right to migrate while the European Convention appears to overlook the rights of migrants. Yet, the migration of peoples has been ubiquitous throughout human history and the Mosaic Law was clear on the rights of 'strangers' along with widows and orphans (Exod 22: 20; Zech 7: 10). In the parable of the last judgement, the king will recall: 'I was a stranger and you made me welcome' (Mt 25: 35) and invite those who did so into his kingdom.

The rights of refugees

Article 1 of the 1951 Refugee Convention defined a refugee as 'a person who is outside his/her country of nationality or habitual residence; has a well-founded fear of persecution because of his/her race, religion, nationality, membership in a particular social group or political opinion; and is unable or unwilling to avail himself/herself of the protection of that country, or to return there, for fear of persecution'.[27] In 2002, the estimated number of Persons of Concern falling under the Mandate of UNHRC was nearly 20 million. Of these some 12 million were refugees, just under 0.5 million were returnees, under 100,000 had been resettled by only 17 countries accepting annual quotas of refugees, 0.9 million were asylum seekers, i.e. have applied for 'the right to be recognized as bona fide refugees and receive the legal protection and material assistance that status implies', and 6.3 million were 'internally displaced persons (IDPs) who "fall between the cracks" of current humanitarian law and assistance'. An estimated 3.9 million Palestinians were covered by a separate mandate of the UN Relief and Works Agency (UNRWA).

What are the root causes of the large-scale forcible migrations which the world has experienced in recent decades? One approach has been offered by Raper and Valcárcel[28] who pointed out that contemporary migration flows are complex and have been caused by a combination of 'political, ethnic, economic, environmental and human rights factors'. People left their homes out of a mixture of fears, hopes and aspirations. Four main causes of forcible displacement were suggested:

- *human rights violations* often with civilians belonging to specific ethnic groups targeted 'as a deliberate tactic of warfare';

---

[27] 'Basic Facts: The 1951 Refugee Convention – Q & A' in http://www.unhcr.ch
[28] Raper and Valcárcel 2000: 44–51.

- *poverty seen as a form of violence* since 'people who live on the margins cannot survive long without a field to cultivate or a market in which to sell their produce';
- *communal conflicts* which result from the breakdown of the nation state, rising religious fundamentalism, and struggles for scarce resources where there are real or perceived inequalities; and
- *the weakening of the nation state* especially in periods of economic decline or as a result of global forces which shift the balance of power within a country.

Many of today's conflicts, all of which increasingly have a global impact, arise out of the complex interplay between such factors as:

- *the persistent search for profit on the part of global capital.* While in the global free market there is freedom of movement for capital, information and goods, 'freedom of movement does not apply to those most desperate to cross borders: refugees and the poor of the world'.[29]
- *the generation of environmental disasters*, such as famines and drought, brought about by changes in agricultural practices and disturbances in the earth's ecosystem;
- *the unresolved power differentials* between different ethnic groups following the ending of the period of uncontrolled imperialism and colonialism;
- *the aftermath of the ending of the Cold War* and the consolidation of the one superpower, the USA, and its economic, political and military dominance;
- *resentments at the growing power and dominance of the USA* and its western allies and client states and their expression in new forms of terrorism; and
- consequentially, *the unlegitimated growth of inequality* both within and between nations, reinforced by major international agencies such as the IMF, WB and WTO, and generating increasing tensions, antagonism and resistance. Refugees arise wherever the grievances and discontents resulting from these complex and interlinking forces explode into violent conflict.

In Britain the powerful tabloid media reinforce a latent xenophobia and refugees of all sorts are frequently subject to hostility and scapegoating. This hostility is 'fuelled by the restrictive asylum policies that have gained ground all over the Western world'. Yet refugees are often traumatized by their experiences of leaving their homes and particular groups, such as

---

[29] *iNexile*, October 2001, Feb/March 2002 and September/October 2002: 4.

children and lesbian and gay refugees, are particularly vulnerable and in need of refuge and a defence of their human rights. Following recent terrorist attacks human rights are 'now often seen as an obstacle to preserving security rather than an essential safeguard'.

In 1982 Pope John Paul II described the problem of refugees as 'a shameful wound of our time'. In a document published by *Cor Unum*[30] it was recalled that experiences of war, expulsion and flight from famine and persecution 'are deeply rooted in the collective memory of every people and are also found in the bible' (Gen 42: 1–3; 2 Kings 25: 21; Mt 2: 13–15; Acts 8:1). Addressing the contemporary situation, the Pontifical Council urged the confrontation of the causes of exile, the cultivation of 'a mentality of hospitality', overcoming indifference which 'constitutes a sin of omission', and taking 'the way of solidarity (which) demands ... the overcoming of selfishness and of fear of the other; ... long range action of civic education ... (and) better concerted action between international institutions and local authorities'. In the first place it was the task of the local Church to offer refugees hospitality, solidarity and assistance according to the demands of the Gospel.

Raper and Valcárcel added the need for ministries of peace and reconciliation; accompanying refugees on their journey; welcome; seeking to find that hope which comes out of suffering and ending dependency; listening and healing; supporting host communities; defending the voluntariness of any return; defending human rights; opposing xenophobia; and addressing root causes of forced displacement.[31] This is a valuable starting point for any response to the shameful evil of the involuntary exile of millions of people.

The rights of asylum seekers

Article 14(1) of the Universal Declaration acknowledged that 'everyone has the right to seek and to enjoy in other countries asylum from persecution' and Article 14(2) noted exceptions in the case of prosecutions for non-political crimes. Article 18 of the EU Charter guaranteed the right to asylum and Article 19(2) that 'no one may be removed, expelled or extradicted to a State where there is a serious risk that he or she would be subjected to the death penalty, torture or other inhuman or degrading treatment or punishment'.

---

[30] Pontifical Council 1992. §§1, 9–10, 16, 24, 26.   [31] Raper and Valcárcel 2000: 67–87.

The UNHCR[32] reported that at the end of 2001 there were 940,800 asylum seekers worldwide whose cases were still pending. The UK was in tenth position in the European league of the number of asylum applicants per 1,000 head of population with 1.5 applications per 1,000 population. Again, to get the figures into proportion, the 'rich' EU received fewer than 400,000 asylum applications in 2001 while 'poor' Pakistan had to cope with some 2.5 million Afghan refugees. In the UK the Refugee Council estimated that around 51 per cent of asylum seekers were successful. In the UK, asylum seekers received only about 70 per cent of mainstream income support. Yet Home Office research has estimated that people born outside the UK, including refugees and asylum seekers, paid £2.5 billion more in taxes than they took out in public services in 2000.[33] There is little doubt that historically the UK has benefited enormously, socially, culturally and economically, from successive waves of asylum seekers over several centuries.

In a recently published review of asylum statistics for the past fifteen years by the Refugee Council, it was evident that flows reflected the emergence of major conflicts such as those in the former Yugoslavia, Africa and Afghanistan. One particularly striking statistic was the financial implications of hosting refugees, especially for developing countries. Thus, for example 'Guinea has 130 people of concern for every million dollars GDP and Tanzania has 80. In comparison, the United States hosts 0.13 and the United Kingdom 0.2 . . . people of concern for every million dollars GDP'.[34]

Bishop O'Donoghue, Chairman of the Office for Refugee Policy of the Bishops' Conference of England and Wales, expressed a number of concerns about asylum policy in his booklet *Any Room at the Inn?*[35] Reflecting on our approaches to asylum seekers he warned that current debates about asylum are 'often based on misrepresentation, prejudice and hostility'. He protested that inflexible Home Office procedures meant that many applications were refused on the grounds of improper submissions rather than because they were unfounded.[36] Finally, he noted that 'concern for refugees

---

[32] http://www.unhcr.ch
[33] Ibid. The Home Office study is entitled 'Migration: An Economic and Social Analysis' and can be located at www.homeoffice.gov.uk/rds/whatsnew1.html; see *iNexile*, February 2001: 3.
[34] Constable 2002: §1.7.   [35] O'Donoghue 2001; also published in *Briefing*, 31(6), 13 June 2001: 29–32.
[36] http://www.asylumaid.org.uk For further information on asylum seekers see *New Internationalist* (No. 350, October 2002); the Refugee Council's *iNexile* and *Update*; and the Medical Foundation's *The Supporter*.

is based on an ancient biblical and historical mandate' requiring aliens to be treated with compassion (Exod 22:21, Lev 19:33, Deut 10: 17–19).

Writing in *Euros Infos*, the monthly publication of COMECE and OCIPE, Felix Leinemann[37] drew attention to the deteriorating standards of treatment of asylum seekers in the EU: 'Many EU States . . . are misusing reception conditions as a method of deterrence'. Ruud Lubbers (UNHCR) 'recently said that it was almost impossible for refugees to seek asylum in the member states of the European Union in a legal manner'. The UNHCR and Caritas Europa have both lobbied in favour of a greater degree of humanity and sensitivity for asylum seekers and stressed the importance of making Europe a 'welcoming society'. But a major task remains 'to address the root causes of migration' whether as a result of oppression, war, internal conflicts, drought or environmental disasters.

The rights of migrant workers

In practice the right to migrate in search of work and economic survival is denied by the major industrial societies today.[38] Yet when it is expedient, the developed societies are only too happy to accept qualified manpower, whether it be Indian computer specialists in the USA or Asian nurses and doctors in the British NHS. Since the sending societies incur a large part of the education costs of these workers, this constitutes a 'brain drain' from developing societies. Other migrant workers do low status and unpleasant jobs which no indigenous worker wants to do. There is evidence of 'the increasing polarisation of labour markets on the basis of skill, and the growing feminisation of international migration'.[39] At the same time there is great opposition to the mobility of labour because of the likely impact on employment opportunities and wage levels. In 1994 the head of the International Organization for Migration (IOM) estimated that there were 120 million migrants of all types, or 2 per cent of the world's population. Some 30 million recent immigrants are foreign workers who are estimated 'to remit over $67 billion annually to their homelands, . . . second only to oil in world trade'. Castles and Miller identified five general tendencies which were likely to play a major role in migration over the next twenty years: the globalization, acceleration (or increasing volume), differentiation, feminization, and politicization of migration.

---

[37] Leinemann 2001.
[38] It is ironic that free marketers want freedom of movement of goods and capital but not of people.
[39] Castles and Miller 1998: xii, 4–5, 8–9, 19–29, 80–81.

What is needed is a comprehensive social analysis of the causes of forced displacement of millions of desperate people. Castles and Miller outlined three main theories which attempt to explain migration flows. Firstly, the *neo-classical economic* approach stressed 'push factors' including 'demographic growth, low living standards, lack of economic opportunities and political repression' and 'pull factors' such as 'demand for labour, availability of land, good economic opportunities and political freedoms'. Such theories have been incapable of explaining some actual migrations and have been regarded as ahistorical and too simplistic and individualistic, failing to take sufficient note of the role of the state as a regulator. Secondly, there was the *historical-structural* approach which 'stresses the unequal distribution of economic and political power in the world economy. Migration is seen mainly as a way of mobilising cheap labour for capital'. These theories were criticized for being too deterministic and for paying insufficient attention to the motivations and actions of the migrants themselves. Thirdly, *migrations systems* theory stressed the close links between two or more countries which exchanged migrants with each other. Such theories took into account former colonial linkages and the important informal support networks which facilitated migration. There was a complex set of factors with a multiplicity of causes necessary to explain migratory processes. In sum 'labour migrants, permanent settlers and refugees have varying motivations and move under different conditions' in response to globalization following colonialism. 'Such fundamental societal changes lead both to economically motivated migration and to politically motivated flight'.

All the same, Raper and Valcárcel were right to point out that systemic 'poverty is a form of violence' and that 'people who live at the margins . . . have to move to keep alive'.[40] The scapegoating of economic migrants and discrimination against them failed to recognize their equal human dignity. One form of discrimination was that expressed in nationality laws which were based on blood ancestry which was exclusionary of foreign migrant workers.[41] The dynamic relationships between migration, citizenship, national identity and nationality have evolved historically over time. The results have been variable as comparisons between Britain, France, Germany and Italy show.[42] The pursuit of social justice for migrant workers, particularly those who have been resident for a significant period of time, requires a careful evaluation of the existing definitions of citizenship and of naturalization.

---

[40] Raper and Valcárcel 2000: 48.   [41] Castles and Miller 1998: 202.
[42] Cesarani and Fulbrook 1996.

In *Mater et Magistra* Pope John XXIII in 1961 insisted on 'the right of the family to migrate' (§45). In *Gaudium et Spes*, the evidence for social forces inducing people to migrate, 'thereby changing their manner of life' (§6), was noted and the work of international agencies which assist migrants and their families (§84) commended. Again, 'the personal right of migration . . . is not to be impugned'. Furthermore, 'discrimination with respect to wages and working conditions must be carefully avoided' while local people and public authorities 'must help them to arrange for their families to live with them and to provide themselves with decent living quarters' (§§ 65–66). The Decree on the Apostolate of the Laity insists on the right of migrants to live together as a family (§11).

In 1967 Pope Paul VI made a brief reference in *Populorum Progressio* to the plight of emigrant workers 'who live in conditions which are often inhuman, and who economise on what they earn in order to send a little relief to their family living in misery in their native land' (§69). He made similar remarks in his Apostolic Letter, *Octogesima Adveniens*, and he proceeded to urge 'people to go beyond a narrowly nationalistic attitude' and to give migrant workers a charter 'which will assure them a right to emigrate, favour their integration, facilitate their professional advancement, and give them access to decent housing where, if such is the case, their families can join them' (§17). The statement from the 1971 Synod of Bishops in Rome condemned 'discriminatory attitudes' and the insecurity and inhuman conditions of the lives of many migrants.[43] In sum, Catholic teaching up to the 1980s stressed:

- the right to emigrate, for example in search of work;
- the right of the migrant not to be discriminated against; and
- the right for the worker's family unit to be retained intact.

Pope John Paul II took the matter further. In 1981 in *Laborem Exercens* he reiterated previous teaching but considered emigration in search of work in a wider context, stressing the loss to the sending country often of its youngest and most active or intelligent people. In other words he recognized a 'brain and energy drain'. He insisted that legislation should be enacted to ensure that permanent or seasonal workers were not subject to 'financial or social exploitation' (§23). Surprisingly, neither of the pope's two social encyclicals *Sollicitudo Rei Socialis* (1978) or *Centesimus Annus* (1991) gave any sustained consideration to the situation of economic migrants. Nor, in spite of its recognition that the USA was basically a society of immigrants, was the plight of today's immigrants a significant

---

[43] In O'Brien and Shannon (eds.) 1992: 291.

theme in the United States Bishops' Pastoral Letter on *Economic Justice for All* (1986).

In his message for World Peace Day, 2001, Pope Paul II wrote that 'the prime value which must be ever more widely inculcated is that of solidarity' and respect for the human dignity of migrants. A month later, in his message for the World Day of Migration, the pope noted that 'the Church recognises this right [to emigrate] in every human person, in its dual aspect of the possibility to leave one's country and the possibility to enter another country to look for better conditions of life'. But, interestingly, he did allow the right of immigration controls on the part of the host country and he continued: 'certainly, the exercise of such a right is to be regulated, because practising it indiscriminately may do harm and be detrimental to the common good of the community that receives the migrant'. In Europe COMECE has encouraged 'the European Commission in its initiative to strengthen cooperation with the countries of origin and thereby to combat the root causes of emigration, which are often detrimental to the society of the countries of origin'. It was not criminal to 'search for better living conditions by legitimate means'.[44]

THE RIGHTS OF THE WEAK: RACISM, SEXISM AND AGEISM

We have noted that the God of Israel warned against the unjust treatment of and discrimination against the weak, in particular, widows, orphans and foreigners. We will now consider the human rights of three categories of weak and vulnerable people: ethnic minorities, females and children.

Ethnic minorities and racism

In the past decade there have been 'multicultural riots' in USA and British cities and in London the police were branded as 'institutionally racist'. Following the London bombings of 7 July 2005 thousands of hate messages were sent to Moslems and mosques were attacked. The 'ethnic cleansing' in the former Yugoslavia is a recent reminder of the continuing evil of racism in contemporary Europe. Refugee hostels in the former East Germany have been violently attacked and gypsies targeted in Eastern Europe. Neo-Nazi extremist parties have attracted significant support in several countries in the EU. Racism threatens social order. Castles and Miller observed that during periods of economic restructuring, immigrants were often seen as

[44] *Briefing*, 31(7), 11 July 2001: 27.

the cause of insecurity and as 'a danger to living standards, life styles and social cohesion'.[45]

The historical roots of racism varied from society to society. In the case of Britain, its roots lay deep in its imperial and colonial past whereas in Germany, they lay rather in its history of nation-building around a strong cultural identity. In our present times migration flows resulted not only from major economic transformations in post-colonial times but also from ethnic conflicts arising out of differential access to resources and power. The outcomes were to be found in both individual forms of prejudice and discrimination, but also institutional and structural forms of civil, economic and political discrimination, marginalization and exclusion. Strong boundaries were constructed between 'insiders' and 'outsiders' whose 'otherness' was stressed and who were stigmatized and scapegoated. Racism was the categorization of social groups on the basis of their physical or cultural characteristics as different or inferior. It involved the use of economic, social or political power to legitimate discrimination, exploitation and exclusion of a minority group.[46]

In 1965 the UN General Assembly adopted the International Convention on the Elimination of All Forms of Racial Discrimination (CERD). It followed the UN Charter's insistence that 'all human beings are equal before the law and are entitled to equal protection of the law against any discrimination' and was based on the conviction that 'any doctrine of superiority based on racial differentiation is scientifically false, morally condemnable, socially unjust and dangerous, and that there is no justification for racial discrimination, in theory or in practice, anywhere'.[47]

Apart from the UNHCR, under whose authority progress across the whole field of human rights, including racial discrimination, internationally is regularly monitored, there is a European Commission Against Racism and Intolerance (ECRI) which regularly monitors the situation in individual member countries of the Council of Europe. In 2000, the ECRI published its second, very detailed report on the United Kingdom.[48] This commended steps taken to counter racism and discrimination, including 'the elaboration of a strategy to counter institutional racism in the police in response to the Stephen Lawrence Inquiry Report'. However, it pointed to 'problems of xenophobia, racism and discrimination ... (which) persist and are particularly acute vis-à-vis asylum seekers and

---

[45] Castles and Miller 1998: 13–14.   [46] Ibid.: 32, 230–238, 263–266. See also Volf 1996.
[47] Preamble and Article 1. See http://www.unhchr.ch/html   [48] http://press.coe.int

refugees. This is reflected in the xenophobic and intolerant coverage of these groups of persons in the media, but also to the tone of the discourse ... [regarding] restrictive asylum and immigration laws. Racial prejudice in the police continue[s] to constitute an element of concern'. The report recommended 'the need to address the hostile climate concerning asylum seekers and refugees', improving criminal law provisions relating to incitement to racial hatred, and ensuring that 'the education system meets the demands of a diverse society'.

Racism is an evil which has to be addressed both at the level of individual prejudices and discrimination but also at the institutional or structural level in terms of citizenship rights and anti-racist legislation. In terms of the Macpherson Report's definition, it is hard to avoid the conclusion that the Catholic Church in this country has been, and arguably still is, institutionally racist.[49] In 1990 the Charter of the Congress of Black Catholics noted their sense of exclusion from the Church in this country. Ten years later they suggested a number of strategies for countering the structural sin of institutional racism.[50] In 1999 the bishops of England and Wales issued guidelines for a review of Catholic organizations and institutions in the light of the Macpherson Report[51] and they have set up a number of working parties over the years to consider the response of the Catholic education system to a multiracial and multicultural society.[52]

In the light of the parable of the Good Samaritan, 'all discrimination, all racism, all prejudice are condemned'.[53] This is reflected in the official Vatican teaching on racism which was presented by the Pontifical Commission 'Iustitia et Pax'.[54] In 2001 the Pontifical Commission reissued the document with a substantial new introduction.[55] This reviewed the situation and noted the paradox of increasing ethnic conflicts at a time of accelerating globalization. It asked pardon for the Catholic Church's racist and discriminatory behaviour in the past and stressed the fundamental importance of education in the struggle against racism and discrimination.

Part III of the earlier document outlined the Christian vision and doctrine of the dignity of every race and the unity of humankind. It quoted *Gaudium et Spes* that, in spite of physical, intellectual and moral differences, 'forms of social or cultural discrimination in basic rights on the grounds of sex, race, colour, social conditions, language or religion, must

---

[49] Kalilombe et al. 1991, and CARJ 2000. [50] CARJ 2000.
[51] 'Serving a multi-Ethnic Society', *Briefing*, 29 (12), 15 December 1999: 20–21. [52] O'Keeffe 1999.
[53] Fuellenbach 1995: 75. [54] Pontifical Commission 'Iustitia et Pax' 1989.
[55] 'Racism, Racial Discrimination, Xenophobia', in *Briefing* 31(10) 10 October 2001: 28–34.

be curbed and eradicated as incompatible with God's design' (§29). Pope John Paul II is quoted as teaching that 'man's creation by God "in his own image" confers upon every human person an eminent dignity; it also postulates the fundamental equality of all human beings ... which ... acquires the dimension of an altogether special brotherhood through the Incarnation of the Son of God'.[56] It quoted prominent scientists who in a 1951 UNESCO report recognized that all human beings living today are descended from one same stock. On the basis of New Testament teaching (Jn 4: 4–42; Mk 7: 24–30; Acts 10: 28, 34) the document stressed 'the unity of humankind' and called on Christians to 'banish all forms of racial, ethnic, national or cultural discrimination from their conduct ... recognise better the newness of the Gospel of reconciliation ... (and) anticipate the eschatological and definitive community of the Kingdom of God'.

The document concluded with a number of suggestions for promoting fraternity and solidarity amongst different races. First must come a 'change of heart', then defence of the victims of racism and discrimination. The role of schools was stressed and the need for appropriate legislation regarding the structuring and functioning of institutions. All citizens must be equal in law and the basic human rights of immigrants and foreign workers safeguarded. International juridical instruments to overcome racism must be constructed. Antagonistic groups must be won over by 'supreme and transcendent values'. This is quite an agenda for action.

Sexism

In 1979 the UN General Assembly adopted the Convention on the Elimination of All Forms of Discrimination Against Women (CEDAW).[57] Robert Drinan, who saw this as 'one of the most important decisions in world history',[58] is right to point to the long history of women's subordination, oppression, exploitation, marginalization, presumed inferiority, spousal abuse, marital rape and wife-beating, the plight of rural women, the practice of genital mutilation, and restrictions to education and medical services, especially in developing societies. It is worth recalling that systematic discrimination in institutional outcomes, whether intended or not, is a form of structural sin. Drinan advocated the mobilization of 'the shame which men and nations increasingly feel for the way societies dominated by men have treated women'.

---

[56] Pontifical Commission 1989: §§17–18, 21–23, 25–26, 28–30, 32.
[57] http://www.un.org/womenwatch/daw/cedaw [58] Drinan 2001: 35–44.

We will consider the claims, in justice, for equal legal, civil, social, cultural and economic rights. During the twentieth century women gradually came to win civil rights. But, in spite of decades of 'equal opportunities' legislation, the evidence shows that women continue to be under-represented in more senior positions and receive only around two-thirds of the wages of men in similar occupations. Furthermore, employed women continue to do 'two jobs', including the bulk of domestic labour and child-rearing. These forms of institutional discrimination constitute structural sins which deserve to be condemned and resisted.

The Convention (CEDAW) dealt with civil rights and the legal status of women in great detail. However, unlike other human rights treaties, the Convention was also concerned with issues of human reproduction as well as the impact of cultural factors on gender relations. In addition to the assertion of equal rights in the choice of spouse and property rights, the Convention demanded shared responsibility for child-rearing and affirmed women's right to reproductive choice'. Article 10h required states to provide 'access to specific educational information to help to ensure the health and well-being of families, including information and advice on family planning'. Article 16e required that they provide 'the same rights to decide freely and responsibly on the number and spacing of their children and to have access to the information, education and means to enable them to exercise these rights'.

As Donal Dorr pointed out, justice for women is one of the major issues on the social justice agenda of the Church.[59] Women are 'poor' in the theological sense, subject to exploitation, oppression, injustice and margin-alization. He suggested 'the elimination of sexist language' in the liturgy because it polluted 'the moral atmosphere'. In his evaluation of the weak-nesses of the tradition of Catholic social teaching he judged that 'perhaps the biggest lacuna . . . is its failure to provide an adequate treatment of the issue of justice for women'.[60]

The Church hardly seems to be a credible authority in this area since it officially continues to insist on an exclusively male priesthood in spite of the extension of liturgical rights to women readers and eucharistic minis-ters. This in spite of the fact that in most parishes, most of the work, of administration, cleaning, counselling, care and support, is undertaken by women. Yet, Jesus challenged all the traditional Jewish boundaries which separated people as his discussions with the Samaritan woman at the well and the Syro-Phoenician woman demonstrated. He had especially close

---

[59] Dorr 1991: 22–24, 108–109, 119–120.   [60] Dorr 1992: 372–4.

relationships with Martha and Mary and it was to a woman that he first revealed himself after his resurrection (Jn 4: 7–29, 11: 1–45, 12: 1–3, 20: 11–18). St Paul stressed in his letter to the Galatians that 'there can be neither male nor female – for you are all one in Christ Jesus' (Gal 3: 28). Most gender divisions are obsolete. This is one area where it seems the Church needs to cultivate some humility. Pope John Paul II attempted to do this in his *Letter to Women*.[61] A more recent statement from the CDF on the collaboration of men and women in the Church and in the world spoke of the importance of feminist values in the life of society and of the Church but was critically received by Catholic feminists.[62]

Ageism: children's rights

The third category of the weak and voiceless, children, is often overlooked in adult presumptions of their immaturity, inferiority, incompetence and dependence. It is, perhaps, only in recent decades that we have become increasingly sensitized to the violence, oppression, appalling physical and sexual abuses, and injustices perpetrated against some of the most vulnerable people on earth. In poor countries street children are too often killed or tortured by police. Children as young as seven are recruited or kidnapped to serve as soldiers. Children may be forced into employment as young as six, often as bonded labourers or in forced prostitution. Refugee children may be separated from their families and brutalized. Children may be abused by teachers, subject to corporal punishment, abuse and sexual violence, and experience discrimination on grounds of race or ethnicity.[63]

In Britain recent cases have drawn attention to the prevalence of domestic violence and the failures of the system of child protection. Within the Catholic community in several western countries including Britain, Ireland and the USA, great scandal has been caused by the evidence of sexual abuse of children by priests and other religious persons. In England and Wales recommendations for the care and protection of children in the life of the Church and in activities in Catholic institutions, such as parishes and schools, made following an independent review by Lord Nolan, have been implemented by the Catholic bishops.

---

[61] John Paul II 1995. *Letter to Women*; see http://www.vatican.va
[62] An abridged version of the document was published in *The Tablet*, 7 August 2004: 30–33. A critical but not unsympathetic review of the document was given by Tina Beattie, 'Feminism, Vatican-Style', in the same issue of *The Tablet*, pp. 4–6.
[63] http://www.hrw.org/children

Children's rights were put on the world's agenda in 1989 when the UN General Assembly adopted the Convention on the Rights of the Child (CRC).[64] It is the most widely ratified international treaty in the world; only the US and Somalia have not ratified it. The treaty applied to all children and young people under the age of eighteen. The Preamble noted that 'the child, by reason of his physical and mental immaturity, needs special safeguards and care, including appropriate legal protection, before as well as after birth'. The Convention laid down that 'every child has the inherent right to life' and it was the task of states to 'ensure to the maximum extent possible the survival and development of the child'.[65] Of particular interest are articles which recognized the child's right to express his or her opinion freely and to have it taken into account in any legal procedures, 'the right to freedom of expression', 'to freedom of thought, conscience and religion', 'to freedom of association and to freedom of peaceful assembly', to protection of privacy, and to access to information sources. The state had an obligation to 'protect the child from all forms of physical or mental violence, injury or abuse, neglect or negligent treatment, maltreatment or exploitation, including sexual abuse'. Other articles dealt with orphans, adoption, refugee children, disabled children and children of minorities and indigenous populations, social security arrangements, 'the right to education', including compulsory and free primary education, the 'right of the child to rest and leisure', protection from narcotic and psychotropic drugs and from sexual exploitation, sale, trafficking and abduction, all forms of exploitation, torture and deprivation of liberty.

Caritas-Social Action, the Catholic Church's voice on social justice and care in England and Wales, recently campaigned for an ending of the physical chastisement (smacking) of children so that, as a matter of justice, they had equal protection in law to that given to adults. It has also joined the End Child Poverty coalition seeking to end child poverty by 2020.[66]

Christine Gudorf[67] notes that the term 'rights of children' had not appeared in Catholic social teaching until recently because of the long-standing papal suspicion of human rights language; because 'children's interests were understood to be protected and promoted through defence of the family'; and because it assumed a hierarchically ordered family with

---

[64] http://www.crin.org/docs/resources/treaties/uncrc.htm A useful summary of the Convention is given by the Children's Rights Alliance for England at http://www.crights.org.uk/law/uncrc.html

[65] UN Convention, §§6.1 and 6.2, 12–17, 19.1, 28.   [66] www.caritas-socialaction.org.uk

[67] Gudorf 1994.

children subordinated to parents who were assumed to care with love for their children. Even so, Gudorf suggested five rights could be identified in papal teaching since Pius XII:

- the right of the unborn to life;[68]
- the right to full-time care by mothers;[69]
- the right to adequate material support and protection;[70]
- the right to education;[71] and
- the right to culture.[72]

Gudorf noted that 'within the family, foetal freedom from direct abortion takes priority over all other rights of children as well as those of the parents' and she is highly critical of 'the romanticism that masks the refusal of the magisterium to analyse its model of the family'. This had failed to reflect contemporary realities such as the increasing awareness of the scale of child abuse by family members. The area of children's rights in Catholic social thought is one which needs substantial development. There is a traditional Catholic insistence that rights are not absolute but must be chosen in accordance with the 'natural law'. This is apparent in the tension between the parental 'right' to know, advise and control and the child's 'right' to independence, for example in the case of independent professional advice to adolescent girls on pregnancy and contraception.

HUMAN RIGHTS IN CATHOLIC SOCIAL THOUGHT

The UN Declaration of Human Rights in 1948 provided an enormous boost to international attempts to achieve minimum standards of human behaviour and to recognize the intrinsic equality of the dignity of each individual human being. The Church has struggled to update its own thinking in this area, notably in the Vatican Council's *Dignitatis Humanae*.

In this chapter we have largely been concerned with legal and political rights. Developments in human rights thinking were apparent when Amnesty announced that the statute defining its work was 'changed to say that AI's work was focused on preventing and ending grave abuses of the rights to physical and mental integrity, freedom of conscience and

---

[68] Paul VI 1968: §14; John Paul II 1981a: §30.
[69] *Gaudium et Spes*, §52; John Paul II 1981b: §19 and 1981a: §§ 23, 25. Gudorf notes that 'there is no attempt in social teaching to restructure men's work or society in general in order to involve men more fully in child care'.
[70] John XXIII 1963: §20; *Gaudium et Spes*: §67; John Paul II 1981b: §19, and 1981a: §41, 46.
[71] John Paul II 1981a: §§36–39, 46.
[72] *Gaudium et Spes*, §§31, 61; Paul VI 1967: §68; John Paul II 1981a: §46.

expression, and freedom from discrimination, within the context of promoting all human rights'. This would enable AI 'to tackle some abuses of economic, social and cultural rights'. Future permanent campaigns would include the death penalty, children's rights and prison conditions and campaigning would be broadened to 'put more pressure on international financial institutions to consider, for example, the human rights impact of their economic reform programs'.[73]

Catholics have always been conscious of the limits of rights discourse, notably when the concept of 'women's rights' is absolutized into 'rights over her own body'. Such claims, which appear to assume the right to have an abortion, are deeply offensive to traditional Catholic thinking which entertains the countervailing notion of the rights of the embryo. There also remains a great deal of discomfort over the notion of 'gay rights' and Cardinal Hume challenged the notion of 'parental rights' in his advocacy of the 'common good' in the case of the Cardinal Vaughan school. And yet, Pope John Paul II suggested that 'respect for this broad range of human rights constitutes the fundamental condition for peace in the modern world: peace both within individual countries and societies and in international relations . . .' (*LE* §16).

What has been referred to as the 'Catholic human rights revolution' has not only surprised many but, on the basis of 'its own distinctive intellectual tradition', has been shown to offer a real alternative to the new liberalism of the 'sovereign individual' and various forms of collectivism which ride roughshod over individual human rights. This is the main thrust of a recent collection of essays on Catholic perspectives on liberalism, communitarianism and democracy. In his review of the teaching of the Second Vatican Council on freedom, Kenneth Grasso[74] demonstrated the continuing and uncompromising rejection by the Church of the liberal model of the sovereign individual. Thus, far from capitulating to a 'belated embrace of liberalism', the Catholic human rights revolution represented a genuine development of doctrine based on the intrinsic worth of the individual human being, created in the image of God, to seek the truth and common good.

It seems appropriate to conclude with Linda Hogan that 'with all its ambiguities the concept of human rights represents the best chance we have of protesting injustice and of protecting human dignity . . . Most importantly however it is a universally recognised way of affirming the inherent worth and dignity of each and every human being'.[75]

---

[73] *Amnesty*, No. 110, November/December 2001:16.　　[74] Grasso 1995: 53–54.　　[75] Hogan 1998: 32.

CHAPTER 7

The family

THE CHANGING CONTEXT

For the first time in Britain the number of households with two parents and their children, what used to be regarded as the standard family, has been overtaken by other forms of household composition. Technological advances in domestic equipment, have revolutionized the domestic work chiefly undertaken by women. Since the 1960s and the increasing availability of the contraceptive pill, women have achieved greater autonomy over child-bearing. The feminist revolution has begun to reverse the systematic subordination of women to male domination. Levels of divorce in the UK are the highest in Europe and it is now estimated that nearly one half of all marriages will end in divorce. The growing awareness of high levels of marital breakdown has led many to avoid formal marriage. Marriage rates have fallen and levels of cohabitation have increased. The long-standing bias against the education of women has begun to be redressed. In Britain, since the Abortion Act of 1967, it is estimated that there have been over five million legal abortions.[1] Homosexuality was decriminalized in Britain in 1967 and attempts have been made to allow single sex couples to adopt children and have the same legal rights as those in traditional families. The 'family' is clearly a more complex phenomenon than a few decades ago.

The family within which children grow up provides the first and most basic form of socialization for their subsequent life as adults. Children are growing up in a world where access to the television and the internet is practically uncontrollable. For adolescents and young adults there are multiple opportunities for drug and alcohol abuse and the dangers of slipping into criminal activities in order to fund addictions. Parenting is becoming recognized as an increasingly vital task in a modern and complex society.

[1] Scarisbrick 1999.

The family, in its various forms, is subject to a variety of pressures and strains including poverty, unemployment and a pervasive sense of insecurity in a rapidly changing economic environment. When tomorrow is uncertain, there is a tendency to live for today. 'Retail therapy' has become the antidote to today's worries. Rising and often unsustainable levels of personal debt are a real social problem with the poorest people subject to horrifying levels of debt repayment from 'loan sharks'. In the modern world good sexual and personal relationships between partners have become more important than legal or contractual obligations. Not surprisingly, therefore, levels of divorce and cohabitation have increased dramatically. Homosexual relationships are regarded as acceptable options.

Recent developments in biotechnology and in genetic engineering have presented Christians with an entirely new set of ethical issues to cope with. These range from the morality of *in vitro fertilization* and the transplanting of human organs to the possibilities of cloning and stem-cell research. Scientific advances require that we look again at such fundamental issues as 'what is a human person?'; 'when does human life begin and end?'; 'are we usurping the proper role of God?' or 'are we using the gifts of intelligence and compassion God has given us to achieve the alleviation of much human misery and suffering?' It may well be the case that the possibilities of genetic engineering will present us with our greatest moral challenges in the twenty-first century. There are fears about creeping legalization of euthanasia.

The place of the family in society is very much a *social* issue and a wide range of public policies influence its health and in consequence the vitality of society. Recent popes have devoted a great deal of attention to the family, the role of women, recent developments in biotechnology and human genetic engineering. Susan Okin points out: 'it is undeniable that the family in which each of us grows up has a deeply formative influence on us . . . This is one of the reasons why one *cannot* reasonably leave the family out of "the basic structure of society", to which the principles of justice are to apply'.[2] Thus it is incumbent on Christians to address perhaps the deepest and most pervasive structural injustice of them all, that of gender inequalities and of our present family structures which largely reproduce these inequalities.

But first, in keeping with the bottom-up, inductive methodology adopted in this book, it is necessary to take seriously the changing social reality of the family and subject it to both social and theological analysis in

---

[2] Okin 1989: 184.

order to respond with some sort of social action and policy proposals. This approach aims to take seriously the fact of emerging scientific knowledge and understanding.

THE CONTEMPORARY FAMILY

In 1998 only 39 per cent of *families* in Great Britain, with a head of household under the age of 60, consisted of a married couple with dependent children. An additional 5 per cent were cohabiting couples with dependent children and a further 16 per cent were lone parent families with dependent children. Twenty per cent were married couples and 8 per cent cohabiting couples with no children. Seven per cent were married couples and 4 per cent lone parent families with non-dependent children only. These figures reflect some rapid changes in recent years. In particular, the proportion of cohabiting couple families has nearly trebled to 14 per cent since 1986 while in the same period the proportion of lone parent families has almost doubled to 20 per cent.[3]

Expressed differently, in the thirty years from 1971 to 2001, *Social Trends*[4] has reported that the proportion of all *households* comprising a couple with dependent children fell from 35 per cent to 23 per cent. Over the same period, the proportion of people living alone doubled from 6 per cent to 12 per cent. In 2001 lone parents, overwhelmingly lone mothers, headed around 22 per cent of all *families* with dependent children, three times the proportion in 1971. There were 159,000 divorces in the UK in 1999. In 2000 around seven in every ten children affected by the divorce of their parents were aged ten or under; around one in four were under the age of five. The latest figures show that around three-fifths of men and women aged 35 to 39, when first married had cohabited with their future partner. The abortion rate for women aged 20–24 in 2000 in England and Wales was 31 per thousand, higher than in any other age group. In 2003/04 28 per cent of children in Britain were living in officially defined poverty.[5]

Other social changes which impact on these outcomes include increasing participation in further and higher education; the continuing failure to build sufficient affordable housing and the consequent high cost of housing in which existing house owners have a vested interest; the steadily increasing proportion of married women working to help finance mortgage payments; increasing insecurity and stress in employment; the

---

[3] *Population Trends* 103. Spring 2001: Table 1, p. 14.
[4] *Social Trends.* 32. Tables 2.1, 2.3, 2.6, 2.8–2.11, 2.19.   [5] Piachaud 2005.

persistent pressures to consume; the postponement of child bearing, reductions in the average family size and the steady ageing of the population; and concerns about adequate pensions for the retired and elderly. These are today's social realities to which Christians are called to respond.

There do appear to be systematic differences in the family and welfare policies of predominantly Catholic and Protestant countries.[6] Thus, in the EU, all the countries having a constitution which recognizes the family and are committed to protecting it are Catholic.[7] One study concluded that 'centre parties in Catholic countries transform the conservative stance of Catholicism in gender-related issues into public policy, such as in family policy, taxation, education, social security and care for children, the elderly and other dependants. These governments thus place priority on the maintenance of traditional patterns of gender differentiation ... That policy, of course, creates powerful disincentives and obstacles to the incorporation of female labour into the economy'.[8] This is reflected in the lower labour force participation rates of married women in Catholic countries and the greater expectation that care of the elderly would be performed by family (mainly female) carers. Another study pointed out that 'Catholicism's subsidiarity principle has always insisted that private organizations (mainly the Church) be prominent in social services'.[9] In general it seems that there was a significant contrast between the more communitarian and family-oriented policies in Catholic countries and more individual citizen-oriented policies in Protestant countries. It is possible that these differences will decline under the pressures of globalization.

CATHOLIC TEACHING ON THE FAMILY

Table 7.1 summarizes the more important Church documents relating to the official teaching on the family as it has responded to social changes in the twentieth century. The family, seen as the vital cell of society, is the first of the seven matters of social concern addressed in the Pontifical Council for Justice and Peace's recently published *Compendium*.[10] This provides a summary of the official teachings of the Church which range in authority from dogmatic statements of the Vatican Council in *Lumen Gentium* to papal teaching in encyclicals and apostolic letters and statements from pontifical congregations.

---

[6] Hornsby-Smith 1999b.   [7] Hantrais 1993.   [8] Schmidt 1993.   [9] Esping-Andersen 1990: 134.
[10] *Compendium*, §§209–254. For a critical review of Catholic social teaching on the family see Farley 1994.

Table 7.1. *Major church documents on the family, 1930–2004*

Year	Author[a]	Document	Key themes	Reference[b]
1930	Pius XI	*Casti Connubii*	Marriage; contraception; eugenics	CTS, Do 113
1964	Vat. II	*Lumen Gentium*	Family as domestic Church	WMA: 14–96
1965	Vat. II	*Apostolicam Actuositatem*	First and vital cell of society	WMA: 486–525
1965	Vat. II	*Gaudium et Spes*	Marriage and the family; conjugal love	OBS, 195–201
1968	Paul VI	*Humanae Vitae*	Birth regulation; responsible parenthood	CTS, Do 411
1974	CDF	*Declaration*	Declaration on Procured Abortion	CTS, Do 545
1981	John Paul II	*Familiaris Consortio*	Family as 'domestic Church'; marriage	CTS, S 357
1983	John Paul II	*Charter on Rights*	Human rights of family; human life	CTS, S 371
1987	CDF	*Donum Vitae*	IVF and fertility treatments	CTS, S 395
1988	John Paul II	*Mulieris Dignitatem*	Dignity of women	CTS, Do 584
1994	John Paul II	*Letter to Families*	Family at centre of civilization of love	CTS, S 434
1995	John Paul II	*Evangelium Vitae*	Value of human life; abortion	CTS, Do 633
1995	John Paul II	*Letter to Women*	Apology for discrimination	CTS, Do 638
1999	PCF	*Family & Human Rights*	Family has human rights	Vat. Website
2004	CDF	*Men and Women*	Collaboration of men and women	Vat. Website

Notes:
[a] CDF: Sacred Congregation for the Doctrine of the Faith. PCF: Pontifical Council for the Family.
[b] OBS: D. J. O'Brien and T. A. Shannon (eds.) 1992. *Catholic Social Thought: The Documentary Heritage*. Maryknoll, New York: Orbis. CTS: Catholic Truth Society; WMA: W. M. Abbott (ed.) 1966. *The Documents of Vatican II*. London: Geoffrey Chapman. Vat. Website: Vatican Website.

The Church's teaching has developed strikingly since the encyclical letter *Casti Connubi* of Pope Pius XI in 1930. He was concerned about attacks on the sancity of life-long marriage, divorce, contraception, abortion and 'injustices committed in the name of eugenics'. In the Vatican Council's Dogmatic Constitution on the Church, the family was referred to as 'the domestic Church' (*LG* §11). In the Decree on the Apostolate of the Laity, the family was referred to as 'the first and vital cell of society'

(*AA* §11). In Part II of the Council's Pastoral Constitution on the Church in the Modern World, the first of the five problems which aroused 'universal concern today' was that of marriage and family life (*GS* §§47–52). In some respects this section of the Constitution seems rather weak and inadequately grounded in real everyday experiences.[11] The controversial matter of contraception was largely by-passed, having been given to a special commission originally set up by Pope John XXIII.[12] There is no serious treatment of the causes of marriage breakdown in the numerous circumstances of stress in the modern world. An idealized picture of sublime marital bliss is offered as a worthy goal but there is no detailed analysis of the particular problems of modern living or of the everyday experiences of married people. On the other hand, the treatment of 'conjugal love' was regarded as 'remarkable'[13] and to have represented a major and highly significant shift in the Church's teaching on marriage and sexuality. In particular, the ancient distinction between the 'primary' end of marriage as procreation and the 'secondary' end of the 'avoidance of concupiscence' was sedulously avoided and due recognition given to the importance of the human relationship between the spouses.

A fuller treatment of these issues was given in Pope Paul VI's encyclical letter *Humanae Vitae* in 1968, which reaffirmed the Church's 'constant doctrine . . . that each and every marriage act must remain open to the transmission of life'(§11),[14] and repeated the traditional condemnation of sterilization and abortion, and in Pope John Paul II's apostolic exhortation *Familiaris Consortio* in 1981 (§29; fn. 83).

Lois Ann Lorentzen (1994) observed that the issue of marriage and family life generated some of the more heated debates of the Council. She noted the 'personalist' flavour in the description of marriage as a 'community of love', an 'intimate partnership of married life and love', which is 'rooted in the conjugal covenant or irrevocable personal consent' (*GS* §§47–48). The teaching on marital fidelity, respect for life, reproduction and birth control remain traditional. However, she also noted major shifts in the discourse and in particular 'the replacement of the notion of marriage as a contract with language of intimate partnership and covenant', that is 'using personalist language to move marriage beyond the earlier

[11] This has been a criticism made over many decades by the Catholic psychiatrist, Jack Dominian; Dominian 1968; 2004.
[12] Kaiser 1987; Marshall 1999.   [13] See fnn. 152 and 155 in Abbott 1966: 249–250.
[14] In doing so, Paul VI rejected the majority view of the Commission on Birth Control, a decision which has created problems for the Church leadership ever since.

legalistic framework' of Canon Law which defined marriage as a contract.[15] Similarly, 'the pastoral constitution views children as the fulfilment of spousal love rather than its purpose'. Joy in sexual intercourse was also viewed more positively than hitherto but many 'regret that the Council chose to avoid difficult issues such as celibacy, divorce, mixed marriages, and a fuller treatment of birth control'.

The Church has always regarded the strength, vitality and independence of the family as essential for the health of society as a whole. It was regarded as the major intermediate institution between the relatively isolated and vulnerable individual and a potentially all-powerful state. Hence the importance of the 'just family wage' and the stress on the principle of 'subsidiarity' in Pius XI's *Quadragesimo Anno* in 1931 (§71). Since the Vatican Council there has been an emphasis on the family as 'the domestic Church'.[16]

An analysis of the historical evolution of Catholic thinking about marriage and the family shows very considerable developments since the ambivalence of New Testament times when the Greco-Roman family was seen as a challenge to the intrinsic inclusiveness of the Christian community and when celibacy was valued more highly than the married state.[17] We can, perhaps, summarize the most recent Catholic social teaching, as expounded by Pope John Paul II in the Apostolic Exhortation *Familiaris Consortio*, in the following points:

- Marriage and family life were willed by God when He created man and woman in His own image and instructed them that the purposes of marriage were to be fruitful, multiply and fill the earth.
- This requires a life-time of commitment to parenting: the raising and education of children. 'The ever faithful love of God is put forward as the model of the relations of faithful love which should exist between spouses (*FC* §12)'. Hence fornication, cohabitation, adultery and divorce are forbidden in the interests of the common good.
- Procreation is the result of sexual intercourse between a male and a female and is a participation in the creative power of God. Any interference with the 'natural' course of sexual intercourse is improper. Thus the teaching rejects IVF where there is a separation of the unitive and procreative purposes of the conjugal act.[18] The norms of natural law are

---

[15] Stressed by Bishop Butler 1981: 192–197 and by Dominian 1968: 243–244; 2004: 73.
[16] *Lumen Gentium*, §11; *Apostolicam Actuositatem* §11; *Familiaris Consortio* §49.   [17] Cahill 2000.
[18] CDF 1987. *Donum Vitae*: §II, B.6.

judged to require that '*each and every marriage act* must remain open to the transmission of life'.[19]

- The 'personalist' aim of sexual intercourse between the spouses is a mutual gift of self-giving which contributes to the strengthening of the relationship between them. 'The indissolubility of marriage ... (is) a fruit ... of the absolutely faithful love that God has for man and that the Lord Jesus has for the Church' (*FC* §20; *GS* §48).
- The Church recognizes the sacramentality of marriage.[20] Like God's love, then, marriage is indissoluble. The pains and sufferings of married life are interpreted as a participation in the saving work of redemption and in the knowledge that after the Cross came the resurrection (*FC* §§9, 13).

Following the UN Declaration of Human Rights in 1948 the Holy See in 1983 presented a *Charter of the Rights of the Family*. The Charter summarized Catholic social teaching on the family as it had developed especially since Vatican II. It insisted that 'the family is based on marriage' and that it existed prior to the State and possessed 'inherent rights which are inalienable' (Preamble). All people had a right to choose whether or not to marry (§1). There is a 'natural complementarity' between man and woman who 'enjoy the same dignity and equal rights' in marriage (§2). 'Human life must be respected and protected *absolutely* from the moment of conception' (§4); hence abortion and 'all experimental manipulation or exploitation of the human embryo' and 'all interventions on the genetic heritage of the human person that are not aimed at correcting anomalies' violate the right to bodily integrity. Parents are the 'foremost educators of their children'. Families have a right to a decent standard of living (§9) and workers have a right to a 'family wage' (§10a). 'The work of the mother in the home must be recognized and respected (§10b)'. 'The family has the right to decent housing' (§11) and 'migrants have the right to the same protection' as other families. Immigrant families 'have the right to respect for their own culture', and the rights of migrant workers and refugees are also affirmed (§12).

In 1994 Pope John Paul II wrote a *Letter to Families* to mark the celebration of the Year of the Family. It is a profound scriptural, theological, philosophical and spiritual meditation and appeal in favour of 'the civilization of love' and against unbounded 'individualism', 'ethical utilitarianism', and the distinctive dualisms of the 'new Manichaeism' and of 'modern rationalism'. Particular attention is paid to the creation stories in

---

[19] *Familiaris Consortio*: §29; *Humanae Vitae*, §11. Emphasis added.
[20] *Casti Connubi*, §§31–43; *Gaudium et Spes* §48; Ephes. 5: 32.

Genesis and the fourth, fifth, sixth and ninth commandments, the marriage at Cana, St Paul's teaching about the ' "great mystery" involved in the creation of man as male and female and the vocation of both to conjugal love, to fatherhood and to motherhood' (§19), and the mystery of the Incarnation and of the Holy Family. The pope suggested that the family was a 'community of persons', 'the first and basic expression of man's *social nature*'. Jesus confirmed 'the *indissoluble character* of marriage as the *basis of the common good of the family*' from 'the dawn of the New Covenant'. The duality of motherhood and fatherhood was 'bestowed by the Creator upon human beings "from the beginning" ' (§7; Mt 19:8). 'The family, which originates in the love of man and woman, ultimately derives from the mystery of God', and the creativity of the Trinity (§8). 'Begetting is the continuation of Creation' (§9).

The pope reiterated previous teaching that '*the two dimensions of conjugal union*, the unitive and the procreative, *cannot be artificially separated* without damaging the deepest truth of the conjugal act itself '. Reaffirming the teaching of *Humanae Vitae*, the pope taught that 'in the conjugal act, husband and wife ... confirm ... the *total gift of self to the other* (which) involves a potential openness to procreation (§12)'. Responsible parenthood was 'an integral part of the "civilization of love" ', a civilization which is not just political but also cultural, so that the family has the task of bringing about the 'humanization of the world'. This led him into a lengthy discussion of the destructiveness of an 'anti-civilization', for example linked to utilitarianism (such as 'the right to choose' and so-called 'safe sex') which simply 'make persons *slaves to their weaknesses*' (§13). The pope meditated on St Paul's '*hymn to love*' which '*endures all things*', the '*Magna Charta* of the civilization of love'. He reflected on 'the Gospel truth about *freedom*' and the way in which '*individualism threaten (s) the civilization of love*' and '*utilitarian happiness*' is 'opposed to the objective demands of the true good' and 'proves a systemic and permanent threat to the family'. Against these threats, 'the love of spouses and parents has ... (a) regenerative force' (§14). It was the task of the family to realize the imperative 'to be human' as citizens of the world (§15). Here the importance of education was indicated. The pope insisted that '*parents are the first and most important educators* of their own children' and that this needed to be recognized by the State according to the '*principle of subsidiarity*' (§16). The pope recalled the duty of Church and State to promote the dignity of marriage and of the family. He defended the institution of marriage and argued against 'other interpersonal unions' (e.g. homosexual partnerships) and 'moral permissiveness' and 'the temptation of a superficial and false modernity'. He regarded unemployment as 'one of the most serious threats to family life' and recognized that the burdensome work women do within the family should be acknowledged and appreciated (§17).

Reflections on the marriage at Cana and Jesus' response to the Pharisees about divorce, led John Paul II to suggest that the *'profound and radical demands'* of marriage and family life have their origins in God's plan of Creation. 'Families are meant to contribute to the transformation of the earth and the renewal of the world, of creation and of all humanity', but in the face of life's challenges, Jesus told them not to be afraid (§18; Jn 14:27). Reflecting on St Paul's reference to the *'great mystery'* of family life he observed that 'love contains the acknowledgement of the personal dignity of the other'. Against the dualism of *'modern rationalism'* he insisted that 'man is a person in the unity of his body and his spirit', with a *'spiritualized body'* and *'an embodied spirit'*. This led him to suggest defiantly that 'the Word made flesh' was the reply to modern rationalism and to reject the 'ethical defeat' of experimentation on embryos and fetuses, and the 'manipulation and exploitation' of human sexuality which could not tolerate the mystery of God's purposes (§19). He appealed to Jesus' demands in the Sermon on the Mount to warn against consumerism and hedonism and the temptations of adultery in the heart (§20; Mt 5: 27–28). He appealed to the infancy Gospel and *'the proclamation of life'* in contrast to the *'threat to life'* posed by abortion, 'killing love by killing the fruit of love' (§21). 'Ultimately', the pope reminded, 'everyone will be judged *on love* (§22)'.[21]

The Pontifical Council for the Family celebrated the fiftieth anniversary of the UN *Universal Declaration of Human Rights* by publishing in 1999 a reflection on *The Family and Human Rights*. This acknowledged the importance of the *Declaration* while indicating reservations about individualism and subjectivism in some human rights discourse (§2). It reiterated the importance of protecting marriage, the rights of the family and the need for the family and marriage to be defended and promoted by the State and society (§9). Challenges from 'the culture of death' must be tackled by a 'conception of human rights that are developed through the family' (§10). It insisted that each person has an innate dignity since 'as the image of God, man has been created through an act of love'. Hence man transcended other created beings (§14). He was 'endowed with an absolute value' and 'is not an instrument, a means or something that can be manipulated' (§19). The document 'recognizes the full equality of every person ... at every

---

[21] The dominant theme in the writings of Jack Dominian.

moment of hisher existence' (§22). Men and women had a reciprocal and complementary relationship to each other (§§24, 26).

Before outlining some of the criticisms which have been levelled at Catholic social teaching on the family, two preliminary points are necessary. Firstly, there has been and there continues to be a multiplicity of family forms both historically over time, and cross-culturally, with different emphases on kinship relations and economic considerations, sexuality and the procreation of children, gender differentiation, and the salience of the personal relationship between the spouses.[22] Secondly, it is important to recognize that in its dialectic with the dominant cultures over time, the emphases of Catholic social teaching on marriage and the family have changed and developed considerably since New Testament times. Lisa Sowle Cahill[23] suggested that the Roman Catholic understanding of marriage and hence its historical and cultural biases has been shaped by four factors:

1) a *Western* historical and social context for understanding sexuality, kinship, and individuality, essentially within a social and patriarchal model, but with a modern emphasis on personal freedom; 2) a *sacramentalizing* tendency, accepting human institutions but also transforming them in distinctive ways (for example, by seeing marriage as permanent); 3) *canon law*, the medium by which Western Christianity has controlled sexuality and protected marriage as an institution via juridical definitions; and 4) a struggle to balance *the physical and the interpersonal* aspects of marriage. Of special current importance is the 'personalism' of the recent magisterium. The latter ambiguously assimilates modern understandings of the person, of freedom, and of interpersonal relationships to a pre-modern emphasis on the physical 'nature' of sex and reproduction, and on the social functions of sexuality and family within a hierarchical and patriarchal order.

According to Cahill there are three ongoing problems with Catholic marriage teaching: (1) 'the dialectic of the social and the personal in marriage', which is both a personal relationship and a social institution involving questions of lineage and kinship ties and economic relationships; (2) assumptions about appropriate gender relationships within marriage, that is, equality or complementarity; and (3) 'the formation of the marital commitment . . . whether by mutual consent or sexual consummation, and as provisional or indissoluble'.

In recent years Catholic theologians have made a number of criticisms of the official teaching of the Church on family matters.[24] Firstly, it has been

---

[22] Cahill 2000.   [23] Cahill 1991: 103–105.
[24] See, e.g., the six chapters on 'The Family in Catholic Social Thought' in Coleman (ed.) 1991a; Cahill 1994; Farley 1994; Buckley 1997; Kelly 1996, 1998; Selling 2001.

suggested that it simply does not take adequately into account the social realities of people's everyday lives, the constraints under which they live, and the difficulties of economic survival, especially in developing societies.[25] Secondly, there are 'serious problems from a feminist perspective'. In particular, the analysis in *Gaudium et Spes* 'provides little insight into the concrete situations of women, demonstrating a blindness to rape, domestic violence, poverty, excessive workload, and so forth'.[26] The awareness of all of these issues has grown considerably over the past forty years. Thirdly, in the past 'the family's influence may have been excessive to the detriment of the fundamental rights of the individual'[27] and to the scriptural teaching that family relationships must 'be subordinated to one's relationships with God'.[28] There is a widespread feeling that the theology of marriage is underdeveloped.

Reservations about the current papal teaching can be seen in the debates about cohabitation, contraception, divorce and gay and lesbian relationships. For example, the papal teaching on cohabitation or 'trial marriages' is to regard them as 'unacceptable' since they are essentially seen as a 'carrying out (of) an "experiment" with human beings' and as a failure to reflect the 'eternally faithful' nature of 'the union of Christ and the Church' (*FC* §80). Kevin Kelly's pastoral moral theology, unlike magisterial documents concerned to enunciate general principles, was altogether more nuanced as a 'No, but . . .'. On the one hand he accepted that cohabitation 'can hardly be conducive to the good of the human person, *integrally and adequately considered*' but on the other hand he argued that it was necessary to start from where people are, often subject to the constraints of structural injustices and sin, such as extreme poverty, shortages of affordable housing, economic insecurity, and an excessive form of individualism, disconnectedness and division in the prevailing culture.[29]

Kelly took a similar 'personalist' line on the matter of contraception. Papal teaching, based on a 'natural law' argument, taught that there must be no impairment of the 'natural capacity to procreate human life' in *every act* of sexual intercourse (*HV* §11; *FC* §29) and a total rejection of 'an anti-life mentality' (*FC* §30). Others have stressed the 'procreative quality of the *whole relationship*'.[30] Kelly's book arose from his passionate concern for people living with HIV/AIDS and the general exploitation of women, especially in Africa. He and others, including several bishops, argued

---

[25] See, e.g., Lorentzen 1994; Dominian 2004: 73–77; Novak 1965.   [26] Lorentzen 1994: 414.
[27] Paul VI 1967: §36.   [28] Howard-Brook 2001: 72–102.   [29] Kelly 1998: 184–187; emphasis added.
[30] Ibid.: 134.

convincingly that safeguarding the health of the sexual partner was a moral issue and justified the use of condoms in order to prevent the spread of the HIV infection.[31] Similar personalist concerns have also been expressed in the matter of marital breakdown and divorce and pastoral responses to the realities of second marriages. While there is a general agreement about the importance of reaffirming faithfulness in marriage, as a sign of God's indissoluble love for the Church, at the same time there is a growing concern in pastoral practices to offer mercy and compassion to those who have experienced the hurts of marital breakdown (*FC* §§83–84).[32]

Another area where a personalist theology has offered a major challenge to traditional Catholic teaching has been that of gay and lesbian relationships. The traditional Catholic position has been to distinguish between homosexual 'orientations', which are somehow 'natural' and therefore have to be allowed for, and practices which have been interpreted as 'contrary to the natural law' and 'intrinsically disordered' (*CCC* §2357). Officially the Church has strongly condemned discrimination against gays and lesbians while ambiguously resisting gay and lesbian human rights legislation.[33] Kevin Kelly asked whether the current position was tantamount to 'denying the Good News to gay men and lesbian women'.[34] He urged 'a more positive approach' based on modern 'biblical exegesis and theological scholarship' and a recognition that their capacity for love is a gift from God. Similarly, Genovesi argued for a more just and less discriminatory approach to the adoption and fostering of children when he argued that 'one's sexual orientation says nothing about one's ability to be a fine parent or guardian'.[35] While these views may not be generally held throughout the Church, they are worthy of serious consideration.

---

[31] Ibid.: 196–206. See also Ackermann 2002 and Greyling 2002. CAFOD's website has a useful outline of its policy at http://www.cafod.org.uk/hivaids/aidsethics.shtml. CAFOD 'does not fund the supply, distribution or promotion of condoms' but does recognize 'that the promotion of harm minimisation is often a necessary and crucial shorter-term strategy' to complement the longer term strategy of change in sexual behaviour.

[32] Kelly 1996 provided a valuable overview. In Appendix 2 he included a wide range of theological and pastoral contributions to the problem of divorce and remarriage. Buckley 1997, following intensive interviews with a wide range of support groups within the Church, considered that the theology of the marriage bond was disputable.

[33] Genovesi 1994: 447–454. See also *Compendium* §228.

[34] Kelly 1998: 64–95.   [35] Genovesi 1994: 452.

GENDER DIFFERENTIATION

It is well known that, in spite of equal opportunities legislation, women continue to be discriminated against in the labour market. They only get around 70 per cent of the wages of men for similar work but also get nowhere near their due share of the more senior or highly rewarded jobs. Traditional forms of the domestic division of labour are also remarkably resilient and, typically, married women workers 'have two jobs'. Patriarchy, that is highly structured forms of gendered inequalities, and ideologies of male superiority or God-given differences and roles which continue to legitimate male dominance, continue to be systemic. This is perhaps the deepest structural injustice of all and our present family structures largely reproduce gender inequalities. In order to address these it is necessary to work for genuine sharing of parenting responsibilities so that gender differentials are eliminated.[36] In the pursuit of justice it is necessary to challenge the institutional Church, in its collusion, through biases in its teaching and structures, in patriarchy and the reproduction of male dominance.

The somewhat idealized picture of the 'happy family' tends to overlook the vulnerability of women in a hierarchical structure of domination and power differentials. In recent years we have become increasingly aware of the subjection of women and children within families to physical and sexual violence, abuse and rape, the economic dependence of women and their financial vulnerability in the event of marriage breakdown. It has been pointed out that 'the family is the most violent group in society with the exception of the police and the military'.[37] One would never guess this from any Vatican document about the family! There is also evidence that women, and especially mothers in full-time employment, work disproportionately long hours compared with men.[38] In developing societies women undertake the bulk of agricultural labour and water-carrying. They are extremely vulnerable to the spread of the HIV/AIDS infection resulting from the migration of male partners. The sexual exploitation of women, female genital mutilation,[39] and the 'feminization of poverty'[40] are commonplace.

Feminist analysts have drawn our attention to the assumption made by social justice theorists, such as John Rawls, that family life is just. Okin, for

---

[36] Okin 1989: 184.
[37] Macionis and Plummer 2002: 445 who noted that most domestic crime went unreported. In the USA 1,300 women die as a result of family violence each year.
[38] Delphy and Leonard 1992: 75–76.   [39] Kelly 1998: 4–8.   [40] Okin 1989: 173.

example, argued that they neglected to apply 'the principles of justice to the realm of human nurturance'.[41] In contemporary industrial societies women are unpaid and exploited workers in the domestic mode of production and overwhelmingly responsible for the tasks of parenting and care of the sick and elderly. To avoid injustice to women and children, family and work institutions 'must encourage the avoidance of socially created vulnerabilities by facilitating and reinforcing the equal sharing of paid and unpaid work between men and women, and consequently the equalising of their opportunities and obligations in general'.

There are, perhaps, some signs of hope in the Church, for example in Pope John Paul II's attempts to dialogue with Catholic feminist theologians. In his message to the Secretary General of the UN Conference on Women in Beijing in 1995, he recognized 'the inherent, inalienable dignity of women' and denounced 'the terrible exploitation of women and girls which exists in every part of the world'.[42] In the Pope's further *Letter to Women* in 1995, he acknowledged and apologized for the participation of the Church in cultural conditioning which failed to acknowledge women's dignity and effectively marginalized them.[43] He called for 'real equality in every area: equal pay for equal work, protection for working mothers, fairness in career advancements, equality of spouses with regard to family rights and the recognition of everything that is part of the rights and duties of citizens in a democratic State'.

Pope John Paul II, following his 1988 encyclical *Mulieris Dignitatem*, referred to 'the "iconic" complementarity of male and female roles'.[44] This view was argued at length in the recent CDF document *On the Collaboration of Men and Women in the Church and in the World*.[45] This based its argument on the biblical vision of the sexually differentiated human person: 'male and female he created them', that is, 'humanity as a relational reality' (§§5–6; Gen 1: 27). The document mentioned 'women's physical capacity to give life', their 'capacity to persevere in adversity' and their special contribution in 'human relationships and caring for others' (§13). From this it urged that attentive recognition be paid to 'the difference and reciprocity between the sexes' (§14). Rather than taking

---

[41] Okin 1989: 108, 169.   [42] Quoted in Kelly 1998: 46 and *Briefing*, 17 August 1995, pp. 16–18.
[43] *Letter to Women* 1995: §§3–4.
[44] Ibid.: §11. Cahill, 2000: 91 refers to the Pope's 'complementarity model of equality'.
[45] CDF, *Letter to the Bishops of the Catholic Church on the Collaboration of Men and Women in the Church and in the World*, 2004 in http://www.vatican.va. An abridged version of this letter was published in *The Tablet*, 7 August 2004: 30–33.

these differences as 'natural', social scientists draw attention to the extent to which they are historically and culturally conditioned.

Tina Beattie, a Catholic feminist theologian, while acknowledging 'the excellent section on work and family', was not unreasonably critical of a 'group of celibate men in an all-male enclave' pronouncing on the psychology and nature of women 'without quoting or referring to any woman's ideas' and without addressing 'domestic abuse and sexual violence as urgent pastoral problems in the Church's dealings with women' or saying 'anything about the responsibilities of men in the home'. But her major criticism was theological. She judged that recent Church teaching on the role of women had been 'a devastating catastrophe' and insisted that 'the belief that there is an essential difference between the sexes is not part of the Catholic tradition'.[46]

Other Catholic women, while acknowledging the pope's attempt to appreciate their special gifts, have been critical of the notion of complementarity.[47] Lisa Cahill, for example, saw the pope's references to women's special genius of nurturing as providing 'a rationale for exclusion from the Church's most respected leadership roles' while Margaret Farley doubted that the Church could provide a prophetic voice until it 'can model in its structures the coequal discipleship which was part of the original vision of Christianity'.[48] Mary Grey[49] pointed out that 'cultural constructions of gender identities – both masculine and feminine – serve the interests of the powerful' and that 'patriarchy is *disordered relationship* spawning diseased patterns of *both* maleness *and* femaleness'. Kevin Kelly suggested that the theory of 'ontological complementarity' was but 'one particular view among many in the area of gender analysis' and that it did not correspond to most women's experiences.[50] Furthermore, it 'is oppressive and deterministic since it implies that we cannot examine critically whether the gender roles we receive today are not, in fact, the end-product of an ongoing process of social construction and therefore open to further transformation in the light of what is in keeping with the dignity of human persons'. He pointed out that 'as Christians we believe we are relational persons created in the image of a relational God' and he argued, with women theologians, in favour of a model for relationship which 'is essentially one of mutuality and interdependence between persons who are equal, though distinct and unique'.

---

[46] Tina Beattie, 'Feminism, Vatican-Style', *The Tablet*, 7 August, 2004: 4–6.
[47] See, e.g., the responses of six Catholic women in *The Tablet*, 15 July, 1995, pp. 920–921.
[48] Cahill 2000: 92, 93.   [49] Grey 2001: 61, 67.   [50] Kelly 1998: 51, 52. 55.

Women theologians have also been critical of the notion, expressed in the Vatican Council's *Dogmatic Constitution on the Church*, and developed further in Pope John Paul II's *Familiaris Consortio*, that 'the family is . . . the domestic Church' (*LG* §11; *FC* §21). Lisa Cahill[51] pointed out that 'historically, the so-called Christian family has often been co-opted by existing social structures, especially those that reproduce economic and gender inequities'. Thus, she judged that despite recent advances, the official Catholic approach to family matters was still 'overly concerned with reproductive issues, not sufficiently attuned to gender and race as intersecting causes of economic inequities that affect families', and too quick to assume that Church or political leaders will do anything about it.

This brief consideration of the systemic injustices ('structural sin') experienced by women globally, and legitimated by long-standing and deeply entrenched ideologies of patriarchy, have only recently been given the attention which is their due by the Roman Catholic Church. It would seem that the Church needs to follow the example of many secular authorities and *listen* to women's stories and experiences.

BIOETHICAL CHALLENGES

In the second half of this chapter we will note that recent advances in the biological sciences, in genetics and in technologies for genetic engineering and reproduction, have presented the Church with an extremely complex set of new ethical challenges. Four main groups of concerns will be considered: organ transplants; abortion; euthanasia; and gene therapy. The aim is to seek an appropriate Christian response faithful to the infinite creativity of God's universe and the radical teaching of Jesus.

The Vatican Council's *Gaudium et Spes* provides the key starting point for the consideration of these issues with its stress on the dignity of the human person made in God's image (*GS* §§3, 12, 35, 76).[52] Kevin Kelly[53] suggested 'the good of the human person, *integrally and adequately considered*' was the basic criterion for moral evaluation and identified eight dimensions. The human person was:

- *a subject*, not to be treated as a means; hence the importance of informed consent in medical interventions;
- *an embodied subject*; this dimension rejected a dualism between body and soul and affirmed the goodness of sexuality;

---

[51] Cahill 2000: 83, 95.   [52] *Compendium* §§34–48.   [53] Kelly 1992: 27–60.

- *part of the material world*; interdependent with the rest of creation and with a full ecological awareness;
- *interrelational with other persons*; this had particular relevance for a more comprehensive view of the purposes of sexual intercourse;
- *an interdependent social being*; this dimension, which was increasingly apparent in a globalizing world, stressed the importance of the common good;
- *historical*; that is with a history of free personal choices but also constrained to some extent by our own time and culture;
- *equal but unique*; self-creating and original but also 'creations of our social, cultural, and familial history' and 'the web of interpersonal relationships';
- *called to know and worship God*; that is open to the experience of transcendence.

These are important considerations which must be borne in mind when evaluating the morality of the wide range of issues which have arisen in recent years.

Organ transplants and surgical procedures enhancing life

In one of the series of very useful pamphlets published recently by the Linacre Centre for Healthcare Ethics, in conjunction with the Catholic Truth Society (CTS), David Jones[54] has provided a brief history of transplant medicine. The classification of blood types goes back to 1900 and the first cornea transplant was carried out in 1905. Kidney transplants had to wait until the 1950s while heart transplants date from the 1960s and 1970s. In 1998 in the UK there were 4903 organ transplant operations, including 264 heart transplants.

Human organ transplantations raise some important ethical issues. Organs may be donated by living donors, in which case due consideration must be given to the wellbeing of the donor, or by dead donors, in which case due attention has to be paid to the difficult issue of diagnosing the death of the donor and to maintaining appropriate respect for the body of the dead person. Other controversial issues include cloning, relying on factory farming human embryos which would later be destroyed, the future development of adult stem-cell technology which might provide ethically acceptable artificial organs, and 'xenotransplantation', that is the transplantation of organs from other species. Jones pointed out that transplant medicine was 'a multi-billion pound industry' and warned that powerful

[54] Jones 2001: 4–6, 19–20, 22–23, 32–35, 40, 52–61.

individuals and institutions involved in transplant medicine had an interest in stifling criticism. This would be 'morally dangerous'.

The development of papal teaching about transplantation can be traced from Pius XII in the 1950s. Pope John Paul II recognized the 'generous impulse' and 'solidarity' with neighbour expressed in blood or organ donation provided there was no 'serious danger or harm to (the donor's) own life or personal identity, and for a just and proportionate reason'. In *Evangelium Vitae* he wrote that one way to 'build up an authentic culture of life ... is the donation of organs, performed in an ethically acceptable manner, with a view to offering a chance of health and even life itself to the sick who sometimes have no other hope (§86)'.[55]

Vital organs, such as hearts, could only be taken from a dead person. This raised the difficult issue of the criteria for ascertaining death. Pope John Paul noted that the death of a person 'results from the separation of the life-principle (or soul) from the corporal reality of the person ... (and) is an event which no scientific technique or empirical method can identify directly'. He then proceeded to acknowledge the legitimate autonomy of medical decisions: 'whether the "encephalic" signs or the more traditional cardio-respiratory signs – the Church does not make technical decisions'. Other ethical issues to which the pope drew attention included the need for 'informed consent' on the part of the donor. The assignment of scarce organs should not be discriminatory or utilitarian 'but made on the basis of immunological and clinical factors'. Finally, 'for a xenotransplant to be licit, the transplanted organ must not impair the integrity of the psychological or genetic identity of the person receiving it; and there must also be a proven biological possibility that the transplant will be successful and will not expose the recipient to inordinate risk'. In the development of the Catholic response to transplants, it can be seen that the Church has been at pains to insist on the human dignity of both the donor and the recipient as subjects and not utilities, and as embodied, interdependent, and equal in dignity and value in the sight of God.

Abortion and related procedures

In the years since the 1967 Abortion Act it is estimated that there have been over five million abortions.[56] Of the 774,000 conceptions in England and

---

[55] See also Pope John Paul's address to the 18th International Congress of the Transplantation Society, 2000, in *Briefing*, 30 (10) 10–11.
[56] Scarisbrick 1999; *Social Trends* No. 32, 2002, Table 2.10.

Wales in 1999, 4 per cent led to legal abortions within marriage and a further 18 per cent to legal abortions outside marriage, a total of 22 per cent of conceptions or some 170,000.

This is a moral issue of the utmost importance. The traditional Catholic view is that 'life begins at conception' and that, hence, given the prohibition on the killing of an innocent human being, abortion is an 'unspeakable crime' (*EV* §58).[57] Robert George offered what seemed to be convincing evidence that human life does in fact begin at conception when he wrote that 'unlike the gametes (that is, the sperm and egg), the zygote is *genetically unique* and *distinct* from its parents. Biologically, it is a *separate organism* ... It possesses, as they do *not*, the active capacity or *potency to develop* itself into a human embryo, fetus, infant, child, adolescent, and adult'.[58] The traditional Catholic condemnation of abortion is consistent with this biology as outlined by George. In *Evangelium Vitae* Pope John Paul, quoting the CDF, claimed that 'the results themselves of scientific research on the human embryo provide "a valuable indication for discerning by the use of reason a personal presence at the moment of the first appearance of a human life: how could a human individual not be a human person?"' (§60).

The Second Vatican Council affirmed that 'from the moment of its conception life must be guarded with the greatest care, while abortion and infanticide are unspeakable crimes (*GS* §51)'.[59] Respect for the human person 'from conception' also explains the rejection of the use of abortifacient contraceptive pills. In *Evangelium Vitae*, Pope John Paul II insisted that even serious and tragic reasons 'can never justify the deliberate killing of an innocent human being (*EV* §58)'. With the unanimous agreement of the bishops he declared solemnly 'that direct abortion, that is, abortion willed as an end or as a means, always constitutes a grave moral disorder, since it is the deliberate killing of an innocent human being (§62)'. This absolutist position creates a challenge, for example in the case of an underage girl pregnant as a result of rape. A parent might claim that it was a greater evil to expect a young girl to bear the burden of an infamous assault throughout the rest of her life.

The openness and integrity of the stance on moral theology taken by Kevin Kelly[60] when considering pastoral cases such as this is attractive and seems to bear the sign of Jesus' compassion. In sum, he seemed to be saying: 'we don't know the answers to everything and, in order to arrive at

---

[57] Watt 2001a.   [58] R. P. George in Gormally (ed.), 2002: 66. All emphases added.
[59] The status of naturally or aborted embryos seems to be glossed over.   [60] Kelly 1992; 1998.

conscientious moral decisions, we must listen to the conversation and dialogue between the developing knowledge and understanding of the sciences, on the one hand, and the developments in scriptural exegesis and moral theology, on the other hand'.

It is important to note, therefore, that a good number of reputable moral theologians do not share the apparent certainty of the current official teaching on the status of the human embryo from the very moment of conception. Kelly[61] has identified three distinct positions, all of which 'are reconcilable with a Christian theology of creation in which we recognise all human persons as "gift" from God and beings of transcendental dignity and not merely of functional worth'. These were:

- *Individuality*: 'as soon as you have an individual human being, you have a being endowed with the full dignity of human personhood'. There are two sub-types differing as to when individuation occurs:
  (a) *the 'fertilization' view*: taught by Pope John Paul II and by the CDF in *Donum Vitae*, sometimes including a 'safety first' gloss.
  (b) *the 'primitive streak' view*: the development of the human individual occurs about fourteen days after fertilization. This view is held by a number of prominent Roman Catholic moral theologians includ-ing Norman Ford who has written: 'instead of viewing development in the first two weeks after fertilization as development of the human individual, ... the process ought to be seen as one of development into a human individual'.
- *Rudimentary Organic Structure* as a prerequisite for self-awareness. This view followed Aristotle and Aquinas and argued 'the need for a biolo-gical grounding of true personhood'. Kelly suggested there are hints of this view in Mahoney's book, *Bioethics and Belief*, and in the philoso-pher, Peter Byrne, who would acknowledge personhood from 'the point where brain and nervous system come to be laid down as differentiated types of tissues', about two months after fertilization.
- *Rudimentary Subjective Experience* which regarded a person as essentially a 'subject' so that development had not reached the personal stage until there was some rudimentary subjective experience. Some have located the beginning of such experience at the time of earliest brainstem activity, that is during the seventh week of development.

It is also relevant here to consider, in the light of the status of the human embryo, some concerns about prenatal tests. Agneta Sutton has written a useful overview of prenatal diagnostic tests. Some of these promoted the

[61] Kelly 1999: 175–188; see also Mahoney 1984: 52–86.

health of the mother and baby but others also aimed to detect foetal abnormalities and raised the possibility of selective abortion. In the latter case the tests were used with a 'eugenic intention'. 'Such an attitude is shameful and utterly reprehensible, since it presumes to measure the value of a human life only within the parameters of "normality" and physical well-being, thus opening the way to legitimizing infanticide and euthanasia as well' (*EV* §63). Sutton[62] summarized the Catholic position, which rejected the view that the unborn child was disposable, in the following terms: 'Only in a society that respects each and every member irrespective of physical or mental disability, riches, power, social status, race or age, can we all live free from fear of being viewed as individuals whose lives are disposable or not worth living'.

Voluntary and involuntary euthanasia

The same general principle of the dignity of the individual human person applies in the case of euthanasia.[63] Recent concerns were expressed when a Bill to 'assist dying' was introduced in the House of Lords. This followed several highly publicized cases including that of Diane Pretty, suffering from an incurable disease, who wished to 'die with dignity', and two other cases where patients travelled to Switzerland to end their lives with a lethal dose of drugs, in one case without proof of terminal illness.[64] On the face of it, the commandment not to kill is sufficiently explicit to prohibit euthanasia. All the same, Christians need to understand where some people are coming from. A correspondent in *The Tablet* recently gave a harrowing and immensely moving account of his experience of the final days of life of his mother. He challenged:

If it had been our dog that had ended up semi-conscious, half-blind, half-deaf, epilectic, incontinent and unable to stand up, and without the faintest chance of recovery, I would not have had the slightest compunction about asking the vet to put it down; nor would anybody have questioned the morality of my action. Was my mother less entitled to a dignified end than our dog?[65]

The Linacre Centre for health care ethics has published a number of contributions on euthanasia.[66] In 1982, a working party under the chairmanship of Fr. J. Mahoney, S. J. summarized the position of euthanasia in

---

[62] Sutton 2002: 44.   [63] Robinson, P. 2003.
[64] Ridge, M. 'Battle over Euthanasia', *The Tablet*, 17 May 2003, pp. 10–11. It is of interest the Human Rights campaigning group *Liberty* supported Diane Pretty's right 'to die at a time of her choosing'.
[65] *The Tablet*, 24 May 2003.   [66] See, e.g., Gormally 1994; Robinson 2003.

clinical practice and thinking in the early 1980s in five specialized fields of care: the newborn, handicapped, terminal care, the elderly and intensive care.[67] The report expressed concern that there was evidence that 'involuntary euthanasia of certain newborn babies is systematic rather than an occasional occurrence in certain paediatric units' and in the case of the terminally ill, 'euthanasia by instalments are still relatively commonplace'. Among the external influences on clinical thinking and practice, the report cites 'the residue of philosophical utilitarianism'; 'possessive individualist' conceptions 'that an infant is not, properly speaking, a person and so lacks human rights'; 'social darwinist notions of human evolution as requiring the elimination of the "unfit"'; moral pluralism and claims such as the 'right to determine the manner of their dying ... with dignity'.

The report was written from a specifically religious perspective which took as axiomatic that there was an essential distinction to be made between human beings and other animals. Because of the intrinsic dignity of the individual human being, the report rejected 'quality of life' judgements which legitimate 'sinister' treatments or the omission of life saving measures both of which are *intended* to hasten death. It is important, however, to note the 'principle of double effect' and distinguish the *intentional* killing of a patient from the hastening of a death as an anticipated *side effect* of, for example, pain control treatments. The current position as summarized in the *Catechism of the Catholic Church* derives from the belief in the sacredness of human life (§2258). Given this premise, the teaching on direct euthanasia which 'consists in putting an end to the lives of handicapped, sick or dying persons (is) morally unacceptable'. Instead, palliative care is encouraged (§§2277–2279).

In 1993 the Linacre Centre presented a submission to the Select Committee of the House of Lords on Medical Ethics on what it saw as the fundamental issues: 'the value of human life, the moral significance of intention, the ethics of killing, the claims of autonomy, the purpose of medicine and its relation to duties of treatment and duties of care'.[68] The submission referred to human life possessing 'an intrinsic dignity and value because created by God in his own image (Genesis 1: 26)' and interpreted this 'in terms of the distinctive *capacity for rational existence* inherent in man's nature ... to develop both the ability to understand what is truly good and the ability to be moved by the desire for what is

[67] Gormally 1994: 21–22, 25, 28–33, 35, 44–48, 95.
[68] Gormally 1994: 116, 118, 123, 133, 150. The Report of the Catholic Union to the House of Lords' Select Committee is given in *Briefing*, 23 (12) 17 June 1993, p. 6.

good'.[69] The submission was critical of Mary Warnock's distinction between 'simply being alive' and 'the specifically human consciousness of having a life to lead' and the suggestion that only the latter has distinctive value. It was also critical of Ronald Dworkin's view that life's inherent value depends on what people 'make of their own lives'. The submission argued that the understanding of human worth advocated by both Warnock and Dworkin 'is a direct attack on the principle of the basic equality-in-dignity of human beings (and hence) is radically subversive of justice'. The submission concluded that 'justifications of voluntary and non-voluntary euthanasia as beneficent rely *essentially* on the judgement that, overall, the present life of the person to be killed is of negative value (not worthwhile). But such a judgement is incompatible with recognizing the ineliminable worth and dignity of the person to be killed'.

Finally, it is worth recording that the submission was highly critical of the 'abdication of the courts' responsibility' by the Law Lords in favour of the discontinuation of treatment and care in the case of Tony Bland who had been in a persistent vegetative state for three years following the Hillsborough disaster. This case was explored at some length by John Keown, Helen Watt and Kevin Kelly.[70] Keown was concerned at the legal revolution and switch of emphasis from 'sanctity of life' to considerations of 'quality of life' and 'autonomy'. He argued that a central objection to the quality of life philosophy was that it denied the ineliminable value of each patient and made arbitrary judgements of worth such as mental or physical disability.[71] He acknowledged that the patient's right to choose merited proper respect but argued that this right was not absolute but required responsibility to promote human flourishing 'in accordance with a framework of moral truths'. He suggested that in the Bland case, the House of Lords decision constituted a shift from the sanctity principle to that of the quality of life. The decision prohibited intentional killing by an act but permitted it by omission. Helen Watt, too, was highly critical of the Bland case which she classified as one of 'involuntary euthanasia', and she urged an awareness of the social significance of feeding patients as 'an expression of solidarity with the person who is being fed ... of showing that the patient is valued ... (as) a fellow human being'.[72]

---

[69] The view that ethical thinking is something basic and distinctive about human beings is stressed by Kelly 1999: 178.

[70] Keown, J. 1999; Watt 2000: Ch.2; Kelly 1999: Ch. 13.   [71] Keown 1999: 239–240, 245–260.

[72] Watt 2000: 38, 40–41 also considers several cases of voluntary and involuntary euthanasis; see also Robinson 2003: 34–36.

However, Kelly[73] rejected 'the position and argumentation of the Linacre Centre' in the case of Tony Bland and insisted that in the field of medical ethics, moral theologians 'have refused to view life as an absolute value'. Normally in the case of a life-threatening condition, medical treatment was an obligation when two conditions were met: '(1) the treatment brings real benefit to the patient; and (2) the treatment is not disproportionately burdensome'. He pointed out that for patients in this condition only '*ordinary*' treatment was obligatory while '*extraordinary*' treatment was optional. Medical intervention should be considered in 'the best interests of the patient as a human person'. An important distinction was that between 'letting die' and 'killing'. Kelly insisted emphatically that the argument 'that intravenous nutrition and hydration should never be withdrawn since it would be withdrawing ordinary human care . . . is certainly not in line with the tradition of moral theology' he had outlined. The *Catechism* rejected direct euthanasia but also 'over-zealous' treatment. Kelly argued with others that persistent vegetative state, such as that of Tony Bland, 'constitutes a fatal pathology'. In such circumstances: 'withholding artificial hydration and nutrition from a patient in an irreversible coma does not induce a new fatal pathology; rather it allows an already existing fatal pathology to take its natural course'.

It was because of the shift from 'sanctity of life' to 'quality of life' arguments that campaigning organizations, such as SPUC, now draw attention not only to abortion issues, but also to the evidence of 'creeping euthanasia' in our society. In view of the growing tolerance in our society for such medical practices, there must also be some concern that the traditional medical ethic of healing might have become corrupted. Having said this, Kelly's rather different judgements also have warrant in the tradition of medical ethics in the Church. Such differences of judgement among moral theologians point to the complexity of the issues and to the need for Christians to take responsibility for their own decisions in awareness of the authoritative teaching of the Church.

Gene therapy and human genetic engineering

Finally, we will consider Catholic responses to the acceleration of developments since the Abortion Act in 1967, in particular in gene therapy and human genetic engineering. The first IVF or 'test-tube' baby was born in 1978. In 1984 the Committee of Inquiry into Human Fertilization and

[73] Kelly 1999: 189–198.

Embryology published its report (the Warnock Report) and in 1990 the Human Fertilization and Embryology Act was passed.[74] Scarisbrick[75] reported that between 1991 and 1994, 300,000 human beings were generated in IVF clinics. Only 7,000 were born alive. 'Most of the rest were either immediately thrown away or died in the womb; 25,000 more were killed in laboratory experimentation ... Thousands more "orphaned" or abandoned embryos have been "culled" regularly since August 1996'.

In 1997 'Dolly', the first cloned sheep was born and there were unconfirmed reports of the first human clone in 2003. The Human Genome project which aimed to 'identify all the approximately 30,000 genes in human DNA' was begun in 1990 and in the USA 'an important feature of this project is the federal government's long-standing dedication to the *transfer of technology to the private sector*'.[76] Scarisbrick feared that the commercialization of genetic engineering and the likely claims of intellectual property rights raised important issues of public accountability and social justice because of the dangers of the 'power to control and manipulate human life'. The economic consequences of developments in biotechnology in the EU were estimated to be worth over 100 billion euros by 2005.[77] Countries of the EU differed somewhat in the extent to which they are prepared to allow research on embryonic stem cells on ethical grounds.

Scarisbrick believed that 'IVF laboratories and deep-freezers have trivialised human life and sexuality' and he is highly critical of the 'impersonal, technical procedures' such as resulted in Diane Blood being inseminated by sperm taken from her dead husband. He argued that children are not prize products or memorials to dead husbands.[78] He pointed out that IVF has a failure rate of about 85 per cent. The fact that many embryos are destroyed in connection with IVF is a key moral objection to the procedure. As we noted above, the official Catholic view is that human life begins at conception. Thereafter development is gradual and continuous. Sutton[79] concluded: 'in short, the Church asks us to treat the human

---

[74] The difficulties of reaching an appropriate Christian response on the morality of such issues as were considered in the Human Fertilization and Embryology Bill were dramatically exposed when the five Roman Catholic Archbishops of England and Wales expressed a totally different viewpoint to that of Lord Habgood, the Archbishop of York, on adjacent pages of *The Times*, 23 April, 1990. The issue is discussed at length in Kelly 1992: 8–26.

[75] Scarisbrick 1999: 301.

[76] http://www.ornl.gov/TechResources/Human_Genome/home.html for information on the Human Genome Project.

[77] Schauer, K. 2003. 'Life Sciences and Biotechnology', *Euro Infos* 45, January: 4. See also her articles in 35, February 2002, 42 October 2002, 45 January 2003, 49 May 2003.

[78] Scarisbrick 1999: 308, 310. I have a great deal more sympathy with Diane Blood than Scarisbrick has.

[79] Sutton 2003: 21, 32–34, 37, 42–43.

embryo as a child, as a member of the human family, as a neighbour in the image of God and as a divine gift'.

Secondly, Sutton regarded IVF as one of a range of treatments for infertility that by-passed sexual intercourse. The Church's opposition to such treatments was based on its view that procreation was properly the fruit of a sexual union of mutual giving in marriage and not the outcome of barter or the intervention or intrusion of a third party, the donor.[80] This constituted 'the depersonalisation of procreation and the commodification of the child'. For the same reasons the Vatican authorities opposed surrogacy 'as a form of baby trade' with the surrogate treated as 'not much more than a hired prenatal incubator'.

The science of human genetics is advancing at an incredibly rapid rate and is posing challenges which demand urgent attention, proper social and theological analysis, and appropriate action in seeking Kingdom values.[81] In a useful introduction to gene therapy Helen Watts pointed out that diagnosis could lead either to treatment, including gene therapy which aimed to replace an abnormal by a normal gene, or lethal forms of discrimination such as induced abortion, where an unborn child was found to have an abnormal gene.[82] Two main types of gene therapy were distinguished: somatic, aimed at affecting an individual only, and germ-line, aiming to affect future generations as well. 'Germ-line therapy would probably be carried out in connection with *in vitro* fertilization ... (and) could involve cloning'.

'Cloning involves the creation of a twin or copy of an individual by replacing the nucleus of an unfertilized ovum with the nucleus of a cell from that individual. The ovum is then stimulated to create an embryo. No sperm is involved and the person created would have no genetic father'. Both Watt and McCarthy stressed that the often-used distinction between 'reproductive' and 'therapeutic' cloning was euphemistic and inaccurate.[83] Both forms were reproductive when an embryo was created, even if it was then destroyed. 'Cloning for research' was seen as a potential source of stem cells which could then be used to repair damaged human organs and for transplantation. Watt argued that 'if it ever became a safe and feasible procedure ... (cloning) would be a form of manufacturing children

---

[80] It seems that not all moral theologians would want to give 'absolute' value to the reasons put forward but would wish to take into account a couple's wish to use the benefits of modern medicine to conceive a child as an expression of their love. See Kelly 1987.

[81] The Pontifical Academy for Life has published a *Declaration on the Production and the Scientific and Therapeutic Use of Human Embryonic Stem Cells*, 2000, CTS (Do 667)

[82] Watt 2001b: 4, 9, 10, 15–18, 35.   [83] Watt 2001b: 16–17; McCarthy 2003: 12.

involving their quality control'. She objected to the attempt to limit the freedom of the child to develop independently from their parents and failure to respect their distinctive identity. McCarthy similarly rejected attempts at 'eugenic selection' grounded in the arbitrariness of the desires of those in power.[84] A more proper response to infertility was the adoption of orphaned or unwanted children.

In sum, there are three main concerns of Catholic moral theology to the new developments of fertility treatments and genetic engineering:

- It is concerned at the use of human embryos and their destruction in huge numbers in research and experimentation. This is based on the fundamental belief, which as we have seen is contested, that the human being exists as a distinct individual from the moment of conception.[85]
- The dignity and respect due to each individual human being is disregarded whenever human beings, for example embryos, are treated as means to achieve some utilitarian purpose, or where their rights are determined by some arbitrary judgement of quality or worth.
- Procreation should properly be confined to a married couple and seen as the fruit of the mutual love of a man and a woman in a relationship which embraces the parenting of any children conceived through their sexual intercourse. (Some moral theologians might wish to qualify this)

It would seem safe to admit with humility that we do not know all the answers and that there is a continuing need for dialogue between theologians and biological scientists and medical specialists.

CONCLUDING REFLECTIONS

A number of commentators have expressed unease at the state of Catholic social thought in the areas of marriage and family life, human sexuality, divorce and remarriage, on the one hand, and developments in the life sciences, on the other. On the former, there is a need to take much more obvious account of the lived experiences of people and the changing social context of family life today, and on the latter for much more dialogue between theologians, philosophers and biological scientists, especially over the issue of the start of human existence and the relationship between the human 'individual' and the human 'person'. In this spirit attention has

---

[84] McCarthy 2003: 53–55.

[85] Some argue that there is a distinction between a human individual and a human person. This is not the standard Catholic position which considers that a human person exists from the moment of conception. But perhaps this is an area where there is scope for much more dialogue between biological scientists, philosophers and theologians.

been drawn to the fact that there are disagreements among moral theologians and biological scientists over the origin of human life.

It has not been possible in this chapter to do justice to the complexity of the ethical challenges arising from new advances in the biological sciences and genetic engineering. The second half of this chapter endeavoured to indicate the broad outlines of a Catholic approach. This takes as axiomatic that in seeking appropriate Christian responses to such issues as the nature of the human person and the beginning and end of life there is no essential conflict between the new discoveries and understandings of science and the revealed truths of Christian faith. Hence it has been suggested that in seeking appropriate moral responses to these new challenges, moral theologians and those seeking to further the values of the kingdom of God, should be engaging in a conversation or continuous dialogue with science, the Church's magisterium, and all other people and sources with relevant contributions to make to our interpretation and understanding. Since much of the Church's 'moral teaching consists of truths which are in principle available to rational inquiry, understanding and judgement', in consequence it 'can properly inform participation in public policy debates in which one aims to secure agreement on the basis of reason rather than on the basis of an authority, the warrant for which is accepted in faith'.[86]

Not that this process guarantees unanimity. We live in a 'fallen world' where evil and sin are ubiquitous. People and corporations have their own agendas and self-interests. What this chapter has endeavoured to show is that the underlying principles of a Catholic approach revolve around the equal dignity of every human being in the sight of God and the need to serve the common good. For these reasons, there is a concern to promote, in collaboration with people of good will, what Pope John Paul II called 'the culture of life' as opposed to what he has labelled 'the culture of death'.[87]

Some, such as Howard-Brook,[88] complain that the Church's official concept of the family is unrealistically 'cosy', while others, such as Winter,[89] complain about 'misguided morality'. Absolutist condemnations, for example of contraception, divorce, homosexuality, or IVF, no longer attract 'authority', in the sociological sense, that is they do not attract a convinced acceptance because they do not always make sense of the social realities experienced in people's everyday lives. In spite of the protestations of the Church leadership that it wishes to dialogue with the

[86] Gormally 1999: 1.   [87] *Evangelium Vitae* 1995.   [88] Howard-Brook 2001: 72–102.
[89] Winter 2002.

world, there is almost invariably no evidence of this in Church documents. This may be because of a clash of epistemologies and the tendency of Church leaders to rely on deductive, top-down approaches, from natural law thinking (as interpreted properly only by the leadership), in contrast to the inductive, experience-based, bottom-up approaches favoured in this book and by liberation theologians.

Given the burgeoning discoveries and advances in the biological sciences, it is important that the Church leadership does not involve itself in a new Galilean situation, unable or unwilling to adapt to God's infinite creativity by responding with wonder, reinterpreting God's call to seek the kingdom of God in new ways and new situations, rather than by relying on blanket condemnations based on understandings of nature which may no longer be adequate. When the Church engages in critical dialogue with these new forms of knowledge in the light of scripture and revelation, new interpretations may result in a deepening or development of doctrine while remaining faithful to the spirit of Jesus' teaching in the totally new circumstances of the third millennium.

In such situations of rapid change, the general approach of moral theologians such as Kevin Kelly who advocates a 'continuing conversation' with science but also *within the Church itself*, as well as with other Christians and other faiths[90] has much to commend it. The key criterion in our moral judgements, from *Gaudium et Spes*, must be the dignity and good of the human person, 'integrally and adequately considered'. Only in this way will the kingdom of God be brought closer to realization. It is hoped that this chapter will contribute in some way to the continuing conversation which Kelly advocates and to the development of a more satisfactory theology of marriage and family life.

[90]   Kelly 1998: 28–60, 96–99.

CHAPTER 8

Economic life

THE SALIENCE OF ECONOMIC ISSUES

In the modern world economic life has become more and more complex. Although great strides have been taken in recent decades in the understanding of the workings of markets and their regulation to ensure that major economic collapses do not occur and that rough equilibrium between supply and demand is maintained, large scale unemployment, usually concentrated among specific subgroups of the population, is still a problem which occurs periodically. This raises such issues as the right to work, in the sense of paid employment, and appropriate social provision for the unemployed.

Some would argue that the capitalist economic system, which is the dominant economic system throughout the world today, is intrinsically unjust and that it treats labour as simply a factor of production to be used or discarded according to the dictates of the market. The power of decision-making is highly asymmetric and reflects the gross inequalities of income and wealth which are to be found both within our own societies and also between developed and developing nations. In Britain, a large majority of the population 'own' their own homes but the ownership of equities is much more skewed and wealth and income disparities have increased significantly in recent years. In our complex world, what does the right to private property mean and what might be its limits? A tiny handful of people in the world between them own immense wealth, and therefore have power of decision-making, which is greater than that of many nation states.

There are also injustices arising out of the nature of authority relations in one's place of employment. There can be major variations in the nature of the employment relationship between owners of capital, managers of enterprises, and other employees. Sometimes workers are little more than 'wage slaves' with little in the way of respect or rights to have any say in the way their skills are employed. Since the early days of the industrial revolution workers have joined together in trade unions to bargain with employers about all aspects of the employment relation, including authority relations, participation in decision-making, and wages.

In 1859 Karl Marx claimed that 'the mode of production in material life determines the general character of the social, political and spiritual processes of life. It is not the consciousness of men that determines their existence, but, on the contrary, their social existence determines their consciousness'.[1] Furthermore, the dominant ideas reflect the material interests of the dominant social classes.[2] While Max Weber in 1904–5 suggested that spiritual beliefs could provide an alternative explanation for the emergence of the 'spirit of capitalism',[3] the overriding importance of economic factors, such as the state of the economy, the levels of employment, the distribution of rewards and costs, and so on, in people's everyday lives can hardly be disputed. All societies have to deal with the production, distribution and consumption of goods and services.[4]

It is not surprising, therefore, that when Abraham Maslow formulated his 'hierarchy of needs',[5] he suggested that primacy was given to survival and security needs before seeking social satisfaction and self-actualization. There is strong evidence that unless existence needs are satisfied, people will not be concerned with higher-order needs. The first concerns of all living animals are for survival and security, that is, how to provide sufficient food by production or through exchange or conquest, or by participation in the labour market, to feed oneself and any dependants, and how to ensure adequate shelter from environmental forces.

Among the many issues in the economic sphere which have given rise to serious concern in recent years are the following:

- *Unemployment*: Access to paid work and employment has been a major concern in recent years and the spectre of unemployment fills many workers and families with fear. Quite apart from the cyclical nature of economic life with successive phases of innovation, expansion, consolidation, overproduction and obsolescence, there has been in all industrial societies a major shift from manufacturing into service sector employment. At the same time there has been an increasing demand for women workers and less demand for male manual workers. During the years of

---

[1] Marx, K. 1859. 'Preface to a Contribution to the Critique of Political Economy' in Bottomore and Rubel (eds.) 1963: 67.
[2] Marx, K. 1845–46. 'The German Ideology' in Bottomore and Rubel 1963: 93.   [3] Weber 1930: 183.
[4] A useful overview of the issues considered in this chapter is to be found in Macionis and Plummer 2002: 346–375.
[5] Maslow, A. K. 1954. *Motivation and Personality*. New York: Harper and Row.

transition, formerly prosperous urban areas have experienced massive decline and high levels of unemployment, typically concentrated in vulnerable groups, especially the young and ethnic minorities.[6]

- *Protection*: The protection of worker rights to just wages and pensions would seem to be essential if human dignity is to be maintained. The vulnerability of workers' pensions in bankrupt firms, as a result of the misappropriation of funds, the collapse of the stock market, or from other contingencies, may result in injustices. As a result of recent failures, some workers face the prospect of having to work until they die. Appropriate safeguards of workers' rights are necessary in the interests of the common good.

- *Demographic change*: The implications of birth rates in Europe which are below replacement levels and the increasing longevity of people in societies with well-developed health and welfare systems has resulted in a rapid ageing of the population.[7] Shortages of labour are likely to be met by migrant labour with its injections of skills, innovation and cultural diversity. But this response also brings with it the dangers of xenophobia, racism and ethnic conflict. Individual workers are beginning to face the prospect of longer working lives and reduced pensions as state policies adjust to the financial implications of the changing demographic circumstances.

- *The changing nature of work*: As a result of the accelerating pace of technological change in recent decades, the notion of a life-time's 'career' seems to have become obsolete. There has been a commodification of labour and a relentless speeding-up of the labour process which have led to a decline in the levels of confidence and trust relations between employers and employees. Increasing insecurity has been reflected in increasing levels of stress.

- *Increasing inequalities*: The widening gap in incomes and wealth between the rich and the poor is increasingly a matter of public concern for social cohesion. Huge inequalities of rewards are widely regarded as obscene[8] and illegitimate as are the severance packages for failed 'fat cat' chief executives.

---

[6] In 2001 the unemployment rate in the 15 countries of the EU was 7.8 per cent, and in the USA 4.3 per cent. Eurostat 2001; quoted in Macionis and Plummer 2002: 364.

[7] The old-age dependency ratio is expected to increase from 29 to 37 elderly people per 100 people aged 18–64 over the next 50 years. Macionis and Plummer 2002: 328.

[8] See, e.g., the analysis of the basic pay, cash bonuses, pensions and other benefits of directors of the FTSE-100 index of top companies which reported a 23 per cent rise in 2002 while average earnings rose by only 3 per cent; *The Guardian*, International Edition, 31 July 2003.

- *Private rights and common good*: The proper balance between the rights of private property and the common good is always a matter of contestation. Not only is there a need to address extreme inequalities of access to private property, but there is also a need to distinguish between the private property of individuals and the corporate property of immensely powerful economic institutions, such as transnational corporations and financial institutions.
- *The power of corporate capital*: There is increasing alarm at the power of corporate capital to control every aspect of social life and behaviour from transport systems, to schools and health and welfare systems, and from retailing to leisure. The global reach of corporate capital has spawned a grass-roots anti-capitalist movement.[9]
- *Effective regulation*: There is a need for the immense power of corporate capital to be effectively regulated in the interests of the common good. Recent revelations about corruption, fraud, irresponsibility, exploitation and extortion on the part of some of the largest corporations, such as Enron and WorldCom, have drawn attention to failures in the systems of regulation and to the need for more effective mechanisms for achieving executive accountability.
- *Trade unions*: The rights of workers to combine in trade unions in defence of their interests have been constrained in recent years and the proportion of workers in unions has declined rapidly.[10] Part-time and home workers, women, and those working in the service sector, especially those from ethnic minorities, asylum seekers and refugees, are often particularly vulnerable to exploitation at the hands of employers.
- *International institutions*: The failure of international institutions to safeguard the rights of poor countries is a concern of development agencies and human rights organizations. In the relentless drive to cut costs, exploitative forms of child labour are often tolerated by major transnational corporations.[11]
- *Just wages and fair prices*: In liberal capitalist economies, prices are largely determined by the market, though both prices and wages can be manipulated where there are concentrations of economic power. The

---

[9] See, e.g., Hertz 2001; Klein 2000, 2002; Montbiot 2000, 2003.

[10] In the UK in 1979 around 55 per cent of the labour force was in trade unions; by the mid-1990s this had fallen to 35 per cent. In the USA, union membership for non-farm workers declined from 25 million in the 1970s to 18 million. Macionis and Plummer 2002: 363.

[11] It is estimated that there are some 400 million working children, especially in Asia and Africa. Macionis and Plummer 2002: 323.

relative rights of farmers, workers, consumers and business enterprises
are in tension and not easy to reconcile.

Catholic approaches to these various issues will be considered over the next
three chapters. This present chapter will note some of the key characteristics of different economic systems and review traditional Catholic criticisms of both unbridled capitalism and totalitarian socialism. It will review
some of the main elements of Catholic social thought as it has developed
since Pope Leo XIII's encyclical on the condition of labour in 1891. It will
show how the focus of this thought has changed in response to historical
contingencies. It will also draw attention to the criticisms of liberal capitalism which have been made, in particular since the collapse of Communist
hegemony and state socialism in Central and Eastern Europe in 1989.

VARIATIONS IN ECONOMIC SYSTEMS

In the eighteenth century, Adam Smith thought that there was an 'invisible
hand' guiding the economy. More recently, Margaret Thatcher, among
others, used to say that you could not 'buck the market'. In other words, in
the last analysis prices of goods and services were determined by the balance
between supply and demand. Common experience indicates that this is far
too simplistic. For one thing, there are market imperfections, such as
inadequate information, and powerful institutions, such as cartels, which
can manipulate the market. Furthermore there are many different forms of
economic system ranging from capitalism – with the private ownership of
property, the pursuit of personal profit, and free competition, consumer
sovereignty and markets – to socialism – with the collective ownership of
property, the pursuit of collective goals, and government control of the
economy.[12]

There are also many different variations of capitalism, ranging from
extreme forms of neo-liberal capitalism which currently hold sway in the
USA to the social market economy of western European countries in recent
years (see Table 2.1). Different liberal democracies have also experimented
with a wide range of welfare state provisions for social security. Will
Hutton has distinguished four different institutional and cultural models
of capitalism: the United States model, social market Europe, East Asian
'Peoplism', and the British model. He analyzed their differences in terms of
their basic organizing principles, the nature of their financial systems,
variations in labour markets, organization of the firm, welfare systems

---

[12] Macionis and Plummer 2002: 354–357.

and government policies. Each system was historically contingent on differences of industrial culture and value system and the historical timing of key events such as the onset of industrialization and the major 'social settlement' between capital and labour.[13]

Michael Novak has offered a robust proclamation of the claimed superiority and virtues of 'democratic capitalism' in his various writings.[14] Francis Fukuyama went further and argued that the collapse of Soviet Communism presaged the inevitable triumph of liberal democracy. Free-market capitalism might be regarded as its economic manifestation.[15] This view is implicitly ethnocentric and it neglects the subtly different forms of economic system to be found in Hindu, Chinese and Islamic societies. Industrial structures and the organization of work are quite different in Japan compared to Anglo-Saxon countries.[16] Samuel Huntington has suggested that Fukuyama's one harmonious world paradigm is 'clearly far too divorced from reality' to fit the realities of the post-Cold War period.[17] Even so, one can hardly deny the hegemony of liberal capitalism in the contemporary world.

Pope John Paul II was cautious in his evaluation of capitalism and the search for an appropriate economic system because 'the answer is obviously complex'. In *Centesimus Annus* he wrote that:

If by *capitalism* is meant an economic system which recognises the fundamental and positive role of business, the market, private property and the resulting responsibility for the means of production, as well as free human creativity in the economic sector, then the answer is certainly in the affirmative ... But if by capitalism is meant a system in which freedom in the economic sector is not circumscribed within a strong juridical framework which places it at the service of human freedom in its totality, and which sees it as a particular aspect of that freedom, the core of which is ethical and religious, then the reply is certainly negative. (§42)

No economic system is perfect and different economic systems have different strengths and weaknesses. Broadly speaking, capitalist economies produce higher growth rates and overall standards of living and also foster formal civil liberties and political freedom but they also generate greater income and wealth inequalities.[18] What can safely be concluded is that the search for a social and economic system that ensures both political liberty

---

[13] Hutton 1996: 257–284.   [14] Novak 1991.   [15] Fukuyama 1992: 44.   [16] E.g. Dore 2000.
[17] Huntington 1998: 32. The 'clash of civilizations' thesis itself grossly exaggerates the uniformity within Islam as well as Christianity and is, in consequence, dangerously misleading.
[18] Macionis and Plummer 2002: 357.

and a reasonable measure of economic equality consistent with the common good is an ongoing challenge to the Christian conscience.

DEVELOPMENTS IN CATHOLIC THOUGHT

In its response to such challenges, the Catholic Church has, over the centuries, developed its analyses and thinking in response to the pressing issues and understandings of the times.[19] As we noted earlier, it was only in recent centuries that the Church condemned the social system of slavery as incompatible with the dignity of each individual human being. The Church has since the times of the Fathers in the fourth century condemned usury, the payment of interest on loans 'where the borrower was a poor man seeking for the means to live and the lender was a rich man who had the necessary resources to help if he would'.[20] However, with the development of money markets, interest on loans for business purposes were increasingly accepted from the Middle Ages onwards. In 1891 Pope Leo XIII angrily condemned 'rapacious usury' (*RN* §2). The problem of debt continues to harm both individuals, through the operation of 'loan sharks', and developing nations, as a result of injudicious bank loans and wild increases in interest rates. A deep-rooted suspicion of socialism from the nineteenth century inhibited the development of a measured response to the emergence of welfare state policies.[21] It was only in the post-war years that a more discriminating acceptance of the role of the welfare state in promoting the common good emerged. A considered response to the problems of development and economic relationships between nations has only come to the fore in the past forty years or so. Issues such as global warming, environmental issues and intellectual property rights are only just coming onto the agenda. As has always been the case, the Church's social teaching continues to develop in response to changing times and challenges.

Contemporary Catholic social thought has traditionally been dated from the publication in 1891 of Pope Leo XIII's encyclical letter *Rerum Novarum* on the condition of labour. Over the succeeding century this official teaching has been developed in response to changing social

---

[19] A summary of current teaching on 'Human Work' is given in the *Compendium* (§§255–322). The section on 'Social Doctrine and the "New Things"' (§§317–322) is particularly insightful. The following chapter (§§323–376) is entitled 'Economic Life'. See also the *Catechism of the Catholic Church* in the section dealing with the seventh commandment (§§2401–2463). A major theme is the universal destination and private ownership of goods.

[20] Charles 1998a: 95, 203, 368.   [21] Coman 1977; Whyte 1981.

circumstances, such as the long struggle between capitalism and communism and the current liberal capitalist hegemony; the two world wars and the subsequent ending of the colonial period; the evidence of unequal development; and rapidly accelerating forms of globalization resulting from technological advances in ICT. It would not be an exaggeration to suggest that in recent decades there has been a noticeable shift from the advocacy of individual charity to those in need (e.g. the 2004 tsunami) to the analysis of the root causes of injustice in order to devise appropriate social responses (e.g. the Make Poverty History campaign). In this section we will briefly trace developments in Catholic social thought on economic life on the basis of nine major documents published in the century from Leo XIII's *Rerum Novarum* to John Paul II's celebration of its centenary, *Centesimus Annus*, in 1991 and two documents published by the Bishops of England and Wales in 1996 and 2004 (see Table 8.1).

Rerum Novarum (Leo XIII 1891)

This encyclical, published forty-three years after Marx and Engels proclaimed the 'Communist Manifesto', attempted to address the condition of the working classes created by the social, technological and economic changes of the Industrial Revolution in Western Europe in the nineteenth century. It is also important to note that in its responses to the political strivings represented by the French Revolution, the Church sought the restoration of the organic unity of society and the old and familiar hierarchical structures of the *ancien regime* and of its own authority and a proper subservience on the part of the State.[22] This fuelled widespread anticlericalism which led to the loss of the Papal States in Italy in 1870.

A key focus of the encyclical was its defence of private property which Leo saw as a natural and reasonable element of proper remuneration for labour, to be protected under the tenth commandment (§8). For this reason he considered that 'the main tenet of socialism, the community of goods, must be utterly rejected' (§12). All the same, he insisted, following Thomas Aquinas, that there was a duty to use and share one's blessings for the benefit of all (§19). He affirmed the dignity of labour and the common brotherhood of all 'children of the common Father' (§21). He considered the Church powerfully restrained 'the lust of possession and the lust of pleasure'(§23) and urged voluntary and self-sacrificing Christian charity

---

[22] See the helpful introduction to the classic texts of Leo XIII and Pius XI in O'Brien and Shannon 1992: 9–13. See also Burns 1994, Charles 1998b, Furlong and Curtis 1994, Misner 1991, Pope 1994.

Table 8.1. *Major church documents on economic life, 1891–1996*

Year	Author[a]	Document	Key themes	Reference[b]
1891	Leo XIII	*Rerum Novarum*	Private ownership; worker dignity	OBS, 14–39
1931	Pius XI	*Quadragesimo Anno*	Reforming capitalism; subsidiarity	OBS, 42–79
1961	John XXIII	*Mater et Magistra*	Role of state; criteria for just distribution	OBS, 84–128
1965	Vat. II	*Gaudium et Spes*	Right of migration; worker participation	OBS, 195–201
1971	Paul VI	*Octogesima Adveniens*	Urbanization and industrialization	OBS, 265–286
1981	John Paul II	*Laborem Exercens*	Human work; capital and labour	OBS, 352–392
1986	US Bishops	*Economic Justice*	Responsible capitalism; process	OBS, 572–680
1987	John Paul II	*Sollicitudo Rei Socialis*	Private property as social mortgage	OBS, 393–436
1991	John Paul II	*Centesimus Annus*	New forms of property; consumerism	OBS, 437–488
1996	CBCEW	*The Common Good*	Structural injustices; social capital	Gabriel
2004	CBCEW	*Taxation*	The state, taxation, public services	Colloquium

Notes:
[a] CELAM: General Conference of Latin American Bishops; CDF: Congregation for the Doctrine of the Faith; CBCEW: Catholic Bishops' Conference of England and Wales.
[b] OBS: O'Brien and Shannon, 1992.

rather than State-organized relief for the support of the needy (§24). The task of the State was to serve the common good while avoiding 'undue interference' and to provide a legal framework of limits to the conditions of employment of men, women and children (§§25–29, 33). He insisted that 'when there is a question of protecting the rights of individuals, the poor and helpless have a claim to special consideration (§29)'. In calling for just wages he insisted 'that each one has a right to procure what is required in order to live; and the poor can procure it in no other way than by work and wages ... remuneration must be enough to support the wage earner in reasonable and frugal comfort' (§34). With a nostalgic memory of workers' guilds, he strongly supported the natural rights of workers to associate for mutual support (§§36–38). In sum, there was in this encyclical an early attempt to articulate the six key principles of Catholic social thought.

From our present perspectives the encyclical is limited in a number of ways. Although it aimed to address the plight of the industrial working class, it referred back inappropriately and nostalgically to an obsolete rural past (§§7–8). Its strong condemnation of socialism was undiscriminating and failed to distinguish social democratic from totalitarian forms. Leo's analysis was overly concerned with injustices perpetrated by individuals (§§15–17) and failed to present an adequate analysis of the *social structural* causes of injustice, exploitation, poverty and need and of huge inequalities in power available to workers in their struggles with employers. One consequence was the interpretation of industrial conflict as the fault of individuals to be resolved by seeking harmony and a return to an acceptance of natural inequalities and 'tranquil resignation' (§20). There was also an inadequate awareness of the role of the democratic welfare state in promoting the common good and ameliorating injustices and excessive inequalities. His notion of the family was emphatically patriarchal as far as authority was concerned and gendered in terms of what he regarded as a natural division of labour (§§9–10). He considered the fertility of the earth to be 'inexhaustible' and did not anticipate subsequent environmental concerns (§6).

Quadragesimo Anno (Pius XI 1931)

Forty years later Pius XI wrote *Quadragesimo Anno* on the need to reconstruct the social order and bring it into conformity with the Gospel precepts. In those forty years the world had changed. The First World War, economic depression and the rise of fascism and communism had shattered liberal confidence and the Church struggled to find an appropriate alternative which would reconcile bitter conflicts and seek social justice, human rights, the common good and human solidarity.[23]

Pius XI began his encyclical by suggesting a number of benefits which could be said to have flowed from *Rerum Novarum*: the development of Catholic social teaching (§20); new laws governing conditions of employment (§28); the growth of trade unions and other forms of associations (§§29–38). The pope next claimed authority to address social and economic problems, not on technical matters, but where they 'have a bearing on moral conduct' (§41). He rehearsed the rights of each individual to private property and recognized both the individual and social dimensions of property, and the obligations implicit in ownership, taking into account the common good (§§44–52). Secondly, the pope condemned the unjust claims of both capital and labour and sought a just distribution of rewards which would minister to the needs of all and promote the common good of all (§§53–57). He concluded somewhat unspecifically that 'each class . . . must receive its due share' and he condemned 'the vast differences between the few who hold excessive wealth and the many who live in destitution' (§58). Thirdly, he showed an interesting early recognition of the 'dispossessed labouring masses' in colonial territories (§59) and pleaded again for a more equitable distribution of the fruits of industrialism (§§60–61). This led, fourthly, to an extended discussion of the just wage (§§63–75) which 'should be sufficient for the support of himself (the workingman) and of his family' (§71).[24] Fifthly, the pope considered the reconstruction of the social order, largely in terms of revitalized associations and the search for social harmony between social classes. In the course of his consideration of the reform of social institutions, he enunciated the principle of subsidiarity that:

One should not withdraw from individuals and commit to the community what they can accomplish by their own enterprise and industry. So, too, it is an injustice and at the same time a grave evil and a disturbance of right order to transfer to the larger and higher collectivity functions which can be performed and provided for by lesser and subordinate bodies. (§79)

This had relevance for the debates about the welfare state and public social policies and, more recently, the relationships between the member nations

---

[23] O'Brien and Shannon 1992: 40–41.

[24] Pius XI went on to suggest that 'mothers should especially devote their energies to the home and the things connected with it'. The gender bias in Catholic social thought was discussed in Ch. 7.

of the EU. The pope continued to suggest the importance of functional groups and associations in the pursuit of social harmony and the common good (§§81–87). He then offered a trenchant criticism of the errors of an excessive individualism. Social unity cannot be built either on class conflict or the 'headstrong and vehement power' of 'rugged competition' which, 'if it is to prove beneficial to mankind, needs to be curbed strongly and ruled with prudence'. What was needed was social justice and social charity (§88). The pope proceeded to make an early plea for 'a healthy economic cooperation by prudent pacts and institutions' between nations (§89). He continued to suggest some advantages in forms of syndicalism and corporatism while also noting some fears of their 'excessively bureaucratic and political character' (§§90–95).

In the final section of the encyclical, the pope reflected on some significant changes in both capitalism and socialism since Leo XIII. He noted that while capitalism 'is not vicious of its very nature ... it violates right order whenever capital so employs the working or wage-earning classes as to divert business and economic activity entirely to its own arbitrary will and advantage without any regard to the human dignity of the workers, the social character of economic life, social justice, and the common good' (§101). He complained that 'immense power and despotic economic domination is concentrated in the hands of a few' who 'hold and control money' and 'govern credit and determine its allotment' (§§105–106). 'This accumulation of power ... is a natural result of unrestrained free competition which permits the survival of those only who are the strongest' (§107). The State became the slave of economic powers rather than the 'supreme arbiter ... intent only upon justice and the common good'(§109). The dangers of both individualism and collectivism were to be avoided and free competition and economic domination must be brought under effective public control in the interests of the common good and the norms of social justice (§110).

The pope distinguished between the more violent form of Communism and a 'mitigated socialism' which retreated from class hatred and showed a concern for justice and the reform of human society similar to Christian principles (§§111–114). But, in the end, Pius XI unconvincingly judged that they could not be reconciled since socialism 'conceives human society in a way utterly alien to Christian truth' (§117). Christian socialism was 'a contradiction in terms' (§120) and he urged efforts 'to reform society ... on a firm basis of social justice and social charity' (§§123–126).

In their consideration of Roman Catholic social teaching in the century following *Rerum Novarum*, O'Brien and Shannon judged that the encyclicals of Leo XIII and Pius XI were too rigid in their theology, too rooted in preindustrial ... ideologies to be directly useful ... (They) were filled with charity and passion for justice, but these qualities were smothered by triumphalist ecclesiology, antidemocratic political values, and a conservative, even negative understanding of natural law. The modern documents (from John XXIII and Vatican II), in contrast, communicate a vision of the Church as servant to humanity, a renewed concern for the human person and human rights, an increasing emphasis on popular participation, and a more open and humble acknowledgement of the historically conditioned character of human life and consciousness ... (Though still) somewhat European-centered (they increasingly) reflect the ideas and perspectives of the emerging Christian communities of the Third World.[25]

Mater et Magistra (John XXIII 1961)

Another thirty years were to pass before John XXIII wrote his encyclical *Mater et Magistra*. In the meantime the Second World War had shattered the world and the dismantling of European colonial empires was well under way. Influential analyses of Christian humanists, such as Jacques Maritain,[26] had been put largely into practice in the early post-war years by Christian Democrat parties. Catholic anti-Communism suited the climate in Western Europe in the Cold War era.[27] John's pontificate represented a turning point in the development of Catholic social thought and in his greater openness to the world. O'Brien and Shannon suggest that he largely accepted the assumptions of the time: 'an acceptance of the Western economic order, a reformist attitude to the status quo, and a wider role for the state'.

In *Mater et Magistra* John provided a lengthy review of both *Rerum Novarum* and *Quadragesimo Anno* and also of a number of wartime contributions of Pius XII. He noted new technological advances in atomic energy, synthetic chemical products, automation, radio and television, transport and space exploration. He confirmed the general teaching that private property was a natural by-product of just wages and wise saving but noted with alarm increasing inequalities between industrial sectors, regions and nations (§§46–49). To address this required the active intervention of the public authorities, bearing in mind the increasing complexity of social

[25] O'Brien and Shannon 1992: 1.
[26] E.g. Maritain 1947, 1951, 1968. For critical reviews of Maritain's thought, see Evans and Ward 1956, Stiltner 1999, Watkins and McInerny 1995.
[27] O'Brien and Shannon 1992: 81–82.

structures and the principle of subsidiarity, in the interests of the common good and social harmony (§§51–58). He accepted the greater intervention of the state in education and health, and on behalf of disadvantaged groups, provided there were appropriate safeguards such as lively intermediate associations (§§59–65). The freedom of individual citizens and the proper regulatory function of the state had to be kept in balance (§66).

He reiterated the need to pay workers a just wage 'sufficient . . . to fulfil family responsibilities properly' but allowed that a number of factors needed to be taken into account: 'First of all, the contribution of individuals to the economic effort; the economic state of the enterprises within which they work; the requirements of each community, especially as regards overall employment; finally, what concerns the common good of all peoples, namely, of the various States associated among themselves, but differing in character and extent' (§71). It is clear from this that the calculus of what exactly is a just wage is not far advanced and there still remains a great deal of scope for disagreement between the different parties.

Considering the common good at the national level, John XXIII noted the relevance of a number of factors including maximizing employment, avoiding the generation of privileged groups, balancing wages and prices, reducing inequalities, ensuring proper provision of public services, adjusting to technological changes and ensuring that their advantages were widely shared and that there was a proper regard for future generations (§79). This is a fine set of criteria which recognized the relevance of state regulation in seeking an appropriate and just balance between different interests and it represented a distinct break with the suspicions of the state expressed by previous popes. Particularly noticeable, too, was the regard for solidarity with future generations, a foretaste, perhaps, of the global ecological concerns which emerged later in the twentieth century.

Pope John next reflected on workplace conditions and suggested that justice was not met where 'the human dignity of workers is compromised, or their sense of responsibility is weakened, or their freedom of action is removed' (§83). This led to a recommendation of various forms of partnership in the affairs of the enterprise in which they worked (§91). In the final section of Part II of his encyclical, the pope returned to the issue of private property, noting further changes in the economy such as the increasing separation of ownership from management and the impact of insurance schemes and social security systems (§§104–108). He emphatically affirmed the permanent validity of the right to private property, 'rooted in the very nature of things' (§109) but also recognized the importance of public property where the common good called for it, providing the principle of subsidiarity was strictly observed (§117). He concluded by reiterating earlier teaching that 'in the right of private property there is rooted a social responsibility' (§119).

It might be observed that there still is, in this encyclical, no serious analysis of the distinctions between personal property, corporate property and the role of the financial markets.

Gaudium et Spes (Vatican II 1965)

The Second Vatican Council initiated by John XXIII marked a major turning point in the relationship between the Church and the secular world. While the Dogmatic Constitution on the Church (*Lumen Gentium*) articulated a shift to a 'People of God' theology, the Pastoral Constitution on the Church in the Modern World (*Gaudium et Spes*) aimed to dialogue directly with the world and its contemporary concerns. O'Brien and Shannon point to its incarnationalist theology and its shift from natural law categories to a doctrine of human rights. They saw it as 'the culmination of the changes begun with *Mater et Magistra*'.[28] In Part I it aimed to dialogue with all people of good will and took as its starting point a concern for the individual human person created in the image of God. Human beings were social beings and, sharing a common Father, were called to live fraternally in community. This was reflected in the evident growing interdependence of humankind promoted by modern technological advances. This required a concern for the common good and its expression in mutual service, solidarity and love. It was the lay person's task to articulate this understanding to the world (§§12–45).

Chapter 3 of Part II addressed the issue of socio-economic life. It recapitulated previous papal teaching (§§63–72) and reiterated a concern about huge economic inequalities between individuals and nations, urging their reduction in the interests of justice and equity. It insisted that economic development should be at the service of humankind and that workers were more than 'mere tools of production'; repeated its rejection of both unrestrained individualism and collectivism; and affirmed the personal right of migration. The worker had a right to work and a duty to labour faithfully. Society had the obligation to provide opportunities for adequate employment. Work ought to be adapted to the needs of people, especially mothers, and workers ought to have sufficient time for rest and leisure. Trade unions were encouraged and 'the active participation of everyone in

---

[28] O'Brien and Shannon 1992: 164–165.

running an enterprise should be promoted'. There should be a proper balance between the distribution of income and the need to provide both present and future employment. Various forms of public ownership had their place.

Medellin (CELAM 1968)

Three years after the end of Vatican II, the Conference of Latin American Bishops held their second meeting in the Columbian city of Medellin. Its conclusions were a remarkable working out of the theology of the Council in the specific context of Latin America and took seriously the rhetoric about the Church serving those in need. It reflected the emergent stream of liberation theology strongly influenced by the social conditions of unfreedom experienced by millions of poor people in Latin America. For the first time the thesis of the Church's 'preferential option for the poor' was articulated.[29] Three years later the Peruvian theologian Gustavo Gutiérrez published the Spanish edition of *A Theology of Liberation*.[30]

Octogesima Adveniens (Paul VI 1971)

In 1971, Pope Paul VI issued his call to action to mark the eightieth anniversary of *Rerum Novarum*. Clearly influenced by his experiences at Medellin, in one of several passages which encouraged the contribution of the social sciences (§§38–40), he recognized that Rome did not have all the answers to local problems so that local Churches must have the courage to discern and act locally. It was

difficult ... to utter a unified message and to put forward a solution which has universal validity ... It is up to the Christian communities to analyse with objectivity the situation which is proper to their own country, to shed on it the light of the Gospel's unalterable words and to draw principles of reflection, norms of judgment and directives for action from the social teaching of the Church (§4).

Pope Paul drew attention to a number of emergent social problems which required close attention including 'human conditions of production, fairness in the exchange of goods and in the division of wealth, the significance of the increased needs of consumption, and the sharing of responsibility' (§7). He was especially concerned about the 'irreversible stage' of urbanization associated with industrialization, and the problems of loneliness and

---

[29] CELAM II 1979: Ch. 14: 7–11, pp. 174–176.   [30] Gutiérrez 1974.

isolation resulting from the 'unceasing flight from the land' as millions of poor farmers left for the big cities in search of a better life. It was the task of Christians 'to create new modes of neighbourliness' and hope (§§8–12). He raised questions about generational relations and the difficulties of 'the handing on of values and beliefs' to present-day youth (§13). In a paragraph which reflected a significant development of thinking, Paul VI asserted women's equal rights and dignity provided it was consistent with 'woman's proper role . . . at the heart of the family'. Legislation should protect 'her proper vocation' while 'recognising her interdependence as a person, and her equal rights to participate in cultural, economic, social, and political life' (§13). The pope reiterated previous teaching on the rights of workers but warned that there were limits to the right to strike if 'the harm caused to society becomes inadmissible' (§14). He pleaded for the new 'poor' and marginalized and those subject to racial discrimination (§§15–16). Finally he again insisted on the 'right to emigrate' and pleaded for the proper integration of migrants into society (§17).

Puebla (CELAM 1979)

The third meeting of CELAM was held at Puebla, Mexico, shortly after the election of Pope John Paul II. At this meeting there were clear signs that the Vatican had concerns about the influence and interpretations of liberation theology.[31] These were later expressed in two documents published by the CDF in 1984 and 1986.

Laborem Exercens (John Paul II 1981)

Pope John Paul II's encyclical letter which commemorated the ninetieth anniversary of *Rerum Novarum* is particularly relevant to the concerns of this chapter. Noticeable is its shift away from a natural law approach and its strong grounding in scripture, especially the Genesis account of the creation of the human person in the image of God and the vocation to subdue the earth (Gen 1: 26–28; 3: 19). The pope noted some recent and anticipated social and technological changes and new concerns with pollution and the democratic participation of the newly independent nations in decision-making (§1). He distinguished the earlier concerns with the 'class' and labour question *within* nations from 1891 to 1931, and the subsequent expansion of concern to world issues and labour relations *between* nations (§2).

---

[31] See, e.g., Smith 1991: 23–24.

He argued that the consistent concern of the Church's social teaching was in making life, including work, more human (§3, quoting *GS* §38). The pope then offered an extended reflection on the philosophy and theology of work in the last quarter of the twentieth century. The Church's special insights were based on the revealed word of God. In carrying out God's mandate to subdue and dominate the whole visible world, 'every human being reflects the very action of the creator of the universe' (§4). This theme that human ingenuity and innovation in the interests of the common good were a sharing in God's creativity is worthy of greater recognition.

Pope John Paul II reflected on objective changes in work resulting from developments in technology (§5) but insisted that more important was the subjective dimension, the ethical nature of work and the dignity of the person doing the work (§6). He repeated former criticisms of capitalism and collectivism insofar as they were 'marked by the premises of materialistic economism' which treated the worker essentially 'as an instrument of production' (§7). He saw the emergence of worker solidarity as 'the reaction against the degradation' of workers and their exploitation in terms of wages, working conditions and social security. But this solidarity in the face of persistent injustices must avoid coercive 'ideological or power systems' and 'must never mean being closed to dialogue and collaboration with others'. In fidelity to Christ, the Church strove to be the 'Church of the poor' (§8). The pope affirmed the wide diversity of forms of work through which the worker, whether manual or intellectual, 'achieves fulfilment as a human being', provided it was not forced and he was not oppressed or exploited (§9). He concluded this section by noting that work 'constitutes a foundation for the formation of family life' and for the wider society which is 'a great historical and social incarnation of the work of all generations' (§10).

The next section of the encyclical reflected on the conflict between capital and labour (§§11–15). The pope gave a realistic historical account of the conflict between workers and entrepreneurs who followed 'the principle of maximum profit (and) tried to establish the lowest possible wages' and 'other elements of exploitation' such as inadequate safety, health and living conditions (§11). Workers benefited from two inheritances: natural resources and the technology and skills developed by previous generations, that is capital. In the light of this, there could be no intrinsic conflict between capital and labour which were 'inseparably linked'. John Paul II stressed 'the primacy of man over things' and reasserted 'the principle of the priority of labour over capital . . . labour is always a primary efficient cause, while capital . . . remains a mere instrument or instrumental cause' which included not only natural resources but also 'the historical heritage of human labour' (§12). The pope rejected the errors of economism, which considered labour 'solely according to its economic purpose', and materialism, which asserted the superiority of the material over the spiritual and personal (§13). He upheld the traditional right to the private ownership of property but stressed that it was 'subordinated to the right to common use, to the fact that goods are meant for everyone (§14)'. For this reason 'one cannot exclude the socialisation, in suitable conditions, of certain means of production' if it was necessary for the common good. He proceeded to teach firmly that 'the position of "rigid" capitalism . . . that defends the exclusive right to private ownership of the means of production as an untouchable "dogma" of economic life' was unacceptable. This right required 'a constructive revision both in theory and in practice' (§14). In sum, the pope's argument was 'personalist' in its affirmation that work had not simply an economic purpose but also had to do with personal values (§15).

The pope continued in the next section to develop thinking about the rights of the worker in the context of human rights generally (§§16–23). In his analysis he distinguished between the worker's 'direct' employer and 'indirect' employer. By the latter the pope meant the various social institutions, such as social contracts and networks of dependence both within and between nations, which provided the social context which regulated but also constrained the relationship between the worker and the direct employer. The concept 'indirect employer' was a significant development in papal teaching (§17). It recognized the constraints on direct employers in a 'system of mutual dependence'. An example would be the owner of a sweat shop who paid low wages because otherwise he would be priced out of the market.

Ian Linden[32] offered a useful discussion of the concept '*indirect employer*'. He suggested that the Polish pope struggled to reconcile his insistence on personal moral responsibility with the reality of 'structural injustice'. John Paul II feared that an emphasis on structures was too Marxist and deterministic. The concept 'puts the consumer, the transnational corporation, the pension fund, the shareholder and the state into the moral dock'. It also 'opens up the possibility of a whole range of action on behalf of justice. The growth of ethical investment, fair trade organizations, consumer lobbies and the quest for "social clauses" in trade agreements' and the insistence on codes of conduct for fair wages, and health and safety

[32] Linden 1998: 92–96. See also Dorr 1992: 290–294.

regulations were all ways in which everyone, as 'indirect employers' can be morally responsible. Linden rightly insisted that simply changing hearts would not do and that 'in reality to bring about change in the direct employers means working through negotiation and pressure on a complex group of indirect employers'.

John Paul II insisted that 'it is respect for the objective rights of the worker . . . that must constitute the adequate and fundamental criterion for shaping the whole economy' at both the level of the individual nation and in the world economic system as a whole (§17). Human work must be 'considered as a fundamental right of all human beings'. Unemployment was always 'an evil' and 'can become a real social disaster', particularly for the young. It was the responsibility of the 'indirect' employer, for example the state, to provide appropriate unemployment benefits and to strive with rational planning and proper organization and coordination to achieve high levels of employment and the right distribution between the different sectors in the interests of the common good (§18). The important regulating function of the state was also recognized in such areas as ensuring appropriate levels of family wage or family allowances, safeguarding the rights of mothers, avoiding discrimination, ensuring adequate minimum working conditions, such as weekly rest, annual holidays and medical care (§19). The pope reaffirmed the workers' right to form trade unions but subtly reinterpreted their role as 'a mouthpiece for the struggle for social justice' *for* the common good rather than *against* others, as Marxist class theory suggested. Strikes may be legitimate as a last resort, within limits, and bearing in mind all the time a concern for the common good (§20). The pope reflected on the exhausting nature of much agricultural labour and the often unjust situations experienced by farmers (§21). He condemned discrimination against disabled people (§22) and against migrant workers and insisted on the right of workers both to leave their native land and to return (§23).

Pope John Paul II concluded *Laborem Exercens* with a short scriptural reflection on a spirituality of work 'which will help all people to come closer, through work, to God, the Creator and Redeemer, to participate in his salvific plan for man and the world and to deepen their friendship with Christ in their lives' (§24). The pope suggested that 'man, created in the image of God, shares by his work in the activity of the creator and . . . within the limits of his own human capabilities, man in a sense continues to develop that activity, and perfects it as he advances further and further in the discovery of the resources and values contained in the whole of creation' (§25).

This quotation serves to illustrate a point which may have been over-looked as we have considered the developments in Catholic social thought in the concrete issues of economic life since *Rerum Novarum*. All the popes, from Leo XIII to John Paul II, have stressed that, however much we seek the kingdom of God in this world, the fullness of justice will only be reached in the world to come. The Christian brings to bear on the issues of economic life not just a secular concern to alleviate social injustices, but also a transcendental awareness of the place of economic life in God's creation and the redemption of this unjust and sinful world by the sacrifice of Jesus. Such an awareness gives Christians the courage to pick up their own crosses and persevere in the struggle for justice while realizing that evil forces will resist and will not be entirely beaten until the end of time.

Economic Justice for All (United States Bishops 1986)

Two features of this great pastoral letter[33], in particular, are worthy of note and might be regarded as exemplary. Firstly, the dialogical nature of the process of its production, with the drafting committee meeting 'with experts and submitting drafts for public consideration',[34] provided a new model for the formulation and development of Catholic social thought when addressing contentious issues. Secondly, their seriousness in partici-pating in a conversation with the secular world was demonstrated by the fact that nearly half of the footnotes related to secular sources: from official government statistics to academic researches in professional journals. This is quite unique in Catholic documents which typically have almost exclu-sively referenced previous papal encyclicals or official Church documents or the writings of favoured authorities such as Thomas Aquinas.

In their introduction the bishops insisted they wrote both as Catholics in the long tradition from the Hebrew prophets, the Sermon on the Mount, and the long tradition of Catholic social teaching, and as Americans grateful for the gift of freedom. As we indicated in 5.3, they enunciated six moral principles for a vision of economic life. These led them to call for a national commitment to full employment and to eradicate poverty. This required conversion and a commitment to become more active in their pursuit.[35]

---

[33] In O'Brien and Shannon 1992: 572–680, and also Gannon 1987: 297ff.
[34] O'Brien and Shannon 1992: 491. See, e.g., Houck and Williams 1984, and Gannon 1987.
[35] In O'Brien and Shannon 1992: 572–578.

The bishops commenced their analysis by noticing that in spite of some 'signs of hope' there were also 'massive and ugly' failures (§3), such as widespread poverty and homelessness, high levels of unemployment, and insecurity both in the USA and the world. They acknowledged the 'pre-eminent role' of the United States 'in an increasingly interdependent global economy' (§10) and expressed concerns about the global 'common ecological environment' (§12), 'stark inequalities across countries' and wide 'disparities of power' in relationships between nations, regarded by many as 'a pattern of dominance and dependence' (§13). They also noticed the 'unequal and unfair way' (§15) unemployment and disadvantage were distributed between different social groups, the damaging effects of economic change on family life and the diversion of scarce resources into arms production (§§6–21). They suggested that economic 'decisions must be judged in light of what they do *for* the poor, what they do *to* the poor, and what they enable the poor to do *for themselves*. The fundamental moral criterion for all economic decisions, policies, and institutions is this: They must be at the service of *all people, especially the poor*' (§24). They felt that no Christian could 'be comfortable in the face of the hunger, homelessness, insecurity, and injustice found in this country and the world . . . [which] challenge us to serious and sustained attention to economic justice' (§27).

Chapter 2 of the pastoral letter presented a Christian vision of economic life. Drawing heavily on the biblical vision of creation, they noted that *'from the patristic period to the present, the Church has affirmed that misuse of the world's resources or appropriation of them by a minority of the world's population betrays the gift of creation since "whatever belongs to God belongs to all"'* (§34; see also fn. 4). Scriptural treatments stress 'that the justice of a community is measured by its treatment of the powerless . . . the widow, the orphan, the poor, and the stranger . . .' (§38). They also provided the basis for the 'preferential option for the poor' (§52; see also §§85–91). The bishops next enunciated a set of ethical norms for economic life: love and solidarity; commutative, distributive and contributive justice; and overcoming the social sins of marginalization and powerlessness and establishing minimum levels of active participation in the economic, political and cultural life of society (§§61–78). In democratic societies where civil and political rights had largely been established, there needed to be a concerted effort to secure social and economic rights (§§79–84).

The pastoral noted that *'the common good demands justice for all, the protection of the human rights of all'* (§85). This meant that Christians were called 'to make a fundamental "option for the poor"' (§87), excluded, vulnerable or economically insecure as a priority (§§85–92). *'Economic and social priorities as well as the organization of the work world should be continually evaluated in the light of their impact on the strength and stability of family life'* (§93). The bishops reiterated traditional Catholic social teaching on institutional pluralism and the principle of subsidiarity, and affirmed the rights to employment, a just wage, decent working conditions, adequate security, minimum provision for rest and recreation, and the elimination of sexual and racial discrimination (§§96–109). 'The freedom of entrepreneurship, business, and finance should be protected, but the accountability of this freedom to the common good and the norms of justice must be assured' (§110). This particularly applied to large corporations and large financial institutions which had considerable power. They 'have the duty to be faithful trustees of the resources at their disposal .... Short-term profits reaped at the cost of depletion of natural resources or the pollution of the environment violate this trust' (§112). The right to own private property was affirmed but this 'does not mean that anyone has the right to unlimited accumulation of wealth' (§115). Finally, there was a recognition that government 'should assume a positive role in generating employment and establishing fair labor practices, in guaranteeing the provision and maintenance of the country's infrastructure ... [and] regulate trade and commerce in the interest of fairness' (§123; see also fn. 74).

The pastoral observed that 'intelligent reflection on the social and economic realities of today is also indispensable in the effort to respond to economic circumstances never envisioned in biblical times' (§61). Chapter 3 proceeded, therefore, to evaluate four major areas of concern in the light of the scriptural, theological and ethical principles identified. Brief consideration of their treatment of employment will be given here.

The bishops commenced by reviewing the position in the USA in the early 1980s when unemployment levels were high and highly skewed against ethnic minorities and young people. They recognized the 'severe human costs' (§141) in terms of self-worth, family disruption, crime, loss of creativity and tax revenues, and so on. They noted recent changes in the labour market as a result of technological changes, including a certain amount of deskilling and the increasing employment of women, greater international competition, the impact of immigration, racial discrimination, the paucity of child care services, the distorting effects of high levels of defence spending, and failures to invest in education and training (§§144–150). They insisted that 'full employment is the foundation of a just economy ... a basic right ... which protects the freedom of all to participate in the economic life of society .... Corresponding to this right is the duty on the part of society to ensure that the right is protected'

(§§136–137). Since 'the market alone will not automatically produce full employment ... the government must act to ensure that this goal is achieved by coordinating general economic policies, [and] by job creation programs' (§154), for example to meet society's unmet needs (§§151–169).

It is instructive to read Archbishop Weakland's revisiting of the pastoral and his reflections on two major critical analyses by Cardinal Ratzinger, now Pope Benedict XVI, in a paper on the 'Market Economy and Ethics' given in 1985, and a comprehensive critique of the US Pastoral from Clodovis and Leonardo Boff in 1987.[36] Weakland observed the growing number of forms of capitalism emerging from quite different cultural contexts where the Enlightenment assumptions underpinning American capitalism did not hold. Ratzinger believed there was a contradiction between individual 'claims of freedom and the deterministic nature of the market system'. The Boffs drew on economic dependency theories to argue that capitalism was intrinsically flawed and led inevitably to systemic exploitation and dominance. They claimed the encyclical failed to address the close relationship between economics and political power. Weakland reflected on the relationship between self-interest and pernicious greed and the systemic issues of recessions, unemployment, monopoly power and ecological concerns, and on individual responsibility and the common good. He concluded that charity 'is not an economic solution' to systemic injustices but insisted that the values of Catholic social thought 'are not outmoded even when the practical solutions demanded seem to change with the times'.

Sollicitudo Rei Socialis (John Paul II 1987)

This encyclical letter, written for the twentieth anniversary of Pope Paul VI's *Populorum Progressio* was important for what it said about private property and the concept of the *'social mortgage'*. John Paul II wrote:

It is necessary to state once more the characteristic principle of Christian social doctrine: the goods of this world are *originally meant for all*. The right to private property is *valid and necessary*, but it does not nullify the value of this principle. Private property, in fact, is under a 'social mortgage', which means that it has an intrinsically social function, based upon and justified precisely by the principle of the universal destination of goods (§42).

---

[36] Weakland 1991: 202, 210.

Centesimus Annus (John Paul II 1991)

To celebrate the centenary of *Rerum Novarum* Pope John Paul II promulgated *Centesimus Annus* which aimed to 'look back' at the original text, 'look around' at the 'new things' in our own times, and 'look to the future' with its uncertainties and promises (§3). After first reviewing the key features of *Rerum Novarum* (§§4–11) the pope proceeded to consider some contemporary 'new things'. Of particular interest was the recognition of inequalities of economic power and hence the responsibility of the state to provide a strong regulatory framework between conflicting parties and protection from the 'nightmare of unemployment' (§15). In a long discussion of the collapse of totalitarian communism in Central and Eastern Europe in 1989, he acknowledged the inefficiency of the centrally controlled economy (§24) and suggested that interdependence among peoples was meant to unite them, not divide them (§27). The next section of the encyclical offered an update on teaching about the right to private property which 'is subordinated to their original common destination as created goods' (§30). This led to an important recognition that there have been three distinct stages in the emergence of property over the past century as land, then capital, and now 'the possession of know-how, technology and skill' (§42).[37] The pope continued to draw attention to the 'human inadequacies of capitalism and the resulting domination of things over people' (§33). While 'the free market is the most efficient instrument for utilising resources and effectively responding to needs' (§34), 'the market (must) be appropriately controlled by the forces of society and by the state, so as to guarantee that the basic needs of the whole of society are satisfied' (§§35, 48). The pope warned against the culture of consumerism and its creation of 'artificial new needs' (§36). Market mechanisms 'carry the risk of an "idolatry" of the market' (§40).[38] There was evidence of new forms of alienation, 'the loss of the authentic meaning of life', as in consumerism, 'when people are ensnared in a web of false and superficial gratifications' (§41).

In sum, while the capitalist economic system has more successfully met people's needs than centrally controlled systems, it continued to present major problems of injustice, inequalities of power and distribution of

---

[37] O'Brien and Shannon note that this recognition of a new form of property remains undeveloped, 1992: 438. The issue is relevant to current concerns about the exploitation of 'intellectual property rights'.

[38] The pope seemed to have in mind common goods such as water and the natural environment.

goods, idolatrous ideologies, and the like, which remained a challenge to the Christian conscience. Appropriate regulatory mechanisms were essential in the interests of the common good.

The Common Good (Bishops of England and Wales 1996)

Three observations in this document are particularly relevant. In their discussion of the 'morality in the market place' the bishops stated that 'the Catholic doctrine of the common good is incompatible with unlimited free-market, or laissez-faire, capitalism, which insists that the distribution of wealth must occur entirely according to the dictates of market forces . . . (This view) can amount to idolatry or a form of economic superstition' (§76). They accepted that centrally commanded economies were inefficient but 'the good functioning of the market requires . . . the embodiment of certain ethical principles within a regulatory and legal framework' (§78). Indeed, they argued that 'unlimited free markets tend to produce what is in effect an "option against the poor"' since 'it gravely disadvantages those who do not have wealth to spend' (§85).

In the section on 'the world of work', the bishops insisted that 'work is more than a way of making a living: it is a vocation, a participation in God's creative activity . . . (and) the primary means whereby humanity was to co-operate with and continue the work of the Creator by responding to God's invitation to "subdue the earth"' (§90). They reiterated traditional Catholic teaching about worker rights, deplored confrontational approaches to industrial relations, but interestingly noted that 'contracts between unequal parties (whether unions of monopoly labour power or large employers) are a potent source of structural injustice' (§93). They affirmed the right to strike but warned that 'it is unfair . . . to use the inflicting of hardship or serious inconvenience on . . . third parties (such as other workers, users or consumers) as deliberate tactics' (§96). They did 'not regard State welfare provision as a desirable substitute for payment of a just wage' (§98).

Finally, in their section on 'ownership and property', they emphasized that 'the economy exists for the human person, not the other way round' (§111). Employers were warned against disregarding, in purely accountancy methods, the 'social capital' represented by the 'reservoir of human effort, wisdom and experience' of their employees. The bishops wrote: 'this dumping of human "social capital", which the Catholic Church must deplore, is a prevalent cause of social injustice in modern society. It often occurs in company "downsizing" operations associated with takeovers, closures and mergers' (§112).

Taxation for the Common Good (CBCEW 2004)

Brief reference is made to this slight document because of the intrinsic importance of the issue and because it touched on the relationship between the individual and the wider society and the common good. Taxation is a contentious issue. It is typically regarded as a necessary evil or as inhibiting the responsibility of families to provide for themselves, or as destructive of choice. Rather, the bishops argued, it should be seen as a necessary contribution to the common good for the provision of public services which individual families were unable to provide for themselves. Furthermore it was one aspect of responsible citizenship and an indication of solidarity with others. The document argued in favour of redistributive justice which 'means that tax is levied according to ability to pay and goods are distributed according to needs and necessities' and for a reduction in inequality which 'will, in the final analysis, mean greater real freedom for everyone' (§§21–23).

MAJOR THEMES AND EVALUATION

To recap, the following are central themes in Catholic social thought particularly as it relates to work and employment:

- *Human dignity*: The key starting point of Catholic social thought is the fundamental dignity of every individual human being created in the image of God and destined for everlasting life with Him. From this flows the primacy of labour over capital, the right to work and to a just wage, decent working conditions, and the right to participate in decision-making.
- *Private property*: From this human dignity and the right to a just wage also flows the right to save and own property and to use this entrepreneurially to extend creation, subject to regulation in the interests of the *common good*. However, the right to private property is not absolute and there is an insistence on the 'universal destination of material goods'.[39] The recent distinction between land, capital and knowledge forms of property, the value of common property, and the concept of the 'social mortgage' remain to be elaborated.
- *The right to associate*: Another corollary of human dignity is the right to associate and form trade unions which are valuable intermediate bodies between the individual and the employer and state.

---

[39] *Centesimus Annus* §§30–43. See also Duchrow and Hinkelammert 2004.

- *The role of the state*: The state has a legitimate role in regulating social and economic affairs in the interests of justice and the *common good* and in seeking a balanced harmony between competing interest groups, subject to the general principle of *subsidiarity*. The regulation of international economic relations remains to be elaborated.
- *The preferential option for the poor*: In social and economic policies preferential concern should be given to those in need. A just distribution of goods, income, wealth and power is necessary in the interests of *solidarity* and the recognition of interdependence.
- *Social harmony*: There is a distinct preference for collaborative, cooperative, and participative structures and policies which encourage social harmony. While social conflict is inevitable in a fallen and imperfect world, everything possible should be done to seek the resolution of differences in a peaceful manner. In other words, there is a *preferential option for non-violence*.
- *Authentic development*: Another corollary of the doctrine of human dignity is the right, of both individuals and nations, to develop themselves to their fullest potential and in *solidarity* with other human beings, both now and with future generations. From this flows a general ecological concern for the environment.

However valuable these criteria are as guidelines for a Christian response to the various problems and issues of economic life, they are always in need of interpretation in real, concrete social situations. This is explicitly recognized by the Church's leaders who claim no technical expertise on economic matters but insist that they have an essential moral dimension which must be taken into account. But it does mean that generally speaking the Church seems to be good on criticism and weak on policy proposals. We have seen that the Church's social thought has developed over twenty centuries and in the face of new challenges. It seems appropriate, therefore, to record three reservations in particular about its state at the beginning of the twenty-first century.

- *Socialism*: Papal teaching about socialism has been one of largely undifferentiated and unqualified hostility. It is certainly the case that over the past century it has softened its antagonism, allowed grudgingly for a 'mitigated socialism' and acknowledged its concern to seek social justice for those in need. But it has rarely distinguished between totalitarian communism and social democracy. The consequence has often been a blanket opposition to 'left-of-centre' politics. The ostensible cause of this hostility is the challenge of socialism to unjust social orders and therefore to that stability of society which the Church needs. There is also a rejection of the atheism of Marxism but similar criticisms of the atheism of neo-conservative liberal economics have always been more muted. Sadly, this hostility has damaged the whole liberation theology movement which has been one of the most fruitful developments in the Church in the past half-century. The huge bias against socialism can be contrasted with one brief criticism of right-wing 'national security regimes' in *Centesimus Annus* (§47).

- *Capitalism*: Here we make the opposite criticism that the Church has been far too uncritical. It has noted the greater efficiency of free-market economics and, since the collapse of Soviet Communism in 1989, has shown itself to be surprisingly sympathetic to the modern business economy and to wealth creation. It insists on the regulation of liberal capitalism and the promotion of the common good. But it has failed to analyze thoroughly the distinctions between the various types of property: land, capital and knowledge; private and public capital; corporate and financial capital; the significance of pension funds; and so on. The implications of instantaneous electronic transfer of speculative funds around the globe and the issue of intellectual property rights are largely unexplored. Power differentials in the regulatory structures and major international institutions such as the IMF, the WB and the WTO have not been scrutinized and evaluated for the capacity they have to control people's lives.
- *Conflict and harmony*: Papal abhorrence of social disorder since the French Revolution and the loss of the Papal States in the nineteenth century has been reflected in a somewhat nostalgic favouring of social harmony and a rejection of conflict. This has given the Church a distinctly 'conservative' face in support of the *status quo* and even, at times, distinctly nasty and tyrannical regimes. This stance has not lain well with rhetoric about a preferential option for the poor. The truth is that conflict is endemic in the human condition and its resolution is often the way to change and innovation in human affairs.

ECONOMIC JUSTICE FOR ALL

In their assessment of Catholic social thought since Leo XIII, O'Brien and Shannon insisted that it reflected an 'ever present tension and pervasive ambiguity' between the concern to promote *both* the 'prophetic integrity of the Church's witness' in the light of Jesus' teaching about the kingdom of God *and* a politically realistic, 'responsible moderation' in order to be a power for good in a pluralistic society. They argued that this tension was reflected in the various documents we have reviewed and urged a continuing 'dialogue about social and political responsibility' taking fully into account the 'social, political and economic problems (which) are the special concerns of the laity'.[40]

As we have seen, the prophetic contribution of Catholic social thought relates in particular to the supreme dignity of the human being created in the image of God and all that derives from that, and also the importance, in justice, of seeking the common good and solidarity between all God's children on earth and with generations to come, giving a preferential option to the poor in order to achieve this, and insisting that the state, important though it is in regulating social and economic affairs in the interests of the common good, does not stifle the activities of individuals and intermediate associations. Work is seen as a participation in God's continuing creative activity and a God-given right. Workers, as God's collaborators in His creative activity, require the respect which is due to their dignity, in their working conditions, remuneration, freedom of association, welfare and security for themselves and their families.

From a prophetic perspective the followers of Jesus constitute a 'counter community' where all were equal, and where 'the politics of oppression and exploitation (were) replaced with the politics of justice and compassion'. This 'counter-system' could be called 'the subversive Kingdom ... in radical obedience to the gospel and in opposition to the powers of the present age'.[41] Serious scriptural analyses of the covenant economics, Luke's systematic challenge, both in his Gospel and in the Acts of the Apostles, to make a radical break with the economics of empire, and John's condemnation in Revelation of the inherent exploitation of the imperial economy in contrast to the treasure of God's creative abundance, all provided evidence of the prophetic and counter-cultural calling of the followers of Jesus to pursue economic exchanges according to the covenant.[42] The sabbath rest had direct relevance as a focus for 'restoring a sense of rhythm between work and rest in our often manic, production-oriented society' while jubilee forms of restitution had direct relevance for debt relief among the developing nations.

On the other hand, the Church's stance of 'responsible moderation' was perhaps reflected in its tolerance of liberal capitalism and its muted and

---

[40] O'Brien and Shannon 1992: 5–7. Note also the somewhat belated acknowledgement of the potential contribution of the human sciences in *Centesimus Annus* §54.

[41] Fuellenbach 1995: 255–256. See also Howard-Brook 2001: 82–85.

[42] Howard-Brook 2001: 72–102; Fuellenbach 1995; Neal 1977: 5–7 and 1987: 10–25. Note also 'the radical Gospel of Mark proclaimed from the margins', as interpreted by Ched Myers 1988.

relatively uncritical judgements about the overwhelming power of corporate capital and the supposedly regulatory bodies which reflected its interests rather than those of the poor. It could be argued that in its emphatic defence of the right to private property and its outspoken and barely qualified antagonism to socialism and, until recently, to the welfare state, the Church failed to keep up with the attempts to create a more just society with more assured security for all its citizens through the construction of the welfare state. It also failed adequately to address the development of corporate property and the huge concentrations of economic power, and the significance of the shift from land to capital to knowledge property. Historically it has been less critical than it should have been of totalitarianisms of the right and 'national security' states, often supported by the leadership of local Churches, of the challenge of transnational corporations and financial institutions, and of the damage done to poor people and developing countries by 'liberal' economic policies imposed by the IMF, WB and WTO. These remain challenges which the Church has yet adequately to address.

CHAPTER 9

Social exclusion

A MULTIDIMENSIONAL CONCEPT

The fourth main area of injustice is that of social exclusion. The term emerged in France in the 1970s, where it referred to those falling through the net of social protection, and was adopted by the European Commission in 1989. The intention was to address wider issues than poverty. While some people criticize the notion of social exclusion as diverting attention from fundamental economic inequalities of income and wealth and both absolute and relative poverty, it alerts to other forms of marginalization in our society such as political participation and influence. Ruth Lister noted that:

> It is a more multidimensional concept than poverty, embracing a variety of ways in which people may be denied full participation in society and full effective rights of citizenship in the civil, political and social spheres . . . Racism, . . . sexism, homophobia and disablism, can . . . operate as mechanisms of exclusion even in the case of those who have adequate material resources.[1]

Four broad dimensions of social exclusion are generally identified:
- impoverishment or exclusion from adequate income or resources;
- labour market exclusion from paid employment;
- service exclusion, for example from education, health and welfare services; and
- exclusion from social relationships, including full participation in political processes and decision-making.[2]

People who are poor often have multiple disadvantages of low or inadequate income, wealth, education, qualifications and skills, poor housing and health, all of which effectively exclude them from full participation in the everyday life of society and in its decision-making processes. Social exclusion from society is effectively a denial of the human rights and

[1] Lister 2000: 38.   [2] Macionis and Plummer 2002: 242.

dignity of those who are excluded and is, therefore, a matter of social injustice. Recent Catholic social thought has drawn attention to it in general terms but without offering much in the way of specific policy proposals.

This chapter offers a Catholic perspective on the controversial issue of distributive justice *within* society. It is suggested that a Christian vision of the dignity of each individual human person, the need to promote the common good of all God's people and solidarity between them, the recognition of the principle of subsidiarity which ensures that social policies properly respect the rights and competencies of individuals, families, and local communities, and the need to take particular account of the needs of the poor, disadvantaged, weak, disabled and marginalized in society, is essential for the full flourishing and development of people in society.

SOCIAL INEQUALITIES IN BRITAIN

The New Policy Institute, with support from the Joseph Rowntree Foundation, has provided the most authoritative overview of recent statistics and trends on poverty and social exclusion in the UK under the eleven headings below.[3] Additional data have been added where appropriate.

Income and wealth

In 1995 the Joseph Rowntree Foundation's *Inquiry into Income and Wealth*[4] showed that income inequality in the UK had grown more rapidly between 1977 and 1990 than in any other industrialized nation except New Zealand. They also noted that 'since 1977 the proportion of the population with less than half the average income has more than trebled'. For male workers, between 1978 and 1992 wages for the lowest paid hardly changed but median wages had grown by 35 per cent while the wages of the top 10 per cent had grown by 50 per cent. In the USA, too, Bureau of Census statistics showed that in 1993 39 million people, 15 per cent of the population, were officially living in poverty.[5]

[3] New Policy Institute, 'Monitoring Poverty and Social Exclusion', http:www.poverty.org.uk/ summary/key_facts.htm. For the full report see Howarth, C. et al. 1999. For an earlier analysis of recent trends, see Russell 1995: 58.
[4] Joseph Rowntree Foundation 1995: Vol. 1: 6, 13–15, 20.
[5] Macionis and Plummer 2002: 244–246.

In 2001/02, 12½ million people were living on incomes below the threshold of 60 per cent of median income, a drop of 1½ million since 1996/97. Using data from the annual *Family Expenditure Survey* from the UK population, the Institute for Fiscal Studies reported[6] that there had been big increases in income inequality in recent decades: 'the income share of the poorest tenth of society has fallen back from 3.7 per cent in 1961–63 to 2.9 per cent in 1991–93, with most of the fall occurring during the 1980s. The share of the richest tenth rose from 21 per cent to 26 per cent over the three decades'. The eightfold increase in unemployment between the early 1960s and the mid-1980s had had a major effect on the income distribution with families with children making up more than half of the poorest decile group in the mid-1990s. 'Throughout the period, the unemployed and lone parents have been at considerable risk of poverty, and the size of both groups has grown markedly'. The Institute of Fiscal Studies concluded that to return to a more equitable income distribution would require 'an economic and political upheaval at least as great as that experienced during the 1980s'. This would run counter to many of the imperatives of economic globalization, the deregulation of the labour market, and involve significant changes in tax policy and social security measures.

Inequalities of wealth in the UK, that is total assets less debts, have also increased in recent decades. The Royal Commission on Income and Wealth showed that the proportion of wealth owned by the top 1 per cent had declined since the 1920s, aided by the growth of home ownership in the post-war period. By 1976 the most wealthy 1 per cent owned 25 per cent of total marketable wealth. This proportion was reduced to 14 per cent when occupational and state pension rights were taken into account.[7] By 1998 the proportion had risen to 23 per cent, or 26 per cent discounting the value of dwellings. The bottom half of the population shared between them only 6 per cent of the total wealth of the nation.[8]

Dominic Hobson[9] argued that it was the public limited company and the MNC and not the State, which was currently 'the chief arbiter of production, consumption, distribution and exchange. Who owns the PLC can truly be said to own the country ... (But these are chiefly) the institutional investors: the pension, insurance and mutual funds which channel the savings of millions of ordinary people into great corporate

[6] Goodman et al. 1997: 86, 112, 253, 281–282.   [7] Royal Commission 1980: 22–23, 26.
[8] Macionis and Plummer 2002: 234–235, quoting *Social Trends* 2001: 109.
[9] Hobson 1999: xxxii–xxiii, 740–742, 755.

enterprises which provide the work and goods and entertainment which fill our lives'. The analysis and interpretation of the huge inequalities in wealth is fraught with difficulties, given its complexity and diversity and the paradoxes, such as the size of trade union pension funds in the shareholdings of many corporations.

Poverty

In the context of modern Britain, poverty is a *relative* concept and is measured in terms of indicators of deprivation of 'what the general public perceives as acceptable minimum standards of living' and income poverty is defined 'in terms of resources which are insufficient to enable an individual to participate in the mainstream of his or her society'. For the European Commission, '"the poor" shall be taken to mean persons, families and groups of persons whose resources (material, cultural and social) are so limited as to exclude them from the minimum acceptable way of life in the Member States in which they live'. In the UK poverty has grown significantly in recent years and by the turn of the century nearly one quarter of the population were officially living in poverty.

The Child Poverty Action Group (CPAG), which periodically publishes evidence about poverty in Britain,[10] reported the results of a number of different national surveys which all pointed to a substantial increase in the proportion of the population living below 50 per cent of mean income or below 60 per cent of median income after housing costs in the last two decades of the twentieth century. In 2001/02, 12.5 million people in Great Britain (22 per cent of the population) were living in households with below 60 per cent of median income after housing costs. This was a substantial increase from 1979 when the comparable figures were 7.1 million (13 per cent of the population).[11] The group with the highest risk was the unemployed, nearly four-fifths of whom were in poverty. Three-fifths of lone parent families, and around one-third of families where there was only part-time worker and also single pensioners were the next most vulnerable groups.[12] One-third of all children, over 4 million, were living in poverty. 'Over the 20-year period from 1979 to 1999/2000, the real incomes of the poorest 10 per cent saw a real rise after housing costs of only 6 per cent compared to a rise of 80 per cent for the mean ... (and) 86 per cent (for the richest 10 per cent)'. In other words, the gap between the rich and

---

[10] Howard et al. 2001: 3, 9, 19, 30, 74.   [11] Flaherty et al. 2004: 31.
[12] Howard et al. 2001: 37–40, 43–44, 47.

the poor was getting much wider. Research using data from the British Household Panel Survey showed that 'certain groups are systematically more at risk of falling into poverty and being in it for longer. These include: large families, lone parents, single people, households with a very young or old family head, those with low levels of educational attainment, people from minority ethnic groups, those living in areas of high unemployment or who are themselves unemployed, retired, disabled or on maternity leave'.

Finally, there have been significant changes in the composition of the poorest 10 per cent of the population (after housing costs) in the past two decades. While the proportion of pensioner couples was down there were significant increases in the proportions who were lone parent families, unemployed, or self-employed or in households with one or more part-time workers.

By the mid-1990s, the UK had child poverty rates higher than any other industrialized nation with the exception of the USA and Russia.[13] In 2001/02 3.8 million children were living in households below the threshold income, a drop of 0.6 million since 1996/97. Two million children lived in workless households. In 1999 Tony Blair announced the aim to end child poverty within a generation. Four groups of measures were to promote this aim: preventive, labour market ('work for those who can'), social protection ('security for those who can't') and neighbourhood regeneration. A recent evaluation reported that some progress had been made in reducing child poverty, though not enough to meet Government targets, but that little progress had been made in reducing poverty as a whole. Indeed, 'even if the 10-year target of halving child poverty by 2010 is reached, levels will still be higher than in 1979'.[14]

What poverty means for children and their parents was investigated by Middleton et al. in the mid-1990s. Taking as their starting point the 1991 UN Convention on 'the right of every child to a standard of living adequate for the child's physical, mental, spiritual, moral and social development' and the need for adequate resources which 'take into account the needs of the child relative to standards which are considered to be acceptable within . . . society',[15] they described the pressures on children to conform to the clothing norms of their peers and the financial pressures on parents to respond to the demands of schools, for trips and holidays and so on. Poorer parents often go without food for their children who may be singled out

---

[13] Howard et al. 2001: 30, 47, 74.   [14] Flaherty et al. 2004: 63–66.
[15] In Middleton et al. 1994: 2, 6–7.

and abused on account of their poverty. It has been estimated that 1.4 million 11–15 year-olds have some paid employment in the UK.

Caritas Europa has recently urged 'the need for family-oriented policies' to tackle poverty and in Britain Caritas-Social Action has joined End Child Poverty, a coalition of organisations committed to policies which would take a million children out of poverty by 2010.[16]

Work

In 2002, there were 3¾ million people who wanted to be in paid work but were not, down from a peak of 5 million in 1993. There were over 2 million long-term workless households, unchanged since 1995. Nearly one half of all lone parents did not have paid work. Around ½ million young adults aged 16–24 were unemployed in 2002 (around 10 per cent), half the number since the peak in 1993, but young adult rates were still more than twice those for older workers. One and a half million people were on temporary contracts in 2002, the same as in 1995. People without qualifications were three times less likely to receive job related training compared with those with some qualifications. The unemployed were more at-risk of poverty than any other group and 'during the 1990s, nearly a half of workless households spent three years in the bottom three-tenths of the income distribution, compared with around one in thirteen households in work'.[17]

Low pay

Over ½ million young adults aged 18–21 and 1½ million adults aged 22 to retirement were paid less than £4.40 per hour in 2002. McNay and Pond noted that 'most of the low paid are women. Many families only avoid hardship through the joint contribution of two breadwinners, and the evidence suggests that the numbers in poverty would rise considerably were it not for the contribution of married women . . . the extra wage often does no more than bring the joint household income up to an acceptable level in compensation for the low wages of one partner'.[18] In a recent memorandum to the Prime Minister, the Zacchaeus Trust drew attention to the International Covenant on Economic, Social and Cultural Rights which included 'the right of everyone to be free from hunger' and argued

[16] Caritas Europa 2004; www.caritas-socialaction.org.uk   [17] Howard et al. 2001: 81.
[18] McNay and Pond 1981: 13.

that 'the UK persistently fails to respect its commitment to the convention in that our statutory minimum incomes force a competition for inadequate weekly money between food and fuel, or clothes, rent, council tax. Hunger is a frequent and scandalous reality in Britain.'[19]

Education

In 2000/01 around 150,000 16-year-olds (25 per cent) got no grades above a D at GCSE and in 2002, 200,000 had no basic qualifications, the same as in 1997 but down by one third since 1992. Smith and Noble traced the evolution of educational policy in this country to equality of access but this had not ensured equality of outcome. With the shift from social engineering to market approaches to schooling in the 1980s and 1990s there was evidence that many children in poor areas continued to experience social and educational disadvantage. While there have been some improvements in school performance in recent years, factors such as race, gender, social class and low income continued to have a significant impact. Smith and Noble concluded: 'It is ... adverse social and economic conditions in income, housing, job opportunities and the local environment which depress performance. Long-term follow-up studies of children born in 1947, 1958 and 1970 provide conclusive evidence of a wide – and sometimes widening – gap in educational performance among children from different social backgrounds'.[20] Factors which undermined children's progress included 'ill-health, financial pressures on the family, family stress and breakdown. Such events are statistically more likely to happen to children from disadvantaged backgrounds, where families may have fewer resources to cope'. There was also evidence that hunger and nutritional deficiencies experienced by many poor children inhibited their performance. There were dangers where children in receipt of free school meals were stigmatized and bullied.[21]

Health

People on below-average incomes are twice as likely to develop a mental illness than those on average and higher incomes. Children from manual social classes are one and a third times more likely to be born underweight

[19] http:www.jcwi.org.uk/campaign/zacchaeus2000trust.pdf
[20] Smith and Noble 1995: 30, 32–33.   [21] McMahon and Marsh 1999: 43.

and 1½ times more likely to die in accidents than children from non-manual social classes. Young men aged 15–24 in the manual social classes are twice as likely to commit suicide as those in the non-manual classes. There has been a series of major reports which have traced health inequalities.[22] These provided strong evidence for the importance of structural factors such as deprivation in pregnancy, infancy and childhood for health inequalities. They concluded that the 'weight of scientific evidence supports a socio-economic explanation of health inequalities' which necessitated steps to reduce income inequalities and improve the living standards of poor households. Mary Shaw et al. summarized the evidence 'that the health gap is widening and that this widening has followed socio-economic polarisation in Britain. As the poor have become relatively poorer and have become concentrated into particular areas of the country, poor health has similarly become more concentrated both by social group and by area over the last twenty years'. The association between poverty and a whole range of health problems for young people has been summarized by Dennehy et al. while the issue of food poverty has been reviewed by Dowler et al. There is growing awareness that 'carers' are often 'paying the price' of poverty and social exclusion. The growing obesity of children has recently created official alarm that there may be a reversal of the long-term increase of life expectancy over the next generation.

Crime

Lone parents and households headed by young people are three times more likely to be burgled than the average. Half of those on low income do not have any household insurance compared to a fifth of households on average income. Households with no household insurance are around three times as likely to be burgled as those with insurance. Dee Cook[23] has reported that there are significant inequalities in the punishment of offenders and 'efforts to combat the race, class and gender biases of the criminal justice system seem to have had little impact . . . Criminal justice is about punishing people – and those people are predominantly the poor, the disadvantaged and the powerless'.

---

[22] Townsend and Davidson 1988; Whitehead 1988; Wilkinson 1996, 2005; Acheson Report 1998; Berridge and Blume 2003: 165, 178–179, 196; Shaw et al. 1999: 107–167; Dennehy et al. 1997: 75–76; Dowler et al. 2001; Howard, 2001.

[23] Cook 1997: 32, 83, 95.

Housing and homelessness

The number of 'rough sleepers' in Britain declined from almost 2000 in 1998 to around 500 in 2004, largely as a result of increasing hostel provision.[24] In June 2003 there were 93,480 households in accommodation arranged by local authorities under homelessness legislation, almost double the number in 1997. Thirty-five per cent of those accepted as meeting the statutory criteria of being eligible for assistance with accommodation 'arose because parents, relatives or friends (mostly parents) were no longer able, or willing, to accommodate them. This proportion has gradually risen since 1997, when it represented around 27 per cent of acceptances'.

In 2000 27 per cent of all households owned their homes outright while 43 per cent were buying their homes on a mortgage. In the same year, 134,000 warrants were issued for repossession and 62,000 were executed. Repossession due to mortgage arrears is a private disaster and results in homelessness. 'Households with younger heads are at greater risk of having mortgage arrears. Older people will in general have had more time to accumulate savings to cushion against times of unexpected financial hardship'.[25] Factors which generate it include unemployment and an increasingly insecure labour market with increasingly flexible and low-paid employment, high interest rates and increased family breakdown.[26]

In spite of some improvements in the 1990s, levels of overcrowding in the social rented sector are 2½ times the level for those with mortgages and households in the private rented sector are twice as likely as other households to be without central heating. In 2001 only 162,000 houses were built, the lowest for 75 years. There is a shortage of affordable housing.

Ethnic minorities

People of Black Caribbean, Bangladeshi and African ethnicity are twice as likely to be out of work and wanting work compared with white people. Black pupils are four times as likely as white pupils to be permanently excluded from school. Black young adults are seven times as likely as white young adults to be in prison. Bangladeshis and Pakistanis are twice as likely not to have a bank or building society account as the rest of the population

---

[24] http://www.odpm.gov.uk Office of the Deputy Prime Minister. Reports on homelessness.
[25] *Social Trends 33*, 2003: Tables 10.18 and 10.27 and p. 177.   [26] Jenkinson 1992.

and are the poorest group in Britain with three times the national average in the poorest fifth of the population.[27] There is considerable educational underachievement on the part of Afro-Caribbean children. Kaushika Amin has recently reviewed the evidence for poverty, inequality and deprivation among the Afro-Caribbean and Asian communities.[28]

Older people

In 1999/2000 there were 1¼ million pensioners who had no income other than the state pension, a number unchanged since at least 1994/95. The proportion of elderly people aged 75 and over who receive support from social services to help them live at home is now two-thirds of what it was at the peak in 1994. Caritas-Social Action has expressed concern that vulnerable old people might 'draw the short straw'.

Communities

The proportion of the poorest fifth of the population not participating in any social, political, cultural or community organization is 1½ times that of the richest fifth. In two-thirds of households in social housing, the head of household is not in paid work. One-sixth of the poorest households did not have any type of bank or building society account in 2001/02. Neighbourhood Management is an important element in the Government's campaign to tackle social exclusion. The early evidence appears to suggest that 'the most effective action is likely to come from strategies which engage effectively at all levels and are able to combine "top-down" (service-led) and "bottom-up" (community-led) forces for change'.[29]

Two other areas can be added to the New Policy Institute list:

Debt

Since the late 1970s 'households have taken a greater amount of new credit each year than has been repaid, and the level of personal indebtedness has

---

[27] Platt 2002: 58.

[28] Amin, K. 1992; see also Platt 2002. It is of interest that CARJ has pointed out that only four of the 5,600 priests in England and Wales with pastoral responsibility are Black British-born and that Black Catholics perceive that they are being excluded; CARJ 2000: 9, 13; see also Kalilombe et al. 1991.

[29] http://www.jrf.org.uk/knowledge/findings reporting on a JRF report, 2000.

therefore risen'.[30] In 1990 the average household had a credit commitment of £1,800. In 1991 4.3 million households had four or more credit commitments. About 2.5 million households in the UK had problems meeting repayments.[31] In 2003 it was reported that the typical household falling into difficulty with repayments owed £25,000 spread across 15 different lenders, compared to £10,000 in 2000. By 2004 UK consumer debt, money owed on credit cards, mortgages, loans and overdrafts, exceeded £1 trillion (i.e. £1,000 billion). The alarming rise in debt is attributed to easy credit and aggressive marketing. 'Loan sharks' or doorstep lenders frequently charge interest rates in excess of 200 per cent APR.[32] Ford argued that most low-income households fell into debt *because* they were poor and because the forms of credit available to them were expensive and discriminatory. Lone mothers were particularly vulnerable.

Multiple economic disadvantage

The evidence suggests overwhelmingly that the poor are subject to multiple economic disadvantages. In 1967 David Caplovitz showed that *The Poor Pay More* in the United States.[33] In the 1970s the CPAG and the National Consumer Council both demonstrated similar findings in Britain.[34] Subsequently, Michael Young drew attention to the important dimension of the distribution of income *within* families. 'Wives of low paid husbands ... have a triple burden to bear. They get less housekeeping money; they are less likely to have had an increase in it over the past year; they pay for more things out of it'.[35] In sum it can be said that in general the poor pay more for less and poorer goods and inferior services.

These bare statistics certainly provide a broad outline of multiple deprivation and social exclusion in our contemporary society. Several studies have attempted to give a flavour of what it must 'feel' like to experience it. Cohen et al. have described what it is like to manage on benefit and the other effects of living in poverty: 'feelings of powerlessness, loss of self-esteem, a sense of guilt and stigma'.[36] Bob Holman who lives alongside the poor in Glasgow's Easterhouse, persuaded seven of them to describe the reality of their lives.[37] The CPAG has published an account of a wide variety of poor people's own analyses of poverty.[38] Polly Toynbee

---

[30] Ford 1991: 1.   [31] McHugh, F. P. 1994: 13, 20, 29.
[32] http://www.church-poverty.org.uk/dticonsultation.htm Debt on Our Doorstep is campaigning for a statutory maximum interest rate.
[33] Caplovitz 1967.   [34] Piachaud 1974, 2005; Young 1975.   [35] Young 1977.
[36] Cohen et al. 1992.   [37] Holman 1998.   [38] Beresford et al. 1999.

has written passionately about her desperate attempt to live in poverty on a Clapham estate not far from her comfortable home in an adjacent affluent area. She noted 'the great social divide to be found within each area, ... rich and poor living in the same postal sectors ... managing to be almost unaware of each other in their parallel space'.[39] In the United States, Barbara Ehrenreich has similarly explored trying to survive on minimum-wage jobs.[40]

The poor and excluded may be 'hidden' and adjacent to affluent areas, as Toynbee has shown, or concentrated in geographical regions[41] where previously dominant industries are in decline. They are invariably concentrated in certain social groups and gender, class and ethnic minority differences are particularly important. What also seems clear is that they are associated with economic, social and political changes, for example in response to the forces of globalization. Alan Walker has suggested that the Thatcher and Major governments pursued a 'strategy of inequality' which they saw as 'an engine of enterprise'. The enterprise culture which they promoted incorrectly assumed there would be a 'trickle down' benefit in the interests of the common good and that 'there is no alternative' to the neo-liberal approach. The result was 'the biggest rise in poverty and social exclusion since the 1930s ... (with) those bearing the largest burden of the government's strategy (being) the very poorest'.[42] That these outcomes were the result of deliberate economic and social policies rather than being the inevitable consequences of economic forces beyond control was evident from international comparisons.[43] 'Deepening inequality marginalises and excludes the poor, and fosters the social isolationism of the rich'.[44] Recent analyses of the 2001 Census returns have shown a dramatic widening of the gap between the rich and the poor in the UK. Yet it is clear that poverty and social exclusion are corrosive of one's sense of worth and dignity as a human being created in the image of God. This is a social injustice.

SOCIAL EXCLUSION AND SOCIAL ANALYSIS

Among the factors which have influenced the recent growth of poverty and inequality have been changes in the global economy, increasing unemployment during recessions, the growth of flexible work and low-pay, the increase of part-time work and the employment of married women,

---

[39] Toynbee 2003: 18–19.   [40] Ehrenreich, B. 2002.
[41] Philo 1995; Brown et al. 2002; for Europe, see Cross 1993.   [42] Walker 1997: 9.
[43] See, e.g., Hutton 1996, 2002; Hornsby-Smith 1999b.   [44] Brown et al. 2002: 163.

changes in families resulting from increased life expectancy, family break-down and divorce, and the increasing number of lone parents. But these are simply descriptions of associated changes. To seek explanations we must go further and locate our interpretation within an understanding of the nature of the aggressive form of neo-liberal capitalism which has been promoted by both the British and American administrations over the past twenty-five years. As Walker and others have pointed out, there was a deliberate strategy to promote the 'enterprise culture', favour the rich by providing incentives, deregulate the labour market, dismantle much of the legislation which protected trade unions and worker rights, squeeze the poor out of a supposed 'dependency culture', and adjust the tax and benefits systems in regressive ways. The deliberate widening of inequality seems so 'unfair'.

Reference was made earlier to John Rawls' theory of justice as fairness,[45] and what means might be appropriate to achieve that, and to Amartya Sen's human capability approach,[46] which put a greater emphasis on basic social outcomes and functioning. Sen distinguished between 'attainment equality' (which might be vulnerable to the criticism of 'levelling down' and the neglect of other attainments such as efficiency) and 'shortfall equality' which allowed for different potentials which reflected human diversity. Sen stressed the importance of asking 'equality of what?'

The variations between different forms of capitalism[47] and welfare states[48] demonstrated clearly that different social and economic choices were possible and gave the lie to the claim that 'there is no alternative' to the neo-liberal version of market capitalism. The fact is that some policy choices are more likely to reduce the different dimensions of inequality and are, therefore, more likely to enhance the capability of realizing fully each individual's equal dignity and favour the values of social justice and equality of substantive citizenship in terms of civil or legal, political, and social and cultural rights. It will also be recalled that extensions of citizenship have historically always been the product of struggle, and have on occasion been reversed.

Thus John Scott has argued that there are three competing models of citizenship: the liberal, social democratic and radical. In recent decades the liberal version has gained in public acceptability along with a strong

---

[45] Rawls 1973.   [46] Sen 1992: 90–93.
[47] Hutton 1996: 257–284, and 2002. See also Gray 1998; Turner 2001; Stiglitz 2002.
[48] See, e.g. Castles 1993; Esping-Andersen 1990; George and Taylor-Gooby 1996; Hornsby-Smith 1999b; Kamerman and Kahn 1978; Kiely and Richardson 1991; Van Kersbergen 1995.

element of fatalism, at the expense of the earlier post-war social democratic version. This has tended to legitimize recent increases in inequality, with the expansion of wealth and privilege at one end of the spectrum and poverty and deprivation at the other, as necessary to encourage enterprise and wealth-creators in the interests of society as a whole. In this liberal version of citizenship great wealth and huge incomes were seen as the legitimate rewards of hard work. At best those who were deprived, for whatever reason, were seen as second-class citizens and as 'undeserving' of more than the minimum of welfare support.[49] Ruth Lister argued convincingly, however, that poverty and deprivation were 'corrosive of citizenship' and that 'poverty spells exclusion from the full rights of citizenship'.[50] But Scott's point that with high levels of inequality the rich and privileged were also excluded from full participation in the common life of society was also important and, indeed, was demonstrated in Toynbee's experiences. The liberal model cannot be reconciled easily with the Christian vision of the equality of human dignity and the corresponding right to participate fully in society.

A number of commentators have addressed various aspects of the dysfunctions of high and increasing levels of inequality associated with an uncompromising form of neo-liberal economics. Jonathan Boswell has presented a strong case in favour of communitarian forms of public co-operation in economic matters.[51] Various forms of corporatism, the social market model, and stakeholding also aimed to promote social inclusion and cohesion. Will Hutton, for example, argued that

At the heart of the welfare state lies a conception of the just society ... it is a symbol of our capacity to act together morally, to share and to recognise the mutuality of rights and obligations ... It is an expression of social citizenship ... It provides boundaries to the operation of markets, underwrites social cohesion and helps produce the values that sustain the co-operation without which successful economies cannot flourish.[52]

Hutton's vision of a stakeholder economy was contested not only by the 'new right' but also by those who sought a 'third way' – a benevolent form of liberal capitalism along with a desirable shifting of the balance towards collective redistribution. Thus Adair Turner, a former Director-General of the CBI, concluded that 'the fundamental issue is how to reconcile a dynamic economy and the liberating effects of individual economic

---

[49] Scott 1994: 147–160. [50] Lister 1990: 68–73.
[51] Boswell 1994a, 1994b. [52] Hutton 1996: 306–307.

freedom with the objective of an inclusive society, recognizing that totally free markets will not achieve that end'.[53]

Ruth Levitas has shown that the concept of 'social exclusion' is 'intrinsically problematic'[54] and is embedded in three distinct discourses which she labelled:

- *Redistributionist egalitarian discourse* (RED), which 'embraces notions of citizenship and social rights' and with a primary concern to address the problem of poverty;
- *Moral underclass discourse* (MUD), which is gendered and which focuses on supposed deficiencies on the part of those, typically young, unemployable, young men and socially irresponsible single mothers, who are said to have excluded themselves; and a
- *Social integrationist discourse* (SID), which focuses in particular on access to paid work.

Levitas argued that the communitarian, stakeholding and social inclusion discourses tended to obscure underlying inequalities and fundamental conflicts of interest and that there was no necessary association between social inclusion and social cohesion in society. She pointed out that 'the term social exclusion presumes that inclusion is beneficial, but it is salutary to remember that even if the unemployed, women, ethnic minorities and disabled people achieve equal opportunities in the labour market, this will still mean participation in a capitalist economy driven by profit, based upon exploitation and fundamentally divided by class'.[55]

Ruth Lister also argued that 'exclusion has to be tackled at both the material and the symbolic level and across a range of dimensions of inequalities ... While social cohesion and social justice are not necessarily incompatible, the promotion of a narrow social cohesion model of inclusion, which ignores inequalities of resources and power, runs the risk of becoming detached from principles of social justice'.[56] In a similar vein, John Gray[57] suggested that the concept of social inclusion represented a social liberal shift away from the social democrat commitment to distributive equality. He went further and argued that both equality and inclusion were incompatible with the project of a global free market. These various writers stressed that the New Labour project to address social exclusion by maximizing access to paid work and education, would not by itself address the issue of widening social inequality.

---

[53] Turner 2001: 376–379.   [54] Levitas 1998: 7.
[55] Levitas 1998: 187–188; see also Askonas and Stewart 2000.
[56] Lister 2000: 51–52.   [57] Gray 2000.

Finally, the difficulties of reconciling the escalating costs of social needs and the increasing resistance to pay for them, especially from the public purse, was explored by Askonas and Frowen who set out to challenge the prevailing 'culture of unconcern' and explore 'ways of modifying the tension between egocentric self-interest in economic behaviour' in favour of the 'enhancement of civic generosity'.[58] This civic generosity was likely to grow where there were closer social relationships but to be destroyed by wide social inequalities. Raymond Plant argued strongly against the assumptions of neo-liberal thought which rejected any sense of *collective* moral obligation and suggested that 'we can collectively be held morally responsible for what are the forseeable consequences of our decisions ... those who are poor as a result of the markets can be said to suffer injustice and thus their position can be regarded as a matter for collective social concern'.[59]

CATHOLIC APPROACHES TO INEQUALITY

Christians believe in the essential equality of dignity of all human beings. It follows that their social concern is with the elimination of those inequalities or conditions which inhibit or detract from the capability of realizing fully that equal dignity. In concrete terms this means that, in spite of inevitable human diversity, some measure of the capability of participating equally in the social, economic, political and cultural dimensions of life in society is necessary in the interest of social justice. The ethical case for equality is that present economic and social structures of inequality inhibit the achievement of that equality of dignity and full participation in society, legally, politically and socially.

We noted previously that Catholic social thought has not devoted a great deal of time to addressing the issue of equality. This is likely to be associated with a distinct preference for a hierarchical ordering of society. This bias is increasingly challenged within the Church, a process which might reasonably be seen as a development of doctrine. The question must be asked: what possible moral justification can there be in a world of global mass production for the huge and growing inequalities in income and wealth? A selection of major Church documents which have addressed various aspects of poverty, inequality and social exclusion has been summarized in Table 9.1.

---

[58] Askonas and Frowen 1997: xi, xv.   [59] Plant 1997: 215.

Table 9.1. *Major church documents on exclusion, 1891–1996*

Year	Author[a]	Document	Key Themes	Reference[b]
1891	Leo XIII	*Rerum Novarum*	Private ownership; worker dignity	OBS, 14–39
1931	Pius XI	*Quadragesimo Anno*	Reforming capitalism; social justice	OBS, 42–79
1961	John XXIII	*Mater et Magistra*	Criteria for just distribution; inequalities	OBS, 84–128
1965	Vat. II	*Gaudium et Spes*	Participation; distribution; migration	OBS, 165–237
1971	Paul VI	*Octogesima Adveniens*	Urbanisation and industrialisation	OBS, 265–286
1986	US NCCB	*Economic Justice*	Responsible capitalism; process	OBS, 572–680
1987	John Paul II	*Sollicitudo Rei Socialis*	Fourth World; poverty; homelessness	OBS, 393–436
1987	J&P Cmsn	*Church and Housing*	Homelessness and housing problem	CTS, S 399
1991	John Paul II	*Centesimus Annus*	New forms of property; consumerism	OBS, 437–488
1994	John Paul II	*Tertio Millennio Adveniente*	Jubilee justice; social doctrine	CTS, Do 627
1996	E&W Bps	*The Common Good*	Structural injustices; social capital	Gabriel

Notes:
[a] NCCB: (US) National Conference of Catholic Bishops; J&P Cmsn: Pontifical Commission 'Iustitia et Pax'; E&W Bps: Conference of Bishops of England and Wales.
[b] OBS: O'Brien and Shannon, 1992; CTS: Catholic Truth Society (London).

Rerum Novarum (Leo XIII 1891)

Leo XIII admitted that 'it is not easy to define the relative rights and the mutual duties of the wealthy and of the poor, of capital and of labour' (§1). The fruits of the earth were intended 'to minister to the needs of all' (§7). He insisted on the right to private property and saw 'socialist' attempts to achieve equality as 'the levelling down of all to the same condition of misery' (§12). This led him to claim 'that humanity must remain as it is' (§14). Inequality was natural and socially necessary though the essential dignity of everyone must be respected (§§15, 20–21). The response to poverty should be 'beautiful charity' rather than 'State-organised relief' (§§24, 45) though it was the job of the state to seek the 'equal distribution of public burdens' in the interests of the 'common good' (§26). 'The poor and helpless have a claim to special consideration' but 'neither justice nor the common good allows anyone to seize that which belongs to another ... under the pretext of futile and ridiculous equality' (§§29–30). In spite of his insistence on the right of the worker to a just wage, Leo XIII seemed more concerned with the potential for coercion by trade unions than by the enormous power differentials in favour of capital (§§34, 38). It could reasonably be said that what Leo sought was the amelioration of social wrongs rather than justice.

Quadragesimo Anno (Pius XI, 1931)

Forty years later Pius XI stressed 'the twofold aspect of ownership ... individual or social' (§45) and was critical of the 'excessive advantages' of capital as well as the 'unjust claims of labour' and the 'alluring poison' of socialism (§§54–55). He wrote that 'the division of goods which is effected by private ownership is ordained by nature itself', though he added that wealth must be distributed so as to serve the common good (§56–57). 'Each class ... must receive its due share ... (in) conformity with the demands of the common good and social justice. For every sincere observer realizes that the vast differences between the few who hold excessive wealth and the many who live in destitution constitute a grave evil in modern society' (§§58, 60).

Pius XI favoured workers becoming sharers in the ownership or management of enterprises and participating in some way in the profits, a form of social inclusion (§65). Amelioration by means of charity needed to be underpinned by social justice. He pleaded that capitalism was not intrinsically violent but insisted that it must have regard for 'the human dignity of workers, the social character of economic life, social justice, and the common good' (§101). The pope complained about the 'immense power and despotic economic domination ... concentrated in the hands of a few' which was 'a natural result of unrestrained free competition which permits the survival of those only who are the strongest' (§§105, 107). The extremes of both individualism and collectivism were to be avoided and 'commutative justice, supported however by Christian charity', should regulate capital-labour relations, and there should be effective public regulation of economic domination according 'to the requirements of the common good, that is, the norm of social justice' (§§110, 120).

Mater et Magistra (John XXIII 1961)

The pontificate of John XXIII is generally recognized to have initiated a new era and openness to the social realities and complexities in the modern world. This encyclical appeared to share the western reformist assumptions of the time.[60] The pope insisted that the determination of wage levels 'cannot be left entirely to unregulated competition ... (or) be decided arbitrarily at the will of the more powerful' (§71). Noting the rapid growth of some economies in the post-war world, he insisted that in justice, 'all classes of citizens will benefit equitably from an increase of national wealth ... (Hence) effective steps (should be) taken that class differences arising from disparity of wealth not be increased but lessened so far as possible ... so that everyone in the community can develop and perfect himself' (§§73–74).

Taking into account the common good at the national level he suggested that income distribution should take into account the need:

To provide employment for as many workers as possible; to take care lest privileged groups arise ...; to maintain a balance between wages and prices; to make accessible the goods and services for a better life to as many persons as possible; either to eliminate or to keep within bounds the inequalities that exist between different sectors of the economy ...; to balance properly any increases in output with advances in services provided to citizens, especially by public authority; to adjust, as far as possible, the means of production to the progress of science and technology; finally, to ensure the advantages of a more humane way of existence not merely subserve the present generation but have regard for future generations as well (§79).

John XXIII appeared to have a not unsympathetic understanding of capitalist economies. He broadened the sense of the just wage, introduced the notion of social development, recognized the role of public property and goods, and the redistributive role of the welfare state, subject to the principle of subsidiarity, in the interest of the common good, introduced the notion of inter-generational justice, and recognized the interdependence of people and countries in the modern world.

---

[60] O'Brien and Shannon 1992: 82.

Gaudium et Spes (Vatican II 1965)

The Pastoral Constitution on the Church in the Modern World developed these themes. At its heart was a theological understanding of the dignity of each individual human person:

Since all men possess a rational soul and are created in God's likeness, since they have the same nature and origin, have been redeemed by Christ, and enjoy the same divine calling and destiny, the basic equality of all must receive increasingly greater recognition ... Although rightful differences exist between men, the equal dignity of persons demands that a more humane and just condition of life be brought about. For excessive economic and social differences between the members of the one human family ... cause scandal, and militate against social justice, equity, the dignity of the human person, as well as social and international peace (§29).

There was a recognition that 'unless his living conditions allow him to become conscious of his dignity' a man cannot participate in society or act responsibly (§31). The challenges of socioeconomic life was one of five contemporary problem areas addressed in Part II of *Gaudium et Spes*. Economic matters should be organized according to the principles of justice and equity in order 'to remove as quickly as possible the immense economic inequalities which now exist' (§§63, 66). A clear warning about the assumptions of liberal capitalism was given: 'theories which obstruct the necessary reforms in the name of a false liberty must be branded as erroneous' (§65). 'The active participation of everyone in the running of an enterprise should be promoted' (§68) and 'the distribution of goods should be directed toward providing employment and sufficient income for the people of today and of the future' (§70). In sum, Vatican II called for greater equality among people but it did not offer much in the way of specific policies.

Octogesima Adveniens (Paul VI 1971)

Pope Paul's apostolic letter was a response to the 'grave problems of our time' notably the 'flagrant inequalities (which) exist' (§2). It was the responsibility of Christians to respond in their own countries (§4) to such problems as the 'human conditions of production, fairness in the exchange of goods and in the division of wealth, the significance of the increased needs of consumption, and the sharing of responsibility' (§7). Pope Paul was particularly concerned about the problems of urbanism, the drift from the land and agriculture, and the hidden misery found in the city

which 'fosters discrimination and also indifference', homelessness, loneliness and exploitation (§10). The pope reflected on the needs of youth and
urged equal cultural, economic, social and political rights for women (§13).
He condemned racial and other forms of discrimination (§16) and insisted
on the right to emigrate, have decent housing and be integrated into the
host society (§17). He acknowledged the two aspirations: to equality and to
participation (§22). 'The Gospel instructs us in the preferential respect due
to the poor . . . (and that) the more fortunate should renounce some of
their rights so as to place their goods more generously at the service of
others' (§§23, 43). He warned that the 'new economic powers', the multinationals, able to 'conduct autonomous strategies' beyond political control, 'can lead to a new and abusive form of economic domination' (§44).
In the light of these challenges to the common good, Pope Paul proclaimed
a 'call to action' to lay people, to conversion, and a 'livelier awareness of
personal responsibility and . . . effective action' (§48) according to local
circumstances.

Economic Justice for All (United States Catholic Bishops 1986)

Poverty was the second of the four economic policy issues addressed in the
United States bishops' pastoral letter. They wrote that 'the norms of
human dignity and the preferential option for the poor' compelled them
to face the fact that one person in seven in the United States in 1986 lived
officially in poverty. 'It is a moral imperative of the highest priority' (§170).
They reviewed the characteristics of poverty, its association with low wages
and unemployment, and its concentration among particular groups
(§§174–182). They noted the 'very uneven distribution of wealth and
income' (§183) and that 'the gap between rich and poor . . . has increased
during the last decade', a reflection of 'the uneven distribution of power' in
United States society (§184; see also fn. 46). They admitted that:

Some degree of inequality not only is acceptable, but also may be considered
desirable for economic and social reasons, such as the need for incentives and the
provision of greater rewards for greater risks. However, unequal distribution
should be evaluated in terms of several moral principles . . .: the priority of meeting
the basic needs of the poor and the importance of increasing the level of participation by all members of society in the economic life of the nation. These norms
establish *a strong presumption against extreme inequality of income and wealth* as
long as there are poor, hungry, and homeless people in our midst. They also
suggest that extreme inequalities are detrimental to the development of social
solidarity and community (§185; emphases added).

In the light of these norms the bishops judged existing inequalities in the USA to be unacceptable and called for economic, political and social reforms to decrease inequities. They proceeded to offer a number of guidelines for action. While these were tailored to the United States situation in the 1980s, they are among the most specific attempts to make concrete policy proposals arising out of Catholic social thought and have continuing relevance. At the heart of their approach were the themes of human dignity, the preferential option for the poor, and the principles of solidarity and participation (§§186–188). They insisted that 'private charity and voluntary action are not sufficient' (§189) and that public taxation and social security policies that adjusted income distribution were necessary (§§189–193). They challenged the common stigmatizing of the poor (§194). They offered proposals for a national strategy to combat poverty and suggested (§§196–214) the need to:

- build a healthy economy providing full employment for all able to work at just wages;
- remove barriers to full and equal opportunities to work for women and minorities;
- foster self-help among the poor by both voluntary and public sectors;
- re-evaluate the tax system in light of its impact on the poor along progressive lines;
- make a stronger commitment to education for the poor;
- ensure that all social policies support families, especially those adversely affected by economic change;
- reform the welfare and income-support policies to encourage recipients to become self-sufficient, give them adequate support, establish national minimum benefit levels, and support for both two-parent and single-parent families.

Sollicitudo Rei Socialis (John Paul II 1987)

The theme of 'authentic development' can be applied *within* as well as *between* nations. Thus among the concerns mentioned by Pope John Paul II in this encyclical were the 'unequal distribution of the means of subsistence originally meant for everybody ... (and) of the benefits deriving from them' (§9), 'the intolerable burden of poverty' (§13), the widening gap in social inequalities (§14), various forms of exploitation, oppression and discrimination (§15), 'economic, financial, and social mechanisms which ... (accentuate) the situation of wealth for some and poverty for the rest' (§16), the 'lack of housing' (§17), 'the phenomenon of unemployment and underemployment' (§18), and the 'Fourth World', that is 'the bands of great or extreme poverty in countries of medium and high income' (§§14, 17 and FN 31). The pope was critical of liberal capitalism (§21) and 'structures of sin . . . rooted in personal sin, and thus always linked to the concrete acts of individuals who introduce these structures, consolidate them and make them difficult to remove' (§36). Among these were 'the all-consuming desire for profit, and . . . the thirst for power . . . (which is) a . . . moral evil, the fruit of many sins which lead to "structures of sin"' (§37). What was needed was a change of spiritual attitudes defining relationships with other people, and 'a firm and persevering determination to commit oneself to the common good . . . because we are all really responsible for all' (§39). The pope looked for an 'authentic liberation' from 'sin and the structures of sin' (§46).

The Church and Homelessness (Pontifical Justice and Peace Commission 1987)

What have You Done to Your Homeless Brother? indicated the huge scale of the housing problem globally. The lack of housing was 'a scandal' and an injustice. It was a structural problem caused by 'an unjust distribution of goods (and) the gap between rich and poor'.[61] The document insisted, following the *UN Universal Declaration of Human Rights* and Pope John Paul II's encyclical *Familiaris Consortio*, that 'the family has the right to decent housing, fit for family life and commensurate to the number of its members in a physical environment that provides the basic services for the life of the family and the community'. The document drew on a wide range of scriptural warrants in both the Old and New Testaments which attributed 'a fundamental value to "housing"'. Finally, the document proposed that a 'fundamental criterion for judging the justice or injustice of political and economic decisions (regarding housing policies) is their effective repercussions on those on the fringes of society'.

Centesimus Annus (John Paul II 1991)

In this encyclical Pope John Paul observed that 'in the countries of the West, different forms of poverty are being experienced by groups which

---

[61] Pontifical Commission 1988, I: 3, II: 3, III: 2 and 4, IV: 1.

live on the margins of society, by the elderly and the sick, by the victims of consumerism, and even more immediately by so many refugees and migrants' (§§57–58). The pope stressed the structural nature of injustice and was critical of the failures of liberal capitalism. The presumed 'equality between the parties' failed to take account of power differentials (§15). The pope noted that: many, possibly most people did not have the means to participate in the productive system. 'They have no possibility of acquiring the basic knowledge which would enable them to express their creativity and develop their potential. They have no way of entering the network of knowledge and intercommunication which would enable them to see their qualities appreciated and utilised' (§33).

Somewhat grudgingly he allowed that the Welfare State had remedied some 'forms of poverty and deprivation unworthy of the human person' but also criticized the 'social assistance state' and insisted that 'the principle of subsidiarity must be respected' (§48). In order for excluded or marginalized people to enter fully into social and economic life required more than 'giving from one's surplus' but rather 'a change of lifestyles, of models of production and consumption, and of the established structures of power', orienting instead to the common good (§58).

Tertio Millennio Adveniente (John Paul II 1994)

This Apostolic Letter, which was a beautiful scriptural reflection, was issued in preparation for the Jubilee year 2000. Pope John Paul recalled 'the custom of Jubilees, which began in the Old Testament and continues in the history of the Church'. All jubilees point to 'the year of the Lord's favour' (§11). He noted that the duty to free slaves and to cancel debts was regulated by detailed prescriptions in the Old Testament (§12; Exod 23: 10–11, Lev 25: 1–28, Deut 15: 1–6). 'The jubilee year was meant to restore equality among all the children of Israel ... Justice ... consisted above all in the protection of the weak ... The riches of Creation were to be considered as a common good of the whole of humanity ... The jubilee year was meant to restore this social justice' (§13). He called for repentance for the 'grave forms of injustice and exclusion' (§§33, 35–36) and concluded by urging a commitment to justice and peace in a world marked by '*intolerable social and economic inequalities*' (§51; emphasis added). The pope's letter was not grounded in any serious social analysis and offered no concrete proposals to address glaring inequalities.

The Common Good (Bishops of England and Wales 1996)

This popular and readable summary of Catholic social teaching was well received as a thoughtful contribution to social policy thinking both inside and outside the Church. Unlike the American bishops' pastoral it was not the product of an open consultative process. It did not draw on reputable official or academic studies or present an in-depth social analysis of the concrete social and economic injustices in the country. Nevertheless, the bishops suggested that 'if any section of the population is in fact excluded from participation in the life of the community ..., then that is a contradiction to the concept of the common good and calls for rectification' (§70). They insisted that governments had a duty to respond to poverty and exclusion, even though they allowed that the level of social security provision necessary for the common good was a political judgement. On inequality they observed that 'there must come a point at which the scale of the gap between the very wealthy and those at the bottom of the range of income begins to undermine the common good. This is the point at which society starts to be run for the benefit of the rich, not for its members' (§71).

They questioned the 'trickle-down' proposition from the wealthy to the poor as 'contrary to common sense as well as to actual experience' (§72). They reasserted the 'option for the poor' in the interests of justice (§73) and suggested that the really poor 'are those without sufficient means to take part in the life of the community ... (and so) are denied the rights of membership. Their choices are circumscribed; they have little personal freedom ... The first duty of the citizen towards the common good is to ensure that nobody is marginalised in this way and to bring back into a place in the community those who have been marginalised in the past' (§§74–75).

As we noted in the previous chapter, the bishops believed that the Catholic doctrine of the common good was incompatible with unlimited free-market capitalism and dismissed belief in Adam Smith's 'invisible hand' as 'idolatry or a form of economic superstition' (§76). On the contrary, market forces must, where necessary, be 'corrected in the name of natural law, social justice, human rights, and the common good' (§77). While market economies were more efficient than centrally commanded economies and accorded to some aspects of freedom and subsidiarity, to function well they required 'a regulatory and legal framework . . . (which) reflects the corresponding principle of solidarity' (§78).[62] The ideology of free market capitalism was likely to encourage individual selfishness so that 'Christian teaching that the service of others is of greater value than the service of self is sure to seem at odds with the ethos of a capitalist economy . . . A wealthy society, if it is a greedy society, is not a good society' (§§79–80). Considering individuals primarily as consumers was 'both contrary to the Gospel and to any rational idea of what a human being really is. It gravely disadvantages those who do not have wealth to spend. Unlimited free markets tend to produce what is in effect an "*option against the poor*"' (§85; emphasis added).

Catholic non-official social thought[63]

A number of other Catholic commentators have added to this body of official teaching. John Collins[64] was concerned about widening inequalities of wealth and called for conversion so that the comfortable 'become aware that the social mortgage has a prior claim, and that new structures of redistribution are needed to provide for restorative justice', and in particular, 'a recipient-based life-time capital receipts tax' for the redistribution of inherited wealth.[65]

However, not all Catholic writers agree with the general drift in recent official Catholic social teaching. Michael Novak, for example, has presented a spirited theological and political defence of 'democratic capitalism' and natural inequalities.[66] Novak contended that 'given the diversity and liberty of human life, no fair and free system can possibly guarantee equal outcomes'. What was important was 'a sense of equal opportunity' and the belief that individuals 'can better their condition', which 'can be realised only under conditions of economic growth'. In contrast to socialist societies which aimed to eliminate inequalities of economic wealth and power, democratic capitalism was most concerned with tyranny, especially state power. 'Under democratic capitalism, inequalities of wealth and

---

[62] 'Uncontrolled and blind market forces favour the powerful and neglect the weak. The free market is an instrument to be respected and used but never given the role of final arbiter of how society is shaped'. Irish Episcopal Conference 1992: §72.

[63] The term comes from Boswell et al. 2000.   [64] Collins 1999: 80–82.

[65] See also the Report of the Commission on Taxation and Citizenship published by the Fabian Society in 2000.

[66] Novak 1991: 15, 83–84, 202, 204–205.

power are not considered evil in themselves' though they are 'potential sources of evil and abuse'. Novak contended that:

The democratic socialist wishes speedily to remove ... inequalities (of wealth) as an offence against nature and morality. The democratic capitalist (on the other hand) sees them as typical of nature, but judges their morality by the benefits they bring (including lack of coercion) to the common good ... In principle, democratic capitalists do not oppose governmental action, but judge it according to whether it generates equalities which bring newcomers into markets or whether it generates dependency.

Novak's defence of 'democratic capitalism' failed to recognize that much, possibly most poverty and inequality was not due to natural misfortune or individual inadequacies or failures but to fundamental structural injustices which unfairly discriminated in favour of those who have or have inherited wealth and power, and hence life chances, to start with. It is to address these structural injustices that concepts such as the 'preferential option for the poor' have been so strongly emphasized in recent Catholic social thought.

Novak believed that since the wealthy have an abiding interest in a stable society, they 'have incentives to be public-spirited, civic-minded, and philanthropic'. Such optimistic judgements, however, have been strongly contested. For example, James Tobin is quoted as pointing out that 'today's inequality of condition is tomorrow's inequality of opportunity'.[67] In response to the claim that economic expansion and growth is a necessary step towards the reduction of inequality,[68] Frank Turner has argued that 'the fundamental (Christian) value which judges economic expansion is that of *fully human life and development* ... economic growth cannot be an intrinsic good or evil at all, still less an *absolute* good or evil, since it is assessed *only* by how it furthers or distorts the deeper human good'.[69]

He argued that 'if increased disparities of income are seen to be a pragmatically inevitable effect of growth, then growth cannot be the most pressing social good'. Like the bishops of England and Wales, he objected to the 'trickle-down' theory since it 'abstracts from the realities of power. The power given by wealth is inherently *power over others*'. The exaggerated claims for philanthropic generosity (or charity) are an inadequate response 'to the asymmetries of vulnerability'. Noting that generosity 'is a random response to the brute facts of human need ... (which) leaves power-relationships untouched', he quoted Reinhold Niebuhr's telling

---

[67] Quoted in Gannon 1987: 181.
[68] See the contributions by Gavin Davies and Stephen Frowen in Askonas and Frowen 1997: 135–143.
[69] Turner 1997: 146, 150–153.

judgement: 'Philanthropy combines genuine pity with the display of power and the latter element explains why the powerful are more inclined to be generous than to grant social justice'.[70] While it must be recognized that the balance between the redistributive social policies of states and the requirements of appropriate incentives to ensure economic growth is a matter of political compromise, as Calvez has observed: 'what must come under judgement ... is the very structure of unequal capitalism. Means must be sought to control capital so that it will be more equally distributed. Perhaps measures can be used to equalise the starting conditions for all, or to revert periodically in some systematic way to a degree of equality'.[71] Some have urged the need to seek solidarity with the poor and a committed participation in their struggles against the structures that cause and perpetuate poverty.[72]

Boswell drew on the analogy with the Trinity of 'three Divine Persons who are (a) diversely distinct, (b) absolutely equal, and (c) perfectly loving and united ... (which) fosters and implies a desire for diversity, parity and love to be combined *even* in the temporal world'.[73] Boswell recognized that in practice conflicts arose 'between pursuits of complex solidarity, pluralistic power sharing, and justice for the poor' and the difficulty of engineering and sustaining 'solidarity-in-diversity'. In the face of disappointments, 'all that social action can do is to remove what appear to be the main obstacles ... (and) tackle the seemingly worst impediments'.

CONTRIBUTIONS FROM OTHER CHRISTIANS

The main aim of this book has been to review Catholic social thought on social injustices. To provide a comprehensive review of the social thought of other Christians is beyond the scope of the present work. Nevertheless, the richness and the prophetic challenges they have offered must be acknowledged. Attention has already been drawn to the insights of Douglas Hicks and Duncan Forrester. Hicks[74] drew on Amartya Sen's notions of human capability and functioning and analyzed the tension between God's universality of care yet preferential concern for those in greatest need. He urged that in situations of unequal power and/or inequality, 'preferential solidarity is required. At the public policy level this calls for special attention to alleviate the relative and absolute deprivations that persons and groups suffer. Attention to the well-being of the most

---

[70] Quoting *Moral Man and Immoral Society*, London: SCM, 1963: 127.   [71] Calvez, J.-Y 2000: 11.
[72] Dorr 1991, 1992, 1994; O'Brien 1994.   [73] Boswell 2000: 109.   [74] Hicks 2000: 195, 235.

disadvantaged is required for achieving social conditions in which moral equality and genuine solidarity operate'. He concluded that 'the commitment to work for an equality of basic capability will require more equality (but not absolute equality) in the sphere of income'.

Forrester[75] acknowledged that the relationship between poverty, inequality and exclusion was complex. He reminded that there can also be 'gated communities' of the rich and powerful and 'ghettos of the privileged'. What was important was to build a society with a high degree of solidarity and mutual responsibility where the weak and poor were not humiliated, shamed and marginalized. Such a community, he insisted, 'requires a high degree of equality'. This led him to review the post-war welfare state as an institutionalized attempt to create 'a more fraternal, just and caring society'. But in an imperfect world, the reality has sometimes been disappointing. He reviewed the attempts of a number of Christian analysts, such as Frank Field, who sought ways of reforming the welfare state. Tawney had 'emphasised the inevitability of confronting the structures of power which sustain inequality'. Bob Holman reminded that it was necessary to allow the poor, unemployed, and deprived people a voice in policy decision-making and that egalitarian principles needed to be expressed in more egalitarian lifestyles. Anglican bishops have viewed the NHS as 'a kind of practical sacrament of the sort of society we believe to be both desirable and possible' and as a 'kind of ritual of civil religion' and collective caring rooted in Jewish and Christian traditions.

At the end of his book, Forrester drew on the parable of the chasm between Dives and Lazarus (Lk 16: 19–31) and likened this to the chasm between comfortable Britain and poor Britain. He argued that to bridge it, it was necessary to 'do justice' and demolish basic structures of inequality. Finally, he pointed out that in the parable of the last judgement (Mt 25: 31–46) it was governments and *nations* rather than individuals that were judged as to whether or not they had responded 'to the needs of the world, particularly the weak and poor and vulnerable'.

Particular attention must be paid to the *Faith in the City* Report on Urban Priority Areas in 1985 which was quite disgracefully dismissed as 'marxist' by the Government of the day. Given the underlying factors of 'unemployment, decayed housing, sub-standard educational and medical provision, and social disintegration' and the interlinking issues of poverty, powerlessness, inequality and polarization, the report's considered view

[75] Forrester 2001: 218, 224, 228, 230, 232–235, 247, 249, 255–256. See also Board of Social Responsibility 1986; Field 1996; Holman et al. 1999.

was that 'the nation is confronted by a *grave and fundamental injustice* in the UPAs'.[76] A Church Urban Fund was set up which supported a large number of projects in deprived inner city areas. In 1990 a progress report had the courage to admit that 'although we cannot do without good institutions in either Church or society, *the present structures of the Church (of England) reflect not a liberative gospel but structures of power and control; we need to ask who it is that the Church serves'*.[77] Roman Catholics could make a similar confession. The *Faith in the City* report also generated some rich theological reflections.[78] In 1997, a Methodist Working Group also published a report on the problems facing many cities.[79]

In 1992 the Bishop of Oxford asked *Is there a Gospel for the rich?* He drew on the parable of the labourers in the vineyard (Mt 20: 1–16) and noted that 'the King, recognizing the need of the labourers and their families, hires as many as he can and pays them all' the same. In the Kingdom of God, 'the law of the market is not the only law'; there is a higher law. 'Living with a sense of God's worth for every single human being will mean, in a great number of situations, ... affirmative action, positive discrimination, in order to help the most vulnerable human beings attain their potential'.[80] A study of the future of employment on behalf of the Council of Churches for Britain and Ireland in 1997 agreed with the Irish Catholic bishops that employment 'is not only the key to new hope for individuals suffering poverty and social exclusion; it is also the key to social harmony and a better life for us all. We do not believe that any other key will fit'.[81]

Hilary Russell[82] reflected on the experiences of poverty and provided a comprehensive social and theological analysis of poverty, inequality and social exclusion in Britain in the mid-1990s. She noted, 'the central problem remains poverty caused by economic restructuring', not individual or neighbourhood characteristics. 'Poverty arises out of people's employment or family circumstances *over which they may have little or no control'*. Since the issues were those of structural injustices, the solutions must inevitably include appropriate political responses. It was false to think that religion can be divorced from politics. Poverty must 'be treated as a systemic problem, not as something marginal. It requires preventive change not just amelioration ... (to) patch matters up rather than attack

---

[76] Archbishop of Canterbury's Commission on Urban Priority Areas 1985: xv.
[77] Archbishop of Canterbury's Advisory Group on Urban Priority Areas 1990: 14. Emphasis added.
[78] See, e.g., Harvey 1989, Sedgwick 1995.
[79] Methodist Church and NCH, *Action for Children*, 1997.   [80] Harries 1992: 110–112.
[81] Council of Churches for Britain and Ireland 1997: 173.   [82] Russell 1995: 118, 158, 248–249. 257.

the root causes'. In a critical review of the Church Urban Fund she concluded that 'structural change, political marginalisation and racial injustice – are not central to most CUF activity'. This may even 'allow the Church to duck the challenge of re-ordering mainstream budget priorities or relinquishing power to people in UPAs', hide behind 'a convenient smokescreen' to carry on as usual 'and thus compound the confusion between "charity" and justice'.

TOWARDS A CHRISTIAN RESPONSE

This chapter set out to reflect on distributive justice within society, particularly in Britain. It has provided a brief overview of evidence of widespread poverty, inequality and social exclusion along a large number of different dimensions. Social analysis suggested that these overwhelmingly have structural causes related to fundamental social and economic transformations in society. They consequently require appropriate political responses, not just to ameliorate the symptoms of poverty and exclusion but also to tackle the causes of injustices which exclude millions of our fellow human beings from full participation in the social life of our society. According to the New Policy Institute, a national strategy for social inclusion requires 'a national mobilisation'.[83]

Apart from the need for a growing consciousness and conversion on the part of individuals, and for a committed political response to ensure the removal of unjust sinful structures which oppress people and prevent their full human flourishing in tune with their essential dignity, there is a third dimension: culture, which also needs to be renewed, reformed and revitalized. This requires the addressing of both the culture of poverty – with its characteristics of demoralization, resignation, fatalism and dependence – and the culture of wealth and its pursuit – indifference, selfishness, misplaced ambition, greed, competitiveness, consumerism and the glorification of celebrities and their lifestyles. This is something which a Christian spirituality and praxis, which take seriously the underlying values and principles which we have identified – human dignity, common good, subsidiarity, solidarity, preferential options for the poor and for non-violence, and also for freedom, equality and participation – can do much to reform.

Care for widows, orphans and strangers, some of the most disadvantaged groups in Old Testament times, was an essential requirement of the

[83] Howarth et al. 2001.

Hebrew *Torah* (Exod 22: 20–23, Lev 19: 34, Deut 14: 29). Jesus urged the rich young man seeking perfection to go and sell his possessions and give the money to the poor (Mt 19: 16–22; Mk 10: 17–22; Lk 18: 18–23). The early Christian community 'owned everything in common; they sold their goods and possessions and distributed the proceeds among themselves according to what each one needed' (Acts 2: 45). St Paul acknowledged the 'generous contribution to the poor' of Jerusalem from the Church in Macedonia and Achaia (Rom 15: 26). In general terms the Christian Church has been concerned about poverty and inequality ever since. Historically, countless Christian individuals and many religious orders have attempted to ameliorate the suffering and address the needs of the poor. Basic health, welfare and educational institutions were originally Christian foundations. But it is perhaps only in recent times that concern has shifted from the *amelioration* of poverty to the search for the *causes* of poverty and the *empowerment* of poor people.

In this chapter Catholic approaches to inequality have been traced from the time of Leo XIII. Official teaching often had a distinct bias towards the *status quo* and stratified social hierarchies which were seen as somehow reflecting God's design, with the poor 'always with us' and yet conveniently and comfortably 'close to God'. The Church was fearful of the potential countervailing power of the modern state and until the post-Vatican period was highly suspicious of welfare state policies. In recent decades there has, however, been a growing awareness of the structural causes of injustice and of individual sin and greed as serving to consolidate and reinforce inequalities. But, on the whole, this has not yet led, save in the analyses of liberation theologians, to sustained attempts by Christians to challenge these structures. Even when injustices are acknowledged, the response tends to be that of 'charity' and amelioration rather than justice and prophetic challenge.

The prophetic challenges are increasingly coming from voluntary NGOs and from ecumenical coalitions rather than confessional organizations. The Commission on Poverty, Participation and Power, for example, insisted on the right of poor people to be heard and listened to.[84] Secular organizations, such as CPAG and Shelter, are in the vanguard of the struggle to seek greater justice for the poor and homeless. Christian organizations such as Church Action on Poverty (CAP), Housing Justice, THOMAS, Zacchaeus Trust and ATD Fourth World are substantially autonomous from the institutional Churches but informed by profound

---

[84] Commission on Poverty, Participation and Power 2000.

scriptural and theological reflection. Their deep involvement with deprived and excluded people and shared experiences with them give them a unique authority to challenge the vast mass of comfortable Christians with the prophetic dimension of their faith. They teach not just about charitable responses to needs but more profoundly, and indeed scripturally, about the Christian calling to break the chains of the enslavement by injustice of so many of our fellow human beings.

CHAPTER 10

Authentic development

INTERNATIONAL INEQUALITIES AND INJUSTICES

The fifth area of concern is that of international distributive justice and authentic development. 'The richest 5 per cent of the world's people receive 114 times the income of the poorest 5 per cent. The richest 1 per cent receive as much as the poorest 57 per cent'.[1] There is evidence that the gap between rich and poor countries has widened in recent years. Whereas the average income per head in the richest country today is around 400 times that in the poorest country, 250 years ago the ratio was around 5:1.[2] Billions of people in developing countries cannot satisfy their elementary needs. They are undernourished and have no access to drinkable water, sanitary and medical services, or schooling. The poorest fifth of the world's population have limited access to credit, capital and technology. Real incomes in the 'post-industrial' world rose at 2.4 per cent a year between 1965 and 1999 compared to 1.6 per cent in the world as a whole. The same countries also consumed half of the world's output of commercial energy and generated half of all carbon dioxide emissions although their proportion of the world's population declined from 32 per cent in 1950 to only 19 per cent today.[3]

While it is true that for decades missionary orders addressed the educational and health needs of many of the former colonial territories, in many ways it is only in recent years that attention has shifted from the amelioration of need to the search for understanding of the root causes of persistent needs and injustices, now regarded as social and structural sins, and to social action such as political advocacy to change unjust structures.

The literature on development is probably greater than that on any of the other areas of injustice considered in this book and it is clear that only a

---

[1] UNDP, *Human Development Report 2003*, 2003: 39. See also *New Internationalist*, No. 364, January/February 2004: 20–21.
[2] Landes 1998: xx.   [3] Martin Wolf, *Financial Times*, 6 November 2001.

rough outline of the relevant issues can be given here. After outlining a number of the economic and political inequalities and injustices between nations, and offering a preliminary consideration of environmental concerns, a critique of the neo-liberal form of capitalism which currently dominates the global economic system will be offered. Catholic criticisms of capitalism date at least from the time of Leo XIII and responses to the development needs of poor nations from the time of John XXIII. There is a manifest need to transform the international economic system in ways which ensure that the evident interdependence of the peoples of the world is regulated in the interests of the common good.

At the Millennium Summit in 2000 'the states of the United Nations reaffirmed their commitment to working toward a world in which sustaining development and eliminating poverty would have the highest priority'.[4] Seven Millennium Development Goals and various targets for 2015 aimed to reduce poverty:

- *Eradicate extreme poverty and hunger* (between 1990 and 2015 the proportions of people whose income is less than $1 a day).
- *Achieve universal primary education* (ensure that by 2015, boys and girls everywhere will be able to complete a full course of primary schooling).
- *Promote gender equality and empower women* (eliminate gender disparity at all levels of education by 2015).
- *Reduce child mortality* (reduce by two-thirds, between 1990 and 2015, the under-five mortality rate).
- *Improve maternal health* (reduce by three-quarters, between 1990 and 2015, the maternal mortality ratio).
- *Combat HIV/AIDS, malaria, and other diseases* (have halted by 2015 and begun to reverse the spread of HIV/AIDS, malaria and other major diseases).
- *Ensure environmental sustainability* (including reversing the loss of environmental resources; halving, by 2015, the proportion of people without sustainable access to safe drinking water; and have achieved, by 2020, a significant improvement in the lives of at least 100 million slum dwellers).

An eighth goal aimed to achieve these goals by means of a '*global partnership for development*'. Among other goals it aimed to 'develop further an open, rule-based predictable, non-discriminatory trading and financial system', 'deal comprehensively with the debt problems of developing countries through national and international measures', 'provide access

---

[4] World Bank 2002, *World Development Indicators 2002*, 3, 16–17.

to affordable essential drugs in developing countries', and 'make available the benefits of new technologies, especially information and communications'.[5]

Trends over the past decade are not very encouraging. Life expectancy at birth for men in Sub-Saharan Africa is 46 compared to 75 in high-income countries; crude death rates are nearly twice as great. Whereas in the UK four-fifths of males survive to age 65, in Botswana only one in eight do so. Child malnutrition rates in Africa have steadily increased over the past twenty years. Mortality rates under-five varied from an average 7 per 1,000 live births in high income countries to 122 in low income countries.[6] Whereas maternal mortality rates in the 1990s in the UK were 7 per 100,000 live births, in several African countries the rate was over 1,000.[7] In 1999 while 0.05 per cent of females aged 15–24 in the UK had HIV, in Botswana the proportion was over one-third. The incidence of tuberculosis in several African countries was over forty times greater than that in the UK. In high income countries health expenditure per capita averaged $2,735 compared to only $21 in low income countries.

World Development Indicators are published by the WB and can be perused on the internet. For example, using the purchasing power parity (PPP) system of comparison, gross national income (GNI) per capita averaged 7,570 international dollars in 2002 across the world. But in Sub-Saharan Africa GNI was only $1,620 compared to $35,060 in the United States and $25,870 in the UK.[8] Depending on which measure of poverty is used, between 1.3 billion and 3 billion people, nearly half the world's population, live in poverty.

The UNDP assessed quality of life using a composite index, the Human Development Index (HDI), taking into account life expectancies, average incomes, rates of adult literacy and years schooling. This index averaged 0.928 in high-income OECD countries but only 0.442 in less developed countries.[9] One indicator of vulnerability used was the proportion of children aged 10–14 in the labour force. In 2000 in Sub-Saharan African countries this was as high as 29 per cent.[10] Whereas the average years of schooling in high income countries in 2000 was 10.0 years, in low income

---

[5] UNDP, *Human Development Report 2003*, 2003: 6–13, 34, 40, 50, 122–124, 228–236.
[6] http://devdata.worldbank.org/external/; World Bank Group, Developing Countries: Health, Nutrition, 2001.
[7] World Bank 2002. *World Development Indicators 2002*, 17, pp. 110–112, 118–120.
[8] http://www.worldbank.org/data; World Bank Indicators database, July 2003.
[9] See also UNDP, *Human Development Report 2003*, 2003: 237–244.
[10] World Bank 2002, *World Development Indicators 2002*, pp. 80, 96, 312–314, 316–318.

countries it was only 4.4 years. Other measures of social capital necessary in the contemporary world indicated sharp gradients between low income and high income countries.

The range of issues which appear to reflect inequalities and injustices is seemingly endless. Brief attention is here drawn to just a few concerns to illustrate inequalities of power and vulnerability between nations. Valuable and readable information is provided on these and other issues by the monthly journal *New Internationalist* and by the major development agencies such as CAFOD, CIIR, Christian Aid, Oxfam and the World Development Movement (WDM).

- *Oil* The three regions of the world, Asia, USA and Western Europe including the UK, which between them consume 71 per cent of the world's oil have only 6 per cent of the estimated reserves.[11] Yet oil economies have only achieved average growth rates of 1.7 per cent per year compared to an average of 4 per cent in non-oil economies. In other words, the rewards of oil production do not benefit local people. Oil drives the global economy and oil companies are among the most powerful in the world. There are numerous links between the oil industry and the present US administration and much evidence that supports the conclusion that current US global strategy is determined by the aim of protecting privileged access to oil sources in the Middle East.

- *Food production and distribution* In 1997–99 there were 815 million people undernourished without sufficient food to meet daily energy requirements. Agriculture provides the main source of income for 2.5 billion people and 96 per cent of the world's farmers live in developing countries. Yet huge, vertically integrated companies increasingly control large parts of the food chain. About three-quarters of the genetic diversity of agricultural crops was lost in the twentieth century. There has been a rapid increase in the production of genetically modified crops and food security is a matter of concern.[12] Whereas developing countries captured 40 per cent of global trade in agricultural products in 1961, by 2001 that had fallen to 35 per cent. EU subsidies for each cow were greater than the daily income of many Africans. Subsidized production of sugar in the EU,[13] dumping of wheat below production costs, and overproduction of coffee pushes down prices but also reduces many farmers in developing countries below subsistence levels. Agriculture consumes 70 per cent of all fresh water used.

---

[11] *New Internationalist 355*, June 2001: 14; *361*, October 2003: 12, 18–19.
[12] Joseph 1999.   [13] *New Internationalist 346, 349, 353, 354, 362, 363*, June 2002–December 2003.

- *Water* In 2000 1.1 billion people, mostly in Asia and Africa, did not have access to a safe water supply. In the mid-1990s two-fifths of the world's population experienced serious water shortages and the proportion is expected to grow to two-thirds by 2025. In the USA the average person uses 500 litres of water each day while in several African countries the average is under 10 litres. Dirty water is the cause of numerous diseases and 2.2 million deaths each year. Malaria, carried by water-breeding mosquitoes kills another 1–2 million each year. Pollution from human and animal waste, naturally occurring toxins, and synthetic chemicals is a major problem. Some 97 per cent of liquid freshwater is stored in underground aquifers but these are becoming depleted at an alarming rate so that currently more is being pumped out than can be recharged. There are big doubts about the utility of big dams which 'do serious environmental damage and mostly benefit the well-heeled'.

- *Drugs and patents* The rapid spread of HIV/AIDS, especially in Africa, has raised the issue of access to cheap drugs and conflicts with powerful pharmaceutical MNCs who argue that high prices and patents are necessary to encourage high research and development costs and protect 'intellectual property rights'. Since the mid-1990s antiretrovirals (ARVs) have been available to control the spread of HIV but drug prices are too expensive for most people in the South. In Brazil, after the Government began producing generic ARVs, prices fell dramatically and AIDS deaths by one half. Concern is growing at the impact of the World Intellectual Property Organization's (WIPO) Patent Co-operation Treaty and the rush to patent common resources, such as plants, animal varieties and even our genes, by a few very large corporations. Developing countries are under-represented in the key international negotiations. Wider patent protection rights under the Trade Related Intellectual Property Rights Agreement (TRIPS) seem unlikely to favour the common good.

- *Debt* Some measure of the difficulties of managing external debt may be gauged from WB data. In 2000 thirty eight countries, two-thirds in Africa, were classified as severely indebted. In eighteen countries the total debt service was over one quarter of their exports of goods and services; in Argentina and Brazil it was well over one half.[14] In 1996 the WB launched the Heavily Indebted Poor Countries (HIPC) initiative. CAFOD helped found the Jubilee 2000 campaign to break the chains of debt.[15]

---

[14] World Bank 2002. *World Development Indicators 2002*, pp. 268–271.
[15] CAFOD 2000. *People Power: Campaigning With CAFOD 1997–2000*, pp. 2–15.

What seems to be apparent from this brief review is that the less developed countries are excluded from full participation in the life of the global community in ways which are an offence to the values of human dignity, the common good and solidarity between nations.

ENVIRONMENTAL SUSTAINABILITY[16]

The seventh millennium development goal aimed to ensure environmental sustainability and to that end proposed a number of targets. This is a huge issue on its own and worthy of fuller treatment than can be given in the context of this present chapter. Here attention will simply be drawn to some of the more obvious problems and an indication given of some social and theological responses to an issue which has climbed rapidly towards the top of the agenda among campaigning groups.

A number of high profile disasters have had major environmental consequences since the London smog killed 4,000 people in 1952 and led four years later to the Clean Air Act. A number of huge oil tankers have spilled their loads around the coasts of the UK since the Torry Canyon in 1967. In 1986 the world's worst nuclear power accident occurred at Chernobyl and many tons of radioactive materials blew north into Belarus which has been declared an international ecological disaster zone. The incidence of some types of cancer in the area increased one hundred fold. The world's worst chemical accident occurred at Bhopal in 1984 when toxic methyl isocyanate gas escaped from a Union Carbide storage tank and 3,000 people died.

The Chernobyl accident and the case of acid rain, caused by smoke emissions from coal-fired power stations in Britain, which destroyed forests in Scandinavia, showed clearly that the harmful effects of accidents in the modern world cannot be contained within national borders. They pointed to the need for effective *international* regulation and response. Secondly, they indicated the involvement of large TNCs, such as oil and chemical companies, in a global capitalist economic system driven in the main by the imperative to maximize profit. Other TNCs are involved in logging operations with very considerable environmental consequences. Flooding in countries like Bangladesh is attributed to deforestation in the Himalayas. Industrialized, large-scale agriculture is likely to exhaust the land and leave insufficient time for it to recover. It also consumes great quantities of water at rates which cannot be sustained. Holes in the earth's

---

[16] See the *Compendium*, 2004, Ch. 10 on 'Safeguarding the Environment', §§451–487.

protective ozone layer have been caused by the use of chlorofluorocarbon (CFC) gas, for example in refrigerators, resulting in increased incidence of skin cancers. Chemical effluents into rivers and seas have caused the deoxygenation of rivers and their inability to support life. Overfishing has resulted in huge reductions of stocks.[17]

Forty years ago Rachel Carson[18] drew attention to the serious consequences of the indiscriminate use of insecticides and pesticides and the persistent poisoning of the environment. Barbara Ward and René Dubos reported to the UN Conference on the Human Environment with the assistance of consultants from fifty-eight countries.[19] Schumacher advocated a shift to intermediate technology.[20] The Brandt Report considered that 'the care of the natural environment is an essential aspect of development'[21] and concluded that 'the strain on the global environment derives mainly from the growth of the industrial economies, but also from that of the (increasing) world's population'. The Brundtland Report[22] drew attention to the loss of the world's forest cover and estimated that renewable energy resources provided only one fifth of all the energy consumed in the world. In thirty years time forests the size of India will have been destroyed and an area the size of Saudi Arabia will have become worthless desert.[23] Scientists have most recently signalled that more than one million species, more than one in ten of all plants and animals, will be lost by 2050.[24]

There has been a quickening of public international concern about the planet's ecosystem and the damage being done to it as a result of current practices and models of development. Particular concern has been expressed at the 30 per cent increase in the level of carbon dioxide in the atmosphere since the start of the industrial revolution as a result of the use of fossil fuels. The predicted global average rise in temperature in the next century of 2–4 °C would be the equivalent of 'half an ice age' but occurring within 100 years rather than a few thousand years. Sea levels are predicted to rise by up to a metre and several islands in the Indian and Pacific Oceans will disappear. There will be both 'more frequent and intense floods and droughts' and significant impacts on health. It is estimated that there will be 150 million 'environmental refugees' in the world by 2050.[25] It should be stressed that global warming is not only a danger to present generations but also to succeeding generations.

[17] Cleary 1989.   [18] Carson 1965.   [19] Ward and Dubos 1972.   [20] Schumacher 1974.
[21] Brandt 1980: 114, 116.   [22] Brundtland 1987.   [23] Quoted in Cleary 1989: 10–11.
[24] *Guardian* 8 January 2004.   [25] Houghton 2004: 13–16.

Over 160 governments agreed the Framework Convention on Climate Change (FCCC) at the Earth Summit in Rio de Janeiro in 1992. Within the FCCC, a start was made through the Kyoto Protocol requiring developing nations to reduce their emissions of greenhouse gases by 2010 by an average of 5 per cent compared with 1990. The UK government in its 2002 White Paper on energy accepted the target of a 60 per cent reduction in carbon dioxide emissions by 2050 recommended by the UK Royal Commission on Environmental Pollution. Yet the British Government has recently announced plans for a huge expansion of air traffic capability with projections of more than doubling of the number of people travelling by 2020.[26] This is in spite of the fact that aircraft are responsible for the bulk of damaging greenhouse gases.[27]

In developed countries such as the UK, access to fresh water is universal and taken for granted. In countries such as Ethiopia, however, only one person in eight in rural areas and just over three-quarters of the urban population have access to 'improved' water sources such as a household connection, public standpipe, borehole or protected well or spring.[28] Access to 'improved' sanitation facilities is clearly essential for the control of disease. In low income countries, however, only 78 per cent of urban populations and 30 per cent of rural populations had such facilities in 2000.

There are huge inequalities in the consumption of non-replaceable resources. For example the USA consumes nearly five times and the UK nearly two and a half times the world average use of commercial energy and electrical power consumption per capita. The ratios are approximately the same when comparing carbon dioxide emissions per capita. In contrast low income countries consume only one third of the world average energy per capita and produce only one quarter of the carbon dioxide emissions per capita. There are also huge differences in access to various facilities such as sewage connection, electricity, telephones and cars.

Lynn White[29] argued that the injunction in Genesis 1 that human beings exercise 'domination' over the earth legitimated the exploitation of the environment. The alternative view in favour of an orientation of the 'stewardship' of God's creation so that it is sustained and passed on in at least as healthy a state as it was received is of relatively recent origin. Thus

---

[26] *Guardian* 17 December 2003.
[27] Juliette Jowit, 'New Labour's Contrail', *Observer*, 4 January 2004.
[28] World Bank 2002. *World Development Indicators 2002*, pp. 150–153, 158–160, 162–164, 170–172, 174–176, 178–180, 182–183, 312–314.
[29] White 1967.

the bishops of England and Wales[30] identified four main problems: damage to the earth's life-sustaining mechanisms; depletion of the world's natural resources; a harmful and unjust impact on the world's poor; and the loss of beauty and diversity. Seeking understanding of the 'signs of the times' they suggested that 'the environmental crisis has revealed the interdependence of all creation' and called for 'ecological conversion' because 'man is no longer the Creator's "steward" but an autonomous despot'.

They suggested that creation had value in itself and was 'good' and revealed God's generosity, majesty, and healing, nourishing and life-giving properties. Human beings were dependent but had the special gift and challenge of sharing responsibly in God's creative activity. But creation also revealed human sin which had distorted the human relationship with the natural world. Catholics were called to 'renew the face of the earth' until there was peace and harmony. In responding to the cry of creation they were called to take up personal responsibilities, educate towards ecological responsibility, experience conversion and choose not to consume what was not needed and what was likely to harm others, act in partnership and solidarity with others, aware that individual and collective greed were contrary to the order of creation.

Nearly two decades ago Sean McDonagh called for a new theology of creation. Both he and Donal Dorr[31] have provided useful overviews of the development of Catholic social thought in response to the environmental crisis as it had developed up to Pope John Paul II's World Day of Peace message for 1990.[32] Both stressed that the Catholic Church was relatively late in its response and certainly lagged behind the work of the World Council of Churches (WCC) and its formula 'Justice, Peace and the Integrity of Creation' (JPIC) based on the idea of servanthood rather than stewardship.[33] McDonagh has called passionately for a new concern 'to care for the earth' as the Creator God's gift to humankind. Drawing on the accounts of creation in scripture and tradition he appealed to the Church to respond to the impending ecological disaster. He was critical of 'dominion theology' and 'anthropocentric bias' in the Church's teaching which viewed the natural world as existing 'primarily for man's exclusive use'. While welcoming Pope John Paul II's statement that Christians should 'realise that their responsibility within creation and their duty

[30] CBCEW 2003: 1–14. See also 1996: §§70, 102, 106; and 2004: §§88–95.
[31] McDonagh 1986; 1990: 175–203; 1994: 104–107, 124–146; Dorr 1991: 73–81; 1992: 333.
[32] http://www.acton.org/policy/environment/theology/rcc.html
[33] See also Duchrow and Liedke 1989.

towards nature and the Creator are an essential part of their faith', he regretted the 'heavy dose of domination theology' in *Centesimus Annus* and called for a more prophetic response from the Church and a 'pastoral ministry of sustainability'.

John Fuellenbach noted that the kingdom of God 'encompasses everything. It aims at the transformation of all human reality including the whole of nature. Animals, plants, and inorganic nature are all destined to participate in the *new earth* and the *new heaven*. The final consummation of the Kingdom will have cosmic dimensions'.[34] We need an 'ecological conversion' and a deeper Christianity.[35] In his more recent writings McDonagh has called for an eco-centred ethics, analyzed the causes and consequences of the global shortage of clean water, and campaigned against the power of TNCs forcing us to eat genetically engineered food.[36] Mary Grey has offered an ecofeminist theology in response to current models of globalization.[37]

In conciliar and papal teaching, it can be seen that an orientation of 'domination' or 'mastery' of the earth was emphasized both in *Gaudium et Spes* (§§33, 35) and Pope Paul's *Populorum Progressio* (§67). In *Octogesima Adveniens* (§21) Pope Paul recognized that 'man is suddenly becoming aware that by an ill-considered exploitation of nature he risks destroying it and becoming in his turn the victim of this degradation'. In *Redemptor Hominis* Pope John Paul II taught that 'it was the Creator's will that man should communicate with nature as an intelligent and noble "master" and "guardian", and not as a heedless "exploiter" and "destroyer"' (§15). In *Sollicitudo Rei Socialis*, the pope drew attention to 'three considerations which alert our consciences to the *moral dimension* of development': firstly, one cannot use animals, plants and natural elements simply according to one's economic needs but must take into account their mutual connections in the 'cosmos'; secondly, since natural resources are limited and not always renewable there must be proper concern for their availability to future generations; thirdly, one must have concern for the quality of life and the risks to health caused by uncontrolled pollution of the environment. In sum, 'the dominion granted to man by the Creator is not an absolute power . . . (but) when it comes to the natural world, we are subject not only to biological laws but also to moral ones' (§34). In his message for the

---

[34] Fuellenbach 1995: 96, 162–167.
[35] See, e.g., http://conservation.catholic.org/creation_spirituality.htm
[36] McDonagh 2003a, 2003b.   [37] Grey 2003.

World Day of Peace in 1990,[38] the pope focused on the ecological crisis which he insisted was a moral problem and a common responsibility. He reflected on the recurring theme in Genesis 'and God saw that it was good'. Man's 'dominion' over the earth must accord with the creator's plan. Key moral criteria were respect for life and the dignity of the human person, including future generations. 'The earth is ultimately *a common heritage*' which must be protected with a *new solidarity*. He urged a serious look at lifestyles so that 'simplicity, moderation and discipline, as well as a spirit of sacrifice . . . become a part of everyday life'. In *Centesimus Annus* (§§37–38, 40) the pope complained about the 'senseless' and 'irrational' destruction of the natural environment and called for an authentic 'human ecology'. He insisted that 'it is the task of the state to provide for the defence and preservation of common goods such as the natural and human environments, which cannot be safeguarded simply by market forces'. These various themes were repeated in *Evangelium Vitae* (§42).

Unlike papal statements which articulated a developing notion of '*domination*', the US bishops called for 'an increased sense of *stewardship*' and the development of 'a new ecological ethic that will help shape a future that is both just and sustainable'.[39] Later in *Renewing the Earth*[40] they pleaded that 'the environmental crisis of our day constitutes an exceptional call to conversion' and reiterated that we are stewards of the earth 'charged with restoring the integrity of all creation'. They suggested that integral dimensions of ecological responsibility included a God-centred and sacramental view of the universe; a consistent respect for life; the affirmation of global interdependence and the common good; an ethic of solidarity; an understanding of the universal purpose of created things; an option for the poor; a conception of authentic development; and the restraint of the voracious consumerism of the developed world. In their statement on *Global Climate Change*[41] they stressed that this 'is about our human stewardship of God's creation and our responsibility to those who come after us'. They observed that 'if we harm the atmosphere, we dishonour our Creator and the gift of creation' and called for 'constructive action to protect God's precious gift of the earth's atmosphere'.

---

[38] John Paul II, 'The Ecological Crisis: A Common Responsibility. Peace with God the Creator, Peace with all of Creation'. Message for the World Day of Peace, 1 January, 1990. At http://www. acton.org/ppolicy/environment/theology/rcc.html

[39] USCBC 1986: §§228, 12.

[40] USCBC. *Renewing the Earth: An Invitation to Reflection and Action on the Environment in Catholic Social Teaching*. See also http://conservation.catholic.org/u_s_bishops.htm

[41] USCBC 2001. *Global Climate Change: A Plea for Dialogue, Prudence, and the Common Good*. See http://www.usccb.org/sdwp/international/globalclimate.htm

In South Africa in 2000 the Catholic Bishops' Conference expressed its concerns over the introduction of genetically engineered food and warned that any 'damage to the environment would be largely irreversible. Once released, genetically engineered organisms become part of our eco-system'.[42] In England and Wales the bishops in *The Common Good*,[43] referred to a 'religious respect for the integrity of creation' and noted that 'our environmental "common goods" are held in trust for the use and enjoyment of future generations'. They called for 'the creation of effective global authorities responsible for the common good at international level'. They added further observations in *The Call of Creation* in 2002 and *Cherishing Life* in 2004.[44]

A CRITIQUE OF LIBERAL CAPITALISM

The dominant economic system throughout the world at the start of the third millennium is capitalism. Alternative centralized state models had proved to be less efficient in terms of the delivery of improving standards of living for their people. While there has been no one single model of capitalism throughout history neo-conservative ideologues propose poli-cies of unregulated economic freedom. Critics have argued that such policies in the major international institutions such as the IMF, WB and WTO, were ideologically driven, promoted an inadequate model of devel-opment which failed to adjust flexibly to the nuances of local needs, failed to deliver on its promises, impoverished poor people still further, and generated an ever-widening gap between rich and poor people and nations.[45]

Development is an extremely complex matter so that some simplifica-tion is inevitable. Broadly speaking, there are two opposing theories which attempted to explain inequalities of wealth, income and power between nations and why so many people in developing countries were so poor.[46] However, the two theories proposed different causal explanations for development with very different policy prescriptions for addressing poverty in less developed nations. On the one hand *modernization theory* attributed global inequality and poverty to different levels of technological develop-ment and traditionalism in the prevailing cultures. Typical prescriptions included the promotion of population control, high-tech farming,

---

[42] http://www.gene.ch/genet/2000/Nov/msg00042.html
[43] CBCEW 1996: §§106–108. See also CCC: §2415.   [44] CBCEW 2003 (first ed. 2002); 2004.
[45] Stiglitz 2002.   [46] Macionis and Plummer 2002: 216–226.

industrialization, and foreign aid. Critics of modernization theory, which was favoured by American theorists and United States dominated institutions such as the IMF, WB[47] and WTO, pointed out that it simply had not worked so that the gap between rich and poor nations had widened alarmingly. They noted that modernization theory glossed over power inequalities between nations, historical colonial linkages and dependencies, was culturally ethnocentric and guilty of blaming the victim.

The alternative *dependency theory* favoured by many analysts in developing nations attributed global inequality to the historical exploitation of poor countries by rich nations and a legacy of colonialism. Political independence of many former colonies in the post-war period had come with new forms of economic neo-colonialism. Rich, 'core' nations continued to exploit poor 'peripheral' nations who supplied cheap labour, ready access to raw materials, and expanding markets for industrial products. In poor countries production was narrow and export-oriented, there was a lack of industrial capacity, foreign debt was excessive and generated a vicious cycle that made rich countries richer and poor ones poorer. Whereas modernization theory focused on the production of wealth, dependency theory focused on the consequences of its distribution. Critics, however, pointed out that wealth creation was not a 'zero-sum' process in which some gained at others' expense and that the world's wealth had expanded five-fold in the second half of the twentieth century. The economies of some countries with strong links to rich nations, such as the 'Asian tigers' had grown rapidly while countries such as Ethiopia, with few links, had been impoverished. Dependency theory tended to neglect factors internal to poor societies such as cultures resistant to change, gender inequality, political corruption and the reckless misuse of available resources.[48]

Adair Turner has argued that 'the market economy . . . *if utilized rather than worshipped*, is the best mechanism available for pursuing both economic dynamism and desirable social goals'.[49] His book aimed to explore how 'to manage and moderate capitalism to make it humane and environmentally responsible'. Against the dogmatism of free market ideologues, Turner argued for a pragmatic, 'liberal *managed* capitalism', a 'redistributive market liberalism' which was right to the extent that it worked. He agreed with critics such as John Gray[50] that the global capitalist system was

[47] World Bank, *World Development Indicators 2002*, 2002: 325–331.
[48] Richard Dowden, 'A Marshall plan will just be more money wasted', *The Observer*, 9 January 2005.
[49] Turner 2001: 8, 276, 345–346, 366; emphases added.   [50] Gray 1998.

imperfect but argued that the response to this should not be pessimistic despair but the pragmatic search for workable policies.

Consistent with Turner's approach was the damning criticism of an ideologically driven emphasis on free markets, deregulation and unrestrained liberalization in terms of its actual consequences for poor nations given by a former WB economist and Nobel prize-winner, Joseph Stiglitz.[51] He pointed out that in the past decade the number of people living in poverty increased by almost 100 million while the total world income increased by an average of 2.5 per cent every year. Western countries were hypocritical, urging the reduction of trade barriers on poor countries while retaining trade barriers and agricultural subsidies themselves or stipulating the elimination of trade deficits when the USA ran a colossal deficit. Since the 1980s, when Ronald Reagan and Margaret Thatcher preached free market ideology with missionary fervour, the 'Washington Consensus' between the IMF, the WB and the United States Treasury, had promoted policies which were an 'unmitigated disaster' for many. Stiglitz proceeded to demonstrate this with detailed analyses of a wide range of case studies of IMF 'market fundamentalism' in countries as diverse as Ethiopia, East Asia and post-communist Russia. The evidence, he concluded, did not support the unsubstantiated *faith* in 'trickle-down' economics and he summarized some of the consequences of Washington Consensus policies:

Trade liberalisation *accompanied by high interest rates* is an almost certain recipe for job destruction and unemployment creation – at the expense of the poor. Financial market liberalisation *unaccompanied by an appropriate regulatory structure* is an almost certain recipe for economic instability – and may well lead to higher, not lower interest rates, making it harder for poor farmers to buy the seeds and fertilizer that can raise them above subsistence. Privatisation, *unaccompanied by competition policies and oversight to ensure that monopoly powers are not abused*, can lead to higher, not lower, prices for consumers. Financial austerity, *pursued blindly*, in the wrong circumstances, can lead to high unemployment and a shedding of the social contract.[52]

---

[51] Stiglitz 2002: 5–7, 12–20, 78–80, 84, 214–252.
[52] References to the social contract appear to refer to political dysfunctions such as relative consensus, social stability and middle class support for the rule of law. Ian Linden has pointed out that the 'Washington Consensus' began to break down in the late 1990s and that since then World Bank policies have altered considerably. Developments in UK Government thinking can be discerned from a series of DTI White Papers: 'A Better Quality of Life: A Strategy for Sustainable Development' (1999), 'Eliminating World Poverty: Making Globalization Work for the Poor' (2000), and 'Making Globalization a Force for Good' (2004).

Just as governments played an essential role in mitigating market failures and promoting social justice, so there was a need for reformed international institutions and governance to combat global poverty and powerlessness.

George Monbiot[53] saw Stiglitz's testimony as so important that he divided the global justice movement into two periods: before and after Stiglitz. However, he criticized Stiglitz for not proposing viable solutions to the problems he reviewed. In particular, he noted the stringent 'conditionalities' on WB lending and the harmful consequences of massive hydro-electric dam projects. Monbiot usefully drew attention to the undemocratic nature of voting strengths in both the IMF and the WB. The 'G8' nations – the USA, Canada, Japan, Russia, the UK, France, Germany and Italy – held 49 per cent of IMF votes and an average 48 per cent of the WB agencies. The USA alone held 17 per cent of IMF votes and 18 per cent WB votes but since all major decisions required an 85 per cent majority, it was able to veto any substantial resolution. In sum, 'both the World Bank and the International Monetary Fund are constitutionally destined to fail'. The problem of debt was illustrated by the case of the nations of sub-Saharan Africa which 'paid twice the sum of their total debt in the form of interest, but they still owed three times more in 1996 than they did in 1980'.

Monbiot described the origins of the Bretton Woods agreement in 1944 where the negotiators for the USA, as the world's biggest creditor, insisted on the United States veto power for the IMF and WB against Keynes's proposal for an International Clearing Union. 'The Americans had won, and engineered a perfect formula for both continued US economic dominance and the permanent indebtedness of the poor nations'. Since the indebted nations had no option but 'to fight or to starve' Monbiot urged them to combine together to set up themselves a Clearing Union along the lines originally proposed by Keynes.

There were signs that the developing nations were beginning to organize themselves to resist the hegemony of the rich nations. World trade negotiations broke down in Cancún, Mexico, in September 2003 when developing nations walked out after failing to secure a reduction in the $1 billion farm subsidies given each day by western countries to their farmers. Twenty important developing countries, including Brazil, China, India and South Africa combined to challenge western nations. Some compromises were reached at renewed WTO talks in Geneva in late July 2004 but NGOs warned that the agreement remained vague and unspecific.

[53] Monbiot 2003: 143, 149–154, 156–157, 168–180, 188–203, 205–207, 222, 226–238, 246.

The global justice movement has come to realize that trade is the only viable way of distributing wealth from rich to poor nations. Oxfam, for example, has shown that 'even under the existing unfair system, the poor world obtains thirty-two times as much revenue from exports as it receives from aid'. But it is important that trade be regulated by laws which do not exploit the poor. At present market fundamentalism has been forced on poor nations while rich nations break rules with huge subsidies to cotton workers in the USA and sugar beet growers in the EU. These subsidies have devastating effects in developing nations, undercutting their crops and forcing them out of business. The granting by the WTO of 'intellectual property rights' to large corporations based in rich countries was estimated to cost poor nations $40 billion a year. Insistence on trade liberalization flew in the face of historical evidence, in Britain, Japan, Taiwan and South Korea, that in the early stages of industrialization, protectionism of infant industries was essential. A powerful group of nations, the 'Quad', i.e. the US, EU, Japan and Canada, determines the agenda of each trade round and 'in practice ... the realities of power' have been reasserted. Monbiot called for an international Fair Trade Organization which would license companies and require them to pay a fair price for the resources they use, including the environmental costs of production and distribution. The poor nations should either demand a new development round of negotiations, controlled by them, or break with the WTO and establish an alternative.

A particularly valuable analysis is that of Amartya Sen who saw development 'as a process of expanding the real freedoms that people enjoy ... Development requires the removal of major sources of unfreedom: poverty as well as tyranny, poor economic opportunities as well as systematic social deprivation, neglect of public facilities as well as intolerance or overactivity of repressive states'.[54] Sen took a pragmatic approach[55] which aimed to contribute to and extend 'the capabilities of people to do things – and the freedom to lead lives – that they have reason to value'. Thus poverty and unemployment were seen as forms of capability deprivation which was more than just income inequality or deprivation and was contingent on such variables as gender, age and location. Literacy, numeracy and health

---

[54] Sen 1999: 3, 85, 94–98, 119.
[55] Sen's approach seems consistent with the Christian understanding of God's great gift of freedom but also that we live in an imperfect world with both good and evil, and the consequences of original sin. Inevitably, therefore, utopias can never be completely realized. Human agency and responsibility are, however, stressed as is a respect for differences of cultural values.

care were important in enhancing economic opportunities.[56] Sen argued convincingly that attention should shift 'from income inequality to the inequality in the distribution of substantive freedoms and capabilities'. This required the need to create basic social opportunities, realizing that public goods, such as environment, health and education, contributed to human capabilities. Minimalist forms of state intervention failed to realize the capabilities of their citizens.

While globalization is not a new phenomenon, in the last two decades it has been greatly accelerated by the liberalization of financial flows, trade and foreign investment.[57] The volume traded in the world foreign exchange market has grown from a daily average of $15 billion in 1973 to over $1000 billion today, much of it speculative. World exports increased from $61 billion in 1950 to $3,447 billion in 1990. However, in spite of a general reduction of trade barriers, 'high tariffs still persist in developed countries in sectors such as agriculture and textiles and for selected manufactured products, which are areas in which developing countries have a comparative advantage'. The proportion of foreign direct investment flows to developing countries had risen from 17 per cent in the 1980s to 32 per cent in the first half of the 1990s. Martin Khor pointed out that 'a major feature of globalization is the growing concentration and monopolization of economic resources and power by transnational corporations and by global financial firms and funds'. Thus while the top 200 TNCs accounted for 24 per cent of world GDP in 1982, by 1992 this proportion had risen to 26.8 per cent.

There has also been a 'globalization of policy-making' and a reduction in the autonomy of national economy policy capacity in favour of international institutions such as the WB, the IMF and the WTO. Exceptions to trade agreements, such as protectionism against competitive products of the weak, have been systematically exploited by the rich and powerful nations. An obvious case in point is the EU Common Agricultural Policy (CAP). Khor points out that while the three institutions 'promote the empowerment of the market, a minimal role for the State and rapid liberalization', most UN agencies, such as the UN Conferences on Trade and Development (UNCTAD), 'operate under the belief that public intervention (internationally and nationally) is necessary to enable basic

---

[56] Thus Sen points to the contrast between the health care systems in the USA and the EU. While the USA has low unemployment, there is also low health insurance and high mortality; in the EU high unemployment is tolerated but health insurance expected, and in consequence low mortality.

[57] Khor 2001: 7–16, 18–19.

needs and human rights to be fulfilled and that the market alone cannot do the job and in many cases hinders the job being done'. Khor summarized some of the consequences of increasing liberalization policies: 'growing wage inequality in both the North and the South between skilled and unskilled workers . . .; capital gaining in comparison with labour . . .; the rise of a new *rentier* class due to financial liberalization and the rapid rise in debt . . .; and the benefits of agricultural price liberalization being reaped mainly by traders rather than farmers'.

Critics of present policies and development processes have argued with much force that present rates of consumption of non-replaceable raw materials, such as fossil fuels, were simply not sustainable and that there was no way in which current rates of consumption in the profligate north could be extended to the whole world. Some control of consumption therefore seemed imperative. Howard Newby[58] has observed that 'environmentalism has provoked a much sharper recognition of the fact that economic well-being in itself does not promote civility, social cohesion or even a sense of enlightened self-interest'. He noted that with 'an increasing awareness that the environmental challenges today are, increasingly, international, global and potentially more life-threatening than in the past . . . we are all . . . environmental citizens now'. Yet there was a problem over the governance of the 'global commons' – ozone layers, oceans, polar ice-sheets, the earth's biosphere, and so on. 'Can human stewardship over the global commons be exercised by more democratically accountable means?'

Critical analyses of development processes, often presented with polemical fervour, are to be found in plenty. Some draw attention to the enormous power of corporate capitalism relative to that of the nation state[59] while others express a partisan view of the globalization debate.[60] A more balanced view would accept the advantages which have accrued as a result of recent technological advances and from capitalist enterprises, the liberalization of trade, and so on, but seek to regulate these processes in the interests of the global common good.

Brief reference ought to be made to two recent studies. The Commission for Africa, the majority of whose members came from Africa, reported in March 2005. They made a number of specific recommendations on such matters as governance, increasing accountability and transparency, tackling corruption, addressing the causes of conflict, investing in people's education and health, improving access to clean water and improving sanitation, tackling HIV and AIDS, investing in infrastructure, agriculture and

[58] Newby 1996: 210, 217–219.   [59] Hertz 2001; Monbiot 2000: 302–330.   [60] Klein 2001; 2002.

small-scale irrigation, improving Africa's capacity to trade, their access to the markets of the rich world, and facilitating their adjustment to new trade regimes.[61] Jeffrey Sachs has suggested a number of ways in which it would be possible to bring an end to poverty in the world including raising the voice of the poor (because the G8 will do nothing if the poor are silent); redeeming the role of the UN in the world and strengthening its agencies; rescuing the IMF and WB from the hands of creditor nations; and each person making personal commitments.[62]

Such critical, yet pragmatic, responses to present inequalities and injustices between rich and powerful nations, on the one hand, and poor and weak nations, on the other, are consistent with Christian approaches which acknowledge the sinfulness of humankind but also their striving towards that kingdom of justice and peace which will never be completely realized in this life but which Christians believe will be reached at the end of time.

CATHOLIC RESPONSES

Catholic social teaching on development[63] has closely followed post-war theories of modernization, dependency and global capitalism. Pope John XXIII was the first pope to consider development issues seriously and in the four decades since, there has been a considerable development of teaching. We can trace this in the sixteen documents indicated in Table 10.1.

Mater et Magistra (John XXIII 1961)

John XXIII was the first pope to insist that 'with the growth of the economy, there occur a corresponding social development' (§73). He was concerned about 'great imbalances between agriculture, industry and . . . services' (§125) and about 'the relationship between economically advanced commonwealths and those that are in the process of development' (§157). He urged that justice and humanity required that 'richer countries come to the aid of those in need' (§161) without seeking to dominate with new forms of colonialism (§§171–172). He was aware that aid, by itself, would not tackle the 'underlying causes of poverty and hunger' (§163) and

---

[61] Commission for Africa 2005: 126–151.   [62] Sachs 2005: 364–368.
[63] See *Compendium* 2004 on 'The Universal Destination of Goods', §§171–184; and 'The "New Things" in the Economic Sector', §§361–376. See also the useful *Rough Guide* series of CAFOD briefings.

Table 10.1. *Major church documents on authentic development, 1961–1997*

Year	Author[a]	Document	Key themes	Reference[b]
1961	John XXIII	*Mater et Magistra*	International aid and cooperation	OBS, 84–128
1963	John XXIII	*Pacem in Terris*	Aid; human dignity; cultural domination	OBS, 131–162
1965	Vat. II	*Gaudium et Spes*	Economic development; inequalities	OBS, 209–215
1967	Paul VI	*Populorum Progressio*	Authentic development; transformations	OBS, 240–262
1968	CELAM II	*Medellin Conference*	Radical transformation; solidarity	NCCB
1971	Paul VI	*Octogesima Adveniens*	Revised relationships between nations	OBS, 265–286
1971	Synod	*Justice in the World*	Interdependence; domination denounced	OBS, 288–300
1975	Paul VI	*Evangelii Nuntiandi*	Development; liberation, justice, peace	OBS, 303–345
1979	CELAM III	*Puebla Conference*	Structural injustice; preferential option	CIIR
1986	US Bishops	*Economic Justice*	Responsible capitalism; option for poor	OBS, 572–680
1986	J&P Cmssn	*International Debt*	Ethical principles; actions; responsibilities	CTS, S 394
1987	John Paul II	*Sollicitudo Rei Socialis*	Authentic development; sinful structures	OBS, 393–436
1991	John Paul II	*Centesimus Annus*	Underdevelopment; deteriorating ecology	OBS, 437–488
1994	John Paul II	*Tertio Millennio Adveniente*	Jubilee; liberation; justice	CTS, Do 627
1996	E&W Bps	*The Common Good*	Poor nations and debt crisis; environment	Gabriel
1997	J&P Cmssn	*Distribution of Land*	Land distribution and agrarian reform	Vat website

Notes:

[a] CELAM: General Conference of Latin American Bishops; Synod: Synod of Bishops; J&P Cmssn: Pontifical Commission 'Iustitia et Pax'; E&W Bps: Bishops' Conference for England and Wales.

[b] OBS: O'Brien and Shannon, 1992; NCCB: US National Conference of Catholic Bishops; CIIR: Catholic Institute for International Relations; CTS: Catholic Truth Society.

advocated increasing international cooperation and a recognition of the growing interdependence of the peoples of the world (§§192, 200).

Pacem in Terris (John XXIII 1963)

Pope John's encyclical letter 'on establishing universal peace in truth, justice, charity and liberty' spoke, for the first time, to 'all men of good will'. He insisted on the equal dignity of all and that there was no justification for racial discrimination (§44). International relations in the post-colonial period should be regulated by justice and the recognition of mutual rights and duties (§91). Economic development should ensure that everyone live 'in keeping with his human dignity' (§122). The pope recognized the growing 'economic interdependence of national economies . . . (as) integral parts of the one world economy' (§130).

Gaudium et Spes (Vatican II 1965)

The Council Fathers noted that while economic development 'could diminish social inequalities' if properly guided and coordinated, 'all too often it serves only to intensify the inequalities . . . (and) the very peace of the world can be jeopardized in consequence' (§§63, 83). The Constitution stressed that the purpose of economic activity was not simply the 'multiplication of products . . . profit or domination' but the service of human beings (§64), bearing in mind 'the universal purpose for which created goods are meant' (§69). The Council quoted the teaching of Aquinas that 'if a person is in extreme necessity, he has the right to take from the riches of others what he himself needs', and recalled the saying of Gratian: 'Feed the man dying of hunger, because if you have not fed him you have killed him'.

Populorum Progressio (Paul VI 1967)

Pope Paul's encyclical[64] was the first to focus specifically on the theme of 'the development of peoples'. While acknowledging some of the benefits brought by colonizers in the past, the pope was alarmed at the widening of the gap between rich and poor peoples, that some have food surpluses while others hunger, that the hardships experienced by many farmers were 'undeserving', and that 'there is also the scandal of glaring inequalities

---

[64] See, e.g., Filochowski 1998, for a useful and sympathetic review of Pope Paul's concern for the poor in his pontificate.

not merely in the enjoyment of possessions but even more in the exercise of power' (§§7–9).

The pope offered a global Christian vision of development in all its 'economic, social, cultural, and spiritual aspects'. 'Development cannot be limited to mere economic growth'. In order to be authentic it had to promote the good of everyone and 'the whole man' (§§13–14). The pope observed that we have inherited from the labours of past generations, benefited from our contemporaries and have obligations towards all, including future generations, in solidarity. He warned against avarice and 'stifling materialism'. Authentic development implied the transition from less human to more human conditions and was promoted by love, friendship, prayer and contemplation. Less human conditions arose where there was individual selfishness and 'oppressive social structures' and an absence of 'cooperation for the common good' (§§17–21).

The pope reiterated the teaching that God intended created goods to be available to all people and affirmed that 'private property does not constitute for anyone an absolute and unconditioned right . . . to the detriment of the common good'. Thus underused landed estates could legitimately be expropriated in the service of the common good (§§22–24). Pope Paul condemned 'unchecked liberalism' and 'the imperialism of money' (§26) and warned that 'bold transformations' and deep innovations aimed at 'complete humanism' were demanded (§§32, 42).

The pope appealed to 'the duty of human solidarity – the aid that rich nations must give to developing countries; the duty of social justice – the rectification of inequitable trade relations between powerful nations and weak nations; the duty of universal charity – the effort to bring about a world that is more human toward all . . . without one group making progress at the expense of the other' (§44). He called for 'great generosity, much sacrifice' from the rich, and a readiness to pay higher taxes and higher prices for imported goods (§47). He proposed a World Fund for aid, funded partly from the 'intolerable scandal' of spending on the arms race and to counter fears of neo-colonial domination. There needed to be a proper dialogue between wealthy donor nations and developing nations to ensure that 'developing nations will . . . no longer risk being overwhelmed by debts' and to ensure that their proper autonomy was respected (§§51–54). What was at stake was 'the future civilization of the world' and 'world peace itself' (§§43. 55, 80).

Inequitable and unjust trade relations which resulted in 'the poor nations remain(ing) ever poor while the rich ones become still richer' was unjust where there were 'excessive inequalities of economic power'

(§§57–58). The pope insisted that the consent of parties to a contract did not guarantee its justice where consent was coerced. He considered that 'in trade between developed and underdeveloped economies, conditions are too disparate and the degrees of genuine freedom available too unequal' (§61) to be just. Social justice required a measure of equality of opportunity which would be facilitated by wide-ranging international agreements to regulate prices and support new industries. The pope appealed to all people of good will to live 'more fraternally' and work for development which was at the service of everyone, for 'the new name for peace is development' (§§79–80, 86–87).

CELAM II at Medellin (1968)

The Latin American bishops developed Pope Paul's vision in the particular circumstances of Latin America.[65] They affirmed the importance of both individual conversion and structural change. 'We will not have a new continent without new and reformed structures, but, above all, there will be no new continent without new men, who know how to be truly free and responsible according to the light of the Gospel'. Among such new structures must be those promoting the participation of all people, especially the lower classes. The bishops denounced both liberal capitalism and Marxist collectivism because 'both systems militate against the dignity of the human person'. Influenced by dependency theorists, they deplored the fact that many workers 'experience a situation of dependence on inhuman economic systems and institutions: a situation which ... borders on slavery'. There was a need to give preference 'to the poorest and most needy sectors ... to sharpen ... our solidarity with the poor ... (This) means that we make ours their problems and their struggles, that we know how to speak with them' and be willing 'to dialogue with the groups responsible' for situations of injustice 'in order to make them understand their obligations'.

Octogesima Adveniens (Paul VI 1971)

In this apostolic letter Pope Paul wrote that he was appalled by the 'flagrant inequalities (which) exist in the economic, cultural, and political development of the nations' (§2) and appealed for more justice globally. He observed that 'man is suddenly becoming aware that by an ill-considered

[65] CELAM II 1979: Justice, §§3, 7, 10–11; Poverty §§9–10.

exploitation of nature he risks destroying it and becoming in his turn the victim of this degradation' (§21). He reiterated previous teaching but warned that 'an overemphasis on equality can give rise to an individualism in which each one claims his own rights without wishing to be answerable for the common good' (§23). Previous 'utopias' had failed: 'bureaucratic socialism, technocratic capitalism, and authoritarian democracy are showing how difficult it is to solve the great human problem of living together in justice and equality' (§37).

Pope Paul pleaded for courage to 'undertake a revision of the relationships between nations', including 'the international division of production, the structure of exchanges, the control of profits, the monetary system . . . the models of growth of the rich nations . . . (and the) new economic powers emerging, the multinational enterprises, which . . . can conduct autonomous strategies which are largely independent of the national political powers, and therefore not subject to control from the point of view of the common good' (§§43–44). This is a valuable check list for action.

Justice in the World (Synod of Bishops 1971)

In their document[66] the Synod bishops produced what is probably the most quoted statement about the centrality of justice-seeking in the lives of Christians:

Action on behalf of justice and participation in the transformation of the world fully appear to us as a constitutive dimension of the preaching of the Gospel, or, in other words, of the Church's mission for the redemption of the human race and its liberation from every oppressive situation.

The pursuit of justice was no optional extra but was central to the Christian vocation. It was a timely antidote to an excessively other-worldly spirituality. It was the Christian's responsibility to liberate those who were oppressed by situations and social structures which enslaved people. The bishops stressed the basic equality and human dignity of all people in this 'interdependent economic world' with its common, 'delicate biosphere', threatened by the arms race and economic injustice and lack of social participation. They affirmed 'the right to development . . . composed both of economic growth and participation' to ensure the maintenance of heritage and culture. The Christian message of love and justice would

---

[66] In O'Brien and Shannon 1992: 289–291, 294–295, 298–300.

lose credibility unless it 'shows its effectiveness through action in the cause of justice in the world'. Christians should examine their lifestyles and collaborate with all people who sincerely sought justice.

Evangelii Nuntiandi (Paul VI 1975)

Reflecting the emergence of liberation theology, Pope Paul taught that Jesus' mission was 'liberation from everything that oppresses man which is above all liberation from sin and the Evil One, in the joy of knowing God and being known by him'. It required struggle and 'a radical conversion, a profound change of mind and heart' (§§9–10). The Church 'has the duty to proclaim the liberation of millions of human beings' from 'famine, chronic disease, illiteracy, poverty, injustices in international relations and especially in commercial exchanges, situations of economic and cultural neo-colonialism'. There were profound links between evangelization and development and liberation (§§30–31) but the Church 'reaffirms the primacy of her spiritual vocation and refuses to replace the proclamation of the Kingdom by the proclamation of forms of human liberation'.[67] While the Church did not wish to 'dissociate herself from man's temporal problems', her mission could not simply be reduced to a temporal project (§§32, 34).

CELAM III at Puebla (1979)

Early in his pontificate Pope John Paul II gave the opening address at the Puebla Conference of Latin American bishops and immediately expressed his intention to amend 'incorrect interpretations' of liberation theology and recent 're-readings' of the Gospel depicting Jesus' mission as a political activist. Even so, the theme of liberation from oppression remained strong in the Final Document which emerged.

Thus, the authentic realization of the human being included 'liberation from all forms of bondage, from personal and social sin', from egotism and idolatry, and from everything that 'tears apart the human individual and society' (§§482, 485). 'God himself is the source of radical liberation from all forms of idolatry'. The Creator had given all earthly goods and everyone had a right to share in their use. 'All other rights, including the right of property and free trade, are subordinate to that right . . . Ownership should be a source of freedom for all, but never a source of domination or

[67] See also CDF 1984, 1986.

special privilege' (§§491–492). The bishops warned against 'the idol of wealth' and regarded both liberal capitalism and Marxist collectivism as 'institutionalised injustice'. They expressed their concerns about uncontrolled industrialization and urbanization, and 'consumptionist tendencies' (§§494–496).

They bemoaned the 'totalitarian use of power (as) a form of idolatry' and grieved at the number of authoritarian and oppressive regimes in Latin America. They condemned the 'ubiquitous' power of multinationals beyond the 'control of governments and even international organisms' (§§500–501; see also §1264). What was needed was to liberate people 'from the idol of absolutized power ... equality for all citizens ... the exercise of their freedoms ... legitimate self-determination ... to organise their lives in accordance with their own genius and history and to cooperate in a new international order (and) the urgent necessity of re-establishing justice ... (with) institutions that are truly operative and adequate to the task' (§§502–506).

While they acknowledged that capitalist liberalism 'has given much encouragement to the creative capabilities of human freedom' they observed that 'the illegitimate privileges stemming from the absolute right of ownership give rise to scandalous contrasts, and to a situation of dependence and oppression on both the national and international levels' (§542). They condemned the Doctrine of National Security as incompatible with a Christian vision (§549). Finally, they noted sadly that since the 1950s, 'the ample hopes for development have come to nothing. The marginalization of the vast majority and the exploitation of the poor has increased' (§1260; see also fn. to §1135). In response the bishops 'affirm the need for conversion on the part of the whole Church to a preferential option for the poor, an option aimed at their integral liberation' (§1134).

Economic Justice for All (US Bishops 1986)

While this pastoral letter primarily addressed domestic economic issues it also recognized that 'the pre-eminent role of the United States in an increasingly interdependent global economy is a central sign of our times' (§10; see also fn. 6). They viewed exclusion created by unjust elites and unjust governments as 'forms of social sin' (§77; see also fn. 34). They acknowledged the power of large corporations and financial institutions and warned that 'short-term profits reaped at the cost of depletion of natural resources or the pollution of the environment violate ... trust' in them (§112). While TNCs and financial institutions could make positive contributions to development and global solidarity, their striving for profit maximization and cost minimization had led to increased inequality and instability (§116). It was important to ask 'how does our economic system affect the lives of . . . all people?' and they affirmed that Third World debt, starvation in sub-Saharan Africa, rising military expenditures and ecological neglect were their problem (§363). They urged that 'we have to move from our devotion to independence, through an understanding of interdependence, to a commitment to human solidarity' (§365).

Following a rehearsal of basic Catholic teaching the bishops suggested that a major moral task was to devise rules for the major actors and for 'reconciling the transnational corporations' profit orientation with the common good that they, along with governments and their multilateral agencies, are supposed to serve' (§256). This led them (in pre-Bush times) to offer 'constructive choices' (§261ff) on the role of the USA in the global economy. They stressed the 'moral obligation' (§263) of the USA to take a lead in reducing poverty in the Third World. They regretted that the USA fell short of offering 'substantial, positive movement toward increasing social justice in the developing world' (§264) in five key areas: development assistance, trade, finance, foreign private investment, and world food. They regretted that the USA lagged proportionately behind most other industrial nations in providing development aid and in shifting from multilateral to bilateral aid which was frequently militarized and security-related. On trade policy they sought agreements on tariffs and trade which 'benefit the poorest countries' (§269). They recognized that United States workers might be 'hurt by the operation of the trading system' and urged much improved 'adjustment assistance programmes' in the USA (§270).

On finance they drew attention to the 'asymmetric character' of the relationship between debtor and creditor countries and the '*dependence* of the developing nations' (§271). Their inability to meet debt payments out of export earnings afflicted and oppressed large numbers of people who were already severely disadvantaged. It was scandalous that the poorest people suffered most from the austerity measures required when a country sought the IMF 'seal of approval' (§274). The bishops also drew attention to 'the impact of US budget and trade deficits on interest rates . . . (which) exacerbate the already difficult debt situation . . . (and) attract capital away from investment in economic development in Third World countries' (§277). They warned lest foreign private investment 'create or perpetuate dependency . . . sustain or worsen inequities . . . help to maintain oppressive elites in power, or . . . increase food dependency by encouraging cash cropping for export at the expense of local needs' (§279). The activities of corporations should be directed towards the common good. 'The Christian ethic is incompatible with a primary or exclusive focus on maximization of profit' (§280).

The bishops next reflected that the 'four resource transfer channels – aid, trade, finance, and investment – intersect' in the international food system. They were aware of the dominant position of the USA and urged that in a world with half a billion hungry people 'we be creatively engaged in sharing the food that sustains life . . . Relief and prevention of . . . hunger cannot be left to the arithmetic of the market-place . . . In . . . poor, food-deficient countries, no less than in our own, the small family farm deserves support and protection' (§§281–283).

Finally, while recognizing that Third World countries were not 'entirely innocent with respect to their own failures', they noted that the international economic order 'is in crisis; the gap between rich and poor countries and between rich and poor people within countries is widening' and called for the restructuring of 'the international order along lines of greater equity and participation and apply the preferential option for the poor to international economic activity [which] will require sacrifices'. They concluded by calling '*for a U.S. international economic policy designed to empower people everywhere and enable them to continue to develop a sense of their own worth, improve the quality of their lives, and ensure that the benefits of economic growth are shared equitably*' (§§288, 290–292).

Reference was made in Chapter 8 to Archbishop Weakland's reappraisal of the pastoral letter and to the criticisms of Clodovis and Leonardo Boff.[68] There was also no sustained analysis and critique of the major international institutions: the IMF, WB and GATT (since replaced by the WTO). Nevertheless, this pastoral letter was an important contribution to the development of Catholic social thinking on development issues.

International Debt (Pontifical Justice and Peace Commission 1986)

This document offered an ethical approach to the international debt question and a framework for the consideration of the responsibilities of all the relevant actors. In particular it advocated seeking solutions to the debt crisis 'in a spirit of dialogue and mutual comprehension' according to the ethical principles of solidarity, which recognized interdependence and equal dignity, the sharing of responsibility, the equitable sharing of the necessary sacrifices, and the requirements of social justice. In emergency

---

[68] Weakland 1991: 201–205.

situations, the document urged 'an ethics of survival' and was critical of some IMF solutions 'imposed in an authoritarian and technocratic way without due consideration for urgent social requirements'.

The larger part of the document discussed the responsibilities of four groups of actors. Firstly, industrialized countries were urged to adopt 'an ethic of expanded solidarity' and modify existing rules of international trade to ensure a more just distribution of its fruits, do away with protectionist policies, avoid erratic fluctuations in exchange rates, and assign a just value to raw materials. Secondly, developing countries had a responsibility to curtail abuses and corruption, to improve structures and a more equitable sharing of goods in the interest of the common good and future generations while avoiding undue nationalism and premature total liberalization of international trade. Thirdly, creditor states should negotiate, according to an international code of conduct, 'reimbursement conditions which are compatible with each debtor State's ability to meet its basic needs ... (and leave) adequate financial leeway for its own growth'. Commercial banks needed 'a type of discernment which transcends the ordinary criteria of profitability and security of capital invested in the form of loans'. Multinational organizations were called to 'coresponsibility and solidarity which is above and beyond their own vested interests'. Fourthly, 'multinational financial organisations will fulfil their role if their decisions and actions are taken in a spirit of justice and solidarity at the service of all'. There should be a 'fair distribution of sacrifices' and these organizations needed to turn from being 'sites of power into centres of dialogue and cooperation for the international common good'. In order to recognize the importance of international solidarity, there was a 'need to increase the representation of developing countries and their participation in the major international economic decisions that affect them'.

Sollicitudo Rei Socialis (John Paul II 1987)

Pope John Paul II insisted that authentic development 'would respect and promote all the dimensions of the human person', social, political, cultural and spiritual as well as economic (§§1, 9, 15). Reviewing developments in the two decades since *Populorum Progressio*, he noted that millions of people still suffered 'under the intolerable burden of poverty' and that there had been a 'widening of the gap' between the developed North and developing South (§§13–14). Both liberal capitalism and Marxist collectivism tended to be 'forms of neocolonialism' and fostered 'wars by proxy' and the arms race which aggravated conflicts and generated millions of refugees and the phenomenon of terrorism (§§20–24). Apart from poverty, John Paul II also drew attention to the prevalence of illiteracy and discrimination, the housing crisis, unemployment and underemployment, and the question of international debt (§§15, 17–19).

The pope proceeded to offer an extended spiritual interpretation of authentic development. Development was not 'automatic'; two world wars had demonstrated that 'a naïve mechanistic optimism' in the Enlightenment notion of 'progress' was unfounded (§27). Alongside 'the miseries of underdevelopment' was to be found an 'inadmissible' form of 'superdevelopment', consumerism, waste, and 'crass materialism'. 'Today's "development" is to be seen as a moment in the story which began at creation, a story which is constantly endangered … especially by the temptation to idolatry'. Improving the lot of man in his totality was a *'difficult yet noble task'* (§30).

Pope John Paul recalled that 'progress is possible only because God the Father has decided from the beginning to make man a sharer of his glory in Jesus Christ risen from the dead …' He invited every human person, institutions and nations to pursue this 'integral human development' and collaborate in this 'duty of *all towards all* … *Peoples* or *nations* too have a right to their own full development'. There was also an *'intrinsic connection* between authentic development and respect for human rights … personal and social, economic and political, including the *rights of nations and peoples'*. The pope continued by suggesting that 'a true concept of development cannot ignore the use of the elements of nature, the renewability of resources and the consequences of haphazard industrialization – three considerations which alert our consciences to the *moral dimension* of development' (§§31–34).

He continued with a 'theological reading' of the obstacles to authentic development and suggested a lack of political will to make *'essentially moral decisions'*. There were 'structures of sin',[69] 'rooted in personal sin, and thus always linked to the *concrete acts* of individuals who introduce these structures, consolidate them and make them difficult to remove'. He pointed to two typical structures of sin: 'the *all-consuming desire for profit* … (and) *the thirst for power*, with the intention of imposing one's will upon others'. This was the true nature of the moral evil which had to be confronted. The pope called for 'conversion' and a change of 'the *spiritual attitudes* which define each individual's relationship with self, with

---

[69] See, e.g., Longley 1998, for an analysis of Pope John Paul II's consideration of 'structures of sin' and free market capitalism.

neighbour, with even the remotest human communities, and with nature itself' in the light of 'higher values such as the *common good*', and a 'growing awareness of *interdependence* among individuals and nations' (§§35–38).

He called for the transformation of international relations in order to give expression to the virtue of 'solidarity': 'The stronger and richer nations must have a sense of moral *responsibility* for the other nations, so that a *real international system* may be established which will rest on the foundation of the *equality* of all peoples and on the necessary respect for their legitimate differences' (§39). The economically weaker countries should be allowed to make their own contribution to the common good. Pope John Paul II continued: '*Solidarity* helps us to see the "other" – whether a *person, people, or nation* – not just as some kind of instrument, with a work capacity and physical strength to be exploited at low cost and then discarded when no longer useful, but as our "neighbour", a "helper", ... to be made a sharer, on a par with ourselves, in the banquet of life to which all are equally invited by God'. '*Solidarity* is undoubtedly a *Christian virtue*' which seeks

to take on the *specifically Christian* dimension of total gratuity, forgiveness and reconciliation. One's neighbour is then not only a human being with his or her own rights and a fundamental equality with everyone else, but becomes the *living image* of God the Father, redeemed by the blood of Jesus Christ and placed under the permanent action of the Holy Spirit ... Solidarity therefore must play its part in the realization of (the) divine plan, both on the level of individuals and on the level of national and international society (§40).

The pope then noted that while 'the Church does not have *technical solutions* to offer', authentic development, 'cannot be reduced to a "technical" problem' (§41). He suggested a number of guidelines such as 'the *option* or *love of preference* for the poor'; 'the goods of this world are *originally meant for all*'; and the right to private property, while valid and necessary, was not absolute (§42). Indeed, 'private property, in fact, is under a "social mortgage", which means that it has an intrinsically social function, based upon and justified precisely by the principle of the universal destination of goods'. He drew attention to the need for 'a *greater degree of international ordering*' and noted in particular: 'The *reform of the international trade system*, which is mortgaged to protectionism and increasing bilateralism; the *reform of the world monetary and financial system* ...; the *question of technological exchanges* and their proper use; the *need* for a *review of the structure of the existing international organisations*, in the framework of an international juridical order' (§43).

The pope urged developing nations to develop 'a spirit of initiative', to collaborate with other nations in the same situation, to develop democratic and participatory political institutions, to promote human rights, and to seek 'the goal of food self-sufficiency'. All this required an awareness of interdependence and solidarity among themselves and a proper autonomy and free self-determination. 'At the same time solidarity demands a readiness to accept the sacrifices necessary for the good of the whole world community' (§§44–45).

This encyclical letter offered a substantial moral framework about human dignity and solidarity with which to judge the consequences of international policies and also an understanding of the vocation of everyone to realize the authentic development of *all* people who share this one world.

Centesimus Annus (John Paul II 1991)

This encyclical celebrated one hundred years of Catholic social teaching since *Rerum Novarum*. Written two years after the collapse of Soviet totalitarianism in Central and Eastern Europe, it analyzed the spiritual inadequacies of atheistic Marxism, regretted the post-war division of Europe and called for 'assistance from ... the countries of Europe which were part of that history and which bear responsibility for it, (since this) represents a debt in justice' (§28). Pope John Paul affirmed that 'the possession of material goods is not an absolute right' because 'God gave the earth to the whole human race'. The pope also interestingly traced three key stages in production based on land, capital and knowledge – 'the possession of know-how, technology, and skill' – though this insight, which has relevance for the controversial issue of intellectual property rights, remains undeveloped (§§30–32).

The pope repeated many of the concerns about the failures of much development in the world today which had been noted by Pope Paul. These pointed to 'the human inadequacies of capitalism'. While the pope acknowledged that 'the free market is the most efficient instrument for utilizing resources and effectively responding to needs ... there are many human needs which find no place on the market. It is a strict duty of justice and truth not to allow fundamental human needs to remain unsatisfied'. Unfortunately, the pope did not subject to critical analysis the major international institutions – the IMF, WB, GATT (now replaced by WTO). While acknowledging the principle that debts should be paid, he added that it was not right to demand or expect payment when the effect would lead to 'hunger and despair for entire peoples' or 'unbearable sacrifices'. It was necessary to find ways 'to lighten, defer or even cancel the debt compatible with the fundamental right of peoples to subsistence and progress' (§§33–35).

The pope also raised concerns about 'the ecological question' and 'the senseless destruction of the natural environment'. He added: 'humanity today must be conscious of its duties and obligations toward future generations' and 'safeguard the moral conditions for an authentic "human ecology"' (§§37–38). He noted that 'economic freedom is only one element of human freedom' and insisted that 'it is the task of the state to provide for the defence and preservation of common goods such as the natural and human environments, which cannot be safeguarded simply by market forces'. He warned that 'the mechanisms of the market ... carry the risk of an "idolatry" of the market ... which ignores the existence of goods which by their nature are not and cannot be mere commodities' (§40). The pope evaluated capitalism in a remarkable paragraph:

If by *capitalism* is meant an economic system which recognizes the fundamental and positive role of business, the market, private property and the resulting responsibility for the means of production, as well as free human creativity in the economic sector, then the answer is certainly in the affirmative ... But if by capitalism is meant a system in which freedom in the economic sector is not circumscribed within a strong juridical framework which places it at the service of human freedom in its totality, and which sees it as a particular aspect of that freedom, the core of which is ethical and religious, then the reply is certainly negative (§42).

In other words, the Church 'recognizes the positive value of the market and of enterprise, but ... at the same time points out that these need to be oriented toward the common good' (§43). In addition, the globalization of the economy 'can create unusual opportunities for greater prosperity ... (but it) ought to be accompanied by effective international agencies which will oversee and direct the economy to the common good, something that an individual state, even if it were the most powerful on earth, would not be in a position to do' (§58). Finally, whereas for Leo XIII the main concern had been the plight of industrial workers, today the main problem was the 'poverty of the developing countries' and the pope called on all people of good will to face up to these new challenges (§61).

Tertio Millennio Adveniente (John Paul II 1994)

This encyclical looked forward to the third millennium and offered a spiritual reflection and invitation to Catholics. It focused on the biblical theme of jubilee and emancipation from debt and slavery and the restoration of equality and social justice (§§11–13). In this spirit he called on 'the European nations to make a serious *examination of conscience*, and to acknowledge faults and errors, both economic and political, resulting from imperialist policies carried out in the (nineteenth and twentieth) centuries vis-à-vis nations whose rights have been systematically violated' (§27). He confessed faults of the Church in the past which were 'ways of thinking and acting which were truly *forms of counter-witness and scandal*' (§33) and in 'our own day, the responsibility shared by many Christians *for grave forms of injustice and exclusion*' (§36). He instanced 'issues of justice and of international economic relations . . . (and) the enormous gap between North and South' (§38). Recalling that Jesus came to 'preach the good news to the poor' and the '*Church's preferential option for the poor and outcast*', he urged that 'a commitment to justice and peace in a world like ours, marked by so many conflicts and intolerable social and economic inequalities' was a necessary condition for the preparation and celebration of the Jubilee (§51).

The Common Good (Bishops of England and Wales 1996)

Three themes have particular relevance for this chapter. Firstly, the principles of solidarity and subsidiarity 'should govern relations between individual states and the wider international community' (§100). Secondly, 'solidarity has an inescapable universal dimension . . . The concept of an international . . . common good demands that no nation should be left incapable of participation in the global economy because it is too poor or too much in debt . . . An international economic order that condemns large sections of the world population to a permanent state of abject poverty is grossly unjust' (§§102–103). The bishops, therefore, urged a return to the UN target of 0.7 per cent GNP for overseas aid and supported attempts to relieve the international debt burden. Thirdly, the bishops expressed concern about the environmental common good which was 'held in trust for the use and enjoyment of future generations' and called for 'the creation of effective global authorities responsible for the common good at international level' (§§106–108).

Towards a Better Distribution of Land (Pontifical Justice and Peace Commission/Council 1997)

Both *Gaudium et Spes* and *Populorum Progressio* had drawn attention to the huge inequalities of land distribution in developing countries and the paradox of un- or under-cultivated lands at the same time that small farmers struggled at subsistence levels. The issues of agrarian reform were addressed in this document which followed statements issued by several conferences of bishops in Latin America. It offered a critical analysis of the failures of previous attempts at reform and made a large number of specific proposals for interlocking reforms, including not only land redistribution but also better infrastructures and social services, education and training in new agricultural skills, legal recognition of ownership rights, access to credit and markets, and so on.

Its chief contribution was its scriptural analysis of the responsibility to subdue the earth according to the requirements of the Creator who cared for the well-being of all and had given the earth to everyone (§§22, 24–25). Ownership of land was not absolute; the Church had steadily developed its teaching about 'the universal destination of goods and private property'. This led to a strong condemnation of 'latifundia', large land holdings held by absentee landowners, and the deprivation of small farmers and indigenous populations from access to land (§§28–34).

International organizations, in their intervention strategies were urged to bear in mind possible 'negative consequences on the fight against poverty and hunger'. The document issued a strong warning about the 'shared responsibility ... of many Christians for grave forms of injustice and exclusion, and the acquiescence of too many of them in the violation of fundamental human rights'. It concluded 'by calling attention to the special and essential significance of justice in the biblical message – that of protection of the weak and of their right, as children of God, to the wealth of creation' and it called for the restoration of 'social justice through a distribution of land ownership carried out in a spirit of solidarity' (§§59–61).

Catholic non-official social thought

Catholic social thought has always been more than papal encyclicals and, indeed, official teaching has historically emerged in response to Catholic individuals and movements.[70] It is the development agencies, such as CAFOD and CIIR, which have been in the forefront of efforts to realize social justice in relations between developed and developing nations. They have a social and moral authority based on their direct experiences of the relevant issues and injustices and the consequences of the policies of

---

[70] Coleman 2000: 266–270; Zahn 1991: 53; Mich 1998.

powerful external agencies – such as TNCs, governments, the IMF, WB and WTO – and their direct contacts with 'partners' in the developing countries. The professionalism of their research and analysis has also put them in a strong position to dialogue with policy makers in, for example, the Department for International Development.[71] Both CIIR, in its *Comment* series, and CAFOD have drawn attention to the damage which the EU Common Agriculture Policy has for poor farmers in developing societies. CAFOD drew public attention to the scale of farm subsidies when it reported that 'in the EU, the average cow now receives total support from EU governments of US $2.20 a day, more than the income of half the world's population'.[72] Both organizations have also grappled with the controversial issue of HIV/AIDS, particularly in Africa.[73] In their everyday work they come into contact with other Christian or secular NGOs which contributes to the refinement of social analyses of the causes of injustices and inequality, and enhances collaborative coalitions which may have greater public persuasiveness for not being overtly 'Catholic'.[74]

This links with two themes identified in the Von Hugel collection. Firstly, Buch was concerned about the 'communicability' of Catholic social thought and argued that 'there is a need for . . . professional expertise and for dialogue and cooperation with experts if Catholic social thought is to make realistic assessments and applications'. What counts is 'practical expertise and social experience as constitutive elements of social ethics'.[75] Secondly, there was a need for 'middle-level' thinking about contemporary trends and social, political and economic contexts with normative value systems about 'human flourishing'.[76] One example was Van Gerwen's analysis of the present system of the 'partial control' of global markets 'through co-ordination by the most powerful and wealthy states (which) has some major setbacks from an ethical perspective'.[77] This led him to suggest a transnational monetary and financial order which would include a transnational central bank, a transnational court, a transnational

---

[71] See, e.g., CAFOD's 'A Development NGO Critique of Globalisation', Submission to the House of Lords Economic Affairs Committee, February 2002, at http://www.cafod.org.uk/policy/hol_economic.shtml

[72] http://www.cafod.org.uk/policy/dumpingonthepoor200209.pdf; Green and Griffith 2002: 9.

[73] See, e.g., the two CIIR pamphlets in the *Comment* series by Ackermann 2002 and Greyling 2002; and CAFOD, 'HIV Prevention, Condoms and Catholic Ethics', November 2001, at http://www.cafod.org.uk/hivaids/aids_ethics.shtml

[74] See, e.g., Jacobs 1996; Madeley 2000; Christie and Warburton 2001; Reed 2001. For such reasons CIIR has changed its name to Progressio the better to reflect what it actually does.

[75] Buch 2000: 143.

[76] See, for example, the chapters by Boswell, Buch, Coleman and McHugh in Boswell et al. 2000.

[77] Van Gerwen 2000: 215, 218–219.

legislator, a transnational executive and transnational supervising bodies. Global regulation along such lines would be relevant for tackling the debt issue as would proposals such as a Tobin Tax on short-term, speculative financial transactions.

The former Director of CIIR has recently published a critical analysis of globalization and the failure to achieve a more just world and alleviate the scandalous injustice of inequality.[78] He warned against the limitations and individualism of human rights discourse and argued passionately for a recovery of the notion of justice to be found in the writings of Thomas Aquinas with its emphasis on the common human heritage and the sacredness of the global common good. To Schumacher's famous phrase 'economics as if people mattered'[79] he added 'politics as if the poor mattered', a perspective which intrinsically invited collaboration with all people of good will.

Linden provided as good an account as there is of 'the dark underside of globalisation' and of how 'criminality is a systemic consequence of the failure to distribute wealth equitably'. After reviewing the history of the 'financialisation of economic life' in the past two decades and pointing out that 'at least half the world is not affected significantly by FDI (foreign direct investment) flows' he concluded that 'this uneven and inequitable distribution of capital, determined mainly by investment decisions of the MNCs, calls into question the realism of any theory of economic development that seeks the "insertion" of the developing world in the global economy'. Unlike the papal encyclicals, Linden provided a sustained critique of 'the political economy of globalisation (which) suffers from the grave asymmetry of global economic power unconstrained by global political order'. He detailed the hypocrisies in trade liberalization policies imposed on poor countries whilst agriculture and cotton were protected by huge subsidies in the USA and EU to the disadvantage of farmers in developing countries, and he reviewed the disastrous consequences of the structural adjustment programmes based on market fundamentalist policies imposed on weak nations by the IMF and WB.

Linden concluded critically that the 'network society' emerging as a result of contemporary economic and technological transformations provided 'no basis for integral human development' because it could not 'create inclusive communities in which people are valued and virtues

---

[78] Linden 2003: ix, 14–76, 91–93, 99, 105, 117–142, 145–146, 151. See, also, the chapters by Brian Davies, Julian Filochowski, Ian Linden and Clifford Longley in Vallely 1998.
[79] Schumacher 1974.

nurtured'. To change this required 'a new ethical politics' which 'encompasses all humanity in its rich diversity and locality' and 'radically reform(s) the global economy in the interests of the poor' by removing 'obstacles to the development of human capabilities'. The moral consequences of the 'misshapen global economy' amounted to 'a persistent abuse of structural power, the shaping of global structures for narrow self-interest and advantage, without concern for the (global) common good'. Given that 'the only moral response to unjust structures is resistance', it was not surprising that a variety of reformist civil society organisations (CSOs) had emerged. Linden described the dilemma they faced of remaining in dialogue with government over reform while believing that 'debt and unfair trade are destroying the preconditions for development' and seeking the radical transformation of the global capital economy.

He bitterly complained of the 'asymmetric world of a single hegemonic superpower'. In the world in which we live 'the bullying, selective unilateral action – and inaction – and arrogance of the USA, have become a grave international problem'. Examples of the important advocacy role of international non-governmental organizations (INGOs) included their successful challenges in cases of national emergencies, of the pharmaceutical trade patenting of drugs, for example retrovirals for the treatment of HIV/AIDs victims, and in the case of diamond smuggling which fuelled civil wars in Africa. The important questions to be addressed were 'how to safeguard the transcendental dignity of the human person in (the) emergent network society? . . . (and) generate a politics fitting for an era of globalization' which was not constrained by notions of national state sovereignty. Linden concluded by insisting that sinful 'structures need to be changed'. But 'structures need virtuous people' who have had an appropriate moral formation. Government policies, schools, Churches, 'communities in which virtues can be learnt by doing, and watching others doing', such as CSOs, parents and families, were all important in learning the practice of the virtues of justice, temperance and fortitude, and the importance of concern for the 'global commons' and the global common good. From such a formation would come a realization, following Aquinas, that 'there is a duty in justice to dispose of superfluous wealth to the poor' and that 'the use of violence to retain such superfluous wealth is injustice'.

Donal Dorr has also challenged the Church to attend to a 'social justice agenda'[80] and take the 'preferential option for the poor'.[81] In the Von Hugel collection he argued that it had two aspects: 'a "solidarity" aspect

---

[80] Dorr 1991.   [81] Dorr 1992.

which was about life-style' springing from compassion, deepened by sharing the suffering of others; and an aspect concerned with careful analysis and discernment and joint political action with the marginalized who 'should be empowered to speak and act on their own behalf'.[82] He was critical of Vatican-inspired attempts to 'tone down' the option's 'basic challenge to the present structures of society'. Finally, Snyder has observed that papal thinking has often 'failed to acknowledge the pivotal role women play in the development process'.[83]

OTHER CHRISTIAN RESPONSES

Christians are essentially people of hope in the redeemability of both individuals and societies and so are suspicious of deterministic explanations of inequalities or injustices such as a strong version of globalization with immense independent causal power to generate social and economic outcomes. They would always want to insist on some measure of social agency or responsibility for action, whether by individuals (such as charismatic political leaders) or nation states, or prophetic individuals or CSOs or international regulatory bodies (such as the UN might promote). What seems clear, however, is that in the past two decades, globalization has been dramatically accelerated by developments in electronic communications technology and satellite transmission. One consequence has been that contemporary problems, such as climate change and terrorism, and indeed collaborative responses to them, are increasingly seen as global in their reach and as demonstrating the interdependence of all people on earth.

The hegemony of liberal capitalism and 'the delusions of global capitalism'[84] have caused much soul-searching and spawned a plethora of anti-globalization coalitions, many of them inspired by their Christian beliefs and values,[85] to protest at the harm being done to many of the poorest people in the world in the name of trade expansion and the assumed advantages of liberalization, such as the claims that the advantages of economic growth will 'trickle down' to poor people. Such protests have increasingly been expressed in mass demonstrations, most recently in Edinburgh. Rather than accept the claim that 'there is no alternative' to economic liberalization, many have sought to find ways in which some form of control and regulation can be put in place, perhaps under United

---

[82] Dorr 2000: 252–253, 255.   [83] Snyder 1994: 279–280.   [84] Gray 1998.
[85] Duchrow 1995; Jacobs 1996; Christie and Warburton 2001.

Nations' auspices, to ensure that the benefits of trade are more fairly distributed and that the poorest and weakest people are not disadvantaged.[86]

The Churches have been challenged by the NGOs. Thus a former Director of Christian Aid has accused the Churches of 'comfortable compassion'.[87] The German theologian, Ulrich Duchrow, has argued that the cultures responsible for present global inequalities and injustices 'are rooted in western Christianity . . . For this reason the Churches have a particular responsibility'.[88] He drew on scriptural sources to suggest alternatives to global capitalism and urged that the Churches should 'use the "conciliar process for justice, peace and the integrity of creation" (that they themselves started) to fulfil their biblical calling and support the people's struggle against pauperisation and environmental degradation'. He argued that the Bible offered two approaches. 'When we were faced with totalitarian systems, resistance based on dissent and small-scale alternatives are both necessary and possible. When political influence can be brought to bear, prophetic intervention is called for'.

There is little doubt that the INGOs, most of which were inspired by their Christian beliefs and values, have done much to raise the level of consciousness of Church members to the existence of famine and poverty in developing nations. Whether they have yet challenged them to go beyond charitable giving and the amelioration of need to a serious analysis of the causes of global inequalities and injustices and to participation in serious political action to change the regulatory framework within which free market capitalism operates is a moot point. On the whole, Church members seem happy with the way things are and it is left to a disparate coalition of critics, some influenced by Church teaching but many by secular humanism and ecological sensitivities, to continue to struggle for a more equitable and just world.

FROM AMELIORATION TO ADVOCACY

In an increasingly interdependent world, global inequalities and injustices are becoming increasingly transparent. The search for global authentic development probably preoccupies more social activists than any other social or political issue. The current social context within which it takes place is dominated by two characteristics:

---

[86] Hirst and Thompson 1999; Turner 2001.   [87] Elliott 1987.   [88] Duchrow 1995: 16, 316.

- the global hegemony of liberal capitalism with all its faults, inequalities and injustices; and
- the social, economic, political, cultural and military supremacy of the USA at the beginning of the twenty-first century.

The so-called anti-globalization movement of the past decade can be seen, at least in large part, as a protest against the global reach of the current brand of neo-liberal economics and the global power of the USA. It has judged that the powerful international institutions, the IMF, the WB and the WTO, have promoted social and economic policies which clearly have not favoured poor nations and poor people throughout the world.

We have noted that Catholic responses to such issues date from the papacy of John XXIII and the Second Vatican Council. In sum, while important values and principles necessary for the pursuit of authentic human development have been enunciated by the Church over the past four or five decades – human dignity, the common good, solidarity, the preferential option for the poor and subsidiarity – the Church has tended largely to accept the global capitalist economy as a social fact and has confined itself to pleading for some amelioration of its substantial consequences in terms of the growing gap between rich and poor people and nations. But important non-official contributions are being made to Catholic social thought as a result of the cumulative experiences of the staff and volunteers in the INGOs working in close collaboration with partners in developing societies. From these sources a significant shift has taken place from aid and amelioration to political advocacy with decision-makers in international agencies, governments and MNCs and to development processes which empower poor people in developing societies. The Catholic NGOs are increasingly collaborating in ecumenical national and global campaigning groups. The 'cancel the debt', 'fair trade' and 'make poverty history' campaigns have successfully mobilized millions of activists across the world and have achieved some limited successes. But while there has been some success in generating a social concern for the poor of the world in the Church, there remains a long way to go before it can truly be said that the rhetoric of justice is being translated into serious action.

At the end of his encyclical *Populorum Progressio* Pope Paul VI wrote that 'the new name for peace is development' (§87). In other words, without authentic human development there is inequality and injustice which are the seeds of conflict and war. It is to these issues of war and peace that we turn in the next chapter.

CHAPTER 11

War and peace

THE UBIQUITY OF CONFLICT

The sixth area of concern is that of war and peace and the related issues of defence strategies, the arms trade and terrorism. Since the Second World War there have been numerous major conflicts, in spite of the efforts of the UN. For four decades there was a dangerous period of nuclear deterrence between the two major superpowers and their associated blocs. Yet the euphoria which attended the collapse of Soviet Communism has not meant the end of war. Recent terrorist atrocities appear to have been provoked by a sense of grievance against the western world's power, arrogance and indifference to the plight of billions of poor people in the developing world.

Auschwitz-Birkenau is a permanent reminder of the attempt by Nazi racists only one lifetime ago to exterminate a whole ethnic group. The conflicts in Northern Ireland, the Balkans, Rwanda and the Holy Land also have their roots in deep ethnic antagonisms and injustices. Other conflicts, such as the two Iraq wars, were related more ambiguously to economic and political interests. Millions of people have been killed or injured in such conflicts since the Second World War. Many more have fled from such conflicts and are to be found in refugee camps all over the world, over-whelmingly in poor countries.

Eric Hobsbawn, has suggested that the twentieth century was the most murderous in recorded history with 187 million deaths, the equivalent of 10 per cent of the world's population in 1913.[1] Paul Rogers has reported that in the 55 years between 1945 and 2000 'there were well over 120 major conflicts killing at least 25 million people and injuring three times that number'.[2] For over forty years during the 'Cold War' the two superpowers fought

[1] Eric Hobsbawn, 'War and Peace', *Guardian Saturday Review*, 23 February 2002.
[2] Paul Rogers in 'Preface' to Elworthy 2004: 4.

numerous proxy wars throughout the world as they struggled for political and economic ascendancy. But with the ending of the Cold War and the supremacy of the United States as the one 'hyperpower' there has been a significant increase in inter-ethnic conflicts and the emergence of terrorism, which has no concern for the constraints of discrimination or proportionality, as a global phenomenon at the start of the twenty-first century.[3] Significant for the Christian tradition of the 'just war' has been the steady 'erosion of the distinction between combatants and noncombatants', at least in terms of practical outcomes. Whereas only 5 per cent of those who died in the First World War were civilians, this increased to 66 per cent in the Second World War and is generally thought to be around 80–90 per cent at the present time.[4] Hobsbawn noted that whereas globalization had advanced economically, technologically, culturally and linguistically, it had failed to do so politically. 'Territorial states remain the only effective authorities' and there is a palpable weakness of governance on a global scale.

This chapter addresses the issue of war in the modern world as a means of resolving conflicts. This is not to overlook the great but largely untapped potential of non-military forms of prevention and strategies for the non-violent resolution of conflicts.[5] Several quite different types of war can be distinguished: civil wars, holy wars or crusades, guerrilla wars, wars of liberation, total war, wars for humanitarian reasons and 'asymmetric' wars. O'Donovan has argued that economic 'sanctions are acts of war which do not involve the direct use of force'.[6] Recently we have experienced the war in Iraq, supposedly to pre-empt the use of 'weapons of mass destruction' by terrorists. Wars may be fought over access to or control of vital raw materials such as oil or clean water.[7] Each of these poses ethical problems which Catholic social thought has attempted to address.

It is a recurring theme in this book that extreme levels of inequality, communal injustices, or structural sins, generate grievances and conflict. These frequently lead to war. So, one important element in any Catholic position, though one which is often underplayed, is the need to seek to understand the causes of conflicts in structural sin and injustices. A second

---

[3] See Rogers 2002 for an excellent overview of current global security issues.

[4] Mary Kaldor suggests that 'at the turn of the (twentieth) century, the ratio of military to civilian casualties in wars was 8:1 . . . this has been almost exactly reversed . . . in the wars of the 1990s . . . (to) approximately 1:8', 1999: 8.

[5] Elworthy 2004. See also Schell 2004; Wink 2003.   [6] O'Donovan 2003: 101.

[7] See, e.g., Marq de Villiers, 'Water wars of the Near Future' at http://www.Itt.com/waterbook/Wars.asp. See, also V. Shiva 2002. *Water Wars: Privatisation, Pollution, and Profit*, South End Press.

important element is support for a 'competent authority'. In the case of disputes between nations it is important to construct some form of transnational authority, such as the UN was intended to be, which will be recognized as having legitimate authority to adjudicate in cases of disputes between nations. More recently an International Criminal Court has been established to bring to justice individuals, including heads of state, responsible for genocide or terrorism and to deter future war criminals.

It is a social fact that conflict has been ubiquitous throughout human history. Both individuals and states have conflicting interests and what is important is how best to manage these conflicts in non-violent ways in the interests of justice and the common good by tackling the underlying causes of grievances and injustices. Theologically, Christians believe that sin and evil are present in this world but also in the redeeming power of Jesus, the saviour, who has called humankind to love enemies and seek the kingdom of justice and peace. Hence the subtitle of a recent book: *eliminating conflict in a nuclear age*[8] is misleading. Eliminating conflict is utopian; what is important is to control it in ways which convey legitimacy.

WAR, STRATEGY AND LEGITIMACY

In line with the four-stage cycle of social reality, reference will first be made to three recent academic analyses of war. This is essential if Catholics are to recognize the 'signs of the times' and engage fruitfully in dialogue with the world as the Second Vatican Council advocated (*GS* §§1, 4). All three analyses concluded that since the collapse of communism in Central and Eastern Europe in 1989, the nature of war has changed significantly as have the appropriate responses. In particular, where the world has one 'hyperpower', there are problems of conflict governance in which the role of the United States is crucial.[9]

Firstly, Mary Kaldor has suggested that since the 1980s 'a new type of organised violence has developed ... which is one aspect of the current globalised era'.[10] In comparison with the 'old wars', characterized by national and ideological conflicts, which were 'construction(s) of the

---

[8] Hinde and Rotblat 2003.
[9] 'U.S. global economic, technological, military and diplomatic influence will be unparalleled among national as well as regional and international organizations in 2015. This power not only will ensure America's pre-eminence, but also will cast the United States as the key driver of the international system'. (US) National Intelligence Council 2000–02, Dec. 2000, *Global Trends 2015: A Dialogue about the Future with Nongovernment Experts*, p. 12; quoted in Bobbitt 2003: 721. See also Chomsky 2004; Hertsgaard 2002; Kagan 2003; Rogers 2002.
[10] Kaldor 1999: 1, 6, 10, 15, 78, 111, 142–152.

centralized, "rationalized", hierarchically ordered, territorialized modern state' or bloc, 'new wars', including the Bosnian War and genocide in Rwanda, were characterized by 'identity politics' arising 'out of the disintegration or erosion of modern state structures, especially centralized, authoritarian states'. Kaldor argued that 'in the context of globalization, ideological and/or territorial cleavages of an earlier era have increasingly been supplanted by an emerging political cleavage between ... cosmopolitanism, based on inclusive, universalist, multicultural values, and the politics of particularist identities'. She argued that 'precisely because the new wars are a social condition that arises as the formal political economy withers, they are very difficult to end'. She rejected the approach of Samuel Huntington's *Clash of Civilisations*[11] in favour of what she called 'cosmopolitan governance' which would 'cross the global/local divide and reconstruct legitimacy around an inclusive, democratic set of values ... counterposed against the politics of exclusivism'.

Secondly, Philip Bobbitt[12] has also suggested that we are living at a time of major constitutional change. He distinguished five 'epochal wars', following each of which a new basis for a peace settlement emerged. The last of these epochal wars was what he called 'the long war' from 1914 to 1990. Since the collapse of Soviet hegemony in Central and Eastern Europe a new form of 'market state' had replaced the 'nation-state'. The nation state was supreme within its borders with respect to its law while externally it 'earns the right of recognition and intercourse to the extent that it can defend its borders'. In the era of nuclear, biological and chemical threats, and limited control over economic strength and cultural integrity, the nation state lost its legitimacy and mutated into a 'market-state'. This required a choice between a number of not very attractive scenarios and from a range of possible wars. Bobbitt believed that 'we face the task of developing cooperative practices that will enable us to undertake a series of low-intensity conflicts. Failing this, we will face an international environment of increasingly violent anarchy and, possibly, a cataclysmic war in the early decades of the twenty-first century'.

Bobbitt pointed to five developments which he argued cast doubt on the entire system of nation states: (1) the recognition of human rights norms; (2) the widespread deployment of weapons of mass destruction; (3) 'the proliferation of global and transnational threats that transcend state borders, such as those that damage the environment, or threaten states through migration, population expansion, disease, or famine'; (4) 'the growth of a

---

[11] Huntington 1998.   [12] Bobbitt 2003: xxii, xxiv, 713, 722–728, 774, 802.

world economic regime that ignores borders in the movement of capital investment to a degree that effectively curtails states in the management of their own economic affairs'; and (5) 'the creation of a global communications network that penetrates borders electronically and threatens national languages, customs, and cultures'. As a result 'a new constitutional order will arise that reflects these five developments' and this 'will also change the constitutional assumptions of the international society of states'.

Bobbitt believed that 'the Long War was won by strategic innovations . . . weapons of mass destruction, the globalization of communications, and the international integration of finance and trade. These strategic innovations have brought with them new challenges that now face the society of states that the end of the Long War is bringing into being'. Bobbitt considered that 'three fundamental choices confront the society of market-states with respect to each of these challenges'. He proposed three general scenarios which might emerge: the 'meadow' or entrepreneurial, the 'park' or managerial, and the 'garden' or mercantile market-states. 'In a meadow all is profusion, randomness, variety. A park is for the most part publicly maintained, highly regulated with different sectors for different uses. A garden is smaller, more inwardly turned – it aims for the sublime, not the efficient or the just'. All three scenarios must cope with trends relating to population, resources, energy, economic growth, technology and events which depend on decisions taken by states such as security, culture and economics.[13] These scenarios 'help us to define what kind of world we really want, among many possible worlds'. He continued to identify:

ten constitutional conditions for a society of market-states: (1) the maintenance of a force structure capable of defeating a challenge to peace; (2) the creation of security structures and alliances capable of dealing with the problems of population control, migration, and ecological stability; (3) a consensus among the great powers on the legitimacy of certain forms of the market-state; (4) a few clear, structural rules for any state's behaviour that are enforced by arms if necessary . . .; (5) provisions for the financial assistance to great powers when . . . (they) intervene on behalf of the peace and security of the society of states as a whole; (6) prohibitions against arms trading in nuclear materials, weapons of mass destruction (WMD), and missile technology . . .; (7) practices for bribing states – by enhancing their security or their wealth – in order to prevent WDM proliferation to any state . . .; (8) prohibitions against wholesale attacks by the state on its own populations; (9) some general prohibition on anticompetitive trade and financial

---

[13] For illustrations of 'possible worlds' see ibid.: 729–771.

practices; (10) a consensus on the rule that no state that meets the standards of the Peace of Paris – free elections, market economy, human rights – ought to be the subject of threats of force.

Both Kaldor and Bobbitt warned against utopian visions and stressed the importance of human agency. Moral choices have to be made in response to the challenges in the real world with real sin and evil. It is the task of Christians to cope with that real world as best they can in the light of Jesus' teaching and praxis.[14]

Thirdly, Paul Rogers has offered an important analysis of global security issues at the beginning of the twenty-first century.[15] He first detailed the nuclear arms race in the post-war period and the absurd air of unreality at the overkill nuclear capacity, with 70,000 nuclear warheads globally in the late 1980s. Targeting policies indicated that the idea that nuclear weapons would only be used as a 'last resort' was false. In 1987, military expenditure was greater than world public expenditure on health and on education and nearly seven times that on health and education in the whole of the developing world. Rogers described the conventional wisdom of the 'old security paradigm', emphatically espoused by the 'neocon' proponents of the 'New American Century'[16] in the Bush administration, as 'liddism':

keeping the lid on dissent and instability . . . by means of public order control that will . . . extend to the use of military force . . . Little attention is paid to the fundamental causes of instability, the economic processes that continue to ensure the marginalization of the majority world and the failure to address core problems of the global environment. The old security paradigm survives – maintain control, maintain the status quo, do not address the underlying problems.

In the 'violent peace' of the post-Cold War period 'it was thought that military postures were adequate to handle this uncertain world and that the Western society would continue to benefit from its dominance of the international economic and financial systems'. But, he argued, this strategy failed to address the innate weaknesses of wealthy nations 'that can be readily exploited in an era of asymmetric warfare' and there was a need to 'come to terms with the changing causes of insecurity'. There were three reasons why a new security paradigm was necessary:

The first is that factors most likely to influence the development of conflict in the coming decades are the socioeconomic divide, environmental constraints and the spread of military technologies, not least weapons of mass destruction. Second,

---

[14] O'Donovan 2003.   [15] Rogers 2002: 34, 37, 40, 102, 112, 118–124, 129, 132–150.
[16] www.newamericancentury/

this is likely to lead to conflicts involving anti-elite action from within the marginalized majority, rapidly increasing migratory pressures and conflict concerning environmental factors, especially strategic resources and climate change, all within the context of middle-ranking states unwilling to accept a Western hegemony. Finally, the Western perception that the status quo can be maintained in such circumstances, by military means if need be, is not sustainable given the vulnerabilities of advanced wealthy states to paramilitary action and asymmetric warfare.

Thus, there was a need for a new paradigm which included measures of arms control, closing the wealthy-poverty divide, and responding to environmental constraints. Yet sadly, the current US response was 'aggressive isolationism' and unilateralism.

CATHOLIC APPROACHES TO WAR AND PEACE[17]

There are two elements in Catholic social thought about war in a sinful world: 'that conflict, but not war is inevitable and that the violence of war is subject to moral restraint'[18] and appropriate institutions of conflict resolution. Joseph Fahey recorded the confusion of a student who did not know 'whether to be a pacifist, a follower of the just war, a crusader, or a world citizen (since) all four seem to be Christian positions'.[19] The crusader view of holy war which drew on Old Testament themes was revived during the medieval period to combat Islam.[20] However, scholastics were reluctant to support the Crusades[21] and support for this view was inconceivable today.[22] At the present time there were roughly three Christian traditions: conscientious pacifism, selective pacifism and the just war.

Fahey gave a useful outline of the historical development of Catholic teaching in response to the dominant concerns of the times.[23] It seemed clear that Jesus stood in the Jewish prophetic tradition of non-violent resistance to injustice and that in the first three centuries 'persecuted Christian communities consistently responded to violence with non-violent love'. After Constantine recognized Christianity as a legitimate religion in the fourth century the institutional Church became more closely linked with the civil authority and began 'to develop an application of the

---

[17] See *Compendium* §§400–401, 488–520. In my view this treatment was disappointing and not as helpful as the US Bishops' pastoral letter.
[18] Himes 1994: 977.　　[19] Fahey 2003.　　[20] Himes 1994: 978.　　[21] Charles 1998a: 236.
[22] Some of President Bush's close associates came close to it.
[23] Fahey 2003: 4–5, 7–9, 11, 14. Attention is also drawn to the much more detailed review of 'Christian Perspectives on War and Peace' in Haleem et al. 1998: 22–59. This source also offers a valuable comparison with Muslim approaches, ibid.: 104–132.

law of love that permitted legitimate defence of the innocent against unjust aggression'. Augustine in the fifth century developed principles for a just war but they were substantially ignored during the atrocities of the Crusades at the end of the eleventh century. Aquinas further developed these principles in the thirteenth century and significant contributions were also made by Francisco di Vitoria and Francisco Suárez[24] in the sixteenth century. In the sixteenth to eighteenth centuries a number of radical pacifist Churches emerged. The First World War saw the mobilization of entire nations for 'total war' and subsequently the plea by Pope Benedict XV for some sort of international 'league' to maintain the independence of nations and safeguard human society. He also stressed that the moral law applied in international affairs as well as to individuals. But within twenty years a Second World War was waging with the genocide of Jews and other minorities, the fire bombings of Hamburg and Dresden, and the nuclear annihilation of Hiroshima and Nagasaki. Recent Church thinking on the issues of war and peace in the era of nuclear weapons of mass destruction and chemical and biological weapons date from Pope John XXIII's encyclical *Pacem in Terris* and the Second Vatican Council's *Gaudium et Spes*. The major Church documents published in recent years have been indicated in Table 11.1. Brief outlines of the key points of each are given below.

Pacem in Terris (John XXIII 1963)

Pope John XXIII introduced a new era of thinking about the just war tradition in the context of modern weapons of mass destruction and the need for nation states to regulate their relationships in accordance with 'the requirements of the universal common good'.[25] *Pacem in Terris* was written shortly after the world had twice been to the nuclear brink in Berlin and Cuba. It was written very much from a natural law perspective, addressed to 'all men of good will', stressing the intrinsic dignity of each individual human being with rights and duties (§§8–38). The task of public authorities was to promote the common good (§§53–57, 98–108). The pope insisted that 'the same natural law, which governs relations between individual human beings, serves also to regulate the relations of nations with one another' (§80). Given the dreadful violence which was the consequence of modern warfare and the dangers of some 'unexpected and unpremeditated act' which might lead to devastating war, the pope

---

[24] O'Donovan 2003.   [25] Himes 1994: 979.

Table 11.1. *Church documents on war, peace and the arms trade, 1963–2004*

Year	Author[a]	Document	Key themes	Reference[b]
1963	John XXIII	*Pacem in Terris*	Disarmament; need for world authority	OBS, 131–162
1965	Vat. II	*Gaudium et Spes*	Total war; arms race; world authority	OBS, 209–215
1967	Paul VI	*Populorum Progressio*	Development: the new name for peace	OBS, 240–262
1971	Synod	*Justice in the World*	Interdependence; domination denounced	OBS, 288–300
1972	Paul VI	*World Day of Peace*	If you want peace, work for justice	Vatican Web
1975	Paul VI	*Evangelii Nuntiandi*	Violence not Christian; fear of revolution	OBS, 303–345
1978	Paul VI	*World Day of Peace*	No to Violence, Yes to Peace	Vatican Web
1982	John Paul II	*World Day of Peace*	Peace: a gift of God entrusted to us	Vatican Web
1983	US Bishops	*Challenge of Peace*	Nuclear war, deterrence, arms trade	OBS, 489–571[c]
1987	John Paul II	*World Day of Peace*	Development and solidarity: two keys	Vatican web
1987	John Paul II	*Sollicitudo Rei Socialis*	Arms trade; terrorism; justice; solidarity	OBS, 393–436
1991	John Paul II	*Centesimus Annus*	Abolish war; reconciliation; solidarity	OBS, 437–488
1994	J&P Cmssn	*International Arms Trade*	Self-defence; international control	CTS, S 438
2002	John Paul II	*World Day of Peace*	No peace without justice, no justice	Vatican web
2004	CBCEW	*Cherishing Life*	War and peace; terrorism; justice	CBCEW/CTS

Notes:

[a] Synod: Synod of Bishops; J&P Cmssn: Pontifical Commission 'Iustitia et Pax'; CBCEW: Catholic Bishops' Conference of England and Wales.

[b] OBS: O'Brien and Shannon, 1992; Vatican web: http://www.vatican.va/holy_father

[c] Also published by CTS/SPCK, 1983.

pleaded for an end to the arms race and an effective programme of disarmament (§§109–116) and 'a peaceful adjustment of relations between political communities on a world level . . . founded on mutual trust, on sincerity in negotiations, on faithful fulfilment of obligations assumed' (§118). The freedom and rights of smaller nations should be respected (§§120–125). In modern circumstances conflicts between states should be settled by negotiation and in the nuclear age, 'it is contrary to reason to hold that war is now a suitable way to restore rights which have been violated' (§§126–127). The pope then reflected on the fact that even with good will, individual states lacked adequate power to ensure the universal common good (§§132–135). This required the efforts of a public authority 'having worldwide power . . . set up by common accord and not imposed by force' (§138). The pope welcomed the establishment of UNO in 1945 and the Universal Declaration of Human Rights in 1948 as important developments towards this goal (§§142–145).

Gaudium et Spes (Vatican II 1965)

The fostering of peace and the promotion of a community of nations was the last of five problems of special urgency addressed in Part II of the Vatican Council's *The Church in the Modern World*. In the first place it was pointed out that 'peace is not merely the absence of war . . . (but) results from that harmony built into human society by its divine Founder, and actualised by men as they thirst after ever greater justice' (§78). The Constitution stressed the need to curb the savagery of war. Only nine years after Pius XII had declared against it, Vatican II recognized the right of conscientious objection and rejected 'blind obedience' to orders from superiors (§79). Since 1965, then, both the pacifist and just war traditions have been regarded as acceptable.

However, the Council warned that modern weapons 'can inflict massive and indiscriminate destruction far exceeding the bounds of legitimate defence'. Accordingly it declared explicitly against total war: 'Any act of war aimed indiscriminately at the destruction of entire cities or of extensive areas along with their population is a crime against God and man himself. It merits unequivocal and unhesitating condemnation' (§80). It bemoaned the 'extravagant sums' spent on the arms race which 'is not a safe way to preserve a steady peace' and declared that 'the arms race is an utterly treacherous trap for humanity, and one which injures the poor to an intolerable degree' (§81). This led them to accept the duty to 'work for the time when all war can be completely outlawed by international consent ... (a) goal (which) undoubtedly requires the establishment of some universal public authority acknowledged as such by all, and endowed with effective power to safeguard, on behalf of all, security, regard for justice, and respect for rights' (§82). The Council then proceeded to urge the construction of appropriate international institutions and encouraged international cooperation at the economic level (§§83–85).

Populorum Progressio (Paul VI 1967)

We have noted Pope Paul's passionate plea for international economic justice and authentic development. He also warned that 'excessive economic, social, and cultural inequalities among peoples arouse tensions and conflicts, and are a danger to peace' (§76). Hence he concluded: 'the new name for peace is development' (§87).

Justice in the World (Synod of Bishops 1971)

The Synod document referred to a crisis of universal solidarity and an awareness of an 'interdependent economic world' in which there were finite resources of air and water and 'the small delicate biosphere of the whole complex of all life on earth ... (which) must be saved and preserved as a rich patrimony belonging to all mankind'. In this context 'the arms race is a threat to man's highest good, which is life ... (which) threatens to destroy all life from the face of the earth'.[26] The bishops wished to foster 'a strategy of non-violence' and a right conscientiously to object to military service.

World Days of Peace (Paul VI 1968–78)[27]

Paul VI wished to celebrate each year a World Day of Prayer for Peace 'as a sign of hope and promise'. Each year's message reflected a particular theme: the promotion of human rights (1969); peace through reconciliation (1970, 1975); the brotherhood of all men (1971); peace as the product of justice (1972) and the defence of life (1977); the possibility of peace (1973) and rejection of violence (1978).

---

[26] O'Brien and Shannon 1992: 289, 298.
[27] http://www.vatican.va/holy_father/paul_vi/messages/peace/documents/

Evangelii Nuntiandi (Paul VI 1975)

Pope Paul had a particular abhorrence of violence and he referred to this in his Apostolic Exhortation on evangelization. He feared the uncontrollable aspect of violence since 'violence always provokes violence and irresponsibly engenders new forms of oppression and enslavement'. He taught that 'violence is not in accord with the Gospel, . . . it is not Christian; and . . . sudden or violent changes of structures would be deceitful, ineffective . . . and certainly not in conformity with the dignity of the people' (§37). One can note here the Vatican concerns about revolutionary means of combating structural injustices which were later developed by Pope John Paul II and by the CDF in their reservations about some aspects of liberation theology.

World Days of Peace (John Paul II 1979–2004)[28]

Pope John Paul II continued Paul VI's annual messages on World Days of Peace. Among the themes mentioned were the need to teach peace (1979, 2004), for truth (1980), and respect for freedom (1981), minorities (1989), all creation (1990), conscience (1991), families (1994), justice (1998), human rights (1999), and dialogue between cultures and nations (1986; 2001). The theme for 1987 was 'development and solidarity: two keys to peace', and for 2002 'no peace without justice; no justice without forgiveness'. The linking of the values of human dignity, the common good and solidarity is apparent and between economic justice, authentic development and peace emphatic. The US bishops' pastoral letter contained numerous references to the various addresses of Pope John Paul II.

The Challenge of Peace (United States Bishops 1983)

In 1971 the United States Catholic bishops 'publicly concluded that the American war in Vietnam could no longer be justified'. In 1983 Cardinal Bernardin had outlined a 'pro-life commitment that linked opposition to abortion, the arms race, capital punishment, and economic injustice'.[29] After a process of public dialogue with a wide range of experts, an extended national debate and three separate drafts, public intervention from the Reagan administration, and consultations with other NATO bishops and

---

[28] http://www.vatican.va/holy_father/john_paul_ii/messages/peace/documents/
[29] O'Brien and Shannon 1992: 489–491.

the Vatican, the bishops published their pastoral letter in 1983. As with their later pastoral on economic justice, which we discussed in earlier chapters, the American bishops introduced a *process* of consultation, debate and dialogue with a wide range of laity and those intimately involved in all aspects of defence policy, which was perhaps unique in the Church but which appeared to offer the most authentic realisation we yet have of the 'People of God' model of the Church.

The pastoral letter was impressively rooted in social reality: the perception that 'nuclear war threatens the existence of our planet . . ... It is neither tolerable nor necessary that human beings live under this threat' (§3). Furthermore, it included an emphatic confession: 'as Americans, citizens of the . . . only [nation] to use [atomic weapons] . . . we have grave human, moral and political responsibilities to see that a "conscious choice" is made to save humanity' (§4). The pastoral letter was divided into four main sections: scriptural and religious perspectives and moral principles; problems of nuclear weapons and deterrence theories; specific proposals to promote peace; and pastoral challenges for the Church.

The bishops started with *Gaudium et Spes* and addressed the wider civil community who were 'equally bound by certain key moral principles' (§17). They commenced with a 'sketch of the biblical conception of peace' (§26). In the Old Testament the warrior image of God 'was gradually transformed' (§31). The prophets had all warned that there was no true peace while injustice and idolatry persisted (§§33–35). In spite of their infidelity to God's covenant, 'God's people clung tenaciously to hope in the promise of an eschatological time when . . . peace and justice would embrace and all creation would be secure from harm' (§38). In the New Testament there was no sign of a warrior God. Rather, the Sermon on the Mount described 'a new reality in which God's power is manifested and the longing of the people is fulfilled' (§45). Jesus described God's reign as 'one in which love is an active, life-giving, inclusive force' (§47). Jesus gave his followers his gifts of peace and his own spirit. They were called to be 'ministers of reconciliation' in seeking the fulfilment of God's plan (§53). The bishops concluded their scriptural reflections by affirming that 'the fullness of eschatological peace remains before us in hope and yet the gift of peace is already ours in the reconciliation effected in Jesus Christ' (§55).

The bishops noted 'not only sinful patterns of domination, oppression or aggression, but the conflict of values and interests which illustrate the limitations of a sinful world' (§61). Consequently tension between the 'already but not yet' of the kingdom of God meant that a permanently peaceful society was utopian (§58). There was a need to make moral choices about 'what contributes to, and what impedes, the construction of a more genuinely human world' (§66). They insisted that 'unconditional and effective respect for each one's ... rights is the necessary condition in order that peace may reign in a society' (§69; see also fn. 23). The Church's teaching 'establishes a strong presumption against war which is binding on all' (§70).

The bishops repeated the teaching of *Gaudium et Spes* that 'governments cannot be denied the right to legitimate defence once every means of peaceful settlement has been exhausted' (§72; quoting *GS* §79). They insisted that the defence of '*a people threatened with an unjust aggression, or already its victim ... is even an obligation for the nations as a whole, who have a duty not to abandon a nation that is attacked*' (§76; see also fn. 27). But at the same time they recognized the alternative view, derived from the example of Jesus, for conscientious opposition to war and a strategy of non-violence, especially given the destructiveness of modern weaponry. Indeed, they believed 'work to develop non-violent means of fending off aggression and resolving conflict best reflects the call of Jesus both to love and to justice' (§78). The bishops described the relationship between the 'two distinct moral responses', pacifism and non-violence and just-war, as 'complementary' (§74), and claimed they 'support and complement one another, each preserving the other from distortion' (§121).

It must be recalled that the pastoral was written some years before the collapse of the Soviet system and the end of the Cold War. It reflected the dominant fears of the times, including accidental and unpremeditated nuclear war. They said that 'both the just-war teaching and non-violence are confronted with a unique challenge by nuclear warfare' (§122). They argued that nuclear war would fail to meet the conditions for a just war, particularly its principles of proportionality and discrimination, so that 'we must refuse to legitimate the idea of nuclear war' (§131), have a conversion of heart, and move 'toward a national policy and an international system which more adequately reflect the values and vision of the kingdom of God' (§134). They proceeded as pastors and teachers, not as politicians or technical experts (§331), to invite a public moral dialogue about four issues.

Firstly, on the use of nuclear weapons, they repeated the teaching of *Gaudium et Spes* that 'no Christian can rightfully carry out orders or policies deliberately aimed at killing non-combatants' (§148; see also *GS* §80). They saw no way of justifying initiating nuclear war and regarded the use of nuclear weapons to counter a conventional attack as 'morally unjustifiable' (§153) because of the recognized danger of escalation. For the same reason they saw 'no moral justification' for risking a limited nuclear war (§161).

Secondly, they examined the morality of deterrence in principle and practice. With seeming reluctance they quoted Pope John Paul's statement to the UN in 1982 that 'in current conditions "deterrence" based on balance certainly not as an end in itself but as a step on the way toward a progressive disarmament, may still be judged morally acceptable' (§173; see also fn. 78). A consideration of US targeting policy and strategic plans for the use of the deterrent led them uncomfortably to 'a strictly conditioned moral acceptance of nuclear deterrence' (§186). They seemed happier to 'raise a prophetic challenge to the community of faith . . . beyond nuclear deterrence, toward more resolute steps to actual bilateral disarmament and peacemaking' (§198).

Thirdly, they offered positive suggestions for peacemaking to 'all men and women of good will': 'effective arms control leading to mutual disarmament, ratification of pending treaties, [and] development of non-violent alternatives' (§202; see also fn. 88).

Fourthly, the bishops pointed to the need for a new world order. Catholic thinking on this had been developed since *Pacem in Terris*. The bishops argued that 'major global problems such as worldwide inflation, trade and payments deficits, competition over scarce resources, hunger, widespread unemployment, global environmental dangers, the growing power of transnational corporations, and the threat of international financial collapse, as well as the danger of world war resulting from these growing tensions – cannot be remedied by a single nation-state approach' (§242). They concluded, therefore, that there was a need for 'a moral as well as a political concept of the international common good . . .. Mutual security and survival require a new vision of the world as one interdependent planet. We have rights and duties not only within our diverse national communities but [also] within the larger world community' (§§243–244). Cold realism required dialogue and the bishops warned against 'hardness of heart' which resisted the necessary changes (§258).

Part IV of the pastoral considered the pastoral implications of the bishops' deliberations and called on Christians to follow Jesus and share in the cross in solidarity with each other. They offered some elements of a pastoral response: peace education, reverence for all life, including the unborn, deeper forms of prayer, and a greater emphasis on reconciliation, penance and conversion. They urged the 'cultivation of the gospel vision of peace as a way of life for believers and as a leaven in society' (§303). They had words of encouragement for men and women in military service: 'where they carry out their duty properly, they are contributing to the maintenance of peace' (§309; see also fn. 119). But they also warned against dehumanizing forms of training which dulled sensibilities and generated hatred towards adversaries (§313). They also addressed those working in the defence industries and scientists.

The bishops noted that 'we are the first generation since Genesis with the power to virtually destroy God's creation' (§331). This presented 'fundamental moral choices' (§332). 'The whole world must summon the moral courage and technical means to say "no" to nuclear conflict; "no" to weapons of mass destruction; "no" to an arms race which robs the poor and vulnerable; and "no" to the . . . indefensible choices of constant terror or surrender. Peacemaking is not an optional commitment. It is a require-ment of our faith' (§333). Finally, the bishops summarized recent Catholic social thinking about interdependence in a global age: 'There is a substitute for war. There is negotiation under the supervision of a global body realistically fashioned to do its job . . . empowered by all the nations to enforce its commands on every nation . . . [yet] so constituted as to pose no threat to any nation's sovereignty' (§334).

The world has changed dramatically since the bishops' pastoral already over twenty years ago and the problems faced today are somewhat dif-ferent.[30] In place of the Cold War between two superpowers, there is one hyperpower. In place of the discussion of how to manage the tension between 'the superpowers in a disordered world' (§§245–258), the need at the beginning of the twenty-first century in a period of intensifying globalization and increasing awareness of the interdependence between nations is to develop Christian responses to global terrorism and the need to reduce the socio-economic inequalities and injustices which fuel griev-ances, resentments and conflicts. It is tragic that the United States administration under George W. Bush, with the collaboration of the UK Blair Government, failed to follow the bishops' advice to 'promote multi-lateral forms of cooperation' (§265) and rather pursued a unilateralist policy of pre-emptive first strike regardless of UN opinion.

In the American celebration of *One Hundred Years of Catholic Social Thought*[31] Part IV considered the issue of peace. Several contributors observed that the origins of the Catholic Church's search for an appro-priate international social order in the age of a global nuclear threat were

---

[30] For American reflections on the United States Peace Pastoral, see, e.g., Reid 1986 and Part IV in Coleman 1991a.
[31] Coleman 1991a.

to be found in various addresses given by Pope Pius XII in the 1950s.[32] Kenneth Himes noted that he had redefined the notion of just cause from the vindication of rights, resisting unjust aggression, and avenging injury, to one cause, defence against aggression. Peaceful means of settling disputes were to be sought and there was a need for some sort of international mechanism for resolving disputes without resort to war. Mary Jegen noted that there had been a shift of emphasis in Catholic thinking about war from 'negative peace', as the absence of violence, to 'positive peace' in which all spontaneously desired the welfare of all. This was reflected, for example, in a growing awareness of unjust socio-economic structures, environmental concerns, and notions of a 'universal common good'. A theology of positive peace resonated with 'a Christology from below' which stressed the humanity of Jesus and historical experiences.[33]

Sollicitudo Rei Socialis (John Paul II 1987)

This encyclical marked the twentieth anniversary of Paul VI's *Populorum Progressio* with its appeal that 'development is the new name for peace' and demand for authentic human development and global justice. In the context of an ever widening gap between the rich and poor nations, John Paul II judged arms production to be 'a serious disorder in the present world'. Arms circulated across the world with almost total freedom and contributed to conflicts which resulted in the tragedy of millions of refugees. As the pope had emphasized at Drogheda in 1979, 'what Christianity forbids is to seek solutions . . . by the ways of hatred, by the murdering of defenceless people, by the methods of terrorism' (§24). The pope considered that 'structures of sin', such as 'exploitation, oppression, and annihilation of others . . . combine to produce the danger of war and an excessive preoccupation with personal security, often to the detriment of the autonomy, freedom of decision, and even the territorial integrity of the weaker nations'. He pleaded for solidarity between people, which 'seeks to go beyond itself, to take on the specifically Christian dimension of total gratuity, forgiveness and reconciliation', regarding one's neighbour as 'the living image of God'. Such solidarity would be 'the path to peace and at the same time to development' (§§39–40).

---

[32] Bernardin, Cardinal J., in Coleman 1991a: 274–275; Jegen 1991: 287; Himes 1991: 331.
[33] Jegen 1991.

Centesimus Annus (John Paul II 1991)

This encyclical celebrated the centenary of *Rerum Novarum*. The pope traced developments in the world over the past century and insisted that 'true peace is never simply the result of military victory, but rather implies both the removal of the causes of war and genuine reconciliation between peoples'. But the peace following the Second World War had been precarious and the world had experienced 'the threat of atomic war', terrorism by 'extremist groups' and 'an insane arms race (which had) swallowed up the resources needed for the development of national economies and for assistance to the less developed nations' (§18). Given 'the terrifying power of the means of destruction' and the likely consequences of war, the pope pleaded: 'No, never again war' (§52). Just as within states the rule of law had replaced a system of private vendetta and reprisal, so there was an urgent need for the rule of law in the international community. Solidarity between all peoples on earth should be promoted by means of authentic development which acknowledged the human dignity of all peoples and the need to seek the 'universal common good'.

The International Arms Trade: an Ethical Reflection (Pontifical Council 1994)

This short document from the Pontifical Council for Justice and Peace repeated previous teaching on the right to legitimate defence but also that it was 'a grave *duty* for someone responsible for another's life, the common good of the family or of the state' (*CCC* §§2265, 2302–2330). It was concerned that the arms trade contributed to 'an endless spiral of violence'.[34] It recapitulated general ethical principles: the presumption against war; the right of legitimate defence; the *duty* to help the innocent; the principle of sufficiency 'by which a State may possess only those means necessary to assure its legitimate defence'; and the need for strict control of arms. The document discussed the responsibility of the state, in both exporting and receiving countries, to control the flow of arms in the interests of the wider common good and not just the profits of arms exporters or the prestige and power of leaders or the political class. It warned against supplying arms to authoritarian regimes which violated human rights, suggested 'a moral presumption against supplying arms to belligerents' and urged the international community 'to find an effective

---

[34] *The International Arms Trade* 1994: 9, 11–16, 26–28, 31, 33.

way to stop the flow of arms to terrorist and criminal groups' and 'likewise give serious consideration to establishing effective and obligatory means for preventing armed conflicts'. The document confirmed the 'need for a public authority having world-wide power "set up by common accord and not imposed by force"' and suggested, as a first step the expansion of the roles of the UN, the International Court of Justice, and regional institutions.

Cherishing Life (Catholic Bishops' Conference of England and Wales 2004)

This document referred briefly to the issues of war and peace (§§195–201) and recapitulated Catholic social teaching on the right to lawful self-defence, just war 'theory' about just cause, self-defence, last resort, legitimate authority, prospect of success and discrimination. It was a scandal that so much money was spent on armaments when there was so much global poverty. It called for a ban on nuclear weapons, and taught that terrorist attacks on innocent people could never be right. It concluded that 'to build a peaceful society, it is necessary to overcome gross economic, social and political inequalities in the world . . . Overcoming war demands establishing a just international order and building up of a culture in which life is cherished' (§201).

Non-official Catholic thought

In their pastoral letter on peace, the United States bishops noted the wide range of views held by Catholics, from selective or general pacifism to just war theories, and judgements regarding nuclear deterrence from conditional acceptable as a temporary measure to outright rejection as intrinsically immoral. An early symposium of Catholic philosophers argued that the possession and use of nuclear weapons was morally unacceptable.[35] Michael Novak, on the other hand, defended nuclear deterrence.[36] In the USA a number of reflections on the United States bishops' pastoral have been published.[37] In Britain, Brian Wicker drew on the teaching of six national hierarchies to summarize Church teaching on nuclear deterrence.[38] Patrick O'Mahony reflected on both the United States Catholic

---

[35] Stein 1965; see also Zahn 1967.
[36] Novak 1983. See also his contribution in Reid 1986: 123–136.
[37] See, e.g., Murnion 1983; Reid 1986.   [38] Wicker 1985.

bishops' letter and the report of the Church of England Working Party under the chairmanship of the Bishop of Salisbury.[39] Oliver McTernan has written a passionate account and analysis of faith-inspired violence.[40]

Mary Jegen's notion of 'negative peace' was reflected in the observation by Archbishop Romero that 'peace is not the silence of cemeteries, . . . the silent result of violent repression . . . (or) the product of terror or fear'. 'Positive peace', rather, was 'the generous, tranquil contribution of all to the good of all'.[41] For John Fuellenbach this biblical notion of *Shalom* was 'wholeness, reconciliation, the harmony of having come to full authenticity concerning our four basic relationships: with ourselves, our neighbour, nature, and God. Shalom is the ultimate state of fulfilment and great gift of the end-time. It means not only the absence of war but the fullness of life'.[42] Thus, as he noted, 'in Hebrew thought the opposite of shalom is not war but injustice'.

PACIFISM AND NON-VIOLENCE

There are two main streams of Catholic thinking about war which appear to be contradictory: pacifism, and just war approaches to conflict. It is important not to draw the line between them too sharply. For example, pacifists point out that in reaching their decisions, they use just war criteria, particularly those of discrimination and proportionality.

In their pastoral letter the United States bishops noted that 'in all of his suffering, as in all of his life and ministry, Jesus refused to defend himself with force or with violence' (§49).[43] In the Sermon on the Mount discourses Jesus is reported to have taught that peacemakers would be blessed and recognized as children of God (Mt 5:9). He advised those who had been offended to turn the other cheek (Mt 5: 38–39). In sum, the warrant for pacifism is to be found in the teaching of Jesus (§§111–121). One version of this would follow from a 'legalistic model' of morality that on issues such as the commandment not to kill, 'there are intrinsically evil acts, exceptionless specific moral norms and inviolable human rights . . . (which are) philosophically defensible and manifestly necessary to preserve the moral substance of Christian ethics'.[44] It was considerations such as these and the conciliar prohibition of total war which led Pax Christ USA to urge

---

[39] O'Mahony 1986; Baker 1982.   [40] McTernan 2003.
[41] Jegen 1991; Romero quote from CAFOD.   [42] Fuellenbach 1995: 168, 171.
[43] One of the authors of *The Challenge of Peace*, Bishop Thomas Gumbleton, has defended the pacifist position and argued for 'peacemaking as a way of life' in Coleman 1991a: 303–316.
[44] Hogan 2001: 30–33.

resistance to 'the impulse to vengeance' and 'courage to break the spiral of violence' after the World Trade Centre atrocity.[45]

Kenneth Himes[46] has pointed out that 'pacifism' has been used in two senses. Some have equated it with non-violence while others have restricted the term to opposition to war. The latter, which was the original sense, did not proscribe individual self-defence. Himes stressed that in Catholic social teaching 'all believers must defend the cause of justice, must protect human rights, must resist evil' and that 'pacifism, like just war, must engage in resistance against aggression'.

In an extended exegesis of Mt. 5: 38–41, Wink[47] has suggested that for Jesus, non-violence did *not* mean passivity and submission as a response to evil. He insisted that 'Jesus abhors both passivity and violence as responses to evil'. Rather, he argued, the examples given by Jesus demonstrated an act of defiance, refusal to be humiliated, protest at exploitation, and discomforting the oppressors. Thus, against the two traditional alternatives of 'flight' or 'fight', Jesus offered a 'third way' involving seizing the moral initiative, finding creative alternatives to violence, asserting one's own humanity and dignity as a person, meeting force with ridicule or humour, breaking the cycle of humiliation, refusing to submit or to accept the inferior position, exposing the injustices of the system, taking control of the power dynamic, shaming the oppressor into repentance, standing one's ground, forcing the 'powers' to make decisions for which they were not prepared, recognizing one's own power, being willing to suffer rather than to retaliate, causing the oppressor to see one in a new light, depriving him of a situation where a show of force was effective, being willing to undergo the penalties for breaking unjust laws, and overcoming fear of the old order and its rules. Wink illustrated this 'third way' of non-violence in the campaigns of Gandhi and Martin Luther King and the overthrow of Marcos in the Philippines. It was significant that the willingness to suffer was an integral part of the non-violent strategy against oppression. For Wink, Jesus' 'third way' was the way of the cross. From this perspective 'the cross means that death is not the greatest evil one can suffer'. Furthermore, non-violent suffering, 'choosing to draw the poison of . . . violence with one's own body rather than perpetuating the downward spiral of hate' required courage.

In his remarkable book Jonathan Schell[48] has suggested that 'the fundamental scientific discoveries of the twentieth century . . . (have) called into

---

[45] Quoted in Pax Christi Press Release, 13 September 2001.   [46] Himes 1994: 706–708.
[47] Wink 2003: 13, 27–28, 85, 88, 93.   [48] Schell 2004: 4, 8–9, 119, 138, 201, 244, 387–389.

question the age-old reliance of politics on violent means'. He argued that there are numerous historical examples which demonstrated that non-violence and grassroots resistance could develop immense power to overthrow oppressive regimes. Schell argued that increasingly there was evidence that compliance *in the long-term* could only be won by the consent of the people. He devoted a complete chapter to the exemplary case of Gandhi and his strategy of 'satyagraha' which 'prescribes non-violent action in which the actors refuse to cooperate with laws that they regard as unjust or otherwise offensive to their consciences, accompanied by a willingness to suffer the consequences'. It is instructive to note that for Gandhi, non-cooperation, civil disobedience and non-violent direct action required considerable courage and self-discipline and needed to be supplemented by positive action in the pursuit of social betterment or the common good.

More recent examples of the power of non-violence included the Civil Rights Movement in the United States and the 'velvet revolution' in Central and Eastern Europe. Martin Luther King observed that 'unearned suffering is redemptive' and that the person 'who acts non-violently in support of justice "lives in the kingdom NOW, and not in some distant day"'. Schell suggested that Václav Havel's 'living in truth' was an inspired translation of 'satyagraha'. Both movements expressed the 'conviction that the prime human obligation is to act fearlessly and publicly in accord with one's beliefs; that one should withdraw cooperation from destructive institutions; (and) that this should be done without violence'. Schell concluded his masterly account by suggesting that cooperative power, popular participation and direct action were the well springs of the people's will in democratic nations. They needed to be pursued locally with love and freedom and a restrained non-violence if survival, not annihilation, was to be our future.

Himes summarized modern Catholic teaching in the following terms:

- Pacifism was an option that individuals may choose. Both conscientious objection and selective conscientious objection were supported by Catholic teaching. The latter was premised on just-war theory, while the former was derived from the legitimacy of pacifism.
- Pacifism required a clear commitment to resist injustice and a desire to promote human rights and the common good.
- The pacifism approved by Catholic social teaching was based on the freedom of the person and the rights of individual conscience. It was not a duty for all but an option for those who discerned a moral call to oppose all war.

The biblical vision of peacemaking in Micah and Isaiah is very appealing: 'They will hammer their swords into ploughshares and their spears into bill-hooks. Nation will not lift sword against nation or ever again be trained to make war. But each man will sit under his vine and fig tree with no one to trouble him' (Mi 4: 3–4; see also Is 2:4). This is clearly God's intention and gift in the fullness of time and Christians are called to struggle to achieve it. Indeed, ever since the era of nuclear weapons and total war, papal teaching has increasingly called for 'no more war' and for the construction of international institutions, with a legitimacy acceptable to all nations, which would facilitate the resolution of conflicts and the reconciliation of the parties concerned without recourse to war. But such institutions do not at present exist.

The pacifist option has usually met with considerable hostility from the hierarchy and Vatican authorities. Michael Winter provided numerous examples throughout the history of the Church.[49] Valerie Flessati reported the hostility of the hierarchy to the Catholic Peace Movement in her history of Pax from 1936 to 1971.[50] Anthony Kenny, Bruce Kent and Owen Hardwicke in their autobiographies all described their own experiences with ecclesiastical superiors and influential Catholic politicians as they grew to challenge the policies of nuclear deterrence and moved towards pacifism.[51] Non-violence is often a heroic and prophetic way of resisting evil or oppression.[52] However, it needs to be stressed that, in spite of a growing shift towards non-violence and a rejection of war in the modern world, official Catholic social teaching, while it recognizes the right of *individuals* to choose a pacifist option, nevertheless emphasizes the *duty* of all to resist injustice.

THE JUST WAR TRADITION

For many Christians the examples of Auschwitz and recent examples of genocide in Cambodia, Bosnia and Rwanda keep them from espousing the pacifist option unreservedly, a position also taken by Schell.[53] What should the international community do in the face of such atrocities? How far should 'turning the other cheek' or appeasement go? How should Christians respond when faced with aggression or injustice or evil, such as genocide, given the 'presumption against war'? O'Donovan's answer to

---

[49] Winter 2002: 169–192.   [50] Flessati 1991.
[51] Kenny 1986: 169–190; Kent 1992; Hardwicke 2001: 212–236.
[52] See Havel 1990. Note the prophetic, non-violent challenges and examples of civil disobedience presented by Catholic Peace Action.
[53] Schell 2004: 9.

these questions was that 'conflict can be brought within the scope of the *authority* on which government may normally call, and ... can be undertaken in such a manner as to *establish* justice'.[54]

It has been suggested that the passage in the Sermon on the Mount where Our Lord urged turning the other cheek referred to harm done to oneself and that what was being excluded was vengeance following the Jewish law of retribution.[55] 'The gospel does not forbid reasonable defence against unjust aggression ... still less opposition to evil in the world'. This leads to the consideration of the alternative Christian approach to conflict: the just war tradition which has arguably dominated official Catholic thinking. Does it stand up under modern conditions?

It seems clear that in its first three centuries the Church espoused the pacifist option of non-violence, though Roger Charles points out that this preference was 'strong but not absolute'.[56] With the coming of the Constantinian era, the Church shifted its concern to the requirements of good citizenship and the early Fathers, Basil, Ambrose and Augustine, began to formulate conditions when it was right to make war in a just cause (*ius belli*) and for its pursuit (*ius in bello*). In the medieval period Aquinas developed Augustine's teaching. For war to be just it must be declared by a proper authority, be fought in a just cause, such as self-defence, and be pursued with the right intention, to avoid evil and not for vengeance. With the emergence of nation states and the decline of a united Christendom following the Reformation in the sixteenth century, neo-scholastic theologians such as Vitoria and Suarez shifted attention to the ways in which war was waged.[57] With the coming of the industrial state, conscript armies, and especially weapons of mass destruction in the twentieth century, the Church had to confront a totally new context. Though the traditional just war position has not entirely been abandoned, the Vatican Council's unequivocal condemnation of modern 'total war', based on traditional just war principles, was perhaps a sign of the way Catholic social thought on war was going.

The just war tradition is perhaps best summarized in the United States Bishops' pastoral letter (§§80–110).[58] They suggested seven criteria for determining when and why recourse to war might be permissible:

- where there was just cause;
- in pursuit of the common good by a competent authority;

---

[54] O'Donovan 2003: 14. [55] *The New Jerusalem Bible*, 1985: 1617, footnote 5p.
[56] Charles 1998a: 66, 96–98, 234–239; see also Fahey 2003: 4–8 and Haleem et al. 1998: 32–41.
[57] Himes 1994: 978; Charles 1998a: 258; Haleem et al. 1998: 42–44.
[58] An alternative formulation can be found in Charles 1998a: 237–239. See also O'Donovan 2003.

- with due concern for comparative justice between the parties to a conflict;
- with the right intention, i.e. pursuit of peace and reconciliation;
- only as a last resort after exhausting all peaceful alternatives;
- there must be a probability of success; and
- there must be proportionality of damage inflicted.

Two principles for the conduct of war were also noted and are particularly relevant today given the enormous destructive potential of modern weaponry:

- proportionality (avoiding escalation of the conflict); and
- discrimination to ensure the innocent are not harmed ('collateral damage' is minimised); it was for this reason the Second Vatican Council rejected policies of 'total war'.

In the light of these principles, the United States bishops rejected strategies of counter-population warfare. They were extremely sceptical about the prospects of controlling a nuclear exchange and hence judged both first use and limited nuclear war strategies to be 'morally unjustifiable'. They were very suspicious of the concept and development of deterrence policy and specifically criticized certain aspects of targeting policies (§§146–199). Summarizing the teaching of several hierarchies on deterrence policy, Brian Wicker concluded that 'nuclear deterrence already stands condemned ... (as) a moral non-starter', though given that 'deterrence has to be recognised as existing', the important issue was how to cope with it 'without making the world an even more dangerous place than it is already'.[59]

In 2003 the USA and UK went to war in Iraq.[60] Attempts made to defend the war using just war principles were unconvincing. It is surely significant that the Vatican, the United States bishops, the UK bishops, the Archbishop of Canterbury, and a former Permanent Under-Secretary of State for Defence[61] all opposed the war on the basis of 'just war' reasoning; a number of criteria were lacking.

ORGANIZED VIOLENCE IN A GLOBAL ERA

In the contemporary period of globalization, three issues, in particular, pose challenges to the Christian conscience and to political leaders:

---

[59] Wicker 1985: 26. Similarly, the United States Bishops make a number of policy proposals for promoting peace, 1983: §§200–273.
[60] For one among many critical analyses, see Chomsky 2004.   [61] Quinlan 2004.

genocide, terrorism and development. As we have seen, since *Populorum Progressio* the Church's official teaching has increasingly drawn attention to the issues of development. However, it might be suggested that the Church's present teaching on war and peace is addressing yesterday's issue, war between nation states, and it has not yet formulated a complete and coherent response to the two great contemporary issues of genocide *within* a nation state and global transnational terrorism. The following reflections are offered tentatively.[62]

(a) Genocide

It seems clear that the pacifist approach was totally incapable of coping with the genocide of Jews and other minorities in the Nazi period. In more recent times, the international community failed to prevent the appalling genocide in Rwanda and only belatedly intervened to prevent a second round of genocide in Kosovo. A tentative judgement would be that in the face of persistent genocide and ethnic cleansing in the Balkans, the European nations have gradually eased their way towards a peacekeeping role which no longer treats the nation state as inviolable. We have noted that resistance against injustices is a Christian obligation. Seen in this light, there is a clear need for peacekeeping forces with a vocation to *prevent* violence, especially genocide, and to offer the structural stability necessary for the resolution of conflicts to be sought through reconciliation and peaceful dialogue between the parties. In many ways UN peacekeepers have performed such a role in numerous conflicts in recent decades.[63] The International Commission on Intervention and State Sovereignty (ICISS), an independent international body designed to support the UN, in 2001 published *The Responsibility to Protect*.[64] This report aimed to promote a comprehensive global debate on the relationship between intervention and state sovereignty and to reconcile the international community's responsibility to act in the face of massive violations of humanitarian norms while respecting the sovereign rights of states.

It does seem to be the case, however, that international law, as presently formulated, inhibits intervention in the internal affairs of any nation state.

---

[62] O'Donovan 2003 offers a robust and convincing case for responsible judgement, taking into account particular circumstances and the requirements of discrimination and proportionality, with the general aim of contributing to a peaceful and stable international authority and the common good.

[63] The Briefing Paper by Scilla Elworthy 2004, is a valuable contribution to the consideration by policy makers of non-military approaches to the prevention of violent conflict and its peaceful resolution.

[64] http://www.dfait-maeci.gc.ca/iciss-ciise/report-en.asp

In a global era, the time is opportune to move towards structures of legitimate global regulatory institutions with the power, resources, commitment and moral authority to intervene in cases of gross injustice such as genocide and to enforce basic human rights. Thus the NATO military intervention in Kosovo in 1999 was justified on humanitarian grounds though it 'violated the U.N. Charter and international law'.[65] Philip Bobbitt quoted Pope John Paul II's statement in 1995 that 'the news and pictures from Bosnia, particularly from Srebrenica and Zepa, testify to how Europe and humanity are still collapsing into the abyss of degradation . . . They are crimes against humanity [which amount to] a defeat for civilization'. Bobbitt interpreted this as providing states with reasons for intervention.[66]

Over forty years ago Pope John XXIII in *Pacem in Terris* called for a universal 'public authority, having worldwide power and endowed with the proper means for the efficacious pursuit of . . . the universal common good . . . set up by common accord and not imposed by force' (§138). More recently, in *Sollicitudo Rei Socialis*, at a time of developing globalization, Pope John Paul II drew attention to the increasing interdependence of people and nations and urged them to commit themselves to the universal common good in solidarity with all people (§§38–40). In pursuit of this there was a need for reformed international institutions.

(b) Terrorism[67]

The atrocities in New York, Washington, Madrid and London, and numerous other acts of terrorism, drew attention to an ugly side of globalizing processes. People and nations all over the world now realize that small numbers of committed terrorists with a perceived grievance and an ideology which justifies violence, for example against 'westernization', could threaten not only large numbers of people anywhere in the world, but also the stability of the global economy itself, and with it the livelihoods of billions of people. The perception of the violence as a global threat to all might have generated a remarkable coalition of previously hostile or suspicious nations in seeking an appropriate response. It also emphasized the interdependence of all people on earth, something which,

---

[65] Charney, J. I., 'Anticipatory Humanitarian Intervention in Kosovo', in *Vanderbilt Journal of Transnational Law* at http://law.vanderbilt.edu/journal/32-05/32-5-1.html. For an extended analysis of the four Balkans wars, including that in Kosovo, see Bobbitt 2003: 416–467.
[66] Bobbitt 2003: 436–437.   [67] See *Compendium* §§513–515.

for Christians, flowed from their common humanity as children of God. The notion of the interdependence of people and nations, both now and across time transgenerationally, is an important theme in the endeavour to seek the Kingdom of God on earth as in heaven.

Sadly, the United States rhetoric after September 11 was one of vengeance: 'take him (Osama Bin Laden) or kill him' and 'if you are not with us you are against us'.[68] The British Government agreed to support the USA in the invasion of Iraq with or without a mandate from the UN. Other European nations were more cautious and gave greater weight to social and cultural considerations, such as not appearing to be involved in a crusade against Islam, and to multilateral approaches which aimed to build transnational solidarity in the struggle against transnational terrorism. In Britain Cardinal Cormac Murphy-O'Connor and Archbishop Kelly, immediately after the World Trade Centre attacks, urged 'justice, not vengeance' and similar pleas were made by many in the Justice and Peace movement.[69] However, Clifford Longley suggested that 'terrorism undermines the whole concept of proportionality' and that 'conventional just war theory starts to buckle under a load it cannot carry'. In a similar vein the Commission of Episcopal Conferences of the European Community (COMECE) said there was a need for 'a rethinking on international relations' and that 'our classical categories of justice seem inadequate to address the terrorist attacks'. Against this view, Brian Wicker has responded that 'on the contrary, it is just war thinking that shows why terrorism is disproportionate'.

Both Kaldor and Bobbitt, in different ways, stressed the importance of human agency, i.e. that people have choices which will determine the sort of world they pass on to their children and grandchildren. Kaldor[70] suggested that the 'new wars' aimed to achieve 'political mobilization on the basis of identity'. The strategy used to achieve this included destabilization 'to foment hatred and fear'. An appropriate response was to create 'islands of civility (which) might offer a counterlogic to the new warfare'. She argued that 'a politics of inclusion needs to be counterposed against the politics of exclusion (achieved by terror and destabilisation); respect for international principles and legal norms needs to be counterposed against the criminality of warlords'. Political authority needed to be reconstructed and top-down diplomacy replaced by a strategy of winning 'hearts and

---

[68] A quote found in Mt. 12: 30. The teaching in Mk. 9: 40 and Lk. 9: 50 seems subtly different.
[69] See *The Tablet*, 29 September 2001, pp. 1358, 1386–1390.
[70] Kaldor 1999: 110–111, 114–115, 123, 141, 147.

minds' 'based on an alliance between international organisations and local advocates of cosmopolitanism in order to reconstruct legitimacy'. In this view, cosmopolitan civic values favouring openness, toleration and participation, were derived from a humanist universalist outlook which crossed the global/local divide so that 'there are no boundaries in a territorial sense'. A similar stress on building international civil society permeated Schell's analysis of non-violent approaches to conflict. Such a secular humanist approach is quite consistent with a Catholic view which seeks the universal common good on the basis of the equal human dignity of all human beings but which is also aware of the reality of evil and the need to build towards the kingdom of justice and peace through individual and collective struggle.

In Bobbitt's analysis[71] we were living in a new and dangerous world of non-state terrorism, nuclear proliferation, and global communications which required new thinking and new alliances to address the new challenges to peace. He offered possible scenarios for each of his three models of market-state, in each case considering how they might cope with security, culture and economics. Ranking the approaches with respect to security, he concluded that 'peace with some justice (the protection of nonaggressors, for example) is to be preferred to simple peace (bought at the price of sacrificing innocent peoples), which is still preferable to a cataclysm that would destroy the innocent and guilty alike'. The core of Bobbitt's contention was that since the Peace of Paris in 1990 which brought an end to the Long War, we were living in a world which required a 'new constitutional order for the society of states in order to cope with the novel challenges'. But it was not easy to achieve consensus since there were, for example, conflicting notions of sovereignty and external responsibility (e.g. over environmental damage).

One particular challenge was addressed at some length: cyberattack on a society's 'critical infrastructure', telecommunications, energy, banking and finance, transportation and government services. At bottom this was not only a national security problem but also increasingly an international security problem. He concluded that defence planners should first 'free themselves from the habits they acquired planning for nuclear strategy'. Instead they 'must learn to think in terms of vulnerabilities instead of threats; of mitigation instead of fortress defence; of reconstitution instead of retaliation'. In the struggle against international terrorism, Bobbitt advocated a strategic shift from retaliatory strategies (nuclear deterrence)

---

[71] Bobbitt 2003: 715–775, 777, 787–795, 805, 815–816.

to vulnerability-based strategies, by preventing the proliferation of weapons of mass destruction, building consensus-creating coalitions, transnational surveillance and cooperation, and sharing information as a means of defence in this 'new age of indeterminacy'.

It is important that the Church is in active dialogue with academic analysts such as Kaldor, Bobbitt and Rogers who are drawing attention to a fundamental shift in the nature of the challenges of the twenty-first century. It seems that the basic framework for development of the Church's teaching on war, defence and peace is in the teaching that:

- Christians have a *duty* to resist evil and come to the aid of the oppressed; and
- in its repeated calls for legitimated international regulatory institutions with power to enforce basic human rights.

International terrorism has drawn attention to the interdependence of people all over the world. It is necessary to collaborate with others in solidarity in pursuit of the universal common good in order to survive and live in a civilized way. As Pope John advocated forty years ago, effective transnational institutions, freely accepted, need to be established with proper powers to enforce compliance to agreed norms of behaviour, properly respectful of the dignity of all human beings and their intrinsic human rights. This will require appropriate changes in the UN Charter and the veto-powers of the permanent members of the Security Council, extension of the legitimacy and powers of enforcement of the International Court of Justice, and some relinquishment of the privileged status of the nation state in favour of a genuine international authority.

(c) Development

Ever since Paul VI in *Populorum Progressio* wrote that 'the new name for peace is development' (§87), the Church has attempted to 'read the signs of the times' and has repeatedly drawn attention to the gross injustices in the world's economic system and the obscenely increasing gap between rich and poor nations. Huge inequalities in access to the fruits of the earth inevitably give rise to resentments and grievances which are the cause of many conflicts and much violence.[72] *Gaudium et Spes* taught that 'peace is not merely the absence of war' or simply 'a balance of power between enemies . . . Instead, it is rightly and appropriately called "an enterprise of justice" (Isaiah 32:7). Peace results from that harmony built into human

---

[72] Rogers 2002.

society by its divine Founder, and actualised by men as they thirst after ever greater justice' (*GS* §78).[73]

In *Sollicitudo Rei Socialis* (§43) Pope John Paul II suggested some guidelines for appropriate reforms in international relations. As we noted previously, he specifically mentioned reform of the international trade system, world monetary and financial system, methods of technological exchanges, the structure of the existing international organizations, and the international juridical order so that they would be 'at the service of the societies, economies and cultures of the whole world'.

George Monbiot has offered a set of proposals for a properly democratic World Parliament, for a Fair Trade Organization and an International Clearing Union which would begin seriously to challenge, through non-violent civil actions, the unjust exploitation of power by a few rich nations, a few MNCs, and a few rich financial speculators. Given their rhetoric about equal human dignity, justice, a preferential concern for the poor, solidarity and the universal common good, it is incumbent on Catholics to engage in serious dialogue with such activists in the World Social Forum and global justice movement generally. As Monbiot noted: 'we can use our agency to change the world, and in changing it, to change ourselves'.[74]

THE ARMS TRADE[75]

The UK is one of the major exporters of arms to developing countries. A Report to the United States Congress on *Conventional Arms Transfers to Developing Nations, 1993–2000* indicated that:

from 1997–2000, the United States, Russia, and France have dominated the arms market in the developing world . . . in the value of arms transfer *agreements* . . . . In 2000, the United States ranked first in the value of arms deliveries to developing nations at $8.7 billion, or 44.8% of all such deliveries. The United Kingdom ranked second at $4.4 billion or 22.7% of such deliveries[76]

with over one quarter of deliveries to countries in the Near East. Elworthy has pointed out that for the £426 million per annum subsidies paid by the British government to arms exporters it would be possible to 'support the setting up of gun collection schemes in every single country where there is local killing' and 'introduce effective boundary controls on gun-running,

---

[73] The current teaching of the Church is summarized in *CCC* §2317; Is 2: 4.
[74] Monbiot 2003: 252.   [75] See *Compendium* §§508–512.
[76] Grimmett 2001. For detailed statistics on defence expenditures and trade in arms see Table 5.7 in *World Development Indicators 2002*: 304–306.

with severe and enforceable penalties; fully support the EU commitment to develop a "Civilian Crisis Management Capacity" by providing training for civilians ready to join'.[77]

The arms trade in the present world was strongly criticized by Pope John Paul II in *Sollicitudo Rei Socialis*. He pointed to the 'strange phenomenon' that 'while economic aid and development plans meet with the obstacle of insuperable ideological barriers, and with tariff and trader barriers, arms of whatever origin circulate with almost total freedom all over the world' (§24). The crisis in the international economic order had been recognized by the United States bishops who urged that 'we should be campaigning for an international agreement to reduce this lethal trade' (*EJA* §289). In its ethical reflection the Pontifical Council for Justice and Peace suggested five general principles as a framework:[78]

- everything possible must be done to avoid war;
- there is a right to legitimate defence;
- there is a duty to help the innocent ('States no longer have a "right to indifference"' and 'the principles of the sovereignty of States . . . cannot constitute a screen behind which torture and murder may be carried out');
- the principle of sufficiency 'by which a State may possess only those means necessary to assure its legitimate defence';
- arms are not like other goods because 'there is a close and indissociable relationship between arms and violence'.

The document urged the extension of international regulation and means of resolving conflicts and there was a strong plea for international solidarity.

The role of the arms trade in fomenting war and perpetuating tyrannical regimes was contested by Philip Towle[79] who argued that Britain needs a viable defence industry in the present uncertain world and that, to ensure this, exporting arms has increased in importance as the armed services have contracted following the end of the Cold War. He suggested that the pursuit of an 'ethical foreign policy'[80], with careful monitoring of arms sales, was easier to pursue in the case of large scale, technologically sophisticated weapons such as warships, aircraft and tanks but that, in any case, these were unlikely to be used by authoritarian or repressive regimes against

---

[77] Elworthy 2004: 16.
[78] Pontifical Council for Justice and Peace, *The International Arms Trade: An Ethical Reflection*, 1994, London: CTS (S 438).
[79] Towle 1998.   [80] For a critique of British foreign policy see Curtis 2004.

their own people. Towle admitted, however, that the trade in small arms which could be used by such regimes was much more difficult to defend. Otherwise his approach was pragmatic, even cynical: arms sales attempted to maintain a stabilizing geo-political balance between nations in conflict. He also argued that there was no correlation between arms sales and the prevalence of warfare, instancing Sub-Saharan Africa where, in the past decade, there had been much devastation as a result of war though arms imports had declined dramatically. Finally, he noted that there was no easy transfer of employment from the defence industry to alternative forms of employment.

Much of this line of argument appears to be special pleading by a powerful interest group. It is difficult to avoid the conclusion that an increasing circulation of small arms is likely to increase their use and hence the risk of serious violence. The Campaign Against the Arms Trade (CAAT) noted that 'by the end of the 1990s nearly 90 per cent of war-victims were non-combatants and at least half of these were children'.[81] It pointed out that 'in 1998, the UK licensed military exports to 30 of the 40 most oppressive regimes in the world' and that many arms customers 'are situated in areas of actual or potential conflict ... Where more than one country is involved, the UK is commonly willing to sell to both, or all, sides'. The UK government is said to be influenced by the 'military-industrial complex' and actively promoted the sale of arms through the Defence Export Services Organization (DESO) and provided various subsidies and export credits.

The International Action Network on Small Arms (IANSA) 'is a global network of NGOs dedicated to preventing the proliferation and unlawful use of small arms by pushing forward the boundaries for international action'.[82] One of the most important aims of the Movement for the Abolition of War (MAW) was to 'combat the culture of violence that pervades our society' and promote a global campaign for peace education which 'educates for peace and non-violence and international cooperation ... A culture of peace will be achieved when citizens of the world understand global problems, have the skills to resolve conflicts and struggle for justice non-violently, live by international standards of human rights and equity, appreciate cultural diversity, and respect the Earth and each other'.[83] A final plea came from the African Synod: 'We turn to our

---

[81] CAAT, *The Arms Trade: An Introductory Briefing*, c 2002.
[82] http://www.abolishwar.org.uk/disarm.shtml   [83] http://www.abolishwar.org.uk/peace.shtml

Christian brothers and sisters and to all people of good will in the northern hemisphere. We request them to intervene with those in responsible political and economic positions in their respective countries as well as those in international organisations. It is imperative that there be a stop to arms sales to groups locked in conflicts in Africa'.[84]

TOWARDS A CULTURE OF PEACE

The issues of war and peace are complex and difficult to resolve in a way which takes seriously the teaching and example of Jesus who lived in a world very different from our own. This is clearly an area where there has been, and is likely to continue to be, a development of doctrine, though the imperatives to love, forgive, be reconciled and to non-violence have always been there, if often hidden. The world of the first Christians was very different from the world of Christendom from the time of Constantine. Initial forms of pacifism were steadily replaced by notions of the just war. The coming of industrialized warfare and the mass mobilization of whole populations in the twentieth century gave the world 'total war' and, with the reckless proliferation of nuclear weapons, brought a threat to the very existence of the planet. In this new situation war is no longer an appropriate way to resolve international conflicts.

Christians have disagreed about the morality of nuclear deterrence but there is a growing consensus that it can no longer be tolerated but must be rejected. This development is scarcely acknowledged but it can be seen, for example, in the shift from Pope John Paul II's acceptance of nuclear deterrence as an interim measure 'towards a progressive disarmament' in 1982[85] to Archbishop Martino's claim in 1993 that it was a 'fundamental obstacle to achieving a new age of global security'.[86] This was even more emphatically stated by Cardinal Danneels, in 1998: 'nuclear weapons, whether used or threatened, are grossly evil and morally wrong. As an instrument of mass destruction, nuclear weapons slaughter the innocent and ravage the environment'.[87]

---

[84] Pax Christi and CAAT leaflet for Arms Trade Day of Prayer, Sunday 6 June 2004.
[85] John Paul II: Papal message to the UN Second Special Session on Disarmament, 1982.
[86] Archbishop Renato Martino, Speech to the UN General Assembly, 25 October, 1993.
[87] 'Act Now for Nuclear Abolition', A Statement addressed to the Nuclear Non-Proliferation Treaty (NPT) Preparatory Committee, 1998, signed jointly by Cardinal Danneels, President Pax Christi International, and Rev. Dr. K. Raiser, General Secretary, World Council of Churches. Located at http://www.nuclearfiles.org/hinonproliferationtreaty/98npt_religious_leaders.html

Arguably, in the twenty-first century, we are entering a totally new world of non-state genocide and global terrorism which present decision-makers with an entirely new set of challenges. As we have seen, the Catholic Church seeks uncomfortably to reconcile the conflicting imperatives of pacifism and just war approaches but has yet to treat comprehensively these new challenges. Humanitarian forms of peacekeeping, non-violent alternatives to war and strategies for the peaceful resolution of conflicts need to be developed. Peace education needs to be given greater prominence. The Dutch bishops in 1969 first expressed the need for this when they wrote in a pastoral letter: 'Looking for peace means: giving peace work a real place, not only as a pious wish in our hearts and on our lips, but in our thoughts, in our interests, in our educational work, in our political convictions, in our faith, in our prayer, and in our budget'.[88]

In his statement to the UN General Assembly in 1998, Archbishop Martino, Apostolic Nuncio and permanent Observer of the Holy See to the UN, referred to easy availability of small arms locking children into a 'culture of violence' and urged a shift to a 'culture of peace' which

Consists in promoting values, attitudes and behaviours reflecting and inspiring social interaction and sharing, based on the principles of freedom, justice and democracy, human rights, tolerance and solidarity. Rather than intervening in violent conflicts after they have erupted and then engaging in post-conflict peace building, it is more human and more efficient to prevent such violence in the first place by addressing its roots.[89]

But, as Archbishop Martino noted two years later, 'a culture of peace is possible, but first we must develop the moral and political will'. He suggested that 'states must work to develop and extend policies that promote human security, new coalitions and negotiations, the rule of law, initiatives at peacemaking, democratic decision-making and humanitarian intervention mandated by the Security Council'. There needed to be a shift of resources from arms and militarization to 'development initiatives and programmes for peace and human security'.[90]

Tentatively, at this point in time, an appropriate Catholic response would appear to include the following elements which flow from a fundamental belief in the dignity of each individual human being and the

---

[88] 'Ban the War', extracts from the Pastoral Letter of the Dutch bishops about peace, Heemstede, March 1969.
[89] Archbishop R. R. Martino, Statement before the First Committee of the 53rd Session of the UN General Assembly, 19 October 1998.
[90] Archbishop R. R. Martino, Statement to the 55th Session of the UN General Assembly, 6 October 2000 at http://www.vatican.va/roman_curia/secretariat_state/documents/

imperative to seek the universal common good in solidarity with the poorest, the weakest, the oppressed and the marginalized:

- a recognition of the reality of sin and evil in the world and the duty of Christians to resist evils such as oppression, social and economic injustices, and genocide;
- actively to seek to address the causes of grievances and conflicts in social, economic, and political inequalities which fail to treat every person and nation with appropriate dignity and respect;
- the establishment of appropriate international institutions for the reconciliation of differences, with legitimacy and the authority to enforce compliance;
- a recognition that an option for non-violence is as important an imperative for Christians as the option for the poor;
- focus more than previously on alternatives to war, the need to promote social justice as an integral element in the following of Jesus, to fund peace education programmes, and so forth;
- the promotion of agreed and internationally regulated arms reduction;
- insofar as armed responses to evils such as genocide are necessary, they should conform to the principles of the just war, and particularly proportionality and discrimination;
- the need for this to be undertaken speedily and effectively by reformed international institutions with legitimacy and powers of enforcement;
- the creation of a strong international civil society with a commitment to human dignity and rights; and
- the promotion of a culture of peace and non-violence through appropriate forms of peace education.

PART IV

Action responses

CHAPTER 12

Catholic responses to injustices

THE GLOBAL SOCIAL CONTEXT

This chapter considers the fourth and final stage of the pastoral cycle: social action responses to the reality of domestic and international injustices (Part III), in the light of the framework for social analysis suggested in Part I and the theological analysis in Part II. After a recapitulation of the argument so far, it will endeavour to suggest ways in which ordinary Christians might respond. In general terms, Christians are called to work in collaboration with all people of good will, through the institutions of civil society – NGOs, campaigning groups, voluntary organizations, and the like – to promote human flourishing, enhance human dignity, the common good and solidarity between all God's people and the integrity of the whole of God's creation. While there are numerous people of good will, members of other faiths and secular humanists, struggling against the same injustices, the focus here is primarily with the beliefs and values which motivate Catholic responses. In spite of the immensity of the tasks to be addressed, there is the reassurance in the parable of the mustard seed that even small contributions grow (Mk 4: 26–32; Mt 13: 31–32; Lk 13: 18–19).

This book has aimed to introduce the reader to the broad thrust of Catholic social thought as it has developed, particularly over the past century in response to changing circumstances and new challenges. The Church's social teaching is a dynamic creation and seeks to address the different moral questions which emerge in each age. There were no weapons of mass destruction, no genetic engineering, no IMF or WTO, when Jesus was teaching. Christians need to work out their responses to these in the light of His teaching and the cumulative reflections of the Church in constant dialogue with critical thinkers and changing circumstances of the times. It is wrong to say the Church never changes. Its teaching develops as it reflects on the teaching of Jesus, the scriptures and secular thought. For example, the teaching on conscientious objection, religious freedom and human rights have all changed in the past half-century. John Fuellenbach conceived of history as 'the "kingdom-process", wherein God's intervention is to be received as a gift and human cooperation is to be understood as a task'.[1] In other words, justice-seeking is primarily the Christian's openness and response to God's call to realize His Kingdom, here on earth as in heaven. It is not apparent that this task has been a priority in much of the Church's history! But in our own times it has been increasingly stressed in the Church's developing social teaching.

One element in Catholic social thought in recent decades has been the development of a methodology: the four-stage cycle of social action, referred to in Chapter 1. In the first stage the active Christian observes the social reality of needs and injustices, both at home and internationally. For the Christian such evils reflect the reality of sin in the world. Some may be due to personal sin but many social ills are the result of sinful *structures*, that is institutional arrangements which operate systematically to exploit or oppress weak or vulnerable people or nations. Examples would include discriminatory legal regulations against minorities or trade arrangements.

In the second stage, the attempt is made to understand and explain the causes of social injustices and seek to interpret these in ways which might lead to corrective measures being taken. In Chapter 2 a framework for such social analysis was offered. Since the collapse of Soviet Communism in 1989, the reality is that the world has one single 'hyperpower' promoting an extreme form of 'market fundamentalism' which is ideologically driven with evangelising fervour by 'neo-cons' in the USA. It is the nature of the currently dominant form of capitalism[2] to seek the maximization of profits through capitalist enterprises with the minimum of regulation, and the liberalization of finance, trade, investment and services in the interests of capitalist enterprises, notably MNCs. Such thinking has also dominated policy thinking in the major international economic institutions, such as the IMF, the WB and the WTO. While this economic system appears to be more efficient than other systems, there has been an increase of inequality both within and between nations.

As a result of recent advances in information and communications technology the context within which capitalist enterprises operate is increasingly global in scope. Thus, the reality is that not infrequently jobs lost in a developed country are transferred to another branch of the

---

[1] Fuellenbach 1995: 56–57.
[2] As Will Hutton points out forcefully, there are other versions such as New Deal capitalism, western European social market capitalism or Asian forms of capitalism.

same MNC in a developing country. In a similar way, decisions about what food to grow in a developing country may be taken by strategists in Washington. Increasingly, the whole world can be meaningfully considered to be a single market and subject to the same media cultural influences and the same terrorist threats. Globalization is a social reality. It highlights the growing interdependence of all people on earth. Many see this as a threat but for Christians it is a demonstration of the common dignity of all human beings.

Two consequences arise from this analysis. Firstly, given the salience of economic forces, there is a close relationship between domestic and international forms of injustice. Depressed areas in developed countries have their parallels in the impoverished areas of developing nations. Ethnic conflicts within nations generate waves of refugees and asylum seekers elsewhere. Massive drift from subsistence agriculture into urban areas in developing nations generates waves of both legal and 'illegal' economic migrants who do the jobs nobody else wants in the developed nations. The underlying social causes of injustices are intrinsic in the economic inequalities generated by unregulated liberal capitalism and the political power inequalities which serve to legitimate, maintain and reinforce those inequalities so that the gap between the rich and poor, people as well as nations, is getting larger. Secondly, just as in the past there was a need for some form of state authority to guarantee security *within* the nation state, so, it is increasingly obvious, there is a need to construct new and effective forms of transnational agencies of social control, order and regulation in the globalized world of the twenty-first century.

SCRIPTURAL AND THEOLOGICAL RESOURCES

The third stage of the cycle of social action is that of theological reflection in the light of scripture and Catholic social thought. We considered these resources in the three chapters of Part II of this book. Chapter 3 was largely devoted to a consideration of the centrality of the notion of the Kingdom of God, both 'now', and 'not yet', in the teaching of Jesus. It closely followed John Fuellenbach's excellent treatment.[3] He stressed the importance of the message of Jesus in today's world. Christians are called to be 'mediators of God's saving activity' as servants for all people and with restored relationships with God, humankind and creation. The realization of the kingdom values of truth, life, justice, love, peace and joy would be

[3] Fuellenbach 1995: 38–39, 58, 69, 79.

truly world-transforming both in terms of personal relationships between people but also at the level of socio-economic structures. Scripture urges the restoration of Covenant relationships and the inclusion of the poor, weak and marginalized. The realization of these kingdom values demands conversion from self-interest and greed for wealth or power.

The theme of citizenship in the kingdom of God was taken up in Chapter 4 which drew on the secular notions of liberty (freedom), equality and fraternity (solidarity). It was argued that all these values were important in the kingdom of God and that it was right that Catholic social thought should be in dialogue with their advocates and incorporate them as appropriate. Following the work of T. H. Marshall, one can usefully distinguish civil and legal, political, and social and economic rights of citizens, originally of the nation state but increasingly, in a developing awareness, of the whole of humanity. The important point about citizenship is that it confers rights but also requires a responsible concern for the common good. It was only at the Second Vatican Council that the Church's historical hostility to the value of freedom was finally overcome. Even so, the Vatican was extremely wary about some aspects of liberation theology and it has been highly critical of neo-liberal forms of capitalism and extreme forms of individualism. Chapter 4 also argued that while the concept of equality of human dignity has been strongly emphasized in Catholic social thought, a sustained and convincing analysis of social, economic and political equality remains to be undertaken. Citizens of the kingdom are diversely distinct, but equal in dignity and esteem in the sight of God, and relate to each other in fraternal love and solidarity. In an era of globalization, there has been a heightened awareness of the interdependence of peoples and of the need to promote solidarity between them.

In Chapter 5 an outline was given of the development of Catholic social thought with its four main sources: scripture; the apostolic tradition as articulated by popes and theologians; the experience of the Church and its members; and the relevant findings of the human and social sciences. Two strands of Catholic social thought are kept in an uneasy tension: scripture, as interpreted by the Church but helpful in ecumenical dialogue; and the natural law tradition, which in principle is reasonable to all people of good will, whether believers or not. The chapter offered an outline of the key Church documents published since Pope Leo XIII's encyclical *Rerum Novarum* in 1891.

It is perhaps inevitable that Catholic social thought has tended to be 'reactive' rather than 'proactive'. It is the task of the Church to discern 'the signs of the times' and offer moral guidance about the problems and needs which emerge to challenge each generation. This book has repeatedly noted that many of these issues, such as the threats of nuclear war or ecological catastrophe or the challenges presented by advances in the biological sciences, have never been faced by human beings before. There is no ready-made store of moral answers to such new questions. The 'people of God' have to work out their responses to each new issue in the light of scripture, the cumulative tradition of the Church, and in dialogue with secular authorities and experiences in the real, concrete world. In recent decades the popes have increasingly focused on development issues and have unambiguously condemned 'total war'. A coherent response remains to be developed on other issues such as the rights of women and children, and social, economic and political equality.

What can be claimed is that Catholic social thought has developed a coherent set of principles with which to guide responses to such issues and challenges. These, while rooted in a faith tradition, nevertheless have appeal to those of a secular frame of mind so that serious dialogue is possible with key decision-makers and opinion-leaders. The intrinsic *dignity* of each individual human being has largely been recognized by the international community, for example in human rights legislation. The importance of the *common good* has been implicitly recognized in the social policies in many countries, though not yet for all peoples on earth. The promotion of the *solidarity* of all people expresses a recognition of the interdependence of all people and a concern for their welfare. The value of the principle of *subsidiarity* is widely accepted as important in the defence of individuals and also nations against the excessive power of states or regional bureaucracies. While the fifth principle, the *preferential option for the poor*, is more strongly rooted in the Judeo-Christian faith tradition it nevertheless has the power to appeal to generous secular hearts and minds. The *preferential option for non-violence* has barely been articulated as a basic principle but it also appeals to a wide spectrum of people concerned with the harmful consequences of uncontrolled military power in the modern world. In sum, these six principles together offer a comprehensive set of criteria with which to judge the morality of social policies and responses to the emergent challenges of the twenty-first century.

One final remark might be made about recent developments in Catholic social thinking. While it is relatively easy to mobilize Catholics for the *amelioration* of suffering, such as famine or homelessness, it is a more challenging task to mobilize them to seek to understand the *causes* of injustices and to take appropriate political action to change institutions and structures responsible for those injustices. Nevertheless, a whole range of NGOs is now engaged in educating the public, not only about the symptoms of injustice, but also in attempting to mobilize them to undertake a range of action responses from lobbying to demonstrating and occasionally direct, non-violent action, in order to put pressure on public authorities, whether governments or commercial organizations, to amend their policies.

DOMESTIC AND GLOBAL INTERCONNECTEDNESS

In Part III of this book six key areas of injustice were considered in the light of Catholic social thought. Nearly all activists in the Justice and Peace Movement are primarily concerned with a single issue of injustice. For example, many people are attracted to Amnesty International and are committed to supporting its campaigns for human rights. Many Catholics support CAFOD and may come to at least some awareness of development issues and injustices. Others in deprived inner-city areas strive to ensure that the voices of the poor are heard, the homeless cared for, or racism combated. Feminists seek to raise consciousness about the injustices experienced by women. Yet others are passionately concerned about peace issues and the arms trade. Every one of these issues is important as a matter of justice. This book has suggested that they are all interlinked so that a greater awareness of the wider causal sinful structures might be developed and lead to more insightful understanding and coordinated responses.

The first issue considered, in Chapter 6, was that of human rights. Here the Church struggled to update its thinking at the Second Vatican Council. While it remains deeply suspicious of some claims, such as 'women's rights' as opposed to embryo rights, for all its ambiguities, human rights thinking is deeply embedded in a recognition of the intrinsic dignity of each individual human being. Thus there are concerns about such issues as the death penalty and freedom from slavery, torture and all forms of discrimination. But at the same time individual rights are not absolute; there is a need to take account of the common good. This awareness has led gradually from a focus on civil and political rights to social and economic rights. Concerns for the wellbeing of particular groups such as refugees, asylum seekers and migrant workers, inevitably draw attention to the wider social, economic and political contexts and the extremities of economic inequalities and asymmetries of economic and political power.

In Chapter 7 the concerns of the Catholic Church for the strength and vitality of the family, as the basic cell of society, and the need to protect it from an over-intrusive state were reviewed. Here the principle of subsidiarity has been traditionally asserted although in recent years there has been a growing recognition that the state has a legitimate and important role to play in protecting the family and promoting the wellbeing and development of all its members. Recent Catholic thought has called for the widest possible employment opportunities in order to promote the independence and health of the family and has urged that, in processes of economic restructuring, workers should not be treated simply as commodities to be disposed of at will. In the second half of the chapter, there was concern about the power of medical or pharmaceutical interests promoting developments in genetic engineering and related fields without due ethical attention being paid to the intrinsic dignity of human beings from conception to death. Scientific developments in biotechnology are among the most challenging issues to be faced by Catholic social thought at the beginning of the twenty-first century.

The issues considered in Chapter 8 were those which first provoked modern popes to address the social and economic consequences of industrialization. From the time of Leo XIII onwards, the Church developed a comprehensive body of social teaching about the rights of the worker to a living wage sufficient to bring up a family at a reasonable standard of living. It insisted on the rights of all, in virtue of their human dignity, to participate fully in the fruits of the earth and to accumulate private property. The Church, in its official teaching, has always been highly critical of extreme forms of economic liberalism and the ways in which capitalism operates. While it has demonstrated an awareness of the injustices resulting from inadequately regulated economic institutions, from MNCs to the IMF, it has not been sufficiently critical of the extreme concentrations of wealth and the power of corporate capital and the sway it holds over both national and international regulatory institutions. This is the contemporary global economic context which must be taken into account.

The issues of domestic distributive justice were considered in Chapter 9. Poverty, unemployment, homelessness, debt, racism and multiple forms of disadvantage cannot be understood and explained apart from an understanding of the underlying social and economic arrangements in society. A wide range of social policies is relevant to the understanding of these

injustices, including taxation and benefits policies, housebuilding strategies, the operation and regulation of the labour and housing markets,
and so on. Social exclusion is an injustice which prevents the full participation of all in the decision-making of society and it is an offence against
human dignity, solidarity and the common good. But reducing inequalities and injustices requires more than piecemeal tinkering which fails to
address the underlying structural features of un- or under-regulated liberal
capitalism.

Similar concerns at the international level were expressed in Chapter 10.
For several decades successive popes have sought to promote 'authentic
development' which would enable poorer developing nations to share
more in the fruits of the earth and participate more equally in the decisions
which affect their struggling peoples. There can be little doubt that present
economic and political arrangements are serving to preserve and reinforce
the advantages of the rich nations and often worsen the conditions for
subsistence farmers in developing countries. Powerful nations hypocritic-
ally impose the liberalization of trade on weak nations while maintaining
blatant protectionism for some of their own industries. Here again, the
problems of developing nations will not be addressed simply by increasing
aid but only by changes in the regulatory framework in a world of asymmetric power.

Chapter 11 considered the Church's developing teaching regarding the
issues of war and peace and outlined the alternative pacifist and 'just war'
positions. It is only fifteen years or so since the Cold War between two
'superpowers' ended in favour of one 'hyperpower' and the triumph of
liberal capitalism. Just over four years ago the situation changed again with
the most dramatic of terrorist attacks on 11 September 2001. The Church's
teaching in this new situation remains to be more fully articulated. For our
present purposes, what is important is to understand the root social,
economic, political and cultural roots of terrorism. The reality is of continuing economic and political power inequalities in the world which are
reinforced in ways regarded as illegitimate by billions of people in developing countries. Such injustices fuel the grievances which lead some to take
the route of terrorism.

One of the main themes of this book has been that domestic and
international issues of injustice are intimately related and have their roots
in the same sinful social structures. In the main, while liberal capitalism
triumphed over totalitarian collectivism at the end of the 1980s, there
remain weaknesses in the present economic arrangements which fail to
achieve legitimacy both domestically and internationally. The result of

unregulated capitalism is to ensure the reinforcement of the wealth and power of the rich and powerful and a growing gap between rich and poor people and nations. Superimposed on this at the international level is the continuing residue of former colonial exploitation. Globalizing processes have failed to reduce economic inequalities and asymmetries of power which are intrinsically undemocratic and unjust. Present economic and political arrangements fail to express the values of equal human dignity and the common good. If Christians are seriously seeking to advance the kingdom of God, here on earth as in heaven, then they must strive to reform the institutional arrangements in which so many of them have such a comfortable stake.

A JUSTICE AND PEACE NETWORK

So how is the rhetoric of Catholic social thought realized in practice? In the remainder of this chapter we will consider what forms of social action might be appropriate.[4] Gordon Zahn pointed out that Leo XIII's *Rerum Novarum* had unanticipated and unintended consequences in promoting Catholic social movements.[5] At the time these were mainly in western European countries[6] but recent examples of 'Catholic social thought from below' would include early post-war Christian democracy,[7] Latin American liberation theology,[8] and the analyses of a multiplicity of Catholic NGOs.[9] Papal encyclicals do not so much formulate Catholic social teaching as articulate the mind of the Church as it has been worked out by numerous grassroots movements. Van Kersbergen, for example, distinguished between the 'grand' tradition of Catholic social teaching, as articulated by Vatican spokesmen, which was still rooted in the moral principles of love and the duties of Christian charity, and a 'little' tradition of Catholic social movements in Western Europe 'which have managed to transcend the "bourgeois" values of love and charity by formulating a distinctive critique of capitalism'[10] in the search not only for the amelioration of poverty and inequality but more radically for social justice through structural change.

[4] *Compendium* §§521–574 on 'Social Doctrine and Ecclesial Action' is a spiritual exhortation rather than a guide to specific forms of social action.
[5] Zahn 1991; see also Mich 1998.
[6] Misner 1991, 1994; Boswell 1994b. These included Marc Sangnier's Sillon movement which was, however, condemned by Rome in 1910.
[7] Fogarty 1957; Buchanan and Conway 1996; Hanley 1996; Papini 1997.
[8] Mainwaring and Wilde 1989; Smith 1991; Cleary and Stewart-Gambino 1992.
[9] Linden 1999; Nevile 1999; and Hogan 2000.   [10] Van Kersbergen 1995: 193.

Johan Verstraeten has drawn attention to the importance of embodying the developing tradition of Catholic social thought in community institutions which are 'carriers' of that tradition. But in changed social circumstances there is a need to create 'a new bearer of that tradition. In other words, when the social context in which Catholic social tradition concretizes itself becomes radically different from the past, when the classic forms of Catholic social movements disappear or become secularized, Catholic social teaching would become meaningless if it refused to adapt and reinterpret its original form and content'.[11]

The point is well made. Over the past fifty years or more, Catholics in the UK have moved out of the fortress model of the Church with its own distinctive culture and institutions.[12] Traditional Catholic organizations, many of which were involved in some form of social action, have declined in recent years[13] while other, largely lay-led organizations have emerged.[14] A good example, typical of many, is the Irish development agency, Trocaire, described by Linda Hogan.[15] She noted that 'there has been a radical change in the nature and orientation' of Catholic social movements and identified some key characteristics. For example, 'they operate with an inductive, praxis-based and context-sensitive approach'. She stressed that official Catholic social teaching, for example in papal encyclicals, 'is but one dimension of the Catholic Church's rich and diverse tradition of social thought'. As far as Trocaire was concerned, she noted the dynamic nature of its mandate, 'constantly being reshaped and reinterpreted in order to respond to the dynamics of global change' and its 'commitment to justice rather than charity' and hence long-term projects of sustainable development. Like development NGOs in Britain, for example CAFOD and CIIR, as well as domestic ecumenical organizations with a strong Catholic involvement such as CAP and Housing Justice, Trocaire was committed to the 'empowerment' of the needy, working with local partners and making strategic alliances.

In this changed social context, can it be said that there is a justice and peace *movement*? Gordon Zahn defines 'a *social movement* as a more or less *organized* effort on the part of a *significant segment* of a population to *change* an existing social order in a manner its participants believe *beneficial to the whole*'.[16] It is helpful to draw on some of the insights of social movement

---

[11] Verstraeten 2000: 66.   [12] Hornsby-Smith 1999a.
[13] Collins and Hornsby-Smith 2002; Eaton 1999.
[14] For an account of the changing nature of Catholic organizations in England, see Nevile 1999.
[15] Hogan 2000: 183–186, 188–190.   [16] Zahn 1991: 49.

theory.[17] Among factors which are likely to be important for a 'Social Movement Organization' (SMO)[18] are:

- The *political opportunities* afforded by the wider society in which the SMO was located. These gave rise to the issues around which collective action might be needed and determined whether or not an organized movement could be established.
- The *mobilizing structures*, that is the SMO's infrastructure through which collective action was made possible. This included factors such as the availability of resources, appropriate leadership, committed members, communication networks, and so on.
- *Framing processes*, that is the way in which the SMO fashioned and maintained a shared ideology and set of goals that motivated social action among the members.

(a) England and Wales

Let us consider first the extent to which it might be argued that these three factors favour the emergence of a strong justice and peace movement in England and Wales. Similar analyses might be undertaken for other countries and, indeed, to evaluate the chances of a global social justice movement emerging.

Political opportunities
There has been a diffuse and general disillusionment with official political processes in the UK in recent years. This has been expressed in low turn-outs in recent elections. Representative democracy seems to be failing and there has been a growing cynicism about politicians in general and a perception that with centrist politics, it will not make much difference which party is elected. There is a widespread perception that real grievances are not being addressed through the formal channels of parliamentary democracy and that the only way to make a difference is through high profile single-issue, interest group politics. Among justice and peace activists there is a growing awareness of high levels of social exclusion, for example of the poor, unemployed, homeless, ethnic and religious minorities, refugees and asylum seekers. There is also widespread concern with current processes of globalization, the debt burden of developing nations and the injustices of the operation of international trade, finance and investment policies and institutions. The war in Iraq was highly

---

[17] Zald and McCarthy 1990; McAdam et al. 1996. [18] McCarthy and Zald 1977.

contentious and there are strong concerns about the implications for civil liberties of the steps being taken to combat terrorism. In sum, at the start of the twenty-first century there are plenty of political opportunities for the emergence of a social movement in pursuit of greater national and international social and economic justice.

Mobilizing structures

In England and Wales there is a multiplicity of organizations concerned with social care or welfare, such as children's homes, or organizations with parish branches such as the St Vincent de Paul Society. I have differentiated between such organizations which are concerned with the *amelioration* of suffering and injustice and those strictly concerned with seeking the *causes* of injustice and working for their removal through political action such as advocacy and lobbying. Apart from the identifiably Catholic organizations and structures, such as CAFOD and CIIR, there has been a significant Catholic contribution to a number of ecumenical campaigning groups, such as CAP, Housing Justice and the Make Poverty History campaign.

It might be noted that there is no single, unified Justice and Peace Movement which can be mobilized behind some centrally agreed goal, with centralized leadership and control of resource allocation, a membership committed to the chosen programme, and a comprehensive communications network to facilitate planning and execution of the movement's strategy for the achievement of its selected goal. The National Justice and Peace Network (NJPN)[19] is largely independent of the Bishops' Conference which might, in theory, have provided a centralized SMO. While recognizing that the bishops have on numerous occasions intervened in matters such as nuclear deterrence, unemployment, homelessness and asylum seekers, and most obviously in their highly regarded statement on *The Common Good*, the long-term trend over the past half-century has been away from the episcopal direction of Catholic social action. Thus the concerns of two lay women led to the founding of CHAS in 1956, ten years before it became one of the founders of the housing charity, Shelter. CIIR grew out of the war-time Sword of the Spirit which was founded by a group of eminent lay people; it has recently changed its name to Progressio to make itself less-explicitly 'Catholic'. CARJ was originally founded in

---

[19] It has been suggested that the NJPN in England and Wales constitutes a more significant network than in other European countries. Yet while it has developed an agreed vision statement and it maintains good working relationships with religious orders and organizations, its resource base is extremely limited.

1984 as a lay organization to achieve independence for Catholics concerned with racial justice from control by the Bishops' Conference. Pax Christi has always been lay-led. Following an initiative by Catholic women for a Family Fast Day to promote overseas development, the bishops developed CAFOD as an agency to distribute to Catholic organizations in developing countries. Caritas-Social Action, which was set up as CASC in 1995, is also lay-led though technically, like CAFOD, it is an agency of the Bishops' Conference. Recent trends have included the active involvement of Catholics in ecumenical campaigning groups such as CAP and Housing Justice and the Make Poverty History campaign.

The theology of the Catholic Church stresses the independent leadership role of the bishop in his own diocese and it seems that bishops, in general, jealously guard their right to operate independently of any national coordination of social action. Inevitably this detracts from the formulation, coordination and implementation of a *national* strategy for the promotion of justice and peace. This is in spite of the obvious fact that effective political decisions and social policies are determined at the national level. Thus there is no official coordination of the work of diocesan Justice and Peace Commissions and funding has recently been withdrawn from the NJPN which for a quarter of a century has provided a forum for liaison between the different elements of the movement. It seems that the bishops are not keen to encourage a grassroots organization which operates relatively independently, and develops and coordinates a national strategy around particular campaigns. The committee structure of the Bishops' Conference mirrors the Vatican's Justice and Peace Commission in focusing on the international dimension. This has the disadvantage of failing to analyze the relationships between and common roots of domestic and international injustices.

Activists generally find it possible, given limitations of time and energy, to retain a commitment to action in only one area at a time (such as homelessness, Amnesty International, or CAFOD). Thus the mobilization structures for a Justice and Peace Movement are weak and uncoordinated. Most organizations and structures have few resources (in terms of funding, full-time staff, publicity, etc.) and there are huge differentials in the resources available for campaigning between CAFOD, which has a sizeable education budget, at one extreme, and CARJ and Housing Justice, at the other.

Framing processes
Thirdly, a successful social movement organization requires appropriate framing processes. These are ways in which the movement fashions and

maintains a shared ideology and set of goals that motivate social action by the members. These processes include (a) a shared vision of a just world; (b) a shared analysis of the causes of injustice; (c) an agreed understanding of social justice and how it might be achieved; (d) the successful resolution of the tensions between radicalism and respectability, and between prophecy and pragmatism. The evidence indicates that there are weaknesses in each of these areas.

There does seem to be an inchoate and latent theory of 'sinful structures' of injustice and inequality which require to be reformed or removed in order to achieve greater justice, which is widely shared among activists, though not among Catholics generally. There is a growing sense of the interconnectedness of domestic and international injustices which is related to concerns with contemporary forms of capitalism and globalization processes. But this analysis is not accepted by many, probably most fellow Catholics. For most Catholics, political choices seem to be determined more by class position or aspirations than by Catholic social teaching.

Among activists there are interesting parallels in methodology, such as advocacy and the empowerment of oppressed or disadvantaged groups, and working with grassroots partners, both domestically (e.g. by CAP) and by those working on development issues (e.g. CIIR and CAFOD). Nevertheless, the Justice and Peace Movement is still highly fragmented and activists more often than not tend to pursue their sectional interests with little concern for other issues. While there are broadly parallel analyses of sectional forms of injustice, there is little evidence of a clear vision of the common good of the global society or overarching theory of social justice and human flourishing which embraces all sectional concerns.

There is also a tension in the relationship between ends and means, between a radical and prophetic response to global sinful structures of injustice and a reformist, respectable and pragmatic response. It can be seen in the ambiguous nature of recent campaigns to bring pressure to bear on the leaders of the most powerful nations of the world to 'Make Poverty History'. Rather than see the capitalist economic system or the processes of globalization as intrinsically evil, a more general view would be to regard them as basically disordered and in need of effective regulation. While most activists would agree that injustices can only be eliminated by a radical transformation of sinful structures, at this moment in time it is utopian to conceive of a world without capitalism. They accept the reality of a sinful world and work for reform in every situation of injustice, wherever it is and wherever they are.

A tentative evaluation

In sum, this analysis of the Catholic Justice and Peace Movement in England and Wales indicates that it fails adequately to meet the socio-logical conditions for a social movement organization. While the current political situation suggests that the opportunities for such a movement are manifest, nevertheless the various components of such a movement remain highly segregated from each other. While there is a more-or-less shared orientation, ideology of justice-seeking and analysis on the part of the elites of increasingly professionalized leadership who are in periodic commu-nication with each other in a loosely connected network, the movement remains highly fragmented, starved of official support and resourcing, and marginalized in the wider body of Catholics.

(b) A global justice movement?

Similar considerations may be thought to apply to the embryonic global justice movement. Again, it might be argued that there are plenty of issues around which such a global SMO might arise. These would include such matters as the increasing gap between rich and poor nations, the harmful consequences for poor farmers of structural adjustment programmes or policies of liberalization of trade imposed on developing nations, the manipulation of protectionist rules which enable the USA and the EU to subsidize their own farmers in ways which harm farmers in developing nations, the overwhelming economic, political and military power of the United States to impose its will on supposedly independent nations, the cynicism of the international trade in arms, the high level of grievances at injustices which are reflected in the large number of ethnic conflicts throughout the world and the large flows of refugees, asylum seekers and migrant workers, and so on.

There are also signs of incipient structures mobilizing in protest, as became clear with mass demonstrations at meetings of the G8 leaders and the WTO. It can also be seen in the success of the Jubilee 2000 campaign and in the emergence of the World Social Forum (WSF) which attracted over 80,000 people from all over the world to its fourth meeting in India in January 2004.[20] The WSF aims to parallel the annual

---

[20] *Guardian*, 17 January, 2004.

meetings of powerful MNCs, governments, the IMF, WB and WTO at the World Economic Forum (WEF) at Davos. It was created to give a voice to peoples' movements seeking alternative forms of people-centred sustainable development and to provide an open forum for debate about the dominant neo-liberal forms of capitalist globalization.[21] The WSF utilizes the availability of rapid communications provided by the internet to achieve a remarkable level of mobilization of grassroots movements. Whether the global justice movement will manage to fashion and maintain a shared ideology and set of goals which will motivate coherent forms of social action remains to be seen. What seems most likely is that there will be a major split between those irrevocably opposed to capitalism and globalization and those who accept these as inevitable, even desirable, but in need of effective international regulation.

A CALL TO ACTION

Pope Paul VI, in his 'call to action' in *Octogesima Adveniens* over thirty years ago, acknowledged the variability of different social and cultural situations and the difficulty of putting forward solutions with universal validity. He urged local Christian communities to analyze the situation in their own country and, in dialogue with others of good will, to determine what responses were appropriate in order to bring about the social, political and economic changes necessary to produce greater social justice (§4). What must be done to change sinful social structures? For the Christian the most important commandment is to love. True love brings conversion and an awareness of the need for that love to be realized effectively through structural changes, such as legislative regulation, which will almost certainly hurt personal interests. Everyone has the agency to act; it is a matter of choice. To act is to demonstrate conversion. Coercive power is sustained by the belief that nothing can be done or 'you can't buck the market'! It is necessary to hasten the reconstruction of the present world order by developing 'a strategic and systematic means of curtailing' what George Monbiot calls 'the Age of Coercion'.[22]

A recurrent theme in the Old Testament is the imperative to seek justice, 'to do what is right' (Mic 6: 8), 'to open the eyes of the blind, to free captives from prison, and those who live in darkness from the dungeon' (Is 42: 7), 'to soothe the broken-hearted, to proclaim liberty to captives,

---

[21] http://www.wsfindia.org/whoweare.php   [22] Monbiot 2003: 255.

release those in prison, to proclaim a year of favour from Yahweh' (Is 61: 2). The Israelites were instructed not to 'cheat the poor ... of their rights', 'oppress the alien' (Exod 23: 6, 9) or exploit the weak or ill-treat the poor (Amos 4: 1). Justice was to be administered impartially (Lev 19: 15). Proper care had to be taken of 'the foreigner, the orphan and the widow' (Deut 14: 29), the weak and vulnerable. This theme of justice-seeking, so easily overlooked in 'other-worldly' or overly-privatized forms of spirituality, continues at the core of the teaching of Jesus. At the very beginning of his mission he announced that God had anointed him 'to bring the good news to the afflicted ... to proclaim liberty to captives, sight to the blind, to let the oppressed go free, to proclaim a year of favour from the Lord' (Lk 4: 18), that is release from debt. When talking about true discipleship Jesus taught bluntly that 'it is not anyone who says to me "Lord, Lord", who will enter the kingdom of Heaven, but the person who does the will of my Father in heaven' (Mt 7: 21). The parable of the last judgement taught that those called to the Kingdom would be those who fed the hungry, gave drink to the thirsty, welcomed the stranger, gave clothes to those without, visited the sick and imprisoned (Mt 25: 31–46). St James insisted that it was through deeds that faith was demonstrated and that 'it is by deeds, and not only by believing, that someone is justified' (Jas 2: 14–26). St Paul reminded that good works reflected the faith that had been given as a free gift (Eph 2: 7–10).

In *Octogesima Adveniens* Pope Paul, drawing on the teaching of Vatican II, recalled that the laity 'should take up as their own proper task the renewal of the temporal order'. He continued:

It is not enough to recall principles, state intentions, point to crying injustices, and utter prophetic denunciations; these words will lack real weight unless they are accompanied for each individual by a livelier awareness of personal responsibility and by effective action. It is too easy to throw back on others responsibility for injustices, if at the same time one does not realize how each one shares in it personally, and how personal conversion is needed first (§48).

In their pastoral letter on the economy, the United States bishops also stressed that 'the Gospel is demanding' and that 'conversion is a lifelong process' (§§23–24). They asked lay people:

to become more informed and active citizens, using your voices and votes to speak for the voiceless, to defend the poor and vulnerable and to advance the common good. We are called to shape a constituency of conscience, measuring every policy by how it touches the least, the lost, and the left-out among us ... (They call) us to conversion and common action, to new forms of stewardship, service and citizenship (§27).

This spelt out what was required not only from citizens of the nation state but also of the world. Christians were called to take the Good News to the poor, not only in their own country, but to all people on earth. Given the obscene inequalities of wealth in the world, it seemed appropriate to cultivate a more modest and egalitarian lifestyle.[23]

At the same time it is necessary to be realistic. The kingdom of God, while here among those striving to do God's will, will only be fully realized at the end of time. That is God's work. The Christian is called to assist and not frustrate its achievement. What is condemned is apathy and self-satisfaction. The message to the Church in Laodicea is apposite: 'since you are neither hot nor cold, but only lukewarm, I will spit you out . . . so repent in real earnest' (Rev 3: 14–22). Christians must start where they are. The important thing is that everyone does something, marvelling, as St Thérèse of Lisieux pointed out, at the contribution of 'little flowers' to the beauty of nature and the wider picture.[24] The parable of the mustard seed (Mt 13: 31–32) is relevant and worth pondering. Contemporary examples of the success of small beginnings over time include the environmental movement and the campaign to cancel the debt of highly indebted poor countries.

So where does a Christian start? George Monbiot recently suggested that:

We can use all the tactics we have deployed in the past – marches, demonstrations, non-violent direct action, letter-writing, petitioning, political lobbying – but with the confidence that we can explain not only what we don't want, but also what we do. We must continue to develop our alternative information networks, and to enhance too the use of the most effective and widespread of all media: word of mouth.[25]

This is a useful summary of methods which can legitimately be employed to challenge existing structures and powers and to seek structural changes. It is up to each individual to decide how to respond and on what to focus. The following are just some of the ways people can become active, depending on their own personal circumstances.

- *Cultivate a spirituality of justice-seeking*: spend some time each day reading scriptures and Catholic social thought with new eyes.
- *Start in a small way doing something*: e.g. a letter of protest or to a prisoner of conscience. The success of campaigns against human rights

---

[23] Forrester 2001: 169–191.
[24] St Thérèse of Lisieux, *Autobiography of a Saint*, London: Fontana, 1960: 26.
[25] Monbiot 2003: 257–258. A classic manifesto for radical activists is Alinski 1946.

abuses in many different countries testify to the sensitivity of oppressive governments to world opinion. Members of Parliament have also testified to the effectiveness of letter-writing campaigns from constituents. Apart from anything else, even the bed-ridden can play a part here. Such campaigns are also valuable in raising the consciousness of participants and directing their attention from initial compassion towards the analysis of power and the search for effective techniques of lobbying of governments, banks and MNCs. Many NGOs circulate postcards to be signed and sent with appeals to governments and large international corporations. In time, when activists become more familiar with the arguments, they will graduate to sending their personally expressed views which are much more impressive and effective. Why not commit to sending one letter each week? Learn also to use the local and national press, radio and TV to initiate or contribute to debates about justice issues.

- *Become an ethically conscious consumer*: Activists can become reflective about their own consumer behaviour and aware of whether or not their lifestyle and consumer choices encourage fair trade practices or are environmentally friendly. They can support Traidcraft and become familiar with trade justice concerns. Boycotts of goods produced by large corporations employing child labour and paying exploitative wages in developing countries have proved to be very effective.

- *Become an ethical investor*: Those with savings and investments can become aware of the ethical investment movement and ethical saving, e.g. with Tridos Bank. They can join others at the annual general meetings of large corporations and monitor their claims of corporate social responsibility.

- *Develop a concern for the environment*: The recycling of paper, glass and metals can be taken seriously and an enthusiasm for the composting of garden and food waste developed. Ways to reduce energy and water consumption can be encouraged and solar energy systems installed and buildings insulated.

- *Seek relationships with marginalized and excluded people*: Some direct contact with oppressed groups seems to be a requirement of discipleship. Examples include homeless people in a local overnight shelter, asylum seekers, the mentally ill, disabled, or ethnic minorities. A local Credit Union or group helping those in difficulty with debt repayments can be supported.

- *Join a group or a campaigning organization*: The problems of injustice in the world cannot be solved on one's own. Activists need to work in collaboration with others, not only ecumenically with other

Christians, but also with those of other faiths or none, who seek the same goals of justice and freedom from oppression and exploitation, at home and abroad. When the disciples told Jesus that they had tried to stop someone who was not 'one of us' healing in his name he said: 'anyone who is not against us is for us' (Mk 9: 40; Lk 9: 50).[26] In this spirit there have been significant moves in the Justice and Peace Movement to work ecumenically and collaboratively in coalitions of people of like mind in a wide range of NGOs. Organizations such as CAP and Housing Justice at home, the Make Poverty History campaign and World Social Forum all reflect a general trend away from advocacy *on their behalf* towards a stress on the *empowerment* of weak or vulnerable groups and the importance of expressing *solidarity with* them.[27] Activists are encouraged to join one of the NGOs or campaigning groups, such as Amnesty International, and gain support, encouragement and knowledge from others with similar concerns.

- *Join or start a parish justice and peace group*: Activists might start by focusing on one particular issue which exercises them and informing themselves about it by contacting relevant organizations and campaigning groups. Their literature can be acquired and the internet surfed for easily available information and campaigning materials. The opportunities of annual prayer intentions or collections (such as for the homeless, refugees, prisoners of conscience, Pax Christi) can be used to raise the awareness of others to the underlying issues. An awareness of the richness of Catholic social thought can be promoted. A familiarity with the pastoral cycle can be developed in the group. A start with the amelioration of suffering and need might lead towards social analysis and the search for the causes of injustices and hence the need to act in order to address them. It is worth remembering that there are many people of other faiths who are just as committed to seeking to promote the Kingdom. Wherever possible collaboration with others locally who share similar goals might be encouraged.

- *Become familiar with Catholic social thought*: Activists should aim to be effective 'carriers' of the distinctive Roman Catholic tradition as they work alongside others. Attendance at the annual NJPN conference at

---

[26] Mt 12: 30 is subtly different: 'anyone who is not with me is against me'.

[27] As the International Ecumenical Congress of Theology in Brazil in 1980 put it: 'Historical liberations incarnate the Kingdom to the degree that they humanize life and generate social relationships of greater fraternity, participation and justice'. Quoted in Fuellenbach 1995: 267.

Swanwick in July will expand the individual's network of people who share their concerns and analysis. Information, resources and experiences of success and failure can be shared with others.

• *Participate in political action*: Apart from letter writing campaigns, in our democratic society demonstrations, marches, collecting and presenting petitions, lobbying and non-violent direct action all have their part to play in raising the awareness of large numbers of people about issues such as homelessness or the arms trade. Participation can lead to the enjoyment of a sense of solidarity with others, affirmation of the worthwhileness of the cause, and a strengthening of the commitment to struggle for a better world.

• *Share gifts with those less fortunate*: An imaginative idea promoted at Christmas time by CAFOD and other charities is to choose to send a 'world gift', such as a voucher for a latrine, a goat, or a shelter, to 'help to change the lives of people in poverty'.

All of these actions contribute to the construction of a 'culture of life' and to a strong 'civil society' imbued with a distinctively Christian morality and values, capable of challenging existing structures of power, seeking ways to alleviate suffering and need, constructing social policies which promote the dignity of each individual human person, and seeking the common good in solidarity with others.

In the final paragraph of his book on *The Wealth and Poverty of Nations*, David Landes writes movingly and wisely: 'The one lesson that emerges is the need to keep trying. No miracles. No perfection. No millennium. No apocalypse. We must cultivate a sceptical faith, avoid dogma, listen and watch well, try to clarify and define ends, the better to choose means'. He follows this with a quotation from Deuteronomy: '... I have set before thee life and death, the blessing and the curse; therefore choose life'.[28] Amen to that; Christians must start where they are, not be afraid of small beginnings.

While it is true that every little 'mustard seed' can grow, and that every contribution to seeking kingdom justice is valuable, it is not the case that such work will be without cost. The cross is at the heart of the Christian call to discipleship. Now is the right time to start. As Jesus proclaimed at the very beginning of his campaign in Galilee: 'the kingdom of God has come near; repent, and believe in the good news' (Mk 1: 15; see also Mt 4: 17, Lk 4: 43). John Fuellenbach noted that we all have a common responsibility to

---

[28] Landes 1998: 524.

contribute to the growth of the Kingdom of God and its final fulfilment in the end-time. He continued:

Wherever and whenever Christians and others stand up for human rights or promote genuine human liberation, especially the rights of the poor and the oppressed, or advocate religious and spiritual values, the Kingdom of God is built up. We all have one common task: the promotion of the Kingdom of God by promoting its basic values: justice, peace, and joy. All those who care for these values are fellow travellers en route toward the fullness of the Kingdom which in its content is the new humanity willed by God for the end-time.[29]

In this task we must be confident and reassured by Jesus' promise: 'Do not let your hearts be troubled . . . I am the Way; I am Truth and life' (Jn 14: 1, 6). So, as Monbiot concludes in his manifesto: 'What are you waiting for?'[30]

[29] Fullenbach 1995: 153.   [30] Monbiot 2003: 261.

Appendix: Selected campaigning organizations

Note: The following list is a fraction of the number of organizations and campaigning groups working in the six broad areas of justice used in this book. Up to date information on all of them can be found on their websites. Organizations listed are, for the most part, campaigning groups which publish appropriate research or informational materials rather than charities mainly concerned with the amelioration of need.

HUMAN RIGHTS

Amnesty International (UK)
Asylum Aid
The Bourne Trust
Catholic Association for Racial Justice (CARJ)
Churches' Commission for Racial Justice (CCRJ)
Commission for Racial Equality (CRE)
Howard League for Penal Reform
Jesuit Refugee Service (JRS UK)
Liberty (National Council for Civil Liberties)
Medical Foundation: Caring for the Victims of Torture
Migration Policy Group (Brussels)
National Catholic Refugee Forum (NCRF)
Prison Reform Trust
Refugee Council

THE FAMILY AND BIOETHICAL ISSUES

Caritas-Social Action
Life
The Linacre Centre
Society for the Protection of the Unborn Child (SPUC)

ECONOMIC LIFE

Ecumenical Council for Corporate Responsibility (ECCR)
Ethical Investment Research Service (EIRIS)
Industrial Christian Fellowship (ICF)
International Christian Union of Business Executives (UNIAPAC)
Movement of Christian Workers (MCW)

SOCIAL EXCLUSION

ATD Fourth World UK
Child Poverty Action Group (CPAG)
Church Action on Poverty (CAP)
Homeless Link
Housing Justice
Shelter
Those on the Margins of Society (THOMAS)

AUTHENTIC DEVELOPMENT

Catholic Agency for Overseas Development (CAFOD)
Christian Aid
Christian Ecology Link (CEL)
Friends of the Earth (FOE)
Greenpeace UK
Intermediate Technology Development Group (ITDG)
International Institute for Environment and Development (IIED)
Jubilee Debt Campaign (JDC)
Médecins Sans Frontières (MSF)
New Economics Foundation (NEF)
One World Week (OWW)
Oxfam
Progressio (formerly Catholic Institute for International Relations,
    CIIR)
Save the Children UK
Scottish Catholic International Aid Fund (SCIAF)
Shared Interest Society
Trócaire
World Development Movement

WAR AND PEACE

Campaign Against the Arms Trade (CAAT)
Campaign for Nuclear Disarmament (CND)
Catholic Peace Action
Christian CND
Christian International Peace Service (CHIPS)
Conscience: The Community
Movement for the Abolition of War (MAW)
Pax Christi
United Nations Association

GENERAL

Center of Concern (Washington, DC)

References

Abbott, W. M. (ed.) 1966. *The Documents of Vatican II*. London: Geoffrey Chapman.

Acheson Report 1998. *Independent Inquiry into Inequalities in Health*. London: HMSO.

Ackermann, D. 2002. *Tamar's Cry: Re-Reading an Ancient Text in the Midst of an HIV/AIDS Pandemic*. London: CIIR.

Alinski, S. 1946. *Rules for Radicals*. New York: Vintage.

Amin, K. 1992. *Poverty in Black and White: Deprivation and Ethnic Minorities*. London: CPAG and Runnymede Trust.

Archbishop of Canterbury's Advisory Group on Urban Priority Areas 1990. *Living Faith in the City: A Progress Report*. London: General Synod of the Church of England.

Archbishop of Canterbury's Commission on Urban Priority Areas 1985. *Faith in the City: A Call for Action by Church and Nation*. London: Church House Publishing.

Askonas, P. and Frowen, S. F. (eds.) 1997. *Welfare and Values: Challenging the Culture of Unconcern*. Basingstoke: Macmillan.

Askonas, P. and Stewart, A. (eds.) 2000. *Social Inclusion: Possibilities and Tensions*. Basingstoke: Macmillan.

Assmann, H. 1975. *Practical Theology of Liberation*. London: Search Press.

Baker, Bishop, J. A. (Chairman) 1982. *The Church and the Bomb: Nuclear Weapons and Christian Conscience: The Report of a Working Party*. London: Hodder and Stoughton/CIO Publishing.

Bauman, Z. 2001. '*Whatever Happened to Compassion?*' in Bentley and Stedman Jones (eds.), pp. 51–56.

Bentley, T. and Stedman Jones, D. (eds.) 2001. *The Moral Universe*. London: Demos.

Beresford, P., Green, D., Lister, R. and Woodard, K. 1999. *Poverty First Hand: Poor People Speak for Themselves*. London: CPAG.

Beretta, S. 2000. '*Ordering Global Finance: Back to Basics*' in Boswell et al. (eds.), pp. 221–238.

Berridge, V. and Blume, S. (eds.) 2003. *Poor Health: Social Inequality Before and After the Black Report*. London: Frank Cass.

Board for Social Responsibility 1986. *Not Just for the Poor: Christian Perspectives on the Welfare State*. London: Church House Publishing.

Bobbitt, P. 2003. *The Shield of Achilles: War, Peace and the Course of History.* London: Penguin.

Boff, L. 1980. *Jesus Christ Liberator: A Critical Christology of Our Time.* London: SPCK.

Boff, L. 1985. *Church, Charism and Power: Liberation Theology and the Institutional Church.* London: SCM.

Boswell, J. 1994a. *Community and the Economy: The Theory of Public Co-operation.* London: Routledge.

Boswell, J. 1994b. '*Catholic Communitarianism and Advanced Economic Systems: Problems of Middle-Level Thinking Since 1891*', in Furlong and Curtis (eds.), pp. 49–69.

Boswell, J. 2000. '*Solidarity, Justice and Power Sharing: Patterns and Policies*', in Boswell et al. (eds.), pp. 93–114.

Boswell, J. S., McHugh, F. P. and Verstraeten, J. (eds.) 2000. *Catholic Social Thought: Twilight or Renaissance?* Leuven: Leuven University Press.

Bottomore, T. B. and Rubel, M. (eds.) 1963. *Karl Marx: Selected Writings in Sociology and Social Philosophy.* Harmondsworth: Penguin.

Brandt, W. (Chairman) 1980. *North-South: A Programme for Survival.* London: Pan.

Brown, R. E. 1997. *An Introduction to the New Testament.* New York: Doubleday.

Brown, R. E., Fitzmyer, J. A. and Murphy, R. E. (eds.) 1991. *The New Jerome Biblical Commentary.* London: Geoffrey Chapman.

Brown, U., Scott, G., Mooney, G. and Duncan, B. (eds.) 2002. *Poverty in Scotland 2002.* London: CPAG.

Brueggermann, W., Parks, S. and Groome, T. H. 1986. *To Act Justly, Love Tenderly, Walk Humbly: An Agenda for Ministers*, New York: Paulist Press.

Brundtland, G. H. (Chair) 1987. *Our Common Future (Report of the World Commission on Environment and Development).* Oxford: Oxford University Press.

Buch, A. J. 2000. '*Catholic Social Thought in Transition: Some Remarks on Its Future Communicability*', in Boswell et al. (eds.), pp. 141–147.

Buchanan, T. and Conway, M. (eds.) 1996. *Political Catholicism in Europe, 1918–1965.* Oxford: Clarendon Press.

Buckley, T. J. 1997. *What Binds Marriage? Roman Catholic Theology in Practice.* London: Geoffrey Chapman.

Bulmer, M. and Rees, A. M. (eds.) 1996. *Citizenship Today: The Contemporary Relevance of T. H. Marshall.* London: UCL Press.

Burns, G. 1994. *The Frontiers of Catholicism: The Politics of Ideology in a Liberal World.* London: University of California Press.

Butler, C. 1981. *The Theology of Vatican II.* London: Darton, Longman and Todd.

Cahill, L. S. 1991. '*Marriage: Institution, Relationship, Sacrament*' in Coleman (ed.), pp. 103–119.

Cahill, L. S. 1994. '*Marriage*' in Dwyer (ed.), pp. 565–570.

Cahill, L. S. 2000. *Family: A Christian Social Perspective.* Minneapolis: Fortress Press.

Calvez, J-Y. 2000. '*Things Old and New: Catholic Social Thought in Retrospect and Prospect*', in Boswell et al. (eds.), pp. 3–11.

Caplovitz, D. 1967. *The Poor Pay More: Consumer Practices of Low-Income Families*. London: Collier-Macmillan.

Caritas Europa 2004. *Poverty Has Many Faces: The Need for Family-Oriented Policies. 2nd Report on Poverty in Europe*. Brussels.

Carson, R. 1965. *Silent Spring*. Harmondsworth: Penguin.

Casanova, J. 1994. *Public Religions in the Modern World*. London: University of Chicago Press.

Casanova, J. 2001. 'Religion, the New Millennium, and Globalization', *Sociology of Religion*. 62: 415–441.

Castles, F. G. (ed.) 1993. *Families of Nations: Patterns of Public Policies in Western Democracies*. Aldershot: Dartmouth.

Castles, S. and Miller, M. J. 1998. *The Age of Migration: International Population Movements in the Modern World*. Basingstoke: Macmillan.

Catechism of the Catholic Church 1994. London: Geoffrey Chapman.

Catholic Association for Racial Justice 2000. *Out-Caste to Authority: A Report on Authority and Governance in the Catholic Church in England and Wales With Particular Reference to the Experience of Black Catholics*. London: CARJ.

Catholic Bishops' Conference of England and Wales 1996. *The Common Good and the Catholic Church's Social Teaching*. Manchester: Gabriel.

Catholic Bishops' Conference of England and Wales 2003. *The Call of Creation: God's Invitation and the Human Response: The Natural Environment and Catholic Social Teaching*. London: Catholic Communications Service.

Catholic Bishops' Conference of England and Wales 2004. *Cherishing Life*. London: Colloquium (CaTEW) and CTS.

CELAM II 1979. *The Church in the Present-Day Transformation of Latin America in the Light of the Council: II Conclusions (Medellin)*. Washington, DC: USCCB.

CELAM III 1980. *Puebla: Evangelization at Present and in the Future of Latin America: Conclusions*. Slough: St Paul Publications.

Cesarani, D. and Fulbrook, M. 1996. *Citizenship, Nationality and Migration in Europe*. London: Routledge.

Charles, R. 1998a. *Christian Social Witness and Teaching: The Catholic Tradition From Genesis to Centesimus Annus, Volume 1: From Biblical Times to the Late Nineteenth Century*. Leominster: Gracewing.

Charles, R. 1998b. *Christian Social Witness and Teaching, Volume 2: The Modern Social Teaching: Contexts, Summaries, Analysis*. Leominster: Gracewing.

Chmielewski, P. J. 1994. '*Copartnership*' in Dwyer (ed.), pp. 237–241.

Christiansen, D. 1984. 'On Relative Equality: Catholic Egalitarianism After Vatican II', *Theological Studies*, 45: 651–675.

Chomsky, N. 2004. *Hegemony or Survival: America's Quest for Global Dominance*. London: Penguin.

Christie, I. and Warburton, D. (eds.) 2001. *From Here to Sustainability: Politics in the Real World*. London: Earthscan.

Churches Together in Britain and Ireland 2005a. *Prosperity With a Purpose: Christians and the Ethics of Affluence*. London: CTBI.

Churches Together in Britain and Ireland 2005b. *Prosperity With a Purpose: Exploring the Ethics of Affluence*. London: CTBI.

Clague, J. 2000. '"*A Dubious Idiom and Rhetoric": How Problematic is the Language of Human Rights in Catholic Social Thought?*' in Boswell et al. (eds.), pp. 125–140.

Cleary, E. L. and Stewart-Gambono, H. (eds.) 1992. *Conflict and Competition: The Latin American Church in a Changing Environment*. London: Lynne Reinner.

Cleary, S. 1989. *Renewing the Earth: Development for a Sustainable Future: An Economic Perspective*. London: CAFOD.

Cohen, R., Coxall, J., Craig, G. and Sadiq-Sangster, A. 1992. *Hardship Britain: Being Poor in the 1990s*. London: CPAG.

Coleman, J. A. (ed.) 1991a. *One Hundred Years of Catholic Social Thought: Celebration and Challenge*. Maryknoll, New York: Orbis Books.

Coleman, J. A. 1991b. '*Introduction: A Tradition Celebrated, Reevaluated, and Applied*', in Coleman (ed.), pp. 1–10.

Coleman, J. A. 2000. '*Retrieving or Re-Inventing Social Catholicism: A Transatlantic Response*', in Boswell et al. (eds.), pp. 265–292.

Collins, J. 1999. *Not Mine But Thine: A Christian Approach to the Redistribution of Wealth and the Reform of Inheritance Tax*. London: Missionary Institute (unpublished dissertation).

Collins, S. and Hornsby-Smith, M. P. 2002. 'The Rise and Fall of the YCW in England', *Journal of Contemporary Religion*, Vol. 17, No. 1, 87–100.

Coman, P. 1977. *Catholics and the Welfare State*. London: Longman.

Commission for Africa 2005. *Our Common Interest: An Argument*. London: Penguin.

Commission on Poverty, Participation and Power 2000. *Listen, Hear: The Right to be Heard*. Bristol: The Policy Press.

Commission on Taxation and Citizenship 2000. *Paying for Progress: A New Politics of Tax for Public Spending*. London: Fabian Society.

Congregation for the Doctrine of the Faith 1984. *Instruction on Certain Aspects of the 'Theology of Liberation' (Libertatis Nuntius)*. Godalming: Ladywell Press.

Congregation for the Doctrine of the Faith 1986. *Instruction on Christian Freedom and Liberation (Libertatis Conscientia)*. London: Catholic Media Office; and CTS (Do 570).

Congregation for the Doctrine of the Faith 1987. *Instruction on Respect for Human Life in its Origin and on the Dignity of Procreation (Donum Vitae)*. London: CTS (S 395).

Constable, J. 2002. *Asylum by Numbers 1985–2000: Analysis of Available Asylum Data from 1985 to 2000*. London: Refugee Council.

Cook, D. 1997. *Poverty, Crime and Punishment*. London: CPAG.

Council of Churches for Britain and Ireland 1997. *Unemployment and the Future of Work: An Enquiry for the Churches*. London: Inter-Church House.

Cross, M. 1993. '*Generating the "New Poverty": A European Comparison*', in Simpson and Walker (eds.), pp. 5–24.

Curran, C. E. 1978. 'Social Ethics: Agenda for the Future', in Tracy et al. (eds.), pp. 146–162.

Curran, C. E. 1991. 'Catholic Social Teaching and Human Morality', in Coleman (ed.), pp. 72–87.

Curran, C. E. 2002. *Catholic Social Teaching 1891–Present: A Historical, Theological, and Ethical Analysis.* Washington, DC: Georgetown University Press.

Curtis, M. 2004. *Unpeople: Britain's Secret Human Rights Abuses.* London: Vintage.

Davies, N. 1996. *Europe: A History.* Oxford: Oxford University Press.

DeBerri, E. P. and Hug, J. E. with Henriot, P. J. and Schultheis, M. J. (2003, 4th ed.) *Catholic Social Teaching: Our Best Kept Secret.* Maryknoll, New York: Orbis Books and Washington, DC: Center of Concern.

Delphy, C. 1984. *Close to Home: A Materialist Analysis of Women's Oppression.* London: Hutchinson.

Delphy, C. and Leonard, D. 1992. *Familiar Exploitation: A New Analysis of Marriage in Contemporary Western Societies.* Cambridge: Polity Press.

Dennehy, A., Smith, L. and Harker, P. 1997. *Not To Be Ignored: Young People, Poverty and Health.* London: CPAG.

Dominian, J. 1968. *Christian Marriage: The Challenge of Change.* London: Libra.

Dominian, J. 2004. *Living Love: Restoring Hope in the Church.* London: Darton, Longman and Todd.

Dore, R. 2000. *Stock Market Capitalism: Welfare Capitalism, Japan and Germany vs. the Anglo-Saxons.* Oxford: Oxford University Press.

Dorr, D. 1991. *The Social Justice Agenda: Justice, Ecology, Power and the Church.* Dublin: Gill and Macmillan.

Dorr, D. 1992. *Option for the Poor: A Hundred Years of Vatican Social Teaching.* Dublin: Gill and Macmillan.

Dorr, D. 1994. 'Poor, Preferential Option for' in Dwyer (ed.), pp. 755–759.

Dorr, D. 2000. 'Option for the Poor Re-Visited' in Boswell et al. (eds.), pp. 249–262.

Dowler, E. and Turner, S. 2001. *Poverty Bites: Food, Health and Poor Families.* London: CPAG.

Drinan, R. F. 2001. *The Mobilization of Shame: A World View of Human Rights.* London: Yale University Press.

Duchrow, U. 1995. *Alternatives to Global Capitalism: Drawn From Biblical History, Designed for Political Action.* Utrecht: International Books.

Duchrow, U. and Liedke, G. 1989. *Shalom: Biblical Perspectives on Creation, Justice and Peace.* Geneva: WCC Publications.

Duchrow, U. and Hinkelammert, F. J. 2004. *Property for People, Not for Profit: Alternatives to the Global Tyranny of Capital.* London: Zed Books and CIIR.

Duffy, E. 1997. *Saints and Sinners: A History of the Popes.* London: Yale University Press.

Dwyer, J. A. (ed.) 1994. *A New Dictionary of Catholic Social Thought.* Collegeville, Minnesota: Liturgical Press.

Eaton, M. 1999. 'What Became of the Children of Mary?', in Hornsby-Smith (ed.), pp. 219–244.

Ehrenreich, B. 2002. *Nickel and Dimed: Undercover in Low-Wage USA.* Granta.

Elliott, C. 1987. *Comfortable Compassion? Poverty, Power and the Church.* London: Hodder and Stoughton.

Elworthy, S. 2004. *Cutting the Costs of War: Non-Military Prevention and Resolution of Conflict.* Oxford: Peace Direct and Oxford Research Group.

Esping-Andersen, G. 1990. *The Three Worlds of Welfare Capitalism.* Cambridge: Polity Press.

Evans, J. W. and Ward, L. R. (eds.) 1956. *The Social and Political Philosophy of Jacques Maritain.* London: Bles.

Fahey, J. 2003. *Peace, War, and the Christian Conscience.* London: Pax Christi.

Farley, M. A. 1994. '*Family*' in Dwyer (ed.), pp. 371–381.

Feuer, L. S. (ed.) 1969. *Karl Marx and Friedrich Engels: Basic Writings on Politics and Philosophy.* Glasgow: Fontana.

Field, F. et al. 1996. *Stakeholder Welfare.* London: IEA.

Filochowski, J. 1998. '*Looking Out to the World's Poor*', in Vallely (ed.), pp. 60–83.

Fimister, G. (ed.) 2001. *An End in Sight? Tackling Child Poverty in the UK.* London: CPAG.

Flaherty, J., Veit-Wilson, J. and Dornan, P. 2004. *Poverty: The Facts.* (5th edn.). London: CPAG.

Flessati, V. 1991. *Pax: The History of a Catholic Peace Society in Britain: 1936–1971.* Unpublished PhD, Department of Peace Studies, University of Bradford (2 vols.).

Fogarty, M. P. 1957. *Christian Democracy in Western Europe 1820–1953.* London: Routledge and Kegan Paul.

Ford, J. 1991. *Consuming Credit: Debt and Poverty in the UK.* London: CPAG.

Forrester, D. B. 1997. *Christian Justice and Public Policy.* Cambridge: Cambridge University Press.

Forrester, D. B. 2001. *On Human Worth: A Christian Vindication of Equality.* London: SCM Press.

Freire, P. 1972. *Pedagogy of the Oppressed.* Harmondsworth: Penguin.

Fuchs, J. 1994. '*Natural Law*', in Dwyer (ed.), pp. 669–675.

Fuellenbach, J. 1995. *The Kingdom of God: The Message of Jesus Today.* Maryknoll, New York: Orbis Books.

Fukuyama, F. 1992. *The End of History and the Last Man.* London: Penguin.

Furlong, P. and Curtis, D. (eds.) 1994. *The Church Faces the Modern World: Rerum Novarum and Its Impact.* Hull: Earlsgate Press.

Gannon, T. M. (ed.) 1987. *The Catholic Challenge to the American Economy: Reflections on the U.S. Bishops' Pastoral Letter on Catholic Social Teaching and the U.S. Economy.* London: Collier Macmillan.

Genovesi, V. J. 1994. '*Homosexuality, Social Implications of*' in Dwyer (ed.), pp. 447–453.

George, V. and Taylor-Gooby, P. (eds.) 1996. *European Welfare Policy: Squaring the Welfare Circle.* Basingstoke: Macmillan.

Giddens, A. 1999. *Runaway World: How Globalization is Reshaping Our Lives.* London: Profile Books.

Goodman, A., Johnson, P. and Webb, S. 1997. *Inequality in the UK*. Oxford: Oxford University Press.

Gormally, L. (ed.) 1994. *Euthanasia, Clinical Practice and the Law*. London: Linacre Centre.

Gormally, L. (ed.) 1999. *Issues for a Catholic Bioethic*. London: The Linacre Centre.

Gormally, L. (ed.) 2002. *Culture of Life–Culture of Death*. London: The Linacre Centre.

Graffy, A. 2001. *Trustworthy and True: The Gospels Beyond 2000*. Blackrock, Co. Dublin: Columbia Press.

Grasso, K. L. 1995. 'Beyond Liberalism: Human Dignity, the Free Society, and the Second Vatican Council', in Grasso et al. (eds.), pp. 29–58.

Grasso, K. L., Bradley, G. V. and Hunt, R. P. (eds.) 1995. *Catholicism, Liberalism, and Communitarianism: The Catholic Intellectual Tradition and the Moral Foundations of Democracy*. London: Rowman and Littlefield.

Gray, J. 1998. *False Dawn: The Delusions of Global Capitalism*. London: Granta Books.

Gray, J. 2000. 'Inclusion: A Radical Critique', in Askonas and Stewart (eds.), pp. 19–36.

Green, D. and Griffith, M. 2002. *Dumping on the Poor: The Common Agricultural Policy, the WTO and International Development*. London: CAFOD.

Grey, M. 2001. 'The Female Experience of Sexuality' in Selling, J. A. (ed.), pp. 61–74.

Grey, M. 2003. *Sacred Longings: Ecofeminist Theology and Globalization*. London SCM Press.

Greyling, C. 2002. *Poverty, HIV and AIDS: The Challenge to the Churches in the New Millennium*. London: CIIR.

Grimmett, R. F. 2001. 'Conventional Arms Transfers to Developing Nations, 1993–2000', CRS Report for Congress, Washington, DC.

Gudorf, C. E. 1994. 'Children, Rights of' in Dwyer (ed.), pp. 143–148.

Gutiérrez, G. 1974. *A Theology of Liberation: History, Politics and Salvation*. London: SCM Press.

Gutiérrez, G. 1991. *The God of Life*. London: SCM Press.

Haleem, H. A., Ramsbotham, O., Risaluddin, S. and Wicker, B. (eds.) 1998. *The Crescent and the Cross: Muslim and Christian Approaches to War and Peace*. Basingstoke: Macmillan.

Hanley, D. (ed.) 1996. *Christian Democracy in Europe: A Comparative Perspective*. London: Pinter.

Hantrais, L. 1993. 'Towards a Europeanization of Family Policy' in Simpson and Walker (eds.), pp. 52–63.

Hardwicke, O. 2001. *Living Beyond Conformity: An Experience of Ministry and Priesthood*. Dublin: Columba Press.

Harries, R. 1990. *Is There a Gospel for the Rich? The Christian in a Capitalist World*. London: Mowbray.

Harrington, D. 1994. 'Kingdom of God', in Dwyer (ed.), pp. 508–513.

Harvey, A. (ed.) 1989. *Theology in the City: A Theological Response to 'Faith in the City'*. London: SPCK.

Hauerwas, S. 1995. '*The Importance of Being Catholic: Unsolicited Advice from a Protestant Bystander*', in Grasso et al. (eds.), pp. 219–234.

Havel, V. 1990. *Disturbing the Peace*. London: Faber and Faber.

Hayek, F. A. 1944. *The Road to Serfdom*. London: Routledge and Kegan Paul.

Hayek, F. A. 1982. *Law, Legislation and Liberty, Vol. II: The Mirage of Social Justice*. (2nd edn.). London: Routledge.

Hayes, Z. 1994. '*Eschatology*', in Dwyer (ed.), pp. 343–348.

Hebblethwaite, P. 1993. *Paul VI: The First Modern Pope*. London: Harper Collins.

Held, D., McGrew, A., Goldblatt, D. and Perraton, J. 1999. *Global Transformations: Politics, Economics and Culture*. Stanford, CA: Stanford University Press.

Henriot, P. J. 2004. *Opting for the Poor: The Challenge for the Twenty-First Century*. Washington, DC: Center of Concern.

Hertsgaard, M. 2002. *The Eagle's Shadow: Why America Fascinates and Infuriates the World*. London: Bloomsbury.

Hertz, N. 2001. *The Silent Takeover: Global Capitalism and the Death of Democracy*. London: Heinemann.

Hicks, D. A. 2000. *Inequality and Christian Ethics*. Cambridge: Cambridge University Press.

Himes, K. R. 1991. '*Pacifism and the Just War Tradition in Roman Catholic Social Teaching*' in Coleman (ed.), pp. 329–344.

Himes, K. R. 1994. '*War*', in Dwyer (ed.), pp. 977–982.

Hinde, R. and Rotblat, J. 2003. *War No More: Eliminating Conflict in the Nuclear Age*. London: Pluto Press.

Hirst, P. and Thompson, G. 1999. *Globalization in Question: The International Economy and the Possibilities of Governance*. Cambridge: Polity Press.

Hobson, D. 1999. *The National Wealth: Who Gets What in Britain*. London: HarperCollins.

Hogan, L. 1998. *Human Rights*. Dublin: Trôcaire, Veritas and CAFOD.

Hogan, L. 2000. '*Trocaire: A Catholic Development Agency Working to Support Communities in Their Efforts to Overcome Poverty and Oppression*', in Boswell et al. (eds.), pp. 183–190.

Hogan, L. 2001. *Confronting the Truth: Conscience in the Catholic Tradition*. London: Darton, Longman and Todd.

Holland, J. and Henriot, P. 1983. *Social Analysis: Linking Faith and Justice*. Maryknoll, New York: Orbis Books.

Hollenbach, D. 1979. *Claims in Conflict: Retrieving and Renewing the Catholic Human Rights Tradition*. New York: Paulist.

Hollenbach, D. 1998. *Justice, Peace and Human Rights: American Catholic Social Ethics in a Pluralistic World*. New York: Crossroads.

Holman, B. 1998. *Faith in the Poor*. Oxford: Lion Publishing.

Holman, B., Stanton, H. and Timms, S. 1999. *Joined-Up Writing: New Labour and Social Inclusion*. London: Christian Socialist Movement.

Hornsby-Smith, M. P. (ed.) 1999a. *Catholics in England 1950–2000: Historical and Sociological Perspectives*. London: Cassell.

Hornsby-Smith, M. P. 1999b. 'The Catholic Church and Social Policy in Europe' in Chamberlayne, P., Cooper, A., Freeman, R. and Rustin, M. (eds.) *Welfare and Culture in Europe: Towards a New Paradigm in Social Policy*. London and Philadelphia: Jessica Kingsley, pp. 172–189.

Houck, J. W. and Williams, O. F. (eds.) 1984. *Catholic Social Teaching and the U.S. Economy: Working Papers for a Bishops' Pastoral*, London: University Press of America.

Houghton, J. 2004. 'Understanding the "Signs of the Times": Global Warming and Climate Change: A Challenge to Scientists and Christians', in R. Williams (ed.), *Faith and the Environmental Imperative: Responding to 'The Call of Creation'*, London: The Newman Association and Christian Ecology Link, pp. 13–22, 25–27.

Howard, M. 2001. *Paying the Price: Carers, Poverty and Social Exclusion*. London: CPAG.

Howard, M., Garnham, A., Fimister, G. and Veit-Wilson, J. 2001. *Poverty: The Facts* (4th edn.) London: CPAG.

Howard-Brook, W. 2001. *The Church Before Christianity*. Maryknoll, New York: Orbis Books.

Howarth, C., Kenway, P., Palmer, G. and Miorelli, R. 1999. *Monitoring Poverty and Social Exclusion 1999*. York: Joseph Rowntree Foundation.

Howarth, C., Kenway, P. and Palmer, G. 2001. *Responsibility For All: A National Strategy for Social Inclusion*. London: New Policy Institute and Fabian Society.

Hughes, G. J. 1994. '*Our Human Vocation*', in Walsh (ed.), pp. 336–356.

Huntington, S. P. 1998. *The Clash of Civilizations and the Remaking of World Order*. London: Touchstone.

Hutton, W. 1996. *The State We're In*. London: Vintage.

Hutton, W. 2002. *The World We're In*. London: Little, Brown.

Irish Episcopal Conference 1992. *Work is the Key: Towards an Economy That Needs Everyone*. Dublin: Veritas.

Jacobs, M. 1996. *The Politics of the Real World: Meeting the New Century*. London: Earthscan.

Jegen, M. E. 1991. '*Peace and Pluralism: Church and Churches*', in Coleman (ed.), pp. 286–302.

Jenkinson, S. 1992. *Repossessed: A Fresh Look at Mortgage Lending Practice*. London: CHAS and National Debtline.

Jeremias, J. 1963. *The Parables of Jesus*. London: SCM Press.

John XXIII, Pope 1961. *Christianity and Social Progress (Mater et Magistra)*, in O'Brien and Shannon (eds.), pp. 82–128.

John XXIII, Pope 1963. *Peace on Earth (Pacem in Terris)* in O'Brien and Shannon (eds.), pp. 129–162.

John Paul II, Pope 1979. *Redemptor Hominis (The Redeemer of Mankind)*, in Walsh and Davies (eds.) 1984, pp. 243–261.

John Paul II, Pope 1980. *Dives in Misericordia (On Divine Mercy)*, in Walsh and Davies (eds.) 1984, pp. 262–270.

John Paul II, Pope 1981a. *Familiaris Consortio (The Christian Family in the Modern World)*. London: CTS (S 357).

John Paul II, Pope 1981b. *Laborem Exercens (On Human Work)* in O'Brien and Shannon (eds.), pp. 350–392.

John Paul II, Pope 1987. *Sollicitudo Rei Socialis (On Social Concern)*, in O'Brien and Shannon (eds.), pp. 393–436.

John Paul II, Pope 1988. *Christifideles Laici (On the Vocation and the Mission of the Lay Faithful in the Church and in the World)*. London: CTS (Do 589)

John Paul II, Pope 1990. 'The Ecological Crisis: A Common Responsibility: Peace with God the Creator, Peace with all of Creation', World Day of Peace Message.

John Paul II, Pope 1991a. *Centesimus Annus (On the Hundredth Anniversary of Rerum Novarum)* in O'Brien and Shannon (eds.), pp. 437–488.

John Paul II, Pope 1991b. *Redemptoris Missio: On the Permanent Validity of the Church's Missionary Mandate*. Vatican City: Libreria Editrice Vaticana.

John Paul II, Pope 1993. *Veritatis Splendor: On Certain Fundamental Questions of the Church's Moral Teaching*. London: CTS (Do 616).

John Paul II, Pope 1994. *Tertio Millennio Adveniente: Apostolic Letter on Preparation for the Jubilee of the Year 2000*. London: CTS (Do 627).

John Paul II, Pope 1995. *Evangelium Vitae: On the Value and Inviolability of Human Life*. London: CTS (Do 633).

John Paul II, Pope 2001. *Novo Millennio Ineunte (At the Beginning of the New Millennium)*. London: CTS (Do 673).

Jones, D. A. 2001. *Organ Transplants and the Definition of Death*. London: CTS.

Joseph, J. 1999. *Food*. Dublin: Trôcaire.

Joseph Rowntree Foundation 1995. *Inquiry into Income and Wealth*. York: JRF.

Kagan, R. 2003. *Paradise and Power: America and Europe in the New World Order*. London: Atlantic Books.

Kaiser, R. B. 1987. *The Encyclical That Never Was: The Story of the Commission on Population, Family and Birth, 1964–66*. London: Sheed and Ward.

Kaldor, M. 1999. *New and Old Wars: Organized Violence in a Global Era*. Stanford, CA: Stanford University Press.

Kalilombe, Bishop P. et al. 1991. *Black Catholics Speak: Reflections on Experience, Faith and Theology*. London: CARJ.

Kamerman, S. B. and Kahn, A. K. (eds.) 1978. *Family Policy: Government and Families in Fourteen Countries*. New York: Columbia University Press.

Kaveny, M. C. 2001. 'The Case of Conjoined Twins: Embodiment, Individuality, and Dependence', *Theological Studies* 62: 753–786.

Kelly, K. T. 1987. *Life and Love: Towards a Christian Dialogue on Bioethical Questions*. London: Collins.

Kelly, K. T. 1992. *New Directions in Moral Theology: The Challenge of Being Human*. London: Geoffrey Chapman.

Kelly, K. T. 1996. *Divorce and Second Marriage: Facing the Challenge*. London: Geoffrey Chapman.

Kelly, K. T. 1998. *New Directions in Sexual Ethics: Moral Theology and the Challenge of AIDS*. London and Washington: Geoffrey Chapman.

Kelly, K. T. 1999. *From a Parish Base: Essays in Moral and Pastoral Theology*. London: Darton, Longman and Todd.

Kenny, A. 1986. *A Path From Rome: An Autobiography*. Oxford: Oxford University Press.

Kent, B. 1992. *Undiscovered Ends: An Autobiography*. London HarperCollins.

Keown, J. 1999. '*The Legal Revolution: From "Sanctity of Life" to "Quality of Life" and "Autonomy"*', in Gormally, L. (ed.), pp. 233–260.

Khor, M. 2001. *Rethinking Globalization: Critical Issues and Policy Choices*. London: Zed Books.

Kiely, G. and Richardson, V. (eds.) 1991. *Family Policy: European Perspectives*. Dublin: Family Studies Centre.

Klein, N. 2001. *No Logo*. London: Flamingo.

Klein, N. 2002. *Fences and Windows*. London: Flamingo.

Landes, D. 1998. *The Wealth and Poverty of Nations: Why Some Are So Rich and Some So Poor*. London: Little, Brown and Co.

Leinemann, F. 2001. 'Seeking Protection in Europe', *Europe Infos*, No. 29, July–August: 6–7.

Leo, XIII, Pope 1891. *Rerum Novarum*, in O'Brien and Shannon (eds.), pp. 14–39.

Levitas, R. 1998. *The Inclusive Society? Social Exclusion and New Labour*. Basingstoke: Palgrave.

Linden, I. 1998. '*People Before Profit: The Early Social Doctrine of John Paul II*', in Vallely (ed.), pp. 84–96.

Linden, I. 1999. '*Social Justice in Historical Perspective*', in Hornsby-Smith (ed.), pp. 139–157.

Linden, I. 2003. *A New Map of the World*. London: Darton, Longman and Todd.

Lister, R. 1990. *The Exclusive Society: Citizenship and the Poor*. London: CPAG.

Lister, R. 2000. '*Strategies for Social Inclusion: Promoting Social Cohesion or Social Justice?*', in Askonas and Stewart (eds.), pp. 37–54.

Longley, C. 1998. '*Structures of Sin and the Free Market: John Paul II on Capitalism*', in Vallely (ed.), pp. 97–113.

Lorentzen, L. A. 1994. '*Gaudium et Spes*' in Dwyer (ed.), pp. 406–416.

McAdam, D., McCarthy, J. D. and Zald, M. N. (eds.) 1996. *Comparative Perspectives on Social Movements: Political Opportunities, Mobilizing Structures, and Cultural Framings*. Cambridge: Cambridge University Press.

McBrien, R. 1994. *Catholicism*. London: Geoffrey Chapman.

McCarthy, A. 2003. *Cloning and Stem Cell Research*. London: CTS/Linacre Centre.

McCarthy, J. D. and Zald, M. N. 1977. 'Resource Mobilization and Social Movements: A Partial Theory', *American Journal of Sociology*, 82: 1212–1241.

McDonagh, S. 1986. *To Care for the Earth: A Call to a New Theology*. London: Geoffrey Chapman.

McDonagh, S. 1990. *The Greening of the Church*. London: Geoffrey Chapman.

McDonagh, S. 1994. *Passion for the Earth: The Christian Vocation to Promote Justice, Peace and the Integrity of Creation.* London: Geoffrey Chapman.

McDonagh, S. 2003a. *Dying for Water.* Dublin: Veritas.

McDonagh, S. 2003b. *Patenting Life? Stop? Is Corporate Greed Forcing Us to Eat Genetically Engineered Food?* Dublin: Dominican Publications.

McHugh, F. P. 1994. *Coping with Debt.* London: CTS (S437).

McHugh, F. P. 2000. '*Muddle or Middle-Level? A Place for Natural Law in Catholic Social Thought*', in Boswell et al. (eds.), pp. 35–57.

McMahon, W. and Marsh, T. 1999. *Filling the Gap: Free School Meals, Nutrition and Poverty.* London: CPAG.

McNay, M. and Pond, C. 1980. *Low Pay and Family Poverty.* London: Study Commission on the Family.

McTernan, O. 2003. *Violence in God's Name: Religion in an Age of Conflict.* London: Darton, Longman and Todd.

Macionis, J. J. and Plummer, K. 2002. *Sociology: A Global Introduction.* Harlow: Pearson.

Macpherson Report 1999. *Stephen Lawrence*, London: Stationery Office. Cm 4262-I.

Madeley, J. 2000. *Hungry for Trade: How the Poor Pay for Free Trade.* London Zed Books.

Mahoney, J. 1984. *Bioethics and Belief: Religion and Medicine in Dialogue.* London: Sheed and Ward.

Mainwaring, S. and Wilde, A. (eds.) 1989. *The Progressive Church in Latin America.* Notre Dame, Indiana: University of Notre Dame Press.

Maritain, J. 1947. *The Person and the Common Good.* New York: Charles Scribner.

Maritain, J. 1951. *Man and the State.* Chicago: Chicago University Press.

Maritain, J. 1968 (fp in French in 1936). *Integral Humanism: Temporal and Spiritual Problems for a New Christendom.* South Bend, Ind.

Marshall, J. 1999. '*Catholic Family Life*', in Hornsby-Smith (ed.), pp. 67–77.

Methodist Church and NCH Action for Children (1997) *The Cities: A Methodist Report*, London: NCH Action for Children.

Meier, J. P. 1991. '*Jesus*', in Brown et al. (eds.), pp. 1316–1328.

Metz, J. B. 1969. *Theology of the World.* New York: Herder and Herder.

Metz, J. B. 1978. '*For a Renewed Church Before a Council: A Concept in Four Theses*', in Tracy, D. et al. (eds.), pp. 137–145.

Mich, M. L. K. 1998. *Catholic Social Teaching and Movements.* Mystic, CT: Twenty-Third Publications.

Middleton, S., Ashworth, K. and Walker, R. (eds.) 1994. *Family Fortunes: Pressures on Parents and Children in the 1990s.* London: CPAG.

Misner, P. 1991. *Social Catholicism in Europe: From the Onset of Industrialization to the First World War.* London: Darton, Longman and Todd.

Misner, P. 1994. '*The Emergence of an International Organization of Christian Labour After Rerum Novarum*', in Furlong and Curtis (eds.), pp. 241–256.

Moltmann, J. 1967. *Theology of Hope.* London: SCM Press.

Monbiot, G. 2000. *Captive State: The Corporate Takeover of Britain*. London: Pan Macmillan.

Monbiot, G. 2003. *The Age of Consent: A Manifesto for a New World Order*. London: Flamingo.

Murnion, P. J. (ed.) 1983. *Catholics and Nuclear War: A Commentary on the Challenge of Peace*. New York: Crossroads Press.

Murray, J. C. 1960. *We Hold These Truths: Catholic Reflections on the American Proposition*. New York: Sheed and Ward.

Murray, J. C. 1966. 'The Issue of Church and State at Vatican II', *Theological Studies*, 27 (4) December: 580–606.

Myers, C. 1988. *Binding the Strong Man: A Political Reading of Mark's Story of Jesus*. Maryknoll, New York: Orbis Books.

Neal, M. A. 1977. *A Socio-Theology of Letting Go: The Role of a First World Church Facing Third World Peoples*. New York, Mahwah: Paulist Press.

Neal, M. A. 1987. *The Just Demands of the Poor: Essays in Socio-Theology*. New York, Mahwah: Paulist Press.

Nevile, M. 1999. 'The Changing Nature of Catholic Organizations', in Hornsby-Smith (ed.), pp. 99–121.

Newby, H. 1996. 'Citizenship in a Green World: Global Commons and Human Stewardship', in Bulmer and Rees (eds.), pp. 209–221.

Nolan, A. 1977. *Jesus Before Christianity: The Gospel of Liberation*. London: Darton, Longman and Todd.

Nolan, A. c1984. *Taking Sides*. London: CIIR and CTS (S372).

Nolan, A. 1988. *God in South Africa: The Challenge of the Gospel*. Grand Rapids, Michigan: Eerdmans.

Novak, M. (ed.) 1965. *The Experience of Marriage: The Testimony of Catholic Laymen*. London: Darton, Longman and Todd.

Novak, M. 1983. *Moral Clarity in the Nuclear Age*. Nashville, Tennessee: Thomas Nelson.

Novak, M. 1991. *The Spirit of Democratic Capitalism*. London: The IEA Health and Welfare Unit.

O'Brien, D. J. 1991. '*A Century of Catholic Social Teaching: Context and Comments*', in Coleman (ed.), pp. 13–24.

O'Brien, D. J. and Shannon, T. A. (eds.) 1992. *Catholic Social Thought: The Documentary Heritage*. Maryknoll, New York: Orbis Books.

O'Brien, J. 1994. '*Poverty*', in Dwyer (ed.), pp. 770–776.

O'Donoghue, P. 2001. *Any Room at the Inn? Reflections on Asylum Seekers*. London: CBCEW Office for Refugee Policy.

O'Donovan, O. 2003. *The Just War Revisited*. Cambridge: Cambridge University Press.

O'Keeffe, B. 1999. '*Reordering Perspectives in Catholic Schools*' in Hornsby-Smith (ed.), pp. 242–265.

Okin, S. M. 1989. *Justice, Gender and the Family*. New York: Basic Books.

O'Mahony, P. J. 1986. *Swords and Ploughshares: Can Man Live and Progress With a Technology of Death?* London: Sheed and Ward.

Papini, R. 1997. *The Christian Democrat International.* London: Rowman and Littlefield.

Paul VI, Pope 1967. *On the Development of Peoples (Populorum Progressio)*, in O'Brien and Shannon (eds.), pp. 239–262.

Paul VI, Pope 1968. *The Regulation of Birth (Humanae Vitae).* London: CTS (Do 411).

Paul VI, Pope 1971. *A Call to Action (Octogesima Adveniens)*, in O'Brien and Shannon (eds.), pp. 265–286.

Paul VI, Pope 1975. *Evangelisation in the Modern World (Evangelii Nuntiandi)*, in O'Brien and Shannon (eds.), pp. 303–345.

Phan, P. 1994. '*Influence of Augustine*', in Dwyer (ed.), pp. 58–63.

Philo, C. (ed.) 1995. *Off the Map: The Social Geography of Poverty in the UK.* London: CPAG.

Piachaud, D. 1974. *Do the Poor Pay More?.* London: CPAG.

Piachaud, D. 2005. 'Child Poverty: An Overview', pp. 3–19 in Preston, G. (ed.). *At Greatest Risk: The Children Most Likely to be Poor.* London: CPAG.

Pius XI, Pope 1930. *Christian Marriage (Casti Connubii).* London: CTS (Do 113).

Pius XI, Pope 1931. *After Forty Years (Quadragesimo Anno)*, in O'Brien and Shannon (eds.), pp. 42–79.

Plant, R. 1997. '*Civic Virtue, Poverty and Social Justice*', in Askonas and Frowen (eds.), pp. 211–219.

Plant, R. (Chairman) 2000. *Paying for Progress: A New Politics of Tax for Public Spending.* London: Fabian Society/ Commission on Taxation and Citizenship.

Platt, L. 2002. *Parallel Lives?: Poverty Among Ethnic Minority Groups in Britain.* London: CPAG.

Pontifical Council for Justice and Peace 2000. *The Social Agenda: A Collection of Magisterial Texts* (edited by R. A. Sirico and M. Zięba), Vatican: Libreria Editrice Vaticana.

Pontifical Council for Justice and Peace 2004. *Compendium of the Social Doctrine of the Church.* Vatican: Libreria Editrice Vaticana.

Pontifical Council for the Pastoral Care of Migrants and Itinerant People ('Cor Unum') 1992. *Refugees: A Challenge to Solidarity*, London: CTS.

Pontifical Justice and Peace Commission 1987. *At the Service of the Human Community: An Ethical Approach to the International Debt Question*, London CTS (S 394).

Pontifical Justice and Peace Commission 1988. *What Have You Done to Your Homeless Brother? The Church and the Housing Problem*, London: CTS (S 399).

Pontifical Justice and Peace Commission 1989. *The Church and Racism: Towards a More Fraternal Society.* London: CTS (S 414).

Pontifical Justice and Peace Commission 1994. *The International Arms Trade: An Ethical Reflection*, London: CTS (S 438) (Authors described by CTS as the Pontifical Council for Justice and Peace).

Pope, S. J. 1994. '*Rerum Novarum*' in Dwyer (ed.), pp. 828–844.

Quinlan, M. 2004. 'Iraq: the Indictment', *The Tablet*, 13 March: 8–10.

Raper, M. and Valcárcel, A. 2000. *Refugees and Forcibly Displaced People*. Dublin: Trocaire, Veritas, CAFOD, SCIAF.

Rawls, J. 1973. *A Theory of Justice*. Oxford: Oxford University Press.

Reed, C. (ed.) 2001. *Development Matters: Christian Perspectives on Globalisation*. London: Church House Publishing.

Reid, C. J. (ed.) 1986. *Peace in a Nuclear Age: The Bishops' Pastoral Letter in Perspective*. Washington, DC: Catholic University of America.

Rico, H. 2002. *John Paul II and the Legacy of 'Dignitatis Humanae'*. Washington, DC: Georgetown University Press.

Rigali, N. J. 1994. '*Magisterium*', in Dwyer (ed.), pp. 559–561.

Robinson, P. 2003. *Euthanasia and Assisted Suicide*. London: CTS/Linacre Centre.

Rogers, P. 2002. (2nd edn.) *Losing Control: Global Security in the Twenty-First Century*, London: Pluto Press.

Royal Commission on the Distribution of Income and Wealth 1980. *An A to Z of Income and Wealth: Everyman's Guide to the Spread of Income and Wealth*. London: HMSO.

Russell, H. 1995. *Poverty Close to Home: A Christian Understanding*. London: Mowbray.

Sachs, J. D. 2005. *The End of Poverty: How We can Make It Happen in Our Lifetime*. London: Penguin.

Saunders, P. 1995. *Capitalism: A Social Audit*. Buckingham: Open University Press.

Scarisbrick, J. J. 1999. '*The Prolife Cause in Great Britain: Reflections on Success and Failure, on the Church's Record and the Present Challenge*' in Gormally (ed.), pp. 300–311.

Schell, J. 2004. *The Unconquerable World: Power, Nonviolence, and the Will of the People*. London: Allen Lane.

Schmidt, M. G. 1993. '*Gendered Labour Force Participation*' in Castles, F. G. (ed.), pp. 179–237.

Schnackenburg, R. 1963. *God's Rule and Kingdom*. Edinburgh and London: Nelson.

Schumacher, E. F. 1974. *Small is Beautiful*. London: Abacus.

Schuck, M. J. 1994. '*Modern Catholic Social Thought*', in Dwyer (ed.), pp. 611–632.

Scott, J. 1994. *Poverty and Wealth: Citizenship, Deprivation and Privilege*. London: Longman.

Sedgwick, P. (ed.) 1995. *God in the City: Essays and Reflections From the Archbishop's Urban Theology Group*. London: Mowbray.

Segundo, J. L. 1977. *The Liberation of Theology*. Dublin: Gill and Macmillan.

Selling, J. A. (ed.) 2001. *Embracing Sexuality: Authority and Experience in the Catholic Church*. Aldershot: Ashgate.

Sen, A. 1992. *Inequality Reexamined*. Oxford: Clarendon Press.

Sen, A. 1999. *Development as Freedom*. Oxford: Oxford University Press.

Shaw, M., Dorling, D., Gordon, D. and Smith, G. D. 1999. *The Widening Gap: Health Inequalities and Policy in Britain*. Bristol: Polity Press.

Simpson, R. and Walker, R. (eds.) (1993) *Europe: For Richer or Poorer?* London: CPAG.

Sirico, R. A. and Zioba, M. (eds.) 2000. *The Social Agenda: A Collection of Magisterial Texts*. Vatican: Pontifical Council for Justice and Peace.

Smith, C. 1991. *The Emergence of Liberation Theology: Radical Religion and Social Movement Theory*. London: University of Chicago Press.

Smith, T. and Noble, M. 1995. *Education Divides: Poverty and Schooling in the 1990s*. London: CPAG.

Snyder, M. H. 1994. '*Development*', in Dwyer (ed.), pp. 278–282.

Sobrino, J. 1978. *Christology at the Crossroads: A Latin American Approach*. London: SCM Press.

Sobrino, J. 1985. *The True Church and the Poor*. London: SCM Press.

Stein, W. (ed.) 1965. *Nuclear Weapons and the Christian Conscience*. London: Merlin Press.

Stiglitz, J. 2002. *Globalization and Its Discontents*, London: Allen Lane.

Stiltner, B. 1999. *Religion and the Common Good: Catholic Contributions to Building Community in a Liberal Society*. Lantham, MD: Rowman and Littlefield.

Sutton, A. 2002. *Prenatal Tests*. London: CTS/Linacre Centre. (also called *Prenatal Diagnosis* inside).

Sutton, A. 2003. *Infertility and Medically Assisted Conception*. London: CTS/Linacre Centre.

Tawney, R. H. 1964. *Equality*. London: Allen and Unwin.

Towle, P. 1998. *Ethics and the Arms Trade*. London: Institute of Economic Affairs.

Townsend, P. and Davidson, N. (eds.) 1988. *Inequalities in Health*. Harmondsworth: Penguin.

Toynbee, P. 2003. *Hard Work: Life in Low-Pay Britain*. London: Bloomsbury Publishing.

Tracy, D., Küng, H. and Metz, J. B. (eds.) 1978. *Toward Vatican III: The Work That Needs To Be Done*. Dublin: Gill and Macmillan.

Turner, A. 2001. *Just Capital: The Liberal Economy*. London: Macmillan.

Turner, B. S. 1986. *Citizenship and Capitalism: The Debate Over Reformism*. London: Allen and Unwin.

Turner, F. 1997. '*Choking on Growth: A Theologian Reflects*', in Askonas and Frowen (eds.), pp. 144–156.

United Nations Development Programme 1992. *Human Development Report 1992*. Oxford: Oxford University Press.

United Nations Development Programme 2003. *Human Development Report: Millennium Goals: A Compact Among Nations to End Human Poverty*. New York: Oxford University Press.

United States Conference of Catholic Bishops 1991. *Renewing the Earth: An Invitation to Reflection and Action on the Environment in Catholic Social Teaching*, Washington, DC: USCCB Publishing.

United States Conference of Catholic Bishops 2001. *Global Climate Change: A Plea for Dialogue, Prudence, and the Common Good*. Washington, DC: USCCB Publishing.

Vallely, P. (ed.) 1998. *The New Politics: Catholic Social Teaching for the Twenty-First Century*. London: SCM Press.

Van Gerwen, J. 2000. '*Global Markets and Global Justice? Catholic Social Teaching and Financial Ethics*', in Boswell et al. (eds.), pp. 201–219.

Van Kersbergen, K. 1995. *Social Capitalism: A Study of Christian Democracy and the Welfare State*. London: Routledge.

Verstraeten, J. 2000. '*Re-Thinking Catholic Social Thought as Tradition*', in Boswell et al. (eds.), pp. 59–77.

Volf, M. 1996. *Exclusion and Embrace: A Theological Exploration of Identity, Otherness, and Reconciliation*. Nashville, Tennessee: Abingdon Press.

Wade, R. H. 2002. 'The American Empire', *The Guardian*, 5 January.

Walker, A. 1997. '*Introduction: The Strategy of Inequality*', in Walker and Walker (eds.), pp. 1–13.

Walker, A. and Walker, C. (eds.) 1997. *Britain Divided: The Growth of Social Exclusion in the 1980s and 1990s*. London: CPAG.

Walsh, M. J. (1984). '*Introduction*', in Walsh and Davies (eds.), pp. xi–xxii.

Walsh, M. J. and Davies, B. (eds.) 1984. *Proclaiming Justice and Peace: Documents From John XXIII to John Paul II*. London: Collins Liturgical Publications.

Walsh, M. J. (ed.) 1994. *Commentary on the Catechism of the Catholic Church*. London: Geoffrey Chapman.

Wansbrough, H. (General Editor) 1985. *The New Jerusalem Bible*. London: Darton, Longman and Todd.

Ward, B. 1962. *The Rich Nations and the Poor Nations*. New York: Norton.

Ward, B. and Dubos, R. 1972. *Only One Earth: The Care and Maintenance of a Small Planet*. Harmondsworth: Penguin.

Watkins, M. and McInerny, R. 1995. '*Jacques Maritain and the Rapprochement of Liberalism and Communitarianism*', in Grasso et al. (eds.), pp. 151–172.

Watt, H. 2000. *Life and Death in Healthcare Ethics: A Short Introduction*. London: Routledge.

Watt, H. 2001a. *Abortion*. London: CTS/Linacre Centre.

Watt, H. 2001b. *Gene Therapy and Human Genetic Engineering*. London: CTS/Linacre Centre.

Weakland, R. G. 1991. '*The Economic Pastoral Letter Revisited*', in Coleman (ed.), pp. 201–211.

Weber, M. 1930. *The Protestant Ethic and the Spirit of Capitalism*. London: Unwin University Books.

White, L. 1967. 'The Historical Roots of Our Ecological Crisis', *Science*, 155: 1203–1207.

Whitehead, M. 1988. *The Health Divide*. London: Penguin.

Whyte, J. H. 1981. *Catholics in Western Democracies: A Study in Political Behaviour*. Dublin: Gill and Macmillan.

Wicker, B. 1985. *Nuclear Deterrence: What Does the Church Teach?* London: CTS (S 374).

Wilkinson, R. G. 1996. *Unhealthy Societies: The Afflictions of Inequality*. London: Routledge.

Wilkinson, R. G. 2005. *The Impact of Inequality: How to Make Sick Societies Healthier*. London: Routledge.

Williams, F. (ed.) 1977. *Why the Poor Pay More*. London and Basingstoke: Macmillan.

Wink, W. 2003. *Jesus and Nonviolence: A Third Way*. Minneapolis: Fortress Press.

Winter, M. M. 2002. *Misguided Morality: Catholic Moral Teaching in the Contemporary Church*. Aldershot: Ashgate.

Woodward, D. 1999. *Contagion and Cure: Tackling the Crisis in Global Finance: A CIIR Comment*. London: CIIR.

World Bank 2002. *World Development Indicators*. Washington, DC: World Bank.

World Council of Churches 1990. *Justice, Peace, Integrity of Creation*. Geneva: WCC.

Wrigley, C. 2001. *The Arms Industry*. London: CAAT.

Young, M. (ed.) 1975. *For Richer, For Poorer: Some Problems of Low-income Consumers*. London: National Consumer Council.

Young, M. 1977. 'Housekeeping Money', in Williams (ed.), pp. 223–234.

Zahn, G. C. 1967. *War, Conscience, and Dissent*. New York: Hawthorn.

Zahn, G. C. 1991. 'Social Movements and Catholic Social Thought', in Coleman (ed.), pp. 43–54.

Zald, M. N. and McCarthy, J. D. 1990. *Social Movements in an Organizational Society: Collected Essays*. New Brunswick: Transaction Publishers.

Index

With Compliments

University of Chester

Learning and Information Services

Direct Line 01244 511234
Fax 01244 511325
lis.helpdesk@chester.ac.uk

University of Chester, Parkgate Road, Chester CH1 4BJ • Tel 01244 511000 • Fax 01244 511300 • www.chester.ac.uk • Registered Charity 525938